the Unofficial Guide® to Washington, D.C.

4th Edition

the Unofficial Guide® to Washington, D.C.

4th Edition

Joe Surkiewicz and
Bob Sehlinger
with Eve Zibart

Macmillan • USA

For Tom Nugent, aka the Enemy of Comfort
—J. S.

To Dick Wood, who infected me with this strange contagion we call book
publishing.
—B. S.

To D.
—E. Z.

Every effort has been made to ensure the accuracy of information throughout
this book. Bear in mind, however, that prices, schedules, etc., are
constantly changing. Readers should always verify information before
making final plans.

Macmillan Travel
A Simon & Schuster Macmillan Company
1633 Broadway
New York, New York 10019-6785

Produced by Menasha Ridge Press
Design by Barbara E. Williams

MACMILLAN is a registered trademark of Macmillan, Inc.
UNOFFICIAL GUIDE is a registered trademark of Simon & Schuster, Inc.

ISBN 0-02-862036-4

ISSN 1071-6440

Library of Congress Catalog Card Number 1071-6440

Manufactured in the United States of America

10 9 8 7 6 5 4 3 2

Fourth edition

CONTENTS

5 Getting around Washington

6 Entertainment and Night Life

7 Exercise and Recreation

8 Shopping in Washington

9 Sight-Seeing Tips and Tours

10 Washington's Attractions

11 Dining and Restaurants

12 Appendix

List of Illustrations

ACKNOWLEDGMENTS

Eve Zibart, author of *The Eclectic Gourmet Guide to Washington, D.C.* and *The Unofficial Disney Companion,* and co-author of *The Unofficial Guide to Ethnic Cuisine and Dining in America, The Unofficial Guide to New Orleans,* and *The Unofficial Guide to Branson, Missouri,* is a feature writer and dining columnist for the Friday "Weekend" section of the *Washington Post*; she drew on her intimate knowledge of D.C.'s diverse after-hours scene and the area's vast array of dining spots when writing our entertainment and restaurant sections. Eve also scoped out where to find the best deals for our chapter on shopping.

Lisa Holland, the media relations pro at the Washington, D.C., Convention and Visitors Association, provided a wealth of up-to-date information and solid advice. Officer Rod Ryan of the Washington Metropolitan Police gave us the straight skinny on how to avoid street crime in Washington, while Jane Gardner at the Information Resources Division of the Smithsonian Institution provided us with timely updates and valuable touring insights for our write-ups on the world's largest museum and research complex. Tara Hamilton, the public affairs manager at the Metropolitan Washington Airports Authority, gave us the latest on terminal expansions at National and Dulles airports.

Metro's Phil Portlock provided photos of the subway system and, among other things, the correct spelling of the U Street–Cardozo station; Gary Barton supplied his detailed knowledge of Washington's streets and spent a Saturday chauffeuring us to suburban Metro stations; renowned bicycling writer (and former D.C. resident) Arlene Plevin shared suggestions on cycling around town; mega-boater Steve Garrison blessed our section on whitewater canoeing; and Ann Lembo pitched in with some last-minute editorial assistance on this revision.

To fulfill their task, the hotel inspection team, Patt Palmer and Grace Walton, endured sore feet, summer crowds, and notoriously bad D.C. traffic.

Finally, many thanks to Barbara Williams, Holly Brown, Robert Clay White, Tim Krasnansky, Ann Cassar, Carolyn Hassett, and The Marathon Group, Inc., the pros who managed to transform all this effort into a book.

Washington without the Hassle

Before we begin rhapsodizing about the joys of visiting Washington, D.C., we have a small confession to make: Sometimes we hate being visitors in D.C.

It's not that we are immune to the spell of this beautiful city on the Potomac. We've done our share of gaping in patriotic awe from the top of the Washington Monument, and have witnessed in utter fascination the histrionics of long-winded U.S. senators ramrodding a pork barrel project through Congress. For us, as for others, the locus of government is intoxicating. We thrive on the constant tension arising from the polarity of powerful people and ideas. Washington, unquestionably, is one of the most exciting cities on the planet.

Where else but in Washington can you watch fire-and-brimstone politicians debate the rights of men and women on the floor of the U.S. Senate or marvel at the eloquence of barristers arguing a case before the Supreme Court—or discover, perhaps, how politics really works by eavesdropping on a couple of veteran lobbyists as they plot strategy over dry martinis in a hip Georgetown pub?

Then, of course, there is the beauty, the magnificence, the majesty of the city. America's capital city boasts some of the most stunning monuments ever created, as well as world-class museums and lush, verdant parks. Broad, shaded boulevards, meticulously laid out by Pierre-Charles L'Enfant, radiate like spokes from the heart of the city, punctuated by stately plazas, ornate bridges, and breathtaking sculpture.

Our problem with D.C. is simple: We cannot stand the peculiarly Washingtonian hassles that routinely get in the way of enjoying this extraordinary city—the sweltering summer heat and humidity, the Rube Goldberg street plan, the agonizing lack of legal parking, the elbow-to-elbow crowds that can wipe out your high spirits before lunch.

In response, we've become absolute fanatics when it comes to warning Washington visitors away from Washington's worst torments. Here's the short list: long lines that never seem to move, lousy food (when D.C. boasts some of the finest restaurants on earth!), industrial-strength traffic jams, outrageous prices for mediocre hotel rooms, bored tour guides that herd tourists like sheep . . .

We do get quite grumpy when things go wrong on a Washington visit. It doesn't have to be this way for you.

This book is the reason why. Its primary purpose can be expressed in exactly ten words: We're going to take the misery out of touring Washington!

While we can't guarantee great weather and small crowds, we'll tell you when you've got the best chances of encountering both, and we'll give you tons of information that will save your feet and your wallet, not to mention your temper.

You'll also find suggestions for things to do and see off the beaten track on hot August afternoons when a stroll on the Mall invites heat stroke and when crowds mob the best-known attractions. At the same time, we'll introduce the best of what D.C. has to offer after the museums close, places where the people who live and work in Washington like to go after hours: the great ethnic restaurants, theaters, and nightspots. We'll also tell you about the best places around to shop, walk, take a hike, get a workout, or ride a bike.

This guide is designed both for folks planning a family trip to Washington to see its famous monuments, halls of government, historic places, and museums, and for business travelers who want to avoid the city's worst hassles. The *Unofficial Guide* also shows how you can see a side of Washington that most visitors miss: a re-creation of a Roman catacomb, $90 million worth of antiques in one place, and the mansion and gardens of a fabulously rich heiress, among others.

The bottom line: We'll help you see Washington like a native. Of course, we can't promise that your D.C. visit will be perfect. But this guidebook can help you eliminate most of the needless irritations that so frequently spoil the fun for Washington tourists.

And who knows? Maybe you'll discover, as we did while researching this book, that there's nothing left to "hate" about being a Washington visitor!

About This Guide

■ How Come "Unofficial"? ■

Most "official" guides to Washington, D.C., tout the well-known sights, promote the local restaurants and hotels indiscriminately, and leave out a lot of good stuff. This one is different.

Instead of pandering to the tourist industry, we'll tell you if the food is bad at a well-known restaurant, we'll complain loudly about D.C.'s notorious high prices, and we'll guide you away from the crowds and lines for a break now and then.

Visiting Washington requires wily strategies not unlike those used in the sacking of Troy. We've sent in a team of evaluators who toured each site, ate in the city's best restaurants, performed critical evaluations of its hotels, and visited Washington's wide variety of nightclubs. If a museum is boring, or standing in line for two hours to view a famous attraction is a waste of time, we say so—and, in the process, hopefully make your visit more fun, efficient, and economical.

■ Creating a Guidebook ■

We got into the guidebook business because we were unhappy with the way travel guides make the reader work to get any usable information. Wouldn't it be nice, we thought, if we were to make guides that are easy to use?

Most guidebooks are compilations of lists. This is true regardless of whether the information is presented in list form or artfully distributed through pages of prose. There is insufficient detail in a list, and prose can present tedious helpings of nonessential or marginally useful information. Not enough wheat, so to speak, for nourishment in one instance, and too much chaff in the other. Either way, these types of guides provide little more than departure points from which readers initiate their own quests.

Many guides are readable and well researched, but they tend to be difficult to use. To select a hotel, for example, a reader must study several pages of descriptions with only the boldface hotel names breaking up large blocks of text. Because each description essentially deals with the same variables, it is difficult to recall what was said concerning a particular hotel. Readers generally must work through all the write-ups before beginning to narrow their choices. The presentation of restaurants, nightclubs, and attractions is similar except that even more reading is usually required. To use such a guide is to undertake an exhaustive research process that requires examining nearly as many options and possibilities as starting from scratch. Recommendations, if any, lack depth and conviction. These guides compound rather than solve problems by failing to narrow travelers' choices down to a thoughtfully considered, well-distilled, and manageable few.

■ How *Unofficial Guides* Are Different ■

Readers care about the authors' opinions. The authors, after all, are supposed to know what they are talking about. This, coupled with the fact that the traveler wants quick answers (as opposed to endless alternatives), dictates that authors should be explicit, prescriptive, and above all, direct. The authors of the *Unofficial Guide* try to do just that. They spell out alternatives and recommend specific courses of action. They simplify complicated destinations and attractions and allow the traveler to feel in control in the most unfamiliar environments. The objective of the *Unofficial Guide* authors is not to give the most information or all of the information, but to offer the most accessible, useful information.

An *Unofficial Guide* is a critical reference work; it focuses on a travel destination that appears to be especially complex. Our authors and research team are completely independent from the attractions, restaurants, and hotels we describe. The *Unofficial Guide to Washington, D.C.* is designed for individuals and families traveling for the fun of it, as well as for business travelers and conventioneers, especially those visiting D.C. for the first time. The guide is directed at value-conscious, consumer-oriented adults who seek a cost-effective, though not Spartan, travel style.

■ Special Features ■

The *Unofficial Guide* offers the following special features:

— Friendly introductions to Washington's most fascinating neighborhoods.

— "Best of" listings giving our well-qualified opinions on things ranging from bagels to baguettes, 4-star hotels to 12-story views.

— Listings that are keyed to your interests, so you can pick and choose.

— Advice to sight-seers on how to avoid the worst of the crowds; advice to business travelers on how to avoid traffic and excessive costs.

— Recommendations for lesser-known sights that are away from the huge monuments of the Mall but are no less spectacular.

— A zone system and maps to make it easy to find places you want to go to and avoid places you don't.

— Expert advice on avoiding Washington's notorious street crime.

— A Hotel Chart that helps you narrow down your choices fast, according to your needs.

— Shorter listings that include only those restaurants, clubs, and hotels we think are worth considering.

— Detailed index and table of contents to help you find things fast.

— Insider advice on crowds, lines, best times of day (or night) to go places, and, our secret weapon, Washington's stellar subway system.

What you *won't* get:

— Long, useless lists where everything looks the same.

— Information that gets you somewhere you want to go at the worst possible time.

— Information without advice on how to use it.

■ How This Guide Was Researched and Written ■

While a lot of guidebooks have been written about Washington, D.C., very few have been evaluative. Some guides come close to regurgitating the hotels' and tourist offices' own promotional material. In preparing this work, nothing was taken for granted. Each museum, monument, federal building, hotel, restaurant, shop, and attraction was visited by a team of trained observers who conducted detailed evaluations and rated each according to formal criteria. Team members conducted interviews with tourists of all ages to determine what they enjoyed most and least during their Washington visit.

While our observers are independent and impartial, they did not claim to have special expertise. Like you, they visited Washington as tourists or business travelers, noting their satisfaction or dissatisfaction.

The primary difference between the average tourist and the trained evaluator is the evaluator's skills in organization, preparation, and observation. The trained evaluator is responsible for much more than simply observing and cataloging. While the average tourist is gazing in awe at stacks of $20 bills at the Bureau of Engraving and Printing, for instance, the professional is rating the tour in terms of pace, how quickly the line moves, the location of rest rooms, and how well children can see the exhibits. He or she also checks out things like other attractions close by, alternate places to go if the line at a main attraction is too long, and the best local lunch options.

Observer teams use detailed checklists to analyze hotel rooms, restaurants, nightclubs, and attractions. Finally, evaluator ratings and observations are integrated with tourist reactions and the opinions of patrons for a comprehensive quality profile of each feature and service.

In compiling this guide, we recognize that a tourist's age, background, and interests will strongly influence his or her taste in Washington's wide array of attractions and will account for a preference for one sight or museum over another. Our sole objective is to provide the reader with sufficient description, critical evaluation, and pertinent data to make knowledgeable decisions according to individual tastes.

■ Letters, Comments, and Questions from Readers ■

We expect to learn from our mistakes, as well as from the input of our readers, and to improve with each new book and edition. Many of those who use the *Unofficial Guides* write to us asking questions, making comments, or sharing their own discoveries and lessons learned in Washington. We appreciate all such input, both positive and critical, and encourage our readers to continue writing. Readers' comments and observations will be frequently incorporated in revised editions of the *Unofficial Guide*, and will contribute immeasurably to its improvement.

How to Write the Authors:
Bob, Joe, Eve
The Unofficial Guide to Washington, D.C.
P.O. Box 43059
Birmingham, AL 35243

When you write, be sure to put your return address on your letter as well as on the envelope—sometimes envelopes and letters get separated. And remember, our work takes us out of the office for long periods of time, so forgive us if our response is delayed.

Reader Survey

At the back of the guide you will find a short questionnaire that you can use to express opinions about your Washington visit. Clip the questionnaire out along the dotted line and mail it to the above address.

■ How Information Is Organized: ■
By Subject and by Geographic Zones

In order to give you fast access to information about the *best* of Washington, we've organized material in several formats.

Hotels Since most people visiting Washington stay in one hotel for the duration of their trip, we have summarized our coverage of hotels in charts, maps, ratings, and rankings that allow you to quickly focus your decision-making process. We do not go on, page after page, describing lobbies and rooms which, in the final analysis, sound much the same. Instead, we concentrate on the specific variables that differentiate one hotel from another: location, size, room quality, services, amenities, and cost.

Restaurants We provide a lot of detail when it comes to restaurants. Since you will probably eat a dozen or more restaurant meals during your stay, and since not even you can predict what you might be in the mood for on Saturday night, we provide detailed profiles of the best restaurants in and around Washington.

Entertainment and Night Life Visitors frequently try several different clubs or nightspots during their stay. Since clubs and nightspots, like restaurants, are usually selected spontaneously after arriving in Washington, we believe detailed descriptions are warranted. The best nightspots and lounges in Washington are profiled by category (see pages 137–65).

Geographic Zones Once you've decided where you're going, getting there becomes the issue. To help you do that, we have divided the city into geographic zones and the suburbs into sub-zones:

Zone 1.   The Mall

Zone 2.   Capitol Hill

Zone 3.   Downtown

Zone 4.   Foggy Bottom

Zone 5.   Georgetown

Zone 6.   Dupont Circle/Adams-Morgan

Zone 7.   Upper Northwest Washington

Zone 8.   Northeast Washington

Zone 9.   Southeast Washington

Zones 10A–D.   Maryland Suburbs

Zones 11A–C.   Virginia Suburbs

All profiles of hotels, restaurants, and nightspots include zone numbers. If you are staying at the Carlyle Suites, for example, and are interested in Japanese restaurants within walking distance, scanning the restaurant profiles for restaurants in Zone 6 (Dupont Circle/Adams-Morgan) will provide you with the best choices.

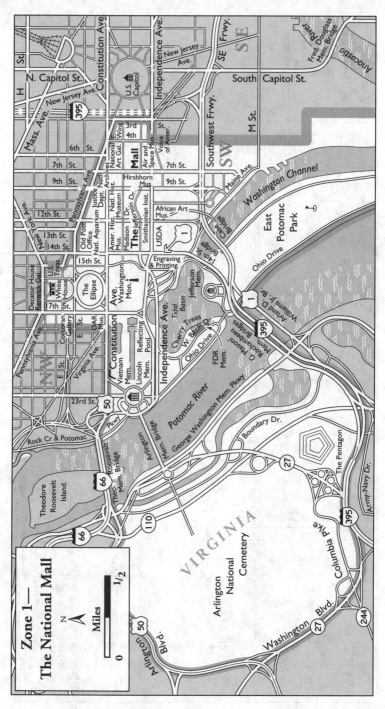

(See pages 82–83 for maps showing all zones combined).

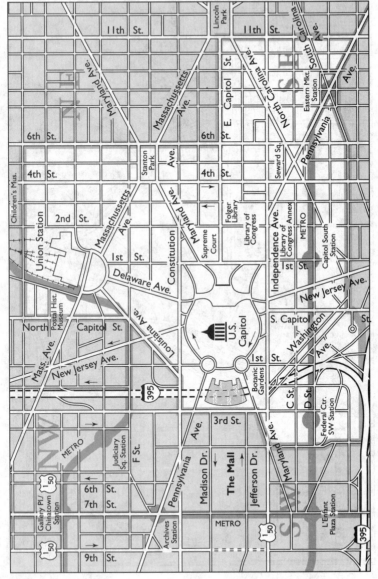

11th St.

Lincoln Park

11th St.

Maryland Ave.

Massachussetts Ave.

E. Capitol St.

North Carolina Ave.

South Carolina Ave.

Ave.

6th St.

6th St.

Stanton Park

Ave.

4th St.

4th St.

Pennsylvania

Seward Sq.

Eastern Mkt. Station

Children's Mus.

2nd St.

Massachussetts Ave.

Constitution

Maryland Ave.

Folger Library

Library of Congress

Independence Ave.

Library of Congress Annex

METRO

Union Station

1st St.

Supreme Court

1st St.

Capitol South Station

Delaware Ave.

Louisiana Ave.

New Jersey Ave.

Postal Hist. Museum

North   Capitol   St.

U.S. Capitol

S. Capitol

St.

Mass. Ave.

New Jersey Ave.

Washington Ave.

1st St.

395

Botanic Gardens

C St.

D St.

Federal Ctr. SW Station

METRO

Judiciary Sq. Station

3rd St.

Maryland Ave.

Gallery Pl./ Chinatown Station

50

F St.

Pennsylvania Ave.

Madison Dr.

6th St.

7th St.

The Mall

Jefferson Dr.

395

Archives Station

METRO

50

9th St.

50

L'Enfant Plaza Station

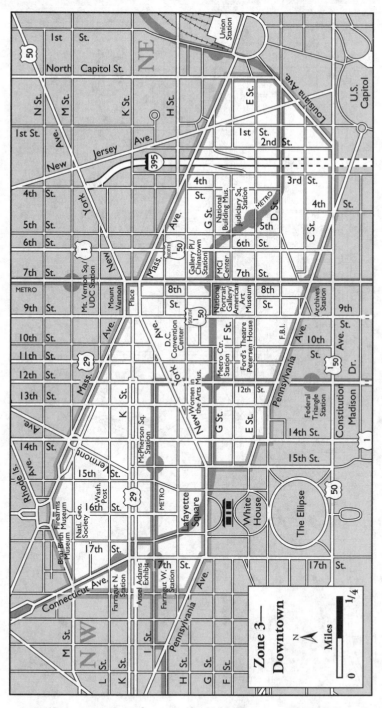

(See pages 82–83 for maps showing all zones combined).

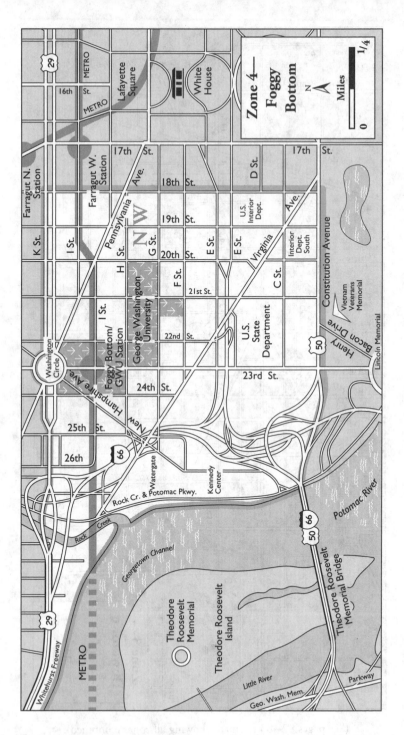

Zone 4—
Foggy
Bottom

N

Miles

0   1/4

Lafayette Square

White House

METRO

16th St.

29

Farragut N. Station

Farragut W. Station

K St.

I St.

Pennsylvania Ave.

H St.

G St.

George Washington University

I St.

Washington Circle

Foggy Bottom/GWU Station

New Hampshire Ave.

24th St.

25th St.

26th

66

17th St.

18th St.

19th St.

20th

21st St.

22nd St.

23rd St.

F St.

E St.

E St.

D St.

U.S. Interior Dept.

Interior Dept. South

17th St.

C St.

Virginia Ave.

U.S. State Department

Constitution Avenue

Henry Bacon Drive

Vietnam Veterans Memorial

Lincoln Memorial

50

Watergate

Kennedy Center

Rock Cr. & Potomac Pkwy.

Rock Creek

Georgetown Channel

Whitehurst Freeway

29

METRO

Theodore Roosevelt Memorial

Theodore Roosevelt Island

Little River

Geo. Wash. Mem.

Potomac River

50 66

Theodore Roosevelt Memorial Bridge

Parkway

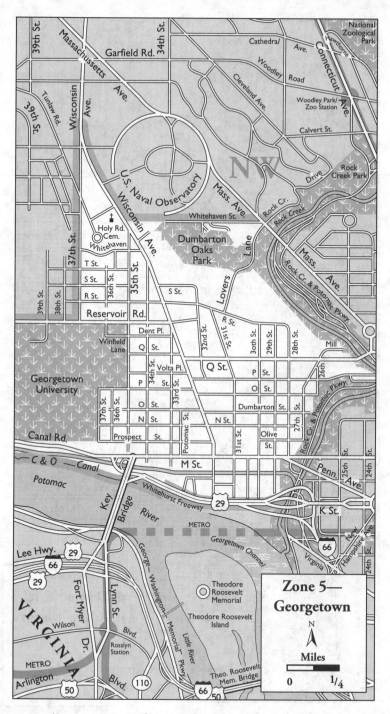

(See pages 82–83 for maps showing all zones combined).

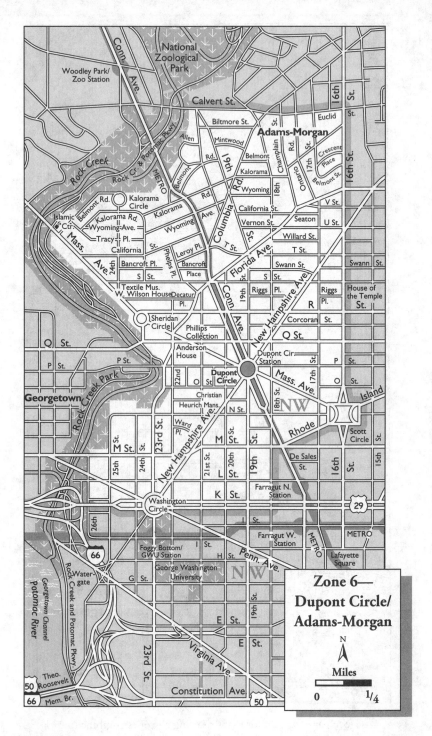

Zone 6—
Dupont Circle/
Adams-Morgan

14

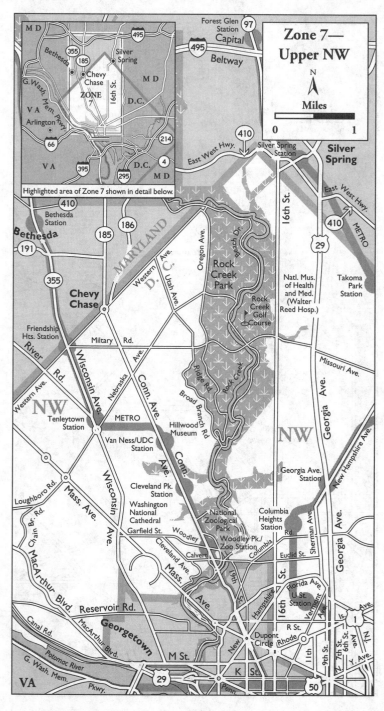

(See pages 82–83 for maps showing all zones combined).

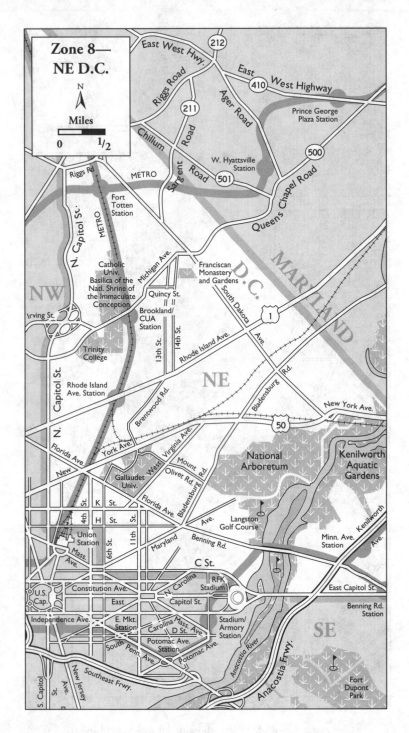

Zone 8—
NE D.C.

N

Miles

0   1/2

East West Hwy.   212

East West Highway   410

Riggs Road

Ager Road   Prince George
Plaza Station

211

Chillum   Sargent Road   500

W. Hyattsville
Station

Riggs Rd   METRO   501   Queen's Chapel Road

N. Capitol St.   METRO   Fort
Totten
Station

Catholic
Univ.
Basilica of the
Natl. Shrine of
the Immaculate
Conception   Michigan Ave.   Franciscan
Monastery
and Gardens   D.C.   MARYLAND

Quincy St.   South Dakota   1

Irving St.   Brookland/
CUA
Station   14th St.

13th St.   Rhode Island Ave.

Trinity
College

NW   NE

Capitol St.   Rhode Island
Ave. Station   Brentwood Rd.   Bladensburg Rd.   New York Ave.

50

N.   York Ave.

Florida Ave.   West Virginia Ave.   Mount   National
Arboretum   Kenilworth
Aquatic
Gardens

New   Oliver Rd.

Gallaudet
Univ.   Florida Ave.   Bladensburg Rd.

K   St.   Ave.   Langston
Golf Course   Kenilworth

4th St.   H   St.   St.   Minn. Ave.
Station   Ave.

Union
Station   6th St.   11th St.   Maryland   Benning Rd.

Mass.
Ave.   C St.

U.S.
Cap.   Constitution Ave.   N. Carolina   RFK
Stadium   East Capitol St.

East   Capitol St.   Benning Rd.
Station

Independence Ave.   E. Mkt.
Station   Carolina   Mass. Ave.   Stadium/
Armory
Station   SE

D St.

Potomac Ave.
Station   Potomac Ave.

South Penn. Ave.   Anacostia River

S. Capitol St.   New Jersey Ave.   Southeast Frwy.   Anacostia Frwy.   Fort
Dupont
Park

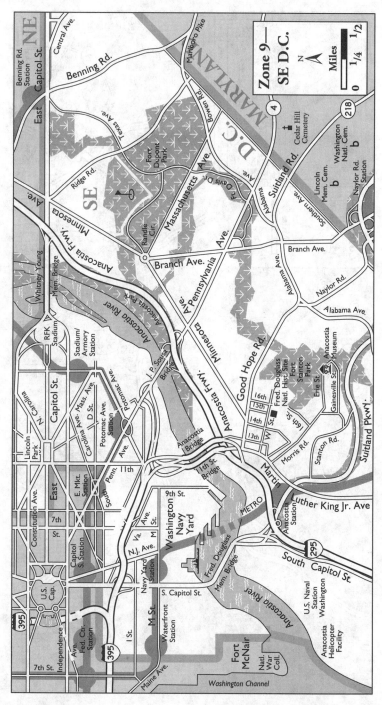

(See pages 82–83 for maps showing all zones combined).

17

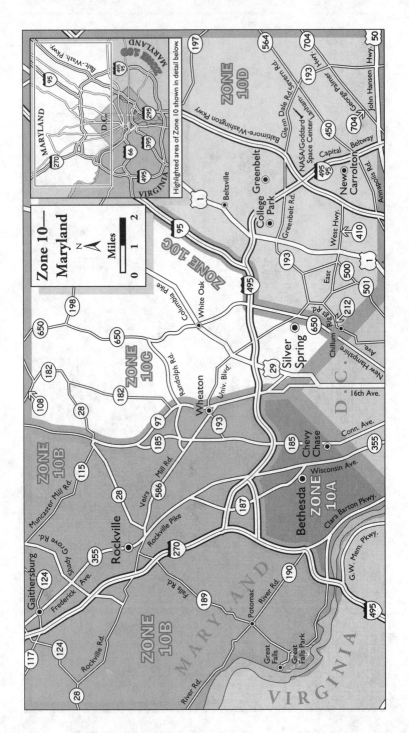

Zone 10—Maryland

N

Miles
0   1   2

ZONE 10D

ZONE 10C

ZONE 10B

ZONE 10C

ZONE 10B

ZONE 10A

D.C.

MARYLAND

VIRGINIA

Gaithersburg
Rockville
Potomac
Bethesda
Chevy Chase
Silver Spring
Wheaton
White Oak
Beltsville
Greenbelt
College Park
New Carrollton
Great Falls
Great Falls Park

Baltimore-Washington Pkwy.
NASA/Goddard Space Center
Lanham
Capital Beltway
Annapolis Rd.
Greenbelt Rd.
West Hwy.
East
Riggs Rd.
Chillum
New Hampshire Ave.
16th Ave.
Conn. Ave.
Wisconsin Ave.
Clara Barton Pkwy.
G.W. Mem. Pkwy.
Columbia Pike
Randolph Rd.
Univ. Blvd.
Veirs Mill Rd.
586
Rockville Pike
Falls Rd.
River Rd.
Muncaster Mill Rd.
Shady Grove Rd.
Frederick Ave.
Rockville Rd.
Glenn Dale Rd.
Good Luck Rd.
George Palmer Hwy.
John Hansen Hwy.

MARYLAND
MARYLAND
D.C.
VIRGINIA

Highlighted area of Zone 10 shown in detail below.

Balt.-Wash. Pkwy.

270
95
95
295
66
395
495

197
564
704
50
193
704
704
450
410
1
500
501
212
650
29
185
355
187
190
189
124
117
28
124
355
28
115
182
108
28
97
185
193
650
650
198
182
1
193
495
95
1
95

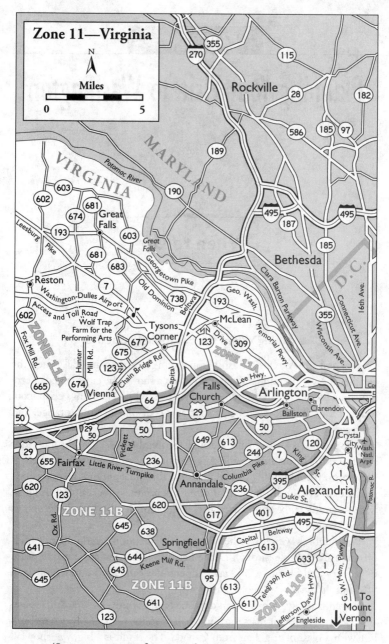

Zone 11—Virginia

N

Miles
0   5

(See pages 82–83 for maps showing all zones combined).

PART ONE

Planning Your Visit to Washington

When to Go

■ Going When the Weather Is Good ■

The best times to visit Washington are in the spring and fall, when the weather is most pleasant and nature puts on a show. The city's fabled cherry blossoms bloom in late March or early April, while fall brings crisp, cool weather and, by mid-October, a spectacular display of gold, orange, and red leaves.

The summers—mid-June through September—can be brutally hot and humid. Visitors in July and August not only contend with the heat as they sprint from building to building, but also must endure the city's over-reliance on air conditioning that often reaches meat-locker chill. August, with its predictably oppressive heat, is the month when Washingtonians leave town in droves.

Washington's winter weather, on the other hand, is erratic. Balmy, mid-60s days are possible through December. While it often gets into the teens in January and February, midday temperatures can climb into the 40s and 50s. This is the season to beat the crowds.

March is tricky. While warm daytime temperatures are frequent, some-times a large, moist air mass moving north from the Gulf of Mexico will col-lide with a blast of frigid air from Canada. The result is a big, wet snowfall that paralyzes the city for days. (It should be noted, in all fairness, that the *pre-diction* of snow can paralyze D.C.)

Washington weather can run the gamut from subzero (rarely) to mild

Washington's Average Monthly Temperatures		
	Degrees Fahrenheit	
	High	**Low**
January	42	27
February	44	28
March	53	35
April	64	44
May	75	54
June	83	64
July	87	68
August	84	66
September	78	60
October	67	48
November	55	38
December	45	30

(most of the winter, some of the summer, and most of the spring and fall) to scorchingly hot and unbearably humid (most of July and August). See the boxed table of the city's average monthly temperatures, in degrees Fahrenheit.

■ Avoiding Crowds ■

In general, popular tourist sites are busier on weekends than weekdays, Saturdays are busier than Sundays, and summer is busier than winter. The best days for avoiding big crowds at Washington's most popular attractions are Monday through Wednesday. Crowds begin to increase as the week progresses, with the volume of visitors peaking on Saturday. During the busiest tourist seasons, spring and summer, major Washington tourist attractions are always crowded between 9:30 A.M. and 3 P.M. For people in town on business, this tourist influx means heavier traffic, congested airports, a packed Metro . . . and a tough time finding a convenient hotel room.

Driving in weekday rush hours, featuring 100,000 frantic, short-tempered bureaucrats clawing their way to office or home, should be avoided at all costs. On weekends, the same government workers and their families become tourists, often creating midday traffic snarls during the warmer months.

If you're driving to Washington, try to time your arrival on a weekend or during a non-rush hour time—before 7 A.M. or during a rather narrow window that opens around 9:30 A.M. and starts to close quickly around 3

P.M. Afternoon traffic doesn't begin to clear up until at least 6:30 P.M. Friday afternoon rush hours are the worst: Don't even think of driving near D.C. until after 8 P.M.

■ **Trying to Reason with the Tourist Season** ■

Whether you're in town on business or pleasure, it's a good idea to be aware of when the big crowds of tourists are likely to be jamming up the Metro, the sidewalk, or the place you've picked for lunch.

The best time to avoid crowds entirely is in winter. On weekdays especially, the Mall is nearly deserted and museums, monuments, and normally crowd-intensive hot spots like the U.S. Capitol are virtually empty—except for the people who work there. Furthermore, the relative scarcity of tourists in the off-season eliminates the worst of D.C.'s traffic gridlock, except during peak rush hours.

After the winter doldrums, crowds begin picking up in late March and peak in early April, when the Japanese cherry trees along the Tidal Basin bloom and Washington is flooded with visitors. Mammoth throngs pack the Mall, and it's elbow to elbow in the National Air and Space Museum. Because of the crowded conditions, we do not recommend touring Washington in the early spring.

Instead, if at all possible, delay your visit until late May or early June. Crowds are more manageable for a few weeks and the weather is usually delightful.

The tourist pace begins picking up again in mid-June as schools let out. July through mid-August are very crowded—and usually the weather is brutally hot and humid. Popular museums such as the Museum of Natural History, the National Air and Space Museum, and the National Museum of American History fill up with masses of elbow-to-elbow people, eating in restaurants becomes a stress-inducing ordeal, and the entire experience becomes exhausting. Driving conditions, never good in Washington, degenerate into gridlock—even on weekends—and the Metro is packed to rush-hour levels all day.

The throngs begin to thin during the last two weeks of August, when kids start returning to school. After Labor Day, the volume of visitors drops off significantly during the week, but weekends remain packed through October—though not as packed as in spring and summer. In November, tourist activity slows down dramatically.

After May and June, the best time to visit Washington is in the late fall and winter. While Thanksgiving Day brings hordes of visitors to popular sights on the Mall, car traffic is light and getting around town from November through March is easy. Winter visitors can't count on balmy weather, but crowds are virtually nonexistent and Washington's elaborate cultural season kicks into full swing. Plays, music, opera, and ballet fill the city's theaters and halls — the Kennedy Center, Arena Stage, the Shakespeare Theater at the Folger, the National Theater, Ford's Theatre, and the Library of Congress. Both business visitors and folks in town to tour the sights will find Washington a lot easier to get around in during the late fall and winter.

The Longest Lines

Unlike Disney World, a tourist destination with which Washington shares some similarities, D.C. has only a handful of attractions that require enduring long queues. Among these are the Bureau of Engraving and Printing (before Easter and after September; otherwise a "time ticket" system is in effect that virtually eliminates long lines), the U.S. Capitol, and the FBI. Even at these, a little judicious planning can virtually guarantee you won't spend hours standing in line.

If your visit to Washington must coincide with the heavy tourist season, read on: There are ways to make it more tolerable, in spite of the record crowds jamming the Mall, the popular museums, eateries, public transportation, and highways. Check Part Five for detailed information on transportation, and Part Nine for pages of sight-seeing tips.

Getting to Washington

Folks planning a trip to our nation's capital have some options when it comes to getting there: car, train, or plane. Your distance from Washington—and your tolerance for hassles such as Capital Beltway gridlock and inconveniently located airports—will probably determine which mode of transportation you ultimately take. (See also Part Four, Arriving and Getting Oriented.)

■ Driving ■

A lot of people who live in the populous Eastern Seaboard or anywhere else within a 12-hour drive of D.C. automatically jump in the family car when embarking on a vacation to Washington. And no wonder: A nearly complete interstate highway system and cheap gasoline make the car trip both easy and inexpensive. The problem, however, is when you arrive in Washington . . . or, to be more exact, when you hit the notorious Capital Beltway that surrounds the city in the Maryland and Virginia suburbs. Arrive on a weekday morning between 7 A.M. and 10 A.M. or in the afternoon from 3 P.M. to 7 P.M. and you'll discover why Washington has a reputation for traffic congestion rivaled only by New York and Los Angeles: Traffic inches along during rush hours and is astonishingly heavy the rest of the day and on warm-weather weekends as well. It only gets worse the closer you get to the Mall. Washington's peculiar geography and eighteenth-century street layout, coupled with unremitting urban and suburban growth, makes touring by car almost impossible. Street parking near popular tourist sights is severely limited, and parking garages, while plentiful in downtown D.C., are expensive and often inconvenient. Our recommendation: If at all possible, leave the car at home. Washington's air and rail connections are excellent, and its Metro subway system is one of the best in the world. And where the Metro won't take you—Georgetown, Mount Vernon, and the Washington National Cathedral come to mind—plentiful cabs and commercial touring outfits will. If you do drive, arrive on a weekend to miss the worst traffic, or very late or early during the week. Stay at a hotel with off-street parking and within easy walking distance to a Metro station. Use public transportation and leave the car parked through most of your stay.

■ Taking the Train ■

Washington's gleaming Union Station, recently refurbished and the city's most-visited tourist attraction (the National Air and Space Museum is number two), is only one of the reasons that taking the train to D.C. is an excellent idea. Another is convenience: Folks living along the East Coast from Boston to Miami are served daily by Amtrak, and lots of people living east of the Mississippi are close to direct rail service into the nation's capital. (In some cases you can board the train in the evening and arrive in Washington in the morning.) From Union Station you're only minutes from a downtown hotel by cab. Because of the city's exasperating traffic—and a public transportation system that virtually eliminates the need for a car—it's the smart way to travel to Washington. We've provided a listing of some major cities with direct Amtrak passenger train service to Washington's Union Station (the frequency of service indicates the number of trains running in both directions).

For schedules and reservations, call Amtrak at (800) 872-7245.

■ Flying ■

Washington, the seat of the federal government and probably the world's most powerful city, is understandably well served by the airline industry. The town boasts three airports, each with its own peculiarities. Washington National Airport is by far the most convenient, located a few miles south of D.C. on the Virginia side of the Potomac River. Yet its closeness to the city has resulted in some odd restrictions: Planes aren't allowed to fly over the White House and other sensitive places, so all approaches and takeoffs are routed over the Potomac River; no planes are allowed to take off or land late at night; only 37 large jets are allowed to land or take off an hour; and a "perimeter rule" restricts nonstop flights to and from National to a distance of 1,250 miles or less. With virtually no international connections, think of National as the "East Coast, short-hop" airport. If you can't get a direct flight into National from your hometown, consider making a connection that will get you into National. It will probably be faster—and certainly more convenient—than flying into either of the other two airports that serve Washington.

While National is our first choice for travelers flying into D.C., its close proximity to the bustling city creates problems for the unwary flyer: It's incredibly congested by heavy traffic. Parking is expensive, long-term parking is a long bus ride away, and renting a car and driving into D.C. can be a drawn-out, frustrating experience. The good news: A new, $1 billion terminal should help reduce the curbside congestion. Cab fares to downtown

Amtrak Passenger Train Service to Washington			
City	**Distance**	**Hours**	**Frequency**
Northeast			
Philadelphia	115 miles	1.5 hours	more than 1/hour
New York City	225 miles	3 hours	more than 1/hour
Boston	400 miles	8 hours	more than 1/hour
South			
Richmond	110 miles	2 hours	7/day
Newport News	187 miles	4 hours	2/day
Raleigh-Durham	305 miles	6 hours	2/day
Charlotte	376 miles	8 hours	2/day
Charleston, S.C.	503 miles	8.5 hours	2/day
Atlanta	633 miles	14 hours	1/day
Birmingham	799 miles	18 hours	1/day
New Orleans	1,155 miles	36 hours	1/day
Jacksonville	753 miles	13 hours	3/day
Tampa	996 miles	18 hours	1/day
Orlando	1,129 miles	16 hours	2/day
Miami	1,166 miles	21 hours	3/day
West			
Pittsburgh	300 miles	8 hours	1/day
Cleveland	440 miles	11 hours	1/day
Toledo	550 miles	13 hours	1/day
Cincinnati	602 miles	14 hours	3/week
Chicago	780 miles	18 hours	10/week

are reasonable, free shuttles can get you to your hotel in a half-hour or so, and National has its own Metro stop.

Dulles International Airport, on the other hand, is rarely congested. No wonder: It's located in the boonies of Virginia, a solid hour from the city by car and with no direct public transportation downtown. Dulles is primarily known as an international hub, although domestic flights are on the increase (spurring a construction project that in 1996 doubled the main terminal's size to 1.1 million square feet). In a sly marketing move a few years back, Baltimore's Friendship Airport became Baltimore/Washington International Airport (BWI). It worked: 1994 was a record-breaking year for this ever-expanding air hub. Southwest, for example, has increased its low-cost service to 20 flights a day, attracting a lot of travelers to Washington who would otherwise drive. BWI is also aggressively pursuing an international market and opened a new, $110 million international pier in the fall of 1997. Yet this busy airport is still closer to Baltimore than to Washington, which means D.C.-bound tourists face at least a 50-minute car or van ride before the Washington Monument comes into view. Another option for folks arriving at BWI is to take the train: Maryland commuter rail service (called MARC) and Amtrak connect BWI to D.C.'s Union Station. The train ride takes almost an hour, though—hardly convenient for tourists itching to explore the marble edifices lining the Mall.

A Calendar of Special Events

Washington hosts a variety of special events throughout the year: fairs, celebrations, parades, shows, festivals, tours, film and jazz festivals, and ceremonies. For exact dates, times, locations, and admission fees, call the phone numbers provided before your visit.

January

Opening of Congress. The first week of January.

Martin Luther King, Jr., Birthday Observance. Wreath-laying ceremony at the Lincoln Memorial accompanied by his "I Have a Dream" speech. Local choirs, guest speakers, and military color guard salute King's memory. Free. (202) 619-7222.

Robert E. Lee's Birthday Celebration. The birthdays of Revolutionary War Colonel Light Horse Harry Lee and his son, Robert E. Lee, are celebrated at the Lee-Fendall House and The Boyhood Home of Robert E. Lee in Alexandria, Virginia. Refreshments, period music, house tours. Admission fee. (703) 838-4200.

February

Black History Month. Special events, various Smithsonian museum exhibits, and cultural programs celebrate the contributions of African-Americans to the quality of American life. Free. (202) 727-0321.

Abraham Lincoln's Birthday. Lincoln's birthday (February 12) is commemorated with an elaborate wreath-laying ceremony and a reading of the Gettysburg Address at the Lincoln Memorial. Free. (202) 619-7222.

Mount Vernon Open House. A wreath-laying ceremony at Washington's tomb is followed by a fife and drum corps performance on the green. Free. (703) 780-2000.

George Washington's Birthday Parade. The nation's largest parade celebrating our first president takes place in Old Town Alexandria. Free. (703) 838-4200.

Washington Boat Show. The latest in pleasure craft and equipment at the Washington Convention Center. Admission fee. (202) 789-1600.

Frederick Douglass Birthday Tribute. The birthday of the great black statesman, orator, and advocate of freedom for blacks and other minorities is observed at the Frederick Douglass National Historic Site (Cedar Hill) in Anacostia. Free. (202) 619-7222.

Chinese New Year's Parade. Chinatown's colorful streets come alive with traditional firecrackers, lions, drums, and dragon dancers in a celebration of the Chinese Lunar New Year. Free. (202) 393-2280 or (202) 638-1041.

March

D.C. Armory Antiques Show. Features more than 185 dealers from 20 states, Canada, and Europe displaying their goods at the D.C. Armory. Admission fee. (301) 738-1966.

St. Patrick's Day Parade/Downtown Washington. The parade goes down Constitution Avenue, with dancers, bands, bagpipes, and floats, at 1 P.M. Free. (202) 637-2474.

Washington Flower & Garden Show. At the Washington Convention Center. Admission fee. (202) 789-1600.

U.S. Botanic Garden's Spring Flower Show. Free. (202) 225-8333.

Smithsonian Kite Festival. Kite makers and flyers of all ages gather at the Washington Monument grounds to compete for prizes and trophies. Free. (202) 357-2700.

National Cherry Blossom Festival. More than 6,000 Japanese cherry trees bloom in late March to early April, bringing springtime splendor to Washington. The Cherry Blossom Festival Parade features princesses, floats, and VIPS. Other events include free concerts, the Japanese Lantern Lighting Ceremony, the Cherry Blossom Ball, and an annual Marathon. The parade hot line is (202) 728-1137.

April

White House Spring Garden Tours. Tour the beautiful gardens of the presidential home. Free. (202) 456-2200.

White House Easter Egg Roll. For children ages 3–6 accompanied by an adult. Eggs and entertainment provided. Children of other ages gather on the Ellipse. Free. (202) 456-2200.

Thomas Jefferson's Birthday. The author of the Declaration of Independence is commemorated with military drills and a wreath-laying ceremony at the Jefferson Memorial. Free. (202) 619-7222.

Smithsonian's Craft Show. A sales exhibition by 100 craftspeople of hand-crafted objects of original design in fiber, ceramics, glass, jewelry, leather, metal, paper, textiles, and wood. Admission fee. (202) 357-2700.

Washington D.C. International Filmfest. International and local films screened at theaters city-wide. Tickets required. (202) 274-6810.

Earth Day. Various events and displays on the National Mall to celebrate our planet. Free. (603) 924-7720.

Duke Ellington Birthday Celebration. Commemorating this native Washingtonian's contribution to American music. Free. (202) 331-9404.

William Shakespeare's Birthday. A day of music, theater, children's events, food, and exhibits at the Folger Shakespeare Library. Free. (202) 544-7077.

Georgetown House Tour. Private homes in the city's oldest neighborhood are open for viewing. Admission fee. (202) 338-1796.

May

Washington National Cathedral Flower Mart. Each year is a salute to a different country, with flower booths, entertainment, and decorating demonstrations. Free. (202) 537-6200.

Goodwill Embassy Tour. Various Washington embassies open their doors to the public. Tour tickets include free shuttle bus. Admission/reservations required. (202) 636-4225.

Capitol Hill House and Garden Tour. See charmingly restored homes in this popular annual tour. Admission fee. (202) 543-0425.

Malcolm X Day. Celebrations honoring the life of the slain civil rights leader and orator. Free. (202) 678-8352.

National Law Enforcement Officers Memorial Candlelight Vigil. Honors America's fallen law enforcement officers; official dedication of new names being added to the memorial, located on E Street between 4th and 5th Streets, NW. Free. (202) 737-3400.

Memorial Day Weekend Concert. The National Symphony Orchestra performs on the West Lawn of the U.S. Capitol, kicking off the summer season. Free. (202) 619-7222.

Memorial Day Ceremonies at Arlington National Cemetery. (May 31) Wreath-laying ceremonies at the Kennedy grave site, a presidential wreath-laying at the Tomb of the Unknowns, and services at the Memorial Amphitheater featuring military bands and a presidential keynote address. Free. (202) 475-0856.

Memorial Day Ceremonies at the Vietnam Veterans Memorial. (May 31) Wreath-laying, speeches, military bands, and a keynote address. Free. (202) 619-7222.

Memorial Day Ceremonies at the U.S. Navy Memorial. (May 31) Wreath-laying ceremonies and an evening concert by the U.S. Navy Band. Free. (202) 737-2300.

June

Alexandria Waterfront Festival. Family-oriented weekend featuring tall ships, ethnic food, entertainment, fireworks, arts and crafts, a 10K run, and the blessing of the fleet. Sponsored by the Red Cross. Admission fee. (703) 549-8300.

Dupont-Kalorama Museum Walk Day. Celebration of collections by six institutions in the area. Activities include textile demonstrations, video programs, interactive tours, hands-on art programs, historic house tours, food, and crafts. Shuttle service provided. Free. (202) 667-0441.

Danceafrica, D.C. Indoor and outdoor performances; African arts, crafts, and food; and evening concerts. Free and admission-fee events. (202) 269-1600.

Kemper Open. Watch the biggest names in professional golf. Admission fee for spectators. (301) 469-3737.

Caribbean Carnival Extravaganza. Judging of Kings, Queens, and Individuals, and a parade ending at Banneker Recreation Park at Georgia Avenue and Barry Place, NW. Free. (202) 726-2204.

July

Festival of American Folklife. More than one million people attend this festival of American music, crafts, and ethnic foods on the Mall each year. Free. (202) 357-2700.

National Independence Day Celebration. (July 4) A full day of dramatic readings, a parade down Constitution Avenue, a demonstration of colonial military maneuvers, entertainment at the Sylvan Theatre, a concert by the National Symphony Orchestra, and a spectacular fireworks display over the Washington Monument. Free. (202) 619-7222.

Virginia Scottish Games. Two-day annual Celtic festival with traditional Highland dancing, bagpiping, animal events, and fiddling competitions. Scottish foods, goods, and genealogy featured. Held at Episcopal High School, 3901 West Braddock Road, Alexandria, Virginia. Admission fee. (703) 838-4200.

Soap Box Derby. Soap-box cars roll down Constitution Avenue, NW, between New Jersey and Louisiana Avenues in Capitol Hill. Free. (301) 670-1110.

August

U.S. Army Band's 1812 Overture Concert. A concert and pageant at the Sylvan Theatre on the Washington Monument grounds. Free. (703) 696-3718.

Georgia Avenue Day. Colorful street fair with a parade, carnival rides, live music, and ethnic food held at Emery Park, Georgia and Missouri Avenues, and Banneker Park at 9th Street and Barry Place, NW. Free. (202) 723-5166.

Summer-Long Activities

U.S. Navy Memorial Concerts on the Avenue Series. Beginning at 8 P.M. on Memorial Day and continuing each Tuesday evening at 8 P.M. through

Labor Day. At the U.S. Navy Memorial on Pennsylvania Avenue. Free. (202) 433-2525.

D.C. World Jazz Festival. Late June through August; various locations. Top national and international jazz artists perform. Free and admission-fee events. (202) 783-0360.

Sunday Polo. (Every Sunday afternoon) Matches on the field east of the Lincoln Memorial at 3 P.M. Free. (202) 485-9880.

C&O Canal Barge Rides. (May through mid-October) Mule-drawn barge rides in Georgetown. Costumed Park Service guides accompany each 90-minute trip, telling the canal's history through stories and song. Admission fee. (202) 653-5190.

U.S. Botanic Garden's Summer Terrace Show. (Mid-May through mid-October) A series of summer gardens in various themes. Free. (202) 225-7099.

Military Band Summer Concert Series. Outdoor concerts held every summer evening (except Saturdays), from Memorial Day through Labor Day, beginning at 8 P.M. Free. U.S. Army Band: (703) 696-3399; "The President's Own" Marine Band: (202) 433-4011; U.S. Navy Band: (202) 433-2525; U.S. Air Force Band: (202) 767-5658.

Monday:	U.S. Navy Band, U.S. Capitol, east side
Tuesday:	U.S. Army Band, Sylvan Theatre
	U.S. Air Force Band, U.S. Capitol, east side
	U.S. Navy Band, Navy Memorial Plaza
Wednesday:	Marine Band, U.S. Capitol, east side
	U.S. Army Band "Twilight Tattoo" at 7 P.M. on the Ellipse (call 202-685-2851 for more information).
Thursday:	U.S. Navy Band, Sylvan Theatre
Friday:	U.S. Army Band, U.S. Capitol, east side
	U.S. Air Force Band, Sylvan Theatre
Sunday:	Marine Band, Sylvan Theatre

September

National Frisbee Festival. The largest noncompetitive Frisbee festival in the United States, featuring world-class Frisbee champions and disc-catching dogs. On the Mall. Free. (202) 645-5043.

International Children's Festival. A two-day, outdoor arts celebration at the Wolf Trap Farm Park for the Performing Arts in Vienna, Virginia. Admission fee. (703) 642-0862.

D.C. Blues Festival. Features top blues performers at Carter Barron Amphitheatre in Rock Creek Park. Free. (202) 828-3028.

Black Family Reunion. A weekend-long celebration of the African-American family offers headline performers, fun, food, and exhibits on the Mall. Free. (202) 737-0120.

Labor Day Weekend Concert. The National Symphony Orchestra closes the summer season with an evening concert on the West Lawn of the U.S. Capitol. Free. (202) 619-7222.

Elderfest. A day-long celebration featuring food, crafts, and entertainment. At Freedom Plaza, 1300 Pennsylvania Avenue, NW. Free. (202) 289-1510, ext. 121.

Adams-Morgan Day Festival. D.C.'s most culturally diverse neighborhood celebrates with live music, crafts, and cuisine. 18th Street and Columbia Road, NW. Free. (202) 332-3292.

Kalorama House and Embassy Tour. Tour selected homes and embassies and the Woodrow Wilson House. Admission fee. (202) 387-4062.

Constitution Day Commemoration. (September 17) Changing of the Joint Services Honor Guard every half-hour from noon to 8 P.M. in the Rotunda of the National Archives building. Free. (202) 501-5000.

Rock Creek Park Day. International and national music, children's activities, food, arts and crafts, exhibits, and demonstrations. Free. (202) 282-1063.

Kennedy Center Open House. The John F. Kennedy Center for the Performing Arts celebrates the arts with free concerts and performances. (202) 467-4600.

October

Supreme Court in Session. First Monday of October. Free. (202) 479-3000.

German-American Day Festival. Music, food, arts and crafts, and entertainment for the whole family. At Union Station on Massachusetts Avenue, NW. Free. (202) 554-2664.

Fall D.C. Antiques Fair. More than 185 dealers from 20 states, Canada, and Europe at the D.C. Armory. Admission fee. (301) 738-1966.

Taste of D.C. Festival. The best of D.C.'s vast array of restaurant food and ethnic cuisine; one of the city's most popular outdoor festivals. Free admission; purchase tickets for food tastings. (202) 724-5430.

Columbus Day Ceremonies. An annual tribute at the Columbus Memorial Plaza in front of Union Station. Free. (301) 434-2332.

Marine Corps Marathon. An annual event that attracts thousands of world-class runners. Starts and finishes at the Iwo Jima Memorial in Arlington. Registration fee. (703) 784-2225.

Washington International Horse Show. One of the country's largest and most important equestrian events, held at the USAir Arena in suburban Landover, Maryland. Admission fee. To reserve tickets, call (202) 432-SEAT after August 15.

White House Fall Garden Tours. See the Rose Garden and the South Lawn to the sounds of a military band. Free. (202) 456-2200.

Design for Living/Washington's Home Show. The area's largest residential design and home products show. Gourmet cooking demonstrations, wine tastings, and more. Washington Convention Center. Admission fee. (301) 261-2180 or (202) 268-8890.

November

Seafaring Celebration. Maritime lore, history, food, arts and crafts, storytelling, and performances at Building 76 in the Washington Navy Yard. Free. (202) 433-4882.

Veterans Day Ceremonies. (November 11) Arlington National Cemetery. Solemn ceremony with military bands to honor the nation's war dead. (202)

475-0843. Additional ceremonies at the Vietnam Veterans Memorial on the National Mall (202) 619-7222, Mount Vernon (703) 780-2000, and the U.S. Navy Memorial on Pennsylvania Avenue (202) 737-2300. Free.

A Christmas Carol. Dickens's holiday classic returns each year to Ford's Theatre. Admission fee. (202) 347-4833.

December

Pearl Harbor Day. (December 7) Wreath-laying ceremony at the U.S. Navy Memorial on Pennsylvania Avenue to commemorate the attack on Pearl Harbor. Free. (202) 737-2300.

Holidays at Mount Vernon. A re-creation of the authentic eighteenth-century holiday season. Visitors may tour the mansion's third floor, which is usually closed to the public. Admission fee. (703) 780-2000.

Scottish Christmas Walk. Featuring a parade through Old Town, bagpipes, Highland dancers, old homes tours, and children's events. Free. (703) 838-4200.

An American Holiday Celebration. A holiday music show by the U.S. Army Band at DAR Constitution Hall. Free, but tickets are required to assure seating. Write to: An American Holiday Celebration, Building 42, Ft. Leslie J. McNair, Washington, D.C. 20319-5050. (202) 685-2851. Do not call or write until after September.

Woodlawn Plantation Christmas Needlework Showcase. Needlework shops decorate the rooms in the mansion. At Woodlawn Plantation, 9000 Richmond Highway, Alexandria, Virginia. Admission fee. (703) 780-4000.

People's Christmas Tree Lighting. Military bands play as the magnificent Christmas tree on the west side of the U.S. Capitol is lighted the day before the Pageant of Peace begins. Free. (202) 224-3069.

National Christmas Tree Lighting/Pageant of Peace. The president lights the giant National Christmas Tree near the White House. Through the end of the year, the Ellipse is the site of nightly choral performances, a Nativity scene, a burning yule log, and a spectacular display of lighted Christmas trees representing each state and territory. Free. (202) 619-7222.

Old Town Christmas Candlelight Tours. Visit Ramsay House, Gadsby's Tavern Museum, the Lee-Fendall House, and the Carlyle House in Old Town Alexandria. Music, colonial dancing, period decorations, and light refreshments. Admission fee. (703) 838-4200.

U.S. Botanic Garden's Christmas Poinsettia Show. More than 3,000 red, white, and pink flowers and other plants in a holiday setting of Christmas wreaths and trees. Free. (202) 226-4082.

Washington National Cathedral Christmas Celebration and Services. Choral performances are part of the special services. Free. (202) 537-6200.

The Nutcracker. (Mid- to late December) The Joffrey Ballet performs this Christmas classic at the Kennedy Center. Free. (202) 467-4600.

White House Christmas Candlelight Tours. Evening tours of the White House Christmas decorations. Free. (202) 619-7222.

Capital Area Auto Show. Introduction of the new models at the Washington Convention Center. Admission fee. (202) 789-1600.

PART TWO

Hotels

Deciding Where to Stay

On weekdays, driving and parking in downtown Washington are nightmarish. On weekends, there is less traffic congestion, but parking is extremely difficult, particularly in the area of the Mall. Because the best way to get around Washington is on the Metro, we recommend a hotel within walking distance of a Metro station. With two rather prominent exceptions, all of Washington's best areas, as well as most of the Virginia and Maryland suburbs, are safely and conveniently accessible via this clean, modern subway system. Only historic Georgetown and the colorful, ethnic Adams-Morgan neighborhood are off-line.

Unless you plan to spend most of your time in Georgetown, we suggest that you pick a hotel elsewhere in the city. If you lodge in Georgetown, you will be reduced to driving or cabbing to get anywhere else. Adams-Morgan, a great neighborhood for dining and shopping, does not offer much in the way of lodging. If you go to Adams-Morgan, especially at night, take a cab.

■ Some Considerations ■

1. When choosing your Washington lodging, make sure your hotel is situated in a location convenient to your recreation or business needs, and that it is in a safe and comfortable area. Please note that while it is not practical to walk to the Washington Convention Center (the major convention venue) from many of the downtown hotels, larger conventions and trade shows provide shuttle service.

2. Find out how old the hotel is and when the guest rooms were last renovated. Request that the hotel send you its promotional brochure. Ask if brochure photos of guest rooms are accurate and current.

3. If you plan to take a car, inquire about the parking situation. Some hotels offer no parking at all, some charge dearly for parking, and a few offer free parking.

4. If you are not a city dweller, or are a light sleeper, try to book a hotel on a more quiet side street. Ask for a room off the street and high up.

5. Much of Washington is quite beautiful, as is the Potomac River. If you are on a romantic holiday, ask for a room on a higher floor with a good view.

6. When you plan your budget, remember that there is a 13% hotel tax (includes sales tax) plus $1.50 per night per room charge in the District of Columbia.

7. Washington is one of the busiest convention cities in the United States. If your visit to Washington coincides with one or more major conventions or trade shows, hotel rooms will be both scarce and expensive. If, on the other hand, you are able to schedule your visit to avoid big meetings, you will have a good selection of hotels at reasonably competitive prices. If you happen to be attending one of the big conventions, book early and use some of the tips listed below to get a discounted room rate. To assist in timing your visit, we have included a convention and trade show calendar.

Getting a Good Deal on a Room

Though Washington, D.C., is a major tourist destination, the economics of hotel room pricing is driven by business, government, and convention trade. This translates to high "rack rates" (a hotel's published room rate) and very few bargains. The most modest Econo Lodge or Days Inn in Washington charges upwards of $50 a night, and midrange chains, such as Holiday Inn and Ramada, ask from $75 to $150.

The good news is that Washington, D.C., and its Virginia and Maryland suburbs offer a staggering number of unusually fine hotels, including a high percentage of suite properties. The bad news, of course, is that you can expect to pay dearly to stay in them.

In most cities, the better and more expensive hotels are located close to the city center, with less expensive hotels situated farther out. There is normally a trade-off between location and price: If you are willing to stay out off the interstate and commute into downtown, you can expect to pay less for your suburban room than you would for a downtown room. In Washington, D.C., unfortunately, it very rarely works this way.

In the greater Washington area, every hotel is seemingly close to something. No matter how far you are from the Capitol, the Mall, and downtown, you can bank on your hotel being within spitting distance of some bureau, agency, airport, or industrial complex that funnels platoons of business travelers into guest rooms in a constant flow. Because almost every hotel and motel has its own captive market, the customary proximity/price trade-off doesn't apply. The Marriott at the Beltway and Wisconsin Avenue, for example, is 30 to 40 minutes away by car from the Mall but stays full with visitors to the nearby National Institutes of Health.

■ Where the Hotel Discounts Are ■

Special Weekend Rates

Although well-located Washington hotels are tough for the budget-conscious, it's not impossible to get a good deal, at least relatively speaking. For starters, some hotels that cater to business, government, and convention travelers offer special weekend discount rates that range from 15 to 40% below normal weekday rates. You can find out about weekend specials by calling individual hotels or by consulting your travel agent.

Getting Corporate Rates

Many hotels offer discounted corporate rates (5 to 20% off rack). Usually you do not need to work for a large company or have a special relationship with the hotel to obtain these rates. Simply call the hotel of your choice and ask for their corporate rates. Many hotels will guarantee you the discounted rate on the phone when you make your reservation. Others may make the rate conditional on your providing some sort of bona fides, for instance a fax on your company's letterhead requesting the rate, or a company credit card or business card on check-in. Generally, the screening is not rigorous.

Preferred Rates

If you cannot book the hotel of your choice through a half-price program, you and your travel agent may have to search for a lesser discount, often called a preferred rate. A preferred rate could be a discount made available to travel agents to stimulate their booking activity, or a discount initiated to attract a certain class of traveler. Most preferred rates are promoted through travel industry publications and so are often accessible only through an agent.

We recommend sounding out your travel agent about possible deals. Be aware, however, that the rates shown on travel agents' computerized reservations systems are not always the lowest rates obtainable. Zero in on a couple of hotels that fill your needs in terms of location and quality of accommodations, and then have your travel agent call for the latest rates and specials.

Hotel reps are almost always more responsive to travel agents, because travel agents represent a source of additional business. There are certain specials that hotel reps will disclose *only* to travel agents. Travel agents also come in handy when the hotel you want is supposedly booked. A personal appeal from your agent to the hotel's director of sales and marketing will get you a room more than half of the time.

Half-Price Programs

The larger discounts on rooms (35 to 60%), in Washington or anywhere else, are available through half-price hotel programs, often called travel clubs. Program operators contract with an individual hotel to provide rooms at deep discounts, usually 50% off rack rate, on a "space available" basis. Space available in practice generally means that you can reserve a room at the discounted rate whenever the hotel expects to be at less than 80% occupancy. A little calendar sleuthing to help you avoid city-wide conventions and special events will increase your chances of choosing a time when the discounts are available.

Most half-price programs charge an annual membership fee or directory subscription charge of $25 to $125. Once enrolled, you are mailed a membership card and a directory listing participating hotels. Examining the directory, you will notice immediately that there are many restrictions and exceptions. Some hotels, for instance, "black out" certain dates or times of year. Others may only offer the discount on certain days of the week, or require you to stay a certain number of nights. Still others may offer a much smaller discount than 50% off rack rate.

Programs specialize in domestic travel, international travel, or both. More established operators offer members between 1,000 and 4,000 hotels to choose from in the United States. All of the programs have a heavy concentration of hotels in California and Florida, and most have a very limited selection of participating properties in New York City or Boston. Offerings in other cities and regions of the United States vary considerably. The programs with the largest selections of Washington hotels are Encore, Travel America at Half Price (Entertainment Publications), International Travel Card, and Quest. Each of these programs lists between 4 and 50 hotels in the greater Washington area.

Encore	(800) 638-0930
Entertainment Publications	(800) 285-5525
International Travel Card	(800) 342-0558
Quest	(800) 638-9819

One problem with half-price programs is that not all hotels offer a full 50% discount. Another slippery problem is the base rate against which the discount is applied. Some hotels figure the discount on an exaggerated rack rate that nobody would ever have to pay. A few participating hotels may deduct the discount from a supposed "superior" or "upgraded" room rate, even though the room you get is the hotel's standard accommodation. Though hard to pin down, the majority of participating properties base discounts on the published rate in the *Hotel & Travel Index* (a quarterly reference work used by travel agents) and work within the spirit of their agreement with the program operator. As a rule, if you travel several times a year, your room rate savings will easily compensate you for program membership fees.

A noteworthy addendum: Deeply discounted rooms through half-price programs are not commissionable to travel agents. In practical terms this means that you must ordinarily make your own inquiry calls and reservations. If you travel frequently, however, and run a lot of business through your travel agent, he or she will probably do your legwork, lack of commission notwithstanding.

Wholesalers, Consolidators, and Reservation Services

If you do not want to join a program or buy a discount directory, you can take advantage of the services of a wholesaler or consolidator. Wholesalers and consolidators buy rooms, or options on rooms (room blocks), from hotels at a low, negotiated rate. They then resell the rooms at a profit through travel agents or tour packagers, or directly to the public. Most wholesalers and consolidators have a provision for returning unsold rooms to participating hotels, but are disinclined to do so. The wholesaler's or consolidator's relationship with any hotel is predicated on volume. If they return rooms unsold, the hotel might not make as many rooms available to them the next time around. Thus, wholesalers and consolidators often offer rooms at bargain rates, at anywhere from 15 to 50% off rack, occasionally sacrificing their profit margin in the process, to avoid returning the rooms to the hotel unsold.

When wholesalers and consolidators deal directly with the public, they frequently represent themselves as "reservation services." When you call, you can ask for a rate quote for a particular hotel, or, alternatively, ask for their best available deal in the area where you prefer to stay. If there is a maximum amount you are willing to pay, say so. Chances are, the service will find something that will work for you, even if they have to shave a dollar or two off their own profit. Sometimes you will have to pay for your room in advance, with a credit card, when you make your reservation. Other times you will pay at the usual time, when you check out. Listed below are several services that frequently offer substantial discounts:

Accommodations Express	(800) 444-7666
Capitol Reservations	(800) 847-4832
Central Reservation Service	(800) 950-0232
Hotel Discounts (online)	www.hoteldiscount.com
Hotel Reservations Network	(800) 964-6835 or www.180096hotel.com
Quikbook	(800) 789-9887
RMC Travel	(800) 782-2674 or (800) 245-5738
Washington, D.C. Accommodations	(800) 503-3338

Bed-and-Breakfasts (B&Bs)

B&Bs offer a lodging alternative based on personal service and hospitality that transcends the sterile, predictable product of chain hotels; however, they can be quirky. Most, but not all, B&Bs are open year-round. Some accept only cash or personal checks while others take all major credit cards. Not all rooms come with private baths. Some rooms with private baths may have a tub, but not a shower, or vice versa. Some allow children but not pets; others, pets but not children. Many B&Bs provide only the most basic breakfast, while some provide a sumptuous morning feast. Still others offer three meals a day. Most B&Bs are not wheelchair accessible, but it never hurts to ask.

Because staying at a B&B is like visiting someone's home, reservations are recommended, though B&Bs with more than ten rooms usually welcome walk-ins. To help you sort out your B&B options, we recommend the following guides. Updated regularly, these books describe B&Bs in more detail than is possible in the *Unofficial Guide.*

Inspected, Rated, and Approved, Bed & Breakfasts and Country Inns, by Sarah W. Sonke, published by the American Bed & Breakfast Association. Covers the entire United States. Call (804) 379-2222 to order.

Bed & Breakfasts—Country Inns and *The Official Guide to American Historic Inns*, by Tim and Deborah Sakach, published by American Historic Inns, Inc. Covers the entire United States. To order, phone (714) 496-6953.

Recommended Country Inns, Mid-Atlantic and Chesapeake Region, by Brenda Boelts Chapin, published by the Globe Pequot Press. Covers Virginia, Delaware, Maryland, Pennsylvania, New Jersey, New York, and West Virginia. To order, phone (800) 243-0495.

For Washington area B&B reservations call *Bed and Breakfast Accommodations Ltd.*, at (202) 328-3510.

■ Helping Your Travel Agent Help You ■

When you call your travel agent, ask if he or she has been to Washington. If the answer is no, be prepared to give your travel agent some direction. Do not accept any recommendations at face value. Check out the location and rates of any suggested hotel and make certain that the hotel is suited to your itinerary.

Because some travel agents are unfamiliar with Washington, your agent may try to plug you into a tour operator's or wholesaler's preset package.

This essentially allows the travel agent to set up your whole trip with a single phone call and still collect an 8–10% commission. The problem with this scenario is that most agents will place 90% of their Washington business with only one or two wholesalers or tour operators. In other words, it's the line of least resistance for them, and not much choice for you.

Travel agents will often use wholesalers who run packages in conjunction with airlines, like Delta's Dream Vacations or American's Fly-Away Vacations. Because of the wholesaler's exclusive relationship with the carrier, these trips are very easy for travel agents to book. However, they will probably be more expensive than a package offered by a high-volume wholesaler who works with a number of airlines in a primary Washington market.

To help your travel agent get you the best possible deal, do the following:

1. Determine where you want to stay in Washington, and if possible choose a specific hotel. This can be accomplished by reviewing the hotel information provided in this guide and by writing or calling hotels that interest you.

2. Check out the hotel deals and package vacations advertised in the Sunday travel sections of the *Washington Post*. Often you will be able to find deals that beat the socks off anything offered in your local paper. See if you can find specials that fit your plans and include a hotel you like.

3. Call the hotels, wholesalers, or tour operators whose ads you have collected. Ask any questions you have concerning their packages, but do not book your trip with them directly.

4. Tell your travel agent about the deals you find and ask if he or she can get you something better. The deals in the paper will serve as a benchmark against which to compare alternatives proposed by your travel agent.

5. Choose from among the options that you and your travel agent uncover. No matter which option you elect, have your travel agent book it. Even if you go with one of the packages in the newspaper, it will probably be commissionable (at no additional cost to you) and will provide the agent some return on the time invested on your behalf. Also, as a travel professional, your agent should be able to verify the quality and integrity of the deal.

■ If You Make Your Own Reservation ■

As you poke around trying to find a good deal, there are several things you should know. First, always call the specific hotel as opposed to the hotel chain's national 800 number. Quite often, the reservationists at the national 800 number are unaware of local specials. Always ask about specials before you inquire about corporate rates. Do not be reluctant to bargain. If you are buying a hotel's weekend package, for example, and want to extend your stay into the following week, you can often obtain at least the corporate rate for the extra days. Do your bargaining, however, before you check in, preferably when you make your reservations.

■ How to Evaluate a Travel Package ■

Hundreds of Washington package vacations are offered to the public each year. Packages should be a win/win proposition for both the buyer and the seller. The buyer has to make only one phone call and deal with just one salesperson to set up the whole vacation: transportation, rental car, lodging, meals, tours, attraction admissions, and even golf and tennis. The seller, likewise, has to deal with the buyer only once, eliminating the need for separate sales, confirmations, and billing. In addition to streamlining sales, processing, and administration, some packagers also buy airfares in bulk on contract like a broker playing the commodities market. Buying a large number of airfares in advance allows the packager to buy them at a significant savings from posted fares. The same practice is also applied to hotel rooms. Because selling vacation packages is an efficient way of doing business, and because the packager can often buy individual package components (airfare, lodging, etc.) in bulk at discount, savings in operating expenses realized by the seller are sometimes passed on to the buyer. In addition to being convenient, such packages can be exceptional values. In any event, that is the way it is supposed to work.

All too often, in practice, the seller cashes in on discounts and passes none on to the buyer. In some instances, packages are loaded up with extras that cost the packager next to nothing but inflate the retail price sky-high. As you may expect, the savings to be passed along to customers evaporate.

When considering a package, choose one that includes features you are sure to use. Whether you use all the features or not, you will certainly pay for them. Second, if cost is of greater concern than convenience, make a few phone calls and see what the package would cost if you booked its individual components (airfare, rental car, lodging, etc.) on your own. If the package price is less than the a la carte cost, the package is a good deal. If the costs are about the same, the package is probably worth buying just for the convenience.

If your package includes a choice of rental car or "airport transfers" (transportation to and from the airport), take the transfers unless you are visiting Washington for the weekend and don't plan to visit the Mall. During the weekend, it is relatively easy to get around by car as long as you don't visit the dreaded "monument alley." During the week, forget it; a car is definitely *not* the way to go. If you do take the car, be sure to ask if the package includes free parking at your hotel.

Tips for Business Travelers

The primary considerations for business travelers are affordability and proximity to the site or area where you will transact your business. Identify the zone(s) where your business will take you on the maps on pages 9–19, and then use the Hotel Chart in the back of the book to cross-reference the hotels located in that area. Once you have developed a short list of possible hotels that are conveniently located, fit your budget, and offer the standard of accommodation you require, you (or your travel agent) can make use of the cost-saving suggestions discussed earlier to obtain the lowest rate.

■ Lodging Convenient to Washington ■ Convention Center

If you are attending a meeting or trade show at Washington Convention Center, look for convenient lodging in downtown Washington, where at least a half-dozen hotels are within walking distance. From most downtown hotels, Washington Convention Center is a five- to eight-minute cab or shuttle ride away. Parking is available at the convention center, but it is expensive and not all that convenient. We recommend that you leave your car at home and use shuttles and cabs.

The Washington Convention Center is about a two-and-a-half-block walk from the nearest Metro subway station. The walk passes through a section of town that is safe during daylight hours.

Commuting to Washington Convention Center from the suburbs or the airports during rush hour is something to be avoided if possible. If you want a room downtown, book early—very early. If you screw up and need a room at the last minute, try a wholesaler or reservation service, or one of the strategies listed below.

■ Convention Rates: How They Work and ■ How to Do Better

If you are attending a major convention or trade show, it is probable that the meeting's sponsoring organization has negotiated "convention rates" with a number of hotels. Under this arrangement, hotels agree to "block" a certain number of rooms at an agreed-upon price for convention-goers. Sometimes, as in the case of a small meeting, only one hotel is involved. In the event of a large, city-wide convention at Washington Convention Center, however, almost all downtown and airport hotels will participate in the room block.

Because the convention sponsor brings a lot of business to the city and reserves a large number of rooms, it usually can negotiate a volume discount on the room rates, a rate that should be substantially below rack rate. The bottom line, however, is that some conventions and trade shows have more clout and negotiating skill than others. Hence, your convention sponsor may or may not be able to obtain the lowest possible rate.

Once a convention or trade show sponsor has completed negotiations with participating hotels, it will send its attendees a housing list that includes all the hotels serving the convention, along with the special convention rate for each. When you receive the housing list, you can compare the convention rates with the rates obtainable using the strategies covered in the previous section. If the negotiated convention rate doesn't sound like a good deal, you can try to reserve a room using a half-price club, a consolidator, or a tour operator. Remember, however, that many of the deep discounts are available only when the hotel expects to be at less than 80% occupancy, a condition that rarely prevails when a big convention is in town.

Here are some tips for beating convention rates:

1. Reserve early. Most big conventions and trade shows announce meeting sites one to three years in advance. Get your reservation booked as far in advance as possible using a half-price club. If you book well before the convention sponsor sends out its hotel list, chances are much better that the hotel will have space available.

2. If you've already got your convention's housing list, compare it with the list of hotels presented in this guide. You might be able to find a hotel not on the convention list that better suits your needs.

3. Use a local reservations agency or consolidator. This strategy is useful even if, for some reason, you need to make reservations at the last minute. Local reservations agencies and consolidators almost always control some rooms, even in the midst of a huge convention or trade show. (See the list of travel clubs on page 42 and the list of wholesalers and consolidators on page 43.)

4. Book a hotel somewhat distant from the convention center, but situated close to the Metro. You may save money on your room rate, and your commuting time underground to the convention

center will often be shorter than if you take a cab or drive from a downtown hotel.

5. Stay in a bed and breakfast, either downtown or near a Metro line. **Bed and Breakfast Accommodations Ltd.**, at (202) 328-3510, can help you locate one.

■ Hotel/Motel Toll-Free 800 Numbers ■

For your convenience, we've listed the toll-free numbers, including TDDs (Telecommunications Devices for the Deaf), for the following hotel and motel chains' reservation lines:

Best Western	(800) 528-1234 U.S. & Canada
	(800) 528-2222 TDD
Comfort Inn	(800) 228-5150 U.S.
Courtyard by Marriott	(800) 321-2211 U.S.
Days Inn	(800) 325-2525 U.S.
Doubletree	(800) 528-0444 U.S.
Doubletree Guest Suites	(800) 424-2900 U.S. & Canada
Econo Lodge	(800) 424-4777 U.S.
Embassy Suites	(800) 362-2779 U.S. & Canada
Fairfield Inn by Marriott	(800) 228-2800 U.S.
Hampton Inn	(800) 426-7866 U.S. & Canada
Hilton	(800) 445-8667 U.S.
	(800) 368-1133 TDD
Holiday Inn	(800) 465-4329 U.S. & Canada
Howard Johnson	(800) 654-2000 U.S. & Canada
	(800) 654-8442 TDD
Hyatt	(800) 233-1234 U.S. & Canada
Loew's	(800) 223-0888 U.S. & Canada
Marriott	(800) 228-9290 U.S. & Canada
	(800) 228-7014 TDD
Quality Inn	(800) 228-5151 U.S. & Canada
Radisson	(800) 333-3333 U.S. & Canada

Ramada Inn	(800) 228-3838 U.S.
	(800) 228-3232 TDD
Residence Inn by Marriott	(800) 331-3131 U.S.
Ritz-Carlton	(800) 241-3333 U.S.
Sheraton	(800) 325-3535 U.S. & Canada
Stouffer	(800) 468-3571 U.S. & Canada
Wyndham	(800) 822-4200 U.S.

Hotels and Motels:
Rated and Ranked

■ What's in a Room? ■

Except for cleanliness, state of repair, and decor, most travelers do not pay much attention to hotel rooms. There is, of course, a discernable standard of quality and luxury that differentiates Motel 6 from Holiday Inn, Holiday Inn from Marriott, and so on. In general, however, hotel guests fail to appreciate that some rooms are better engineered than others.

Contrary to what you might suppose, designing a hotel room is (or should be) a lot more complex than picking a bedspread to match the carpet and drapes. Making the room usable to its occupants is an art, a planning discipline that combines both form and function.

Decor and taste are important, certainly. No one wants to spend several days in a room where the decor was dated, garish, or even ugly. But beyond the decor, certain variables determine how "livable" a hotel room is. In Washington, D.C., we have seen some beautifully appointed rooms that are simply not well-designed for human habitation. The next time you stay in a hotel, pay attention to the details and design elements of your room. Even more than decor, these are the things that will make you feel comfortable and at home.

It takes the *Unofficial Guide* researchers about 40 minutes to inspect a hotel room. Here are a few of the things we check that you may want to start paying attention to:

Room Size While some smaller rooms are cozy and well-designed, a large and uncluttered room is generally preferable, especially for a stay of more than three days.

Temperature Control, Ventilation, and Odor The guest should be able to control the temperature of the room. The best system, because it's so quiet, is central heating and air conditioning, controlled by the room's own thermostat. The next best system is a room module heater and air conditioner, preferably controlled by an automatic thermostat, but usually by manually operated button controls. The worst system is central heat and air without any sort of room thermostat or guest control.

The vast majority of hotel rooms have windows or balcony doors that have been permanently secured shut. Though there are some legitimate safety and liability issues involved, we prefer windows and balcony doors that can be opened to admit fresh air. Hotel rooms should be odor free and smoke free, and should not feel stuffy or damp.

Room Security Better rooms have locks that require a plastic card instead of the traditional lock and key. Card and slot systems allow the hotel to change the combination or entry code of the lock with each new guest who uses the room. A burglar who has somehow acquired a room key to a conventional lock can afford to wait until the situation is right before using the key to gain access. Not so with a card and slot system. Though the largest hotels and hotel chains with lock and key systems usually rotate their locks once each year, they remain vulnerable to hotel thieves much of the time. Many smaller or independent properties rarely rotate their locks.

In addition to an entry lock system, the door should have a deadbolt and preferably a chain that can be locked from the inside. A chain by itself is not sufficient. Doors should also have a peephole. Windows and balcony doors should have secure locks.

Safety Every room should have a fire or smoke alarm, clear fire instructions, and preferably a sprinkler system. Bathtubs should have a nonskid surface, and shower stalls should have doors that either open outward or slide side-to-side. Bathroom electrical outlets should be high on the wall and not too close to the sink. Balconies should have sturdy, high rails.

Noise Most travelers have been kept awake by the television, partying, or amorous activities of people in the next room, or by traffic on the street outside. Better hotels are designed with noise control in mind. Wall and ceiling construction are substantial, effectively screening routine noise. Carpets and drapes, in addition to being decorative, also absorb and muffle sounds. Mattresses mounted on stable platforms or sturdy bed frames do not squeak even when challenged by the most passionate lovers. Televisions enclosed in cabinets, and with volume governors, rarely disturb guests in adjacent rooms.

In better hotels, the air conditioning and heating system is well maintained and operates without noise or vibration. Likewise, plumbing is quiet and positioned away from the sleeping area. Doors to the hall, and to adjoining rooms, are thick and well-fitted to better keep out noise.

Darkness Control Ever been in a hotel room where the curtains would not quite come together in the middle? In cities where many visitors stay up way into the wee hours, it's important to have a dark, quiet room where you can sleep late without the morning sun blasting you out of bed. Thick, lined curtains that close completely in the center and extend beyond the dimensions of the window or door frame are required. In a well-planned room, the curtains, shades, or blinds should almost totally block light at any time of day.

Lighting   Poor lighting is an extremely common problem in American hotel rooms. The lighting is usually adequate for dressing, relaxing, or watching television, but not for reading or working. Lighting needs to be bright over tables and desks and alongside couches or easy chairs. Since so many people read in bed, there should be a separate light for each person. A room with two queen beds should have an individual light for four people. Better bedside reading lights illuminate a small area, so if you want to sleep and someone else prefers to stay up and read, you will not be bothered by the light. The worst situation by far is a single lamp on a table between beds. In each bed, only the person next to the lamp will have sufficient light to read. This deficiency is often compounded by light bulbs of insufficient wattage.

In addition, closet areas should be well lit, and there should be a switch near the door that turns on lights in the room when you enter. A seldom seen but desirable feature is a bedside console that allows a guest to control all or most lights in the room from the bed.

Furnishings   At bare minimum, the bed(s) must be firm. Pillows should be made with nonallergenic fillers and, in addition to the sheets and spread, a blanket should be provided. Bedclothes should be laundered with a fabric softener and changed daily. Better hotels usually provide extra blankets and pillows in the room or on request and sometimes use a second top sheet between the blanket and the spread.

There should be a dresser large enough to hold clothes for two people during a five-day stay. A small table with two chairs, or a desk with a chair, should be provided. The room should be equipped with a luggage rack and a three-quarter- to full-length mirror.

The television should be color, cable-connected, and ideally have a volume governor and remote control. It should be mounted on a swivel base and preferably enclosed in a cabinet. Local channels should be posted on the set, and a local TV program guide should be supplied.

The telephone should be touchtone, conveniently situated for bedside use, and should have, on or near it, easily understood dialing instructions and a rate card. Local white and yellow pages should be provided. Better hotels have phones in the bath and equip room phones with long cords.

Well-designed hotel rooms usually have a plush armchair or a sleeper sofa for lounging and reading. Better headboards are padded for comfortable reading in bed, and there should be a nightstand or table on each side of the bed(s). Nice extras in any hotel room include a small refrigerator, a digital alarm clock, and a coffeemaker.

Bathroom   Two sinks are better than one, and you cannot have too much counter space. A sink outside the bath is a great convenience when one person dresses as another bathes. Sinks should have drains with stoppers.

Better bathrooms have both tub and shower with a nonslip bottom. Tub and shower controls should be easy to operate. Adjustable shower heads are preferred. The bath needs to be well lit and should have an exhaust fan and a guest-controlled bathroom heater. Towels should be large, soft, and fluffy, and provided in generous quantities, as should hand towels and washcloths. There should be an electrical outlet for each sink, conveniently and safely placed.

Complimentary shampoo, conditioner, and lotion are a plus, as are robes and bathmats. Better hotels supply their bathrooms with tissues and extra toilet paper. Luxurious baths feature a phone, a hair dryer, sometimes a small television, or even a jacuzzi.

Vending   There should be complimentary ice and a drink machine on each floor. Welcome additions include a snack machine and a sundries (combs, toothpaste) machine. The latter are seldom found in large hotels that have 24-hour restaurants and shops.

■ Room Ratings ■

To separate properties according to the relative quality, tastefulness, state of repair, cleanliness, and size of their **standard rooms**, we have grouped the hotels and motels into classifications denoted by stars:

★★★★★	*Superior Rooms*	Tasteful and luxurious by any standard
★★★★	*Extremely Nice Rooms*	What you would expect at a Hyatt Regency or Marriott
★★★	*Nice Rooms*	Holiday Inn or comparable quality
★★	*Adequate Rooms*	Clean, comfortable, and functional without frills—like a Motel 6
★	*Super Budget*	

Star ratings in this guide do not necessarily correspond to ratings awarded by Mobil, AAA, or other travel critics. Because stars have little relevance when awarded in the absence of commonly recognized standards of comparison, we have tied our rating to expected levels of quality established by specific American hotel corporations.

Star ratings apply to *room quality only* and describe the property's standard accommodations. For most hotels and motels a "standard accommodation" is a hotel room with either one king bed or two queen beds. In an all-suite property, the standard accommodation is a one- or two-room suite. In addition to standard accommodations, many hotels offer luxury rooms and special suites that are not rated in this guide. Star ratings for rooms are assigned without regard to whether a property has restaurant(s), recreational facilities, entertainment, or other extras.

In addition to stars (which delineate broad categories), we also employ a numerical rating system. Our rating scale is 0–100, with 100 the best possible rating, and zero (0) the worst. Numerical ratings are presented to show the difference we perceive between one property and another that may be in the same star category. Rooms at One Washington Circle Hotel, Ritz-Carlton Washington, D.C., and Henley Park Hotel, for instance, are all rated as ★★★★ (four stars). In the supplemental numerical ratings, the Washington Circle and the Ritz-Carlton Washington, D.C., are rated 88 and 87, respectively, while the Henley Park Hotel is rated 83. This means that within the four-star category, One Washington Circle and the Ritz-Carlton are comparable, and that both have somewhat nicer rooms than the Henley Park Hotel.

The location column identifies the greater Washington area (by zone) where you will find a particular property.

■ How the Hotels Compare ■

Cost estimates are based on the hotel's published rack rates for standard rooms. Each "$" represents $30. Thus, a cost symbol of "$$$" means a room (or suite) at that hotel will cost about $90 a night.

Below is a hit parade of the nicest rooms in town. We've focused strictly on room quality and excluded any consideration of location, services, recreation, or amenities. In some instances, a one- or two-room suite can be had for the same price or less than that of a hotel room.

If you used previous editions of this guide, you may notice that many of the ratings and rankings have changed. These changes reflect the inclusion of new properties, as well as guest room renovations or improved maintenance and housekeeping in previously listed properties. A failure to properly maintain guest rooms or a lapse in housekeeping standards can negatively affect the ratings.

Finally, before you begin to shop for a hotel, take a hard look at this letter we received from a couple in Hot Springs, Arkansas:

> *We cancelled our room reservations to follow the advice in your book [and reserved a hotel room highly ranked by the* Unofficial Guide*]. We wanted inexpensive, but clean and cheerful. We got inexpensive, but [also] dirty, grim, and depressing. I really felt disappointed in your advice and the room. It was the pits. That was the one real piece of information I needed from your book! The room spoiled the holiday for me aside from our touring.*

Needless to say, this letter was as unsettling to us as the bad room was to our reader. Our integrity as travel journalists, after all, is based on the quality of the information we provide our readers. Even with the best of intentions and the most conscientious research, however, we cannot inspect every room in every hotel. What we do, in statistical terms, is take a sample: We check out several rooms selected at random in each hotel and base our ratings and rankings on those rooms. The inspections are conducted anonymously and without the knowledge of the management. Although it is unusual, it is certainly possible that the rooms we randomly inspect are not representative of the majority of rooms at a particular hotel. Another possibility is that the rooms we inspect in a given hotel are representative but that by bad luck a reader is assigned a room that is inferior. When we rechecked the hotel our reader disliked, we discovered that our rating was correctly representative but that he and his wife had unfortunately been assigned to one of a small number of threadbare rooms scheduled for renovation.

The key to avoiding disappointment is to snoop around in advance. We recommend that you ask for a photo of a hotel's standard guest room before you book, or at least get a copy of the hotel's promotional brochure. Be forewarned, however, that some hotel chains use the same guest room photo in their promotional literature for all hotels in the chain; a specific guest room may not resemble the brochure photo. When you or your travel agent call, ask how old the property is and when your guest room was last renovated. If you arrive and are assigned a room that does not live up to the brochure's promises, demand to be moved to another room.

How the Hotels Compare

Hotel	Zone	Quality Rating	Star Rating	Cost
Westin Hotel of Washington	5	96	★★★★★	$$$$$$–
Ritz Carlton Pentagon City	11	95	★★★★½	$$$$$$+
Jefferson Hotel	3	94	★★★★½	$$$$$$$$+
Park Hyatt	5	94	★★★★½	$$$$$$$$$$–
Four Seasons Hotel	5	93	★★★★½	$$$$$$$$$$$$–
Hay-Adams Hotel	3	93	★★★★½	$$$$$$$$$+
Willard Inter-Continental	3	93	★★★★½	$$$$$$–
Watergate Hotel	4	92	★★★★½	$$$$$$+
ANA Hotel	5	92	★★★★½	$$$$$$–
Loew's L'Enfant Plaza	1	91	★★★★½	$$$$+
Renaissance Mayflower Hotel	3	91	★★★★½	$$$$$$$+
Sheraton Premiere Tysons Corner	11	91	★★★★½	$$$$$$+
Sheraton Suites Alexandria	11	91	★★★★½	$$$$$
Capitol Hilton	3	90	★★★★½	$$$$$$$+
Carlton Hotel	3	90	★★★★½	$$$$$$$+
Morrison-Clark Inn	7	90	★★★★½	$$$$–
Washington Vista Hilton	3	90	★★★★½	$$$$$$–
Grand Hyatt Washington	3	88	★★★★	$$$$$$$$
Hotel Sofitel	6	88	★★★★	$$$$$$–
Lincoln Suites	3	88	★★★★	$$$$–
One Washington Circle Hotel	4	88	★★★★	$$$$
Doubletree Guest Suites Pennsylvania Ave.	5	87	★★★★	$$$$–
Embassy Row Hilton	6	87	★★★★	$$$$+
Embassy Suites Downtown	6	87	★★★★	$$$$$$$–
Ritz-Carlton Washington DC	6	87	★★★★	$$$$$$$+
Washington Court Hotel	3	87	★★★★	$$$$$$+
Canterbury Hotel	6	86	★★★★	$$$$–
Embassy Suites at Tysons Corner	11	86	★★★★	$$$$+

How the Hotels Compare (continued)

Hotel	Zone	Quality Rating	Star Rating	Cost
Embassy Suites Chevy Chase	10	86	★★★★	$$$$$$+
Embassy Suites Crystal City	11	86	★★★★	$$$$$+
Hyatt Regency Bethesda	10	86	★★★★	$$$$$$+
J.W. Marriott Hotel	3	86	★★★★	$$$$$$$+
Marriott Crystal Gateway	11	86	★★★★	$$$$$$+
Marriott Metro Center	3	86	★★★★	$$$$$$+
Morrison House	11	86	★★★★	$$$$$
Residence Inn Bethesda	10	86	★★★★	$$$$$$−
Residence Inn Pentagon City	11	86	★★★★	$$$$$+
St. James	4	86	★★★★	$$$$$−
Embassy Suites Alexandria	11	85	★★★★	$$$$$$−
George Washington University Inn	4	85	★★★★	$$$$$−
Georgetown Inn	5	85	★★★★	$$$$$+
Latham Hotel Georgetown	5	85	★★★★	$$$$+
Marriott Crystal City	11	85	★★★★	$$$$$$+
Marriott Tysons Corner	11	85	★★★★	$$$$$+
Omni Shoreham Hotel (renovated rooms)	7	85	★★★★	$$$$$$$−
River Inn	4	85	★★★★	$$$$+
Sheraton City Centre	6	85	★★★★	$$$$+
Doubletree Hotel National Airport	11	84	★★★★	$$$$$−
Sheraton Washington Hotel	7	84	★★★★	$$$+
Courtyard Crystal City	11	83	★★★★	$$$$−
Doubletree Guest Suites Alexandria	11	83	★★★★	$$$$
Henley Park Hotel	3	83	★★★★	$$$$+
Hyatt Regency Crystal City	11	83	★★★★	$$$$$$+
Washington Marriott Hotel	6	83	★★★★	$$$$$+
Washington Renaissance Hotel	3	83	★★★★	$$$$$$$−
Wyndham Bristol Hotel	5	83	★★★★	$$$$$

How the Hotels Compare (continued)

Hotel	Zone	Quality Rating	Star Rating	Cost
Doubletree Guest Suites New Hampshire	4	82	★★★½	$$$$–
Holiday Inn Hotel and Suites	11	82	★★★½	$$$$$–
Hotel Lombardy	4	82	★★★½	$$$+
Madison	3	82	★★★½	$$$$+
Washington National Airport Hilton	11	82	★★★½	$$$$+
Hyatt Arlington	11	81	★★★½	$$$$$$–
Hyatt Regency Capitol Hill	3	81	★★★½	$$$$$$
Arlington Virginia Hilton	11	80	★★★½	$$$$+
Courtyard New Carrollton	10	80	★★★½	$$$–
Courtyard Rosslyn	11	80	★★★½	$$$–
Georgetown Dutch Inn	5	80	★★★½	$$$$+
Radisson Plaza at Mark Center	11	80	★★★½	$$$$+
Sheraton Crystal City	11	80	★★★½	$$$$$$$–
Washington Hilton	6	80	★★★½	$$$$$$+
Marriott Hotel Key Bridge	11	79	★★★½	$$$$$+
Courtyard Alexandria	11	78	★★★½	$$$$–
Embassy Square Summerfield Suites	6	78	★★★½	$$$$$+
Sheraton National Hotel	11	78	★★★½	$$$$–
Courtyard Washington	6	77	★★★½	$$$$$–
Holiday Inn Arlington	11	77	★★★½	$$$–
Hotel Washington	3	77	★★★½	$$$$+
State Plaza Hotel	4	77	★★★½	$$$$–
Clarion Hampshire Hotel	6	76	★★★½	$$$$+
Holiday Inn Chevy Chase	10	76	★★★½	$$$$–
Radisson Barceló Hotel	6	76	★★★½	$$$$–
Savoy Suites Hotel	7	76	★★★½	$$$$$+
The Governor's House	6	76	★★★½	$$$+
Doubletree Hotel Park Terrace	7	75	★★★½	$$$+
Doubletree Hotel Tysons Corner	11	75	★★★½	$$$$$–

How the Hotels Compare (continued)

Hotel	Zone	Quality Rating	Star Rating	Cost
Tabard Inn	6	75	★★★½	$$$$+
Holiday Inn Georgetown	7	74	★★★	$$$$$−
Holiday Inn Old Town	11	74	★★★	$$$$$+
Holiday Inn Bethesda	10	72	★★★	$$$+
Ramada Hotel Bethesda	10	72	★★★	$$$$+
Crowne Plaza	3	71	★★★	$$$$+
Holiday Inn Silver Spring	10	71	★★★	$$$$−
Ramada Plaza Hotel Old Town	11	71	★★★	$$$+
Channel Inn Hotel	1	70	★★★	$$$$+
Holiday Inn Capitol	2	70	★★★	$$$$+
Kalorama Guest House	6	70	★★★	$$$
Marriott Hotel Bethesda	10	70	★★★	$$$$$+
DuPont Plaza Hotel	6	69	★★★	$$$$+
Hampton Inn Alexandria	11	69	★★★	$$$+
Holiday Inn Central	7	68	★★★	$$$+
Howard Johnson Hotel and Suites	7	68	★★★	$$$−
Holiday Inn Franklin Square	3	67	★★★	$$$$
Holiday Inn National Airport	11	67	★★★	$$$$−
Best Western New Hampshire Suites	6	66	★★★	$$$$−
Phoenix Park Hotel	2	66	★★★	$$$$$$+
Washington Plaza Hotel	3	66	★★★	$$$$$−
Holiday Inn and Suites	11	65	★★★	$$$$−
Holiday Inn on the Hill	3	65	★★★	$$$−
Comfort Inn Washington Gateway	11	64	★★½	$$+
Days Inn Downtown	3	64	★★½	$$$+
Howard Johnson National Airport	11	64	★★½	$$$$−
Bethesda Court Hotel	10	63	★★½	$$$−
Carlyle Suites Hotel	6	63	★★½	$$$$$−
Days Hotel Crystal City	11	63	★★½	$$$+
Holiday Inn Westpark	11	63	★★½	$$$$−
Quality Hotel Downtown	6	63	★★½	$$$−

		Quality	Star	
Hotel	Zone	Rating	Rating	Cost
Quality Inn Iwo Jima	11	63	★★½	$$$+
Best Western Key Bridge	11	62	★★½	$$$$+
Comfort Inn Arlington	11	62	★★½	$$$$
Days Inn Camp Springs	10	62	★★½	$$$−
Quality Inn College Park	10	62	★★½	$$$−
Ramada Seminary Plaza Pentagon	11	62	★★½	$$$−
Holiday Inn Camp Springs	10	61	★★½	$$+
Best Western Skyline Inn	9	60	★★½	$$$$−
Best Western Tysons Westpark	11	60	★★½	$$$$−
Days Inn Connecticut Ave.	7	60	★★½	$$$+
Normandy Inn	6	60	★★½	$$$$−
Omni Shoreham Hotel (Parkview rooms)	7	60	★★½	$$$$$$$−
Red Roof Inn Downtown	3	60	★★½	$$$$−
Best Western Arlington Inn	11	58	★★½	$$$−
Quality Hotel Silver Spring	10	58	★★½	$$$+
Comfort Inn Alexandria	11	57	★★½	$$+
Econo Lodge National Airport	11	57	★★½	$$+
Econo Lodge West Arlington	11	57	★★½	$$$−
Embassy Inn	6	57	★★½	$$$−
Travelodge City Center	7	57	★★½	$$$+
Windsor Park Hotel	6	57	★★½	$$$+
Comfort Inn Vienna	11	56	★★½	$$$+
Washington Premier Hotel	4	56	★★½	$$$+
Adams Inn	7	55	★★	$$+
American Inn of Bethesda	10	55	★★	$$$+
Comfort Inn Landmark	11	55	★★	$$+
Best Western Old Colony Inn	11	54	★★	$$$−
Days Inn Alexandria	11	53	★★	$$−
Connecticut Woodley Guest House	7	31	★	$$+

How the Hotels Compare (continued)

■ Good Deals and Bad Deals ■

Having listed the nicest rooms in town, let's reorder the list to rank the best combinations of quality and value in a room. As before, the rankings are made without consideration of location or the availability of restaurant(s), recreational facilities, entertainment, or amenities. Once again, each lodging property is awarded a value rating on a 0–100 scale. The higher the rating, the better the value.

A reader recently complained to us that he had booked one of our top-ranked rooms in terms of value and had been very disappointed in the room. We noticed that the room the reader occupied had a quality rating of ★★½. We would remind you that the value ratings are intended to give you some sense of value received for dollars spent. A ★★½ room at $30 may have the same value rating as a ★★★★ room at $85, but that does not mean the rooms will be of comparable quality. Regardless of whether it's a good deal or not, a ★★½ room is still a ★★½ room.

Listed below are the best room buys for the money, regardless of location or star classification, based on averaged rack rates. Note that sometimes a suite can cost less than a hotel room.

The Top 30 Best Deals in Washington, D.C.				
Hotel	Zone	Quality Rating	Star Rating	Cost
Morrison-Clark Inn	7	90	★★★★½	$$$$–
Sheraton Washington Hotel	7	84	★★★★	$$$+
Courtyard Rosslyn	11	80	★★★½	$$$–
Lincoln Suites	3	88	★★★★	$$$$–
Courtyard New Carrollton	10	80	★★★½	$$$–
Loew's L'Enfant Plaza	1	91	★★★★½	$$$$+
Courtyard Crystal City	11	83	★★★★	$$$$–
Holiday Inn Arlington	11	77	★★★½	$$$–
One Washington Circle Hotel	4	88	★★★★	$$$$
Doubletree Guest Suites Pennsylvania Ave.	5	87	★★★★	$$$$–
Canterbury Hotel	6	86	★★★★	$$$$–
Hotel Lombardy	4	82	★★★½	$$$+
Doubletree Hotel Park Terrace	7	75	★★★½	$$$+
Westin Hotel of Washington	5	96	★★★★★	$$$$$–

The Top 30 Best Deals in Washington, D.C. (continued)

Hotel	Zone	Quality Rating	Star Rating	Cost
Doubletree Guest Suites Alexandria	11	83	★★★★	$$$$
Sheraton Suites Alexandria	11	91	★★★★½	$$$$$
The Governor's House	6	76	★★★½	$$$+
Latham Hotel Georgetown	5	85	★★★★	$$$$+
River Inn	4	85	★★★★	$$$$+
Sheraton City Centre	6	85	★★★★	$$$$+
Embassy Row Hilton	6	87	★★★★	$$$$+
Doubletree Guest Suites New Hampshire	4	82	★★★½	$$$$−
Henley Park Hotel	3	83	★★★★	$$$$+
Radisson Barceló Hotel	6	76	★★★½	$$$$−
Doubletree Hotel National Airport	11	84	★★★★	$$$$$−
ANA Hotel	5	92	★★★★½	$$$$$$−
Washington Vista Hilton	3	90	★★★★½	$$$$$$−
Courtyard Alexandria	11	78	★★★½	$$$$−
Willard Inter-Continental	3	93	★★★★½	$$$$$$−
George Washington University Inn	4	85	★★★★	$$$$$−

Visiting Washington on Business

Not All Visitors Are
Headed for the Mall

While most of the more than 21 million people who come to Washington each year are tourists, not everyone visiting the city has an itinerary centered around the Mall. In fact, almost 1.5 million visitors are convention-goers attending shows at the Washington Convention Center, located in downtown Washington. In addition, as the seat of the United States government, the city draws another 4.5 million visitors from around the world who fly in to conduct business with both federal agencies and a wide array of private organizations headquartered here.

The city is also a center of higher education. The District is home to George Washington University, Georgetown University, American University, Howard University, and the Catholic University of America, among others. As a result, Washington attracts a lot of visiting academics, college administrators, and students and their families.

In many ways, the problems facing business visitors on their first trip to Washington don't differ much from the problems of folks in town intent on hitting the major tourist attractions. People visiting on business need to locate a hotel that's convenient, want to avoid the worst of the city's traffic, face the same problems getting around an unfamiliar city, must figure out how to buy a Metro ticket, and want to know the locations of the best restaurants. This book can help.

For the most part, though, business visitors aren't nearly as flexible about the timing of their visit as folks who pick Washington as a vacation destination. While we advise that the best times for coming to D.C. are spring and fall, the necessities of business may dictate that January is when you pull into town—or, even worse, early April, when the city is mobbed for the Japanese cherry blossom festivities.

Yet much of the advice and information presented in the *Unofficial Guide* is as valuable to business visitors as it is to tourists. As for our recommendations on seeing the city's many sights . . . who knows? Maybe you'll be able to squeeze a morning or an afternoon out of your busy schedule, grab this book, and spend a few hours exploring some of the attractions that draw the other 17 million people who visit Washington each year.

The Washington Convention Center

The Washington Convention Center is an 800,000-square-foot, two-level structure located five blocks from the White House on a 9.7-acre site bounded by New York Avenue, 9th, H, and 11th Streets, NW. The center can accommodate 26,000 convention-goers, contains 37 meeting rooms, and features three exhibit halls with 100,000 square feet, 105,000 square feet, and 150,000 square feet of space, respectively. The Center provides all food and beverage services on the premises, including catered meals, 11 permanent concession stands, a 500-seat cafeteria, and a 250-seat cocktail lounge.

For both exhibitors and attendees, the Washington Convention Center is an excellent site for a meeting or trade show. Large and small exhibitors can set up their exhibits with a minimum of effort. Twelve loading docks and huge bay doors make unloading and loading quick and simple for large displays arriving by truck. Smaller displays transported in vans and cars are unloaded in the same area, entering from New York Avenue. Equipment can be carried or wheeled directly to the exhibit area. The exhibit areas and meeting rooms are well marked and easy to find. For more information call (202) 789-1600.

■ Lodging within Walking Distance ■
of the Convention Center

While participants in city-wide conventions lodge all over town, a couple of hotels are within easy walking distance of the Convention Center: the Grand Hyatt and Crowne Plaza. The Grand Hyatt, directly across the street from the Center, features 891 rooms and 60 suites. The Crowne Plaza, two blocks away at Metro Center, has 318 rooms, each supplied with a minibar, and 13 suites.

Other hotels within a few blocks of the Washington Convention Center are:

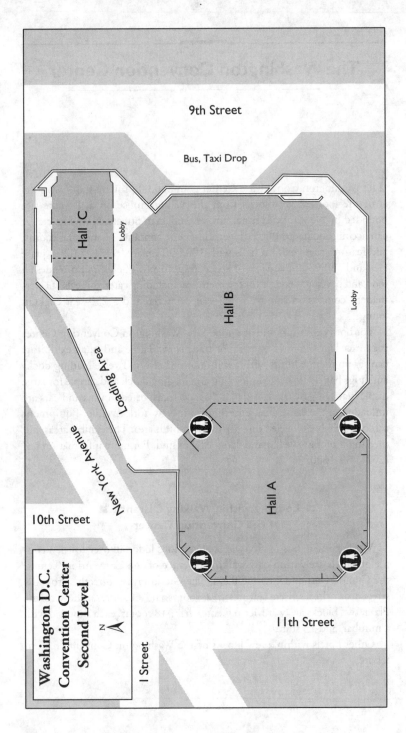

Washington D.C.
Convention Center
Second Level

N

I Street

10th Street

11th Street

9th Street

Bus, Taxi Drop

Hall C

Lobby

Hall B

Lobby

Hall A

New York Avenue

Loading Area

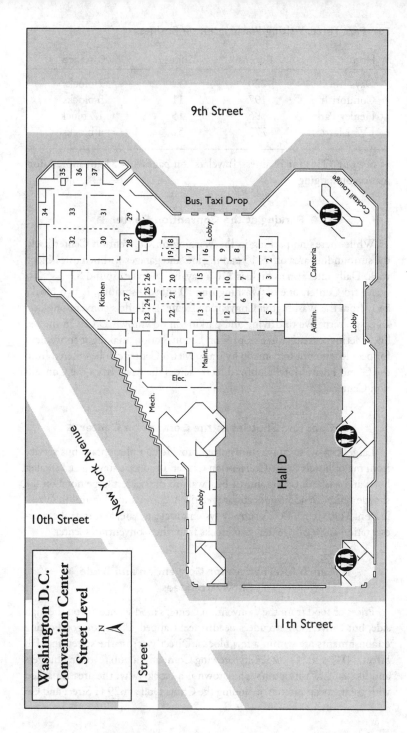

Washington D.C. Convention Center
Street Level

Hotel	Rooms	Suites	Distance
Days Inn	220	12	2 blocks
Comfort Inn	197	11	3 blocks
Henley Park	96	15	1½ blocks
J.W. Marriott	773	52	4 blocks

See our "Tips for Business Travelers" on pages 48–51 for more information on lodging.

■ Parking at the Convention Center ■

While there's no parking in the Washington Convention Center itself, the surrounding area offers 15 parking lots and garages within a three-block walk. Daily rates run as high as $10 a day, but average around $7.

Metro Center, one of Washington's 70 subway stations, is two blocks away from the Washington Convention Center and offers convention-goers an easy alternative to driving and parking in downtown D.C. On the red line, Metro Center is three stops from Union Station, making it convenient for people who opt to come in by train. Metro Center can be entered from the Grand Hyatt Hotel's lobby, directly across the street from the Convention Center.

■ Cabs and Shuttles to the Convention Center ■

Large, city-wide conventions often provide complimentary bus service from major hotels to the Convention Center. If you are staying at a smaller hotel and wish to use the shuttle bus, walk to the nearest large hotel on the shuttle route. In addition, cabs are relatively cheap and plentiful in Washington. The Metro, D.C.'s subway system, is clean, safe, and fast; the nearest station is Metro Center, two blocks from the Convention Center.

■ Lunch Alternatives for Convention and Trade ■ Show Attendees

Prices of food from the Convention Center's food service are on the high side, but convention attendees needn't feel trapped: Plenty of good eating establishments are within a few blocks. Directly across the street on 11th Street, NW, is the Capitol City Brewing Company, a pub featuring burgers and like fare. Washington's Chinatown is a block away; the area is packed with good, cheap eateries, including the China Doll at 629 H Street and Go

Lo's at 604 H Street. For a quiet business lunch, the Old Ebbitt Grill at 675 15th Street should fill the bill. For more exotic tastes, try the Moroccan fare at Marrakesh at 617 New York Avenue, or the Burmese cuisine at Burma, 740 6th Street. For fast food, choose from Hardee's, McDonald's, Taco Bell Express, and the Shops at National Place, a three-level mall located at 13th and F Streets, NW, that features a food court.

■ Convention and Special Events Calendar ■

The city's considerable convention business (1.4 million delegates in 1996) can make it hard to get a hotel room in and around the city. Use the following list of major 1998 and 1999 convention dates to plan your trip to Washington.

Dates	Convention/Event	Attendees
1998		
Jan. 7–8	Pampered Chefs Leadership Conference	5,000
Jan. 27–29	Communications Networks	31,000
Feb. 22–23	National Capital Food Service Expo	10,000
Mar. 6–8	Luggage and Leather Goods Manufacturers	6,000
Mar. 24–26	FOSE, American Information Technology Forum	60,000
Apr. 2–4	National Council of Teachers of Math	10,000
Apr. 19–22	Softbank Expos	5,200
Apr. 28–30	CardTech/SecurTech	3,000
May 4–7	Sybase, Inc.	4,000
May 18–21	American Society of Biochemistry & Molecular Biology	5,000
June 9–11	Armed Forces Communications	20,000
June 27–30	American Library Association	23,000
Sept. 16–19	Congressional Black Caucus Weekend	10,000
Oct. 8–10	Transcatheter Cardiovascular Therapeutics	5,000
Oct. 19–21	American Society of Clinical Pathologists	5,000
Nov. 1–4	Choice Hotels International	3,500
Nov. 15–18	American Public Health Association	12,000
1999		
Jan. 26–28	Communications Networks	31,000
Mar. 16–18	FOSE, American Information Technology Forum	60,000

Dates	Convention/Event	Attendees
Apr. 1–2	Softbank Expos	5,200
Apr. 9–11	Mobile Electronics Show	4,000
Apr. 17–21	Federation of American Societies for Experimental Biology	13,000
May 16–19	American Psychiatric Association	16,000
June 7–9	American Physical Therapy Association	4,000
June 15–17	Armed Forces Communications & Electronics	20,000
Aug. 16–20	International Society on Thrombosis and Haemostasis	8,000
Sept. 15–18	Congressional Black Caucus Foundation	10,000
Sept. 23–25	Transcatheter Cardiovascular Therapeutics	5,000
Oct. 1–3	Emergency Nurses Association	3,500
Oct. 9–12	American Academy of Pediatrics	9,000
Oct. 18–24	Urban Land Institute	4,500
Oct. 28–31	National Automatic Merchandising Association	7,700
Dec. 12–15	American Society for Cell Biology	7,500

PART FOUR

Arriving and Getting Oriented

Coming into the City

■ By Car ■

If you drive, you will most likely arrive on one of three freeways: Interstate 95 from the north, I-95 from the south, or I-70 from the northwest. Other routes that converge in Washington are I-66 from the west (which links up with I-81 in Virginia's Shenandoah Valley), US 50 (which hooks up with Annapolis, Maryland, US 301, and Maryland's Eastern Shore), and the Baltimore-Washington Parkway, which parallels I-95 between the two cities' beltways.

All these routes have one common link: They connect with Washington's Capital Beltway, a ribbon of concrete encircling the city. Now for an introduction to how unfriendly D.C. freeways can be to unsuspecting motorists: Part of the Beltway is numbered both I-95 and I-495.

Why? Since I-95 doesn't cut directly through Washington (the way it does in Richmond to the south and Baltimore to the north), it's rerouted along the southern half of the Beltway. It's quite confusing to visitors, and it's only the first of many Washington driving horrors you'll encounter.

Drivers coming from the north and I-70 and headed downtown should take the Beltway to the Baltimore-Washington Parkway and exit south. Bear right onto New York Avenue where the Parkway splits; it goes straight to downtown, near Union Station.

From the south and west, motorists can take either I-66 or I-395 (what I-95 becomes after it crosses inside the Beltway). Both get you across the Potomac and into D.C. near the center of the tourist hubbub.

Our advice to drivers unfamiliar with Washington is to sit down with a

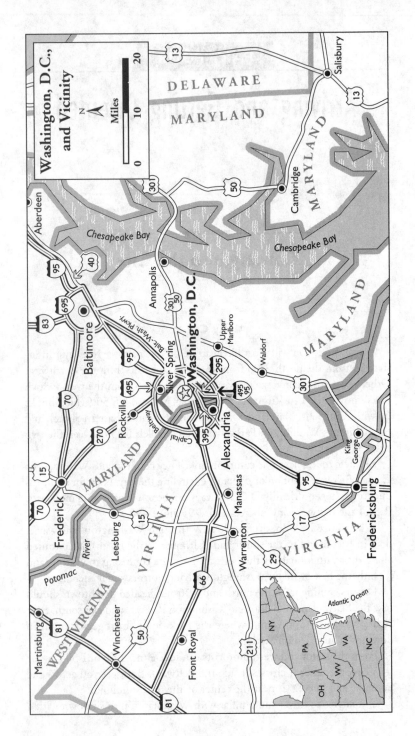

Washington, D.C., and Vicinity

N

Miles

0   10   20

DELAWARE

MARYLAND

MARYLAND

MARYLAND

MARYLAND

Salisbury

Cambridge

Chesapeake Bay

Chesapeake Bay

Aberdeen

Annapolis

Baltimore

Balt.-Wash. Pkwy.

Silver Spring

Washington, D.C.

Upper Marlboro

Waldorf

Rockville

Beltway

Capital

Alexandria

King George

Frederick

Leesburg

VIRGINIA

Manassas

Fredericksburg

Potomac River

WEST VIRGINIA

Martinsburg

Winchester

Warrenton

VIRGINIA

Front Royal

Atlantic Ocean

NY

PA

OH

WV

VA

NC

map before you leave home and carefully trace out the route to your destination. If you need to make a phone call or two for directions, do it then. And don't try to fight the weekday rush hour traffic (between 6:30 and 9:30 A.M. or 3 and 7 P.M.).

■ By Plane ■

Washington National Airport. While Washington officially has three major airports, this is the most convenient by far for domestic flyers, just a few miles south of the city on the Virginia side of the Potomac. Don't ask a friend to pick you up: Parking is terrible at this cramped facility. A courtesy van service can whisk you from the Virginia side of the Potomac. A new $1 billion, one-million-square-foot main terminal that opened in the summer of 1997 should improve National's notorious reputation as a cramped, hard-to-get-in-and-out-of airport. The new terminal features seamless connection between ground transportation, parking, buses, and D.C.'s subway. (It also boasts a food court, 32 elevators, 26 escalators, 12 baggage carousels, dozens of retail stores, and a great view of the nation's capital across the Potomac River.) Along with 6,500 new parking spaces, new roadways, and expanded curb space and travel lanes (eight lanes for lower-level baggage claims, five lanes for upper-level ticket counters), the new facility should make things much easier for travelers.

Nearly 5,000 parking spaces are housed in a new parking garage directly across from the new terminal and are reached via moving sidewalks. Two new Metro mezzanines connect D.C.'s subway system to the terminal via two pedestrian bridges spanning the airport's roads. Two ground transportation centers located on the baggage claim level provide information on Metro, taxi service, SuperShuttle vans and Washington Flyer bus service, and rental cars.

Cab fares to nearby downtown Washington are reasonable ($12–$15). SuperShuttle shared-service vans leave every 15 (or fewer) minutes to any destination in the D.C. area. Fares range from $6 to $13 to any address in Washington and from $6 to more than $30 in the Virginia and Maryland suburbs. Three SuperShuttle ticket counters are located at National; look for the "Washington Flyer/SuperShuttle" signs posted throughout the airport. For more information, exact fares, and reservations for return pick-up to National, call (800) BLUE VAN (258-3826).

Washington Flyer operates an interairport shuttle service between Washington National and Dulles (located way out in the boonies of Northern Virginia). Buses leave on the hour from 5 A.M. to 11 P.M. during the week and less frequently on weekends and holidays. The fare for the 45-minute

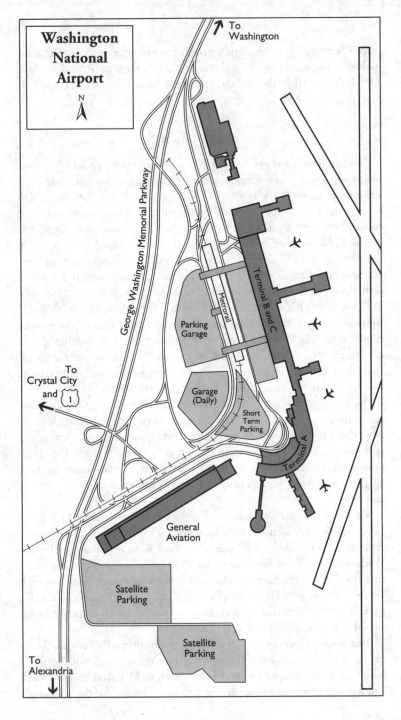

Washington
National
Airport

N

To
Washington

George Washington Memorial Parkway

Metrorail

Terminal B and C

Parking
Garage

To
Crystal City
and
①

Garage
(Daily)

Short
Term
Parking

Terminal A

General
Aviation

Satellite
Parking

Satellite
Parking

To
Alexandria

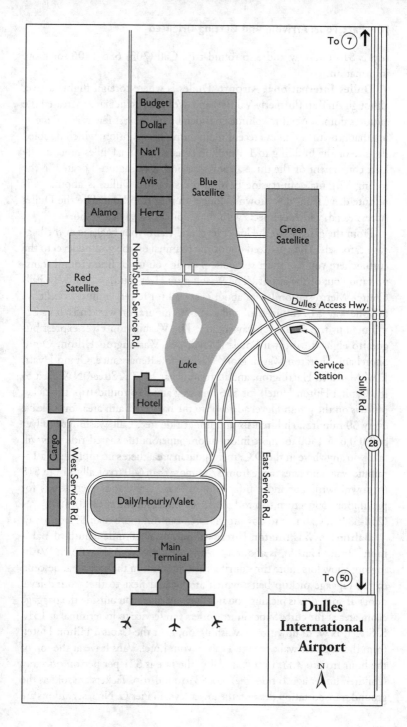

To ⑦ ↑

Budget
Dollar
Nat'l
Avis
Hertz

Blue
Satellite

Green
Satellite

Alamo

Red
Satellite

North/South Service Rd.

Dulles Access Hwy.

Lake

Service
Station

Sully Rd.

㉘

Hotel

Cargo

West Service Rd.

East Service Rd.

Daily/Hourly/Valet

Main
Terminal

To ㊿ ↓

✈ ✈ ✈

**Dulles
International
Airport**

N
↑

trip is $16 one-way and $26 round-trip. Call (703) 685-1400 for more information.

Dulles International Airport. Dulles is where foreign flights arrive, although AirTran (formerly ValuJet) and Western Pacific have increased the airport's domestic traffic volume considerably in the last few years. Reflecting that growth is Dulles's recent main terminal expansion, which doubled the size of the building to 1.1 million square feet. Yet Dulles remains the least convenient of the three airports serving Washington. Located in the rolling Virginia countryside beyond the suburbs, Dulles is about a 45-minute drive from downtown—longer during rush hour. Use the Dulles Access Road, which connects with the Capital Beltway and I-66.

From the gate, go to the lower level and claim your baggage at the baggage carousels. Then proceed out of the terminal on the ground level to the curb, where you can meet someone picking you up or find ground transportation out of the airport. The Washington Flyer shuttle to the West Falls Church Metro station leaves about every 30 (or fewer) minutes weekdays ($8 one-way, $14 round-trip) and every 30 minutes on weekends; it's a 22-minute bus trip to the subway station. The Washington Flyer express bus goes to eight downtown hotels (Mayflower, Washington Hilton, Omni Shoreham, Sheraton Washington, Washington Renaissance, Grand Hyatt, J. W. Marriott, Harrington, and its terminal at 1517 K Street, NW, next to the Capital Hilton Hotel) for $16 one-way and $26 round-trip; the ticket office is on the ground level adjacent to the baggage claim area. Buses leave every 30 minutes; children six and under ride free. Call Washington Flyer at (703) 685-1400 for more information. SuperShuttle shared-ride vans will take you anywhere in the D.C. metropolitan area; there's no more than a 15-minute wait, and fares range from $7 to more than $40 (typically $15 to $18 to downtown). For more information, exact fares, and reservations for pickup for your return trip to Dulles, call SuperShuttle at (800) BLUE VAN (258-3826). Cab fare to downtown D.C. can run more than $50 one-way.

Baltimore-Washington International. BWI, 10 miles south of Baltimore's Inner Harbor, is about a 50-minute drive from downtown Washington; allow lots more time during rush hour. From the gate area, descend to the luggage pickup belts, which are located next to the ground-level doors. If someone is picking you up, they can meet you outside the baggage claim area at the curb. SuperShuttle offers van service to its terminal at 1517 K Street, NW, in downtown Washington, near the Capitol Hilton Hotel; from there, either walk or take a cab to your hotel. Vans leave at the top of the hour from 6 A.M. to 9 P.M. daily; the fare is $21 per person one-way (children under age 6 ride free) and $31 round-trip. Tickets are sold at the ground transportation desk on the lower level in Pier C. No reservations are

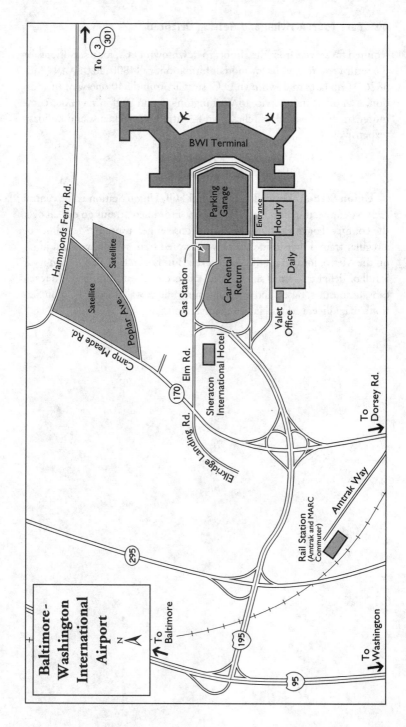

Baltimore-
Washington International
Airport

N

To
Baltimore

To
Washington

To
Dorsey Rd.

BWI Terminal

Parking
Garage

Entrance

Hourly

Daily

Valet
Office

Car Rental Return

Gas Station

Satellite

Satellite

Poplar Ave.

Hammonds Ferry Rd.

Camp Meade Rd.

Elm Rd.

Sheraton
International Hotel

Elkridge Landing Rd.

170

Rail Station
(Amtrak and MARC
Commuter)

Amtrak Way

295

195

95

To 3
301

79

required for service from the airport to downtown D.C.; for reservations for the return trip to BWI or for more information, call (800) BLUE VAN (258-3826). Cab fares to downtown D.C. start at around $40 one-way. In addition, BWI offers train service to Washington's Union Station via MARC commuter trains on weekdays (cheap) and Amtrak on weekends and holidays (expensive).

■ By Train ■

Union Station. Located near Capitol Hill, Union Station is the central Amtrak connecting point in Washington. From here, trains go out all over the country. For most routes you can choose either a speedy Metroliner or a regular train. Once inside the newly restored train station, you can jump on the Metro, located on the lower level. But, not so fast! The station itself is full of delights—small shops, cafes, and even a theater complex. To reach cabs, limousines, buses, and open-air tour trolleys, walk through Union Station's magnificent Main Hall to the main entrance.

A Geographic Overview
of Washington

■ **City and Two States** ■

Washington, D.C., is a city of about 600,000 people located near the southern end of the East Coast megalopolis stretching from Boston to Richmond. George Washington chose the city's site, where the Anacostia River flows into the Potomac, upriver from his Mount Vernon plantation. Maryland and Virginia donated wedges of land from both sides of the Potomac to make the 100-square-mile diamond called the District of Columbia. In 1846, Virginia snatched its lands back; today, the planned city of Washington sits on the former Maryland acreage on the river's east bank.

Washington proper is surrounded by bustling, congested suburbs. Across the Potomac, Arlington County, the town of Alexandria, and Fairfax County crowd D.C. from the south and west, while the Maryland counties of Montgomery and Prince George's surround Washington's northwestern and eastern borders. All the suburbs surrounding D.C. are experiencing exponential growth. Rockville, for example, a few miles north of the D.C. line, has become Maryland's second-largest city, after Baltimore.

Washington's most important geographical feature, the Potomac River, is a natural impediment to both tourists and suburban commuters. The few bridges that cross the river from Virginia to Washington are rush-hour bottlenecks. While driving across the border to the Maryland suburbs is nominally easier, D.C.'s intense traffic and concentration of government and tourist sites near the river makes for a long trek into Maryland.

■ **D.C.'s Street Plan** ■

While Washington's reputation as a tough city to get around in is well deserved—at least for first-time visitors—the city's layout is actually fairly logical. Downtown streets are arranged in a grid, with numbered streets running north/south and lettered streets going east/west. The loose cannons in the scheme are streets named after states, which cut across the grid diagonally and meet in traffic circles that are the nemesis of Washington drivers.

Our advice: Ignore the state-named streets on your map and you'll dis-

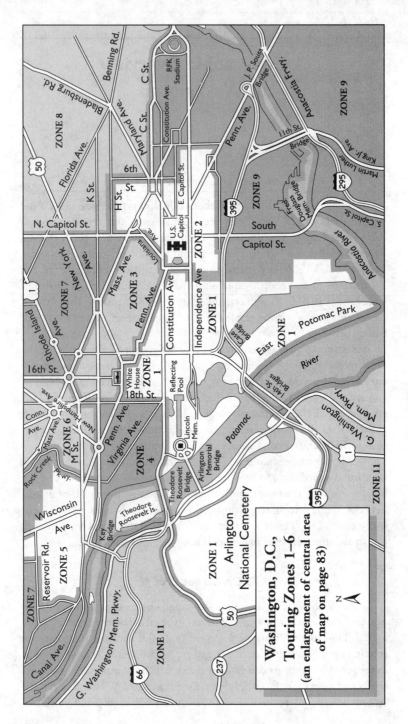

Washington, D.C., Touring Zones 1–6 (an enlargement of central area of map on page 83)

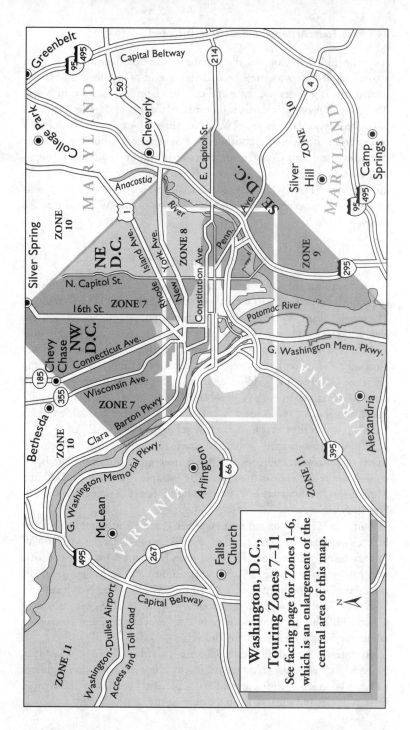

Washington, D.C., Touring Zones 7–11
See facing page for Zones 1–6, which is an enlargement of the central area of this map.

cover the underlying logic of the system. If your destination is, in fact, on a street named after a state, the underlying grid of number- and letter-named streets will get you there and can even help you locate your block. An example: A popular destination for both tourists and power seekers is 1600 Pennsylvania Avenue, NW. Since this well-known street snakes a course from the poor neighborhoods of Southeast Washington through downtown and into Georgetown, pinpointing an exact address is tough. The clue, however, is in the street address: The White House is near the intersection of Pennsylvania Avenue and 16th Street. Note: The two blocks of Pennsylvania Avenue immediately in front of the White House are closed to vehicles.

■ Finding Your Way ■

Once you get the hang of it, finding your way around Washington is a snap. You'll have a head start if you know the basics of how D.C. is arranged. The roughly diamond-shaped city's four corners point north, south, east, and west. Inside the diamond, Washington is laid out in a rectilinear gridlike plan and divided into four pie-wedge-shaped quadrants: Northwest (NW), Northeast (NE), Southwest (SW), and Southeast (SE); in the center of the pie is the U.S. Capitol building. Separating the quadrants and running in compass directions from the Capitol are North Capitol Street, East Capitol Street, and South Capitol Street. What happened to West Capitol Street? It's the Mall, which runs west from the Capitol to the Potomac River.

Within each quadrant, numbered streets run north-south, and lettered streets run east-west. Addresses on lettered streets give a clue to the numbered cross street at the end of the block. For example, the National Building Museum at 401 F Street, NW, is located on F Street between 4th and 5th Streets, NW.

Surprise: Washington has four 1st Streets, four E Streets, and so on, one for each quadrant. As a result, addresses must bear designations such as NW to prevent utter confusion. The good news for short-term visitors is that they can virtually ignore the quadrants: Almost all tourist sights, hotels, restaurants, and night life are in Northwest Washington. Northeast and Southeast Washington, with the exception of the middle-class enclave of Capitol Hill, are predominantly poor and less commercially developed, while tiny Southwest is mostly middle-class.

Avenues are named after states (Connecticut, Massachusetts, Wisconsin, etc.) and cut diagonally across the street grid. Some are major thoroughfares and do a good job of disrupting the traffic pattern. Downtown, the avenues meet at circles and squares, the most noteworthy of which are:

- *Dupont Circle* (Connecticut, Massachusetts, and New Hampshire Avenues)

- *Washington Circle* (New Hampshire and Pennsylvania Avenues)

- *Scott Circle* (Massachusetts and Rhode Island Avenues, and 16th Street)

- *Mount Vernon Square* (Massachusetts and New York Avenues)

Here's a rundown of some major roads that visitors will encounter in the city:

- *Pennsylvania Avenue* runs from Southeast and Capitol Hill through downtown and into Georgetown. The two blocks of Pennsylvania Avenue immediately in front of the White House are closed to vehicles.

- *Wisconsin Avenue* starts in Georgetown and leads north to the Maryland suburbs.

- *Connecticut Avenue* runs from Lafayette Square, in front of the White House, through Dupont Circle, past the National Zoo, and into Chevy Chase, Maryland.

- *16th Street, NW*, heads due north from the White House through Adams-Morgan and merges with Georgia Avenue in the Maryland suburbs.

- *K Street, NW*, is a major east-west downtown business artery.

- *Constitution and Independence Avenues* run east-west along the Mall.

- *New York Avenue* is a major artery that runs from the White House to Northeast Washington and turns into US 50 and the Baltimore-Washington Parkway.

- *14th Street, SW*, is a major point of egress to and from the Virginia suburbs.

- *Massachusetts Avenue* runs from Union Station through Dupont Circle, up Embassy Row, and past Washington National Cathedral and American University on its way to Maryland.

Things the Natives
Already Know

■ The Metro: An Introduction ■

The first section of Washington's clean, modern, safe, and efficient subway system opened in 1976, just in time for the nation's bicentennial celebrations. As the five-line system has expanded over the years, the rave reviews keep coming. The stations all follow the same brown-and-beige color scheme, with high, curved ceilings made of square concrete panels that fade into the distance. Monotonous, maybe, but the stations are safe and make the lives of visitors infinitely easier.

The trains themselves are clean, quiet, carpeted, virtually crime-free, and air-conditioned. They run so often that carrying a schedule isn't necessary. With two notable exceptions (trendy Georgetown and hip Adams-Morgan), the Metro delivers visitors within easy walking distance of everywhere they might want to go inside the city and into the suburbs.

Even if, like a lot of Americans, you're not comfortable with the idea of relying on public transportation, Washington provides a strong argument for seriously reconsidering your love affair with your car. The Metro system is easy, even fun, to ride. There's really no excuse not to use it. Later, in Part Five, we include a chapter on how.

■ Taxis ■

Washington's cab fares are low, but the fare system is weird: Fares are based on zones, not a meter. You can go 2 blocks from one zone to another and be charged more than for a 12-block ride within one zone. It helps to know the zones.

Washington has more cabs per capita than any other American city. But other than for schlepping your luggage to and from National Airport or Union Station, or dining out in subway-free Georgetown and Adams-Morgan, cabs are superfluous, thanks to the Metro. Take the train instead.

In our experience, Washington cabbies are polite and friendly. Yet it's a good idea to ask for a receipt at the beginning of the ride, just to let the driver know that you're not some inexperienced out-of-towner and you won't tolerate being charged for a roundabout route through many zones.

Most sight-seeing attractions and hotels are in Zone 1. Note: In late 1998, cabs are scheduled to scrap the zone system and switch to meters. (The strange hows, whats, and wheres of taxi travel in D.C. are discussed in more detail in Part Five.)

■ Traffic ■

If at all possible, avoid driving during your stay in Washington. If you arrive by car, make sure your hotel has parking and is either within walking distance to a Metro station (more on that in Part Five) or offers convenient shuttles to one. Park your car and, with few exceptions, don't plan on moving it until you leave.

Here's why: Driving in Washington is infuriating, and trying to park your car near major tourist sites and government buildings is usually hopeless. The city is a bewildering mix of traffic circles, diagonal boulevards, and one-way streets that change direction depending on the time of day. To make matters worse, some avenues change names for no apparent reason. And the volume of traffic? The *Washington Post* doesn't call its regular traffic column "Dr. Gridlock" for nothing.

One last note: You'll see a lot of cars with cute red, white, and blue license plates imprinted with the word "Diplomatic." The driver of such a car is associated with a foreign embassy and has diplomatic immunity from many local laws—including traffic violations. Give these cars a wide berth. (We cover driving in more detail in Part Five.)

■ The Neighborhoods ■

Arguably, Washington is the most important city in the world. When most people think of D.C., they conjure up an image of the Mall, anchored by the U.S. Capitol at the east end and the Lincoln Memorial on the other. On its east end alone, the Mall features at least 11 major museums and attractions. In the center is the Washington Monument, with the White House just to the north.

While there's much to see and do on the Mall, visitors who don't get beyond the two-mile strip of green are missing a lot of what this vibrant, international city has to offer: brick sidewalks in front of charming colonial-era row houses in Georgetown, the bohemian cafes of Adams-Morgan, stately townhouses and mansions near Dupont Circle, the glitter and overflowing street life in the "new downtown" along K Street, NW. At the very least, a foray off the Mall can elevate your trip beyond the level of an educational grade-school field trip and give you a taste of the lively city itself.

All the neighborhoods that follow are safe for visitors to explore on foot, except where noted. For more details on zones, see pages 7–8, "Geographic Zones."

Adams-Morgan (in Zone 6)

An ethnic neighborhood with a heavy emphasis on the Hispanic and African, Adams-Morgan is where young and cool bohemians migrated after the price of real estate zoomed around Dupont Circle in the '70s and '80s. While it doesn't offer much in the way of large museums or monuments, the neighborhood is full of ethnic restaurants, eclectic shops, and night-clubs. Parking, alas, is a severe problem: Adams-Morgan isn't served by the Metro. Don't let that stop you; take a cab.

Dupont Circle (in Zone 6)

Dupont Circle is the center of one of the city's most fashionable neigh-borhoods, where you'll find elegantly restored townhouses, boutiques, restaurants, cafes, bookstores, and art galleries. A stroll down Embassy Row (along Massachusetts Avenue) leads past sumptuous embassies and chan-celleries, as well as some of Washington's best visitor attractions: Anderson House, the Phillips Collection, Woodrow Wilson House, and the Islamic Center. You can recognize an embassy by the national coat-of-arms or flag; a pack of reporters and TV cameras may indicate that international unrest has erupted somewhere in the world.

Capitol Hill (in Zone 2)

The neighborhood surrounding the Capitol is a mix of residential and commercial, with plenty of restored town houses and trendy bars. Called "The Hill" by natives, here congressional staffers, urban homesteaders, and poor people commingle—sometimes not so successfully: Street crime can be a problem. Blocks can change character abruptly from one end to the other, but if you don't wander far from the Capitol itself you'll be okay.

Downtown (in Zone 3)

Directly north of the Mall is "old downtown," full of department stores, government office buildings (including the FBI), shops, street vendors, hotels, restaurants, two Smithsonian museums, Ford's Theatre, a tiny Chi-natown, and the Washington Convention Center. To the west is "new downtown," the glittery glass and steel office buildings where D.C.'s legions of lobbyists and lawyers do their thing. Both areas offer visitors plenty of choices for shopping, dining, and sight-seeing.

Foggy Bottom (in Zone 4)

Located west of the White House, Foggy Bottom got its name from the swampy land on which it was built. Today, it's home to George Washington University, the U.S. Department of State ("Foggy Bottom" is journalese for "State"), the Kennedy Center, and the Watergate. Closer to the Mall, massive government office complexes such as the Department of the Interior and the Federal Reserve crowd the White House.

Georgetown (in Zone 5)

A river port long before Washington was built, Georgetown is now the epitome of swank. From the distance, Georgetown is immediately identifiable by its skyline of spires. The neighborhood of restored townhouses is filled with crowded bars and shops, and the streets pulse with crowds late into the night. An overflow of suburban teenagers on weekends makes for traffic congestion that's intense, even by Washington standards; lack of a Metro station only makes it worse. Georgetown University marks the neighborhood's western edge. The Chesapeake and Ohio Canal and its famous towpath begin in Georgetown and follow the Potomac River upstream for 184 miles to Cumberland, Maryland. When you've had enough of the city, rent a bike and see how far you can get.

Upper Northwest (in Zone 7)

Here's where the Washington National Cathedral, the National Zoo, the Hillwood Museum, the city's best private schools, and its wealthiest citizens are found. Without clear boundaries to separate them, Tenleytown, Glover Park, Woodley Park, and Cleveland Park are full of Victorian houses that are homes to members of Congress, rich lobbyists, and attorneys. Attention, joggers: This is where you go for a nighttime run.

Rock Creek Park (in Zone 7)

It's not a neighborhood, but a managed forest in the heart of Washington well worth knowing about. Hikers, joggers, in-line skaters, equestrians, mountain bikers, and anyone wishing an escape from the city can escape here. In the summer, it's ten degrees cooler than the rest of the city.

The Southwest Waterfront (in Zone I)

A fascinating array of private yachts is on view in Washington's waterfront area, a stretch along Maine Avenue that features marinas, seafood restaurants, and the Wharf Seafood Market, where visitors can sample fresh fish and Chesapeake Bay delicacies such as oysters on the half shell. Here's where you can take a scenic river cruise to Mount Vernon on the *Potomac Spirit*. It's easy to get to the waterfront: Take the subway to the Waterfront Metro station.

Anacostia (in Zone 9)

The city's first suburb today sits in the midst of a war zone of drive-by shootings, drug dealing, and random violence. When Washington is called "Murder Capital of the U.S.," the reference is usually to a large swath of Northeast and Southeast Washington across the Anacostia River from downtown. While Anacostia is well off the beaten tourist path, there are two attractions visitors should take the time to explore: Cedar Hill, the home of nineteenth-century abolitionist Frederick Douglass, and the Smithsonian's Anacostia Museum. Either drive or ride special tourist buses (not public transportation) to visit these attractions.

■ Customs and Protocol ■

Dress   In spite of its status as a world capital, Washington is a fairly relaxed town under the surface. The city's laid-back Southern heritage and the vestiges of an inferiority complex relative to older East Coast cities mean that Washingtonians, by the way they dress and socialize, aren't an ostentatious crowd. For men, suits and ties remain the uniform of work, while most women stick to power suits with padded shoulders in neutral colors for office wear.

Tourists have diplomatic immunity from this dreary dress code, however. In daytime and around the major tourist areas, it's perfectly okay to look the part: If it's hot, wear a T-shirt and bermudas as you stroll the Mall with three cameras around your neck. You won't be alone.

For forays up Connecticut Avenue and into Georgetown, though, leave the cameras and loud Hawaiian print shirts in your hotel room. The crowds are better dressed and hipper, and if you don't follow suit, you'll really stand out in the crowd.

Washington, we're glad to report, is quite informal after 5 P.M.—which makes it easy on visitors. With few exceptions, men needn't worry about going out to a restaurant without a tie, and women can feel comfortable wearing slacks. If there's a casual, after-work uniform in this city, it's probably the preppie look: chinos, Docksiders, and an Izod shirt for men and similar attire for women.

Eating in Restaurants   Washington, as an international city, is full of inexpensive ethnic restaurants—Ethiopian, Thai, Vietnamese, Lebanese,

Greek, Afghani . . . the list goes on. Most are casual and you needn't feel intimidated about unfamiliar menus—just ask the waiter or waitress for a recommendation. Since Washington doesn't take itself as seriously as, say, New York, you won't be made to feel uncomfortable in a Japanese restaurant if you request a spoon for your miso soup. Expect to be elbow to elbow with other diners in the crowded eateries, since dining out seems to be a full-time activity for a lot of Washingtonians.

Tipping   Is the tip you normally leave at home appropriate in Washington? The answer is yes. Just bear in mind that a tip is a reward for good service. Here are some guidelines:

Porters and Redcaps. At least 50 cents per bag and $2–3 for a lot of baggage.

Cab Drivers. 15% of the fare. Add an extra dollar if the cabby does a lot of luggage handling.

Valet Parking. A dollar.

Bellmen. At least 50 cents per bag and $2–3 for a lot of baggage.

Waiters. 15–20% of the pretax bill.

Bartenders. 10–15% of the pretax bill.

Chambermaids. A dollar a day.

Checkroom Attendants in Restaurants and Theaters. A dollar per garment.

Going Where the Locals Go   During the week, you'll have to get away from the Mall or the Washington Convention Center if you want to rub shoulders with native Washingtonians. But not too far—Capitol Hill bars and restaurants are crowded with congressional aides, lobbyists, secretarial staff, and even the odd congressperson or two. During the lunch hour on weekdays (but not weekends and holidays), L'Enfant Plaza is jammed with bureaucrats from the myriad concrete-enclosed agencies located south of Independence Avenue.

North of the White House, the "new downtown" (roughly from 15th Street, NW, west to Rock Creek Park) is an area of glass-enclosed office buildings where lawyers, lobbyists, and other professionals ply their trades—and take their clients to lunch. Dupont Circle, formerly Washington's bohemian quarter, remains headquarters to Washington's artists, international, and gay communities.

How Not to Look Like a Tourist   If it's important to you not to look like A Visitor on Holiday in Our Nation's Capital, we offer the following advice:

1. Never say "Washington"—it's "D.C." to the natives. If you must say the full name of the city, pronounce it "Worshington."

2. Be obsessive, if not maniacal, about the Redskins.

3. For men, wear a coat and tie, and carry a briefcase at all times. For women, wear power suits with padded shoulders.

4. Tuck a *Washington Post* under your arm and march up Connecticut Avenue with a determined stride.

5. Be blasé about Washington's tourist attractions: Deny ever going to the Mall except in the company of small children.

6. Clutch an espresso, latte, or cappuccino in one hand and a just-baked, multigrain olive loaf in the other: The natives are wild about fresh bread and coffee bars.

■ **Tips for the Disabled** ■

Washington is one of the most accessible cities in the world for the disabled. The White House, for example, has a special entrance on Pennsylvania Avenue for visitors arriving in wheelchairs, and White House guides usually allow visually handicapped visitors to touch some of the items described on tours. Each Metro station is equipped with an elevator, complete with Braille number plates.

All Smithsonian museum buildings are accessible to wheelchair visitors, as are all museum floors. For a copy of "Smithsonian Access" call (202) 357-2700 (voice) or (202) 357-1729 (teletypewriter [TTY]). Folks headed to the National Zoo can get a copy of the Zoo Guide for Disabled Visitors by calling (202) 673-4717 (voice) or (202) 673-4823 (TTY). The Lincoln and Jefferson Memorials and the Washington Monument are equipped to accommodate disabled visitors. Most sight-seeing attractions have elevators for others who want to avoid a lot of stair climbing. See our section "People with Special Needs" on pages 121–22 in Part Five for more information.

■ **The Local Press** ■

Washington is a city of news junkies, and the *Washington Post* is the opiate of choice. Visitors should make a point of picking up Friday's editions, which include the paper's "Weekend" section. It's loaded with information on things to do in and around Washington; if you can, grab a copy of a Friday *Post* on your way into town for the weekend.

The *Washington Times*, D.C.'s other daily newspaper, offers a more conservative slant on national and world events.

City Paper, a free weekly "alternative" newspaper, is another good source of information on arts, theater, clubs, popular music, and movie reviews. It's available from street-corner vending machines and stores all over town.

The *Washingtonian*, a monthly magazine, is strong on lists (top 10 restaurants, etc.) and provides a calendar of events, dining information, and feature articles.

Where/Washington is one of several free publications that list popular things to do around town.

Visitors looking for the latest information on Washington theater, night life, restaurants, special exhibitions, and gallery shows in advance of their trip should call or write:

Where/Washington Magazine, 1225 19th Street, NW, Suite 510, Washington, D.C. 20036-2411. Phone (202) 463-4550.

The *Washingtonian*, 1828 L Street, NW, Suite 200, Washington, D.C. 20036. Phone (202) 331-0715.

■ Telephones ■

The Washington area is served by three area codes: (202) inside the District, (703) in the Northern Virginia suburbs across the Potomac River, and (301), which connects you with the Maryland suburbs. To dial out of D.C. to suburbs beyond the city's limits, it's necessary to dial the right area code. While calls to Arlington, Alexandria, and most of Fairfax County in Virginia and to Montgomery and Prince George's Counties in Maryland are dialed as if they're long distance, they are charged as local calls (25 cents from pay phones).

■ Rest Rooms ■

Field researchers for the *Unofficial Guide* are selected for their reporting skills, writing ability, . . . and small bladders. When we enter a marble edifice, you can be sure we're not just scrutinizing the layout, the flow of the crowd, and the aesthetics: We're also nervously eyeing the real estate for the nearest public facility where we can unload that second cup of coffee.

So how does Washington rate in the rest room department? Actually, pretty well. That's because of the huge number of museums, monuments, federal office buildings, restaurants, bars, department stores, and hotels that cover the city. Most rest rooms are clean and conveniently located.

Leading any list of great rest room locations should be the National Air and Space Museum on the Mall. For women who claim there's no justice in the world when it comes to toilet parity, consider this: There are three times as many women's rest rooms as there are men's rest rooms. "And the men don't seem to notice," says a female Smithsonian employee who works at the information desk.

Other facilities of note on the Mall include those at the National Gallery of Art, the Arthur M. Sackler Gallery, the Hirshhorn Museum and Sculpture Garden, and the National Museum of African Art. The rest rooms in the National Museum of Natural History are inconveniently located on a lower level. At the Arts and Industries Building, facilities are located far away from the front entrance. On the other hand, the rest rooms in The Castle, the Smithsonian's visitor center, are easy to find and usually not very crowded.

Virtually all the monuments are rest room–equipped, including the Lincoln and Jefferson Memorials and the Washington Monument. One notable exception is the White House, a place infamous for long lines. Downtown, hotels, restaurants, and bars are good bets. (The rest rooms off the huge lobby of the Stouffer Mayflower Hotel on Connecticut Avenue are both convenient and elegant.) Avoid the few public rest rooms located in parks, such as the ones on the grounds of the Washington Monument and at Dupont Circle; they're usually dirty. Nor will you find rest rooms in Metro stations, although a few stations are located in complexes that do provide rest rooms, including Union Station, Metro Center, Farragut North, and L'Enfant Plaza.

How to Avoid Crime and
Keep Safe in Public Places

■ Crime in Washington ■

The combination of a widespread crack epidemic and the availability of high-powered weaponry put Washington on the map for a dubious distinction: "Murder Capital of the United States." Anyone who watches the evening news or reads a newspaper knows about Washington's grim murder rate. So the question arises, as you contemplate a trip to D.C.: Just how safe is Washington anyway? Am I going to end up just another statistic?

"It's very safe," says Officer Rod Ryan of D.C.'s Metropolitan Police Department, as long as you stay in proscribed areas. Ryan, a three-year veteran of the force who has worked special anticrime details around the Mall and popular tourist sites, explains, "Washington patrols its main visitor areas very strongly, because tourism is all the city has for income."

To get an idea of how much protection the average tourist or business visitor gets, consider this fact: It's not just Officer Ryan and the rest of D.C.'s finest patrolling the city. Contributing to the task are a number of other law enforcement agencies whose jobs include protecting visitors: The U.S. Park Police patrols the monuments, the U.S. Capitol Police protects the Capitol and the 20-square-block area around it, and the Secret Service patrols the area around the White House. Plus, the Metro has its own police force for protecting people riding public transportation.

"Police are patrolling on bicycles, on horseback, on small motorcycles, on foot, and in unmarked cars," explains Officer Ryan. "And the Smithsonian has its own police force—highly trained federal officers—who patrol inside the buildings and around the grounds. Anyone who knows what he's looking for can spot five police patrols from anywhere on the Mall."

Statistics support his claim: D.C.'s overall crime rate, as defined by the FBI, is actually fairly low. In the summer of 1991, FBI statistics ranked Washington 21st in overall rate of crime among major U.S. cities. Moreover, in 1995 the D.C. Metropolitan Police reported a declining murder rate: Homicides dropped during the first six months of the year by over 18% over the same period in 1994—a year that saw an overall decline in murders of 12% over 1993. Overall, the Metropolitan Police Department reports that city-wide crime dropped 3% in 1996 when compared with the previous year.

So, who's on the receiving end of all that automatic weapons fire? Most of the victims are either young drug dealers in shootouts with competitors or people involved in violent domestic disputes. Random murders are rare events in D.C., despite its reputation, and police say the odds here are about the same as anywhere else. Furthermore, the mayhem usually occurs in sections of the city visitors do not normally frequent: low-income, residential areas that are removed from the city center and business/tourist districts. The worst areas are in Northeast and Southeast Washington across the Anacostia River from downtown and the major visitor areas. You'd have to go to quite an effort to get there, even by mistake.

"Tourists should never wander across the bridge over the Anacostia River," says Officer Ryan, who should know: He leads a newly formed mountain bike patrol that has helped reduce street crime by 75% in one of the worst sections of Southeast Washington. "Visitors should stay within the boundaries of the Mall, Georgetown, upper Northwest, Dupont Circle, Adams-Morgan, and downtown."

Even Capitol Hill, which gained notoriety when a legislative aide was murdered on the street a few years ago, is as safe for visitors as any other area that out-of-towners frequent. Ryan explains, "Too many powerful congressmen live in Capitol Hill for it not to be well patrolled."

■ Having a Plan ■

Random violence and street crime are facts of life in any large city. You've got to be cautious and alert and plan ahead. When you are out and about, you must work under the assumption that you must use caution because you are on your own; if you run into trouble, it's unlikely that police or anyone else will be able to come to your rescue. You must give some advance thought to the ugly scenarios that might occur, and consider both preventive measures that will keep you out of harm's way and an escape plan just in case. Not being a victim of street crime is sort of a survival of the fittest thing. Just as a lion stalks the weakest member of the antelope herd, muggers and thieves target the easiest victim. Simply put, no matter where you are or what you are doing, you want potential felons to think of you as a bad risk.

On the Street   For starters, you always present less of an appealing target if you are with other people. Second, if you must be out alone, act alert, be alert, and always have at least one of your arms and hands free. Felons gravitate toward preoccupied folks, the kind found plodding along staring at the sidewalk, with both arms encumbered by briefcases or packages. Visible jewelry (on either men or women) attracts the wrong kind of attention. Men, keep your billfolds in your front trouser or coat pocket or in a fanny pack. Women, keep your purses tucked tightly under your arm; if you're wearing a coat, put it on over your shoulder bag strap.

Here's another tip: Men can carry two wallets, including one inexpensive one, carried in your hip pocket, containing about $20 in cash and some expired credit cards. This is the one you hand over if you're accosted. Your real credit cards and the bulk of whatever cash you have should be in either a money clip or a second wallet hidden elsewhere on your person. Women can carry a fake wallet in their purse and keep the real one in a pocket or money belt.

If You're Approached   Police will tell you that a felon has the least amount of control over his intended victim during the few moments of his initial approach. A good strategy, therefore, is to short-circuit the crime scenario as quickly as possible. If a felon starts by demanding your money, for instance, quickly take out your billfold (preferably your fake one) and hurl it in one direction while you run shouting for help in the opposite direction. The odds are greatly in your favor that the felon will prefer to collect your silent billfold rather than pursue you. If you hand over your wallet and just stand there, the felon will likely ask for your watch and jewelry next. If you're a woman, the longer you hang around, the greater your vulnerability to personal injury or rape.

Secondary Crime Scenes   Under no circumstance, police warn, should you ever allow yourself to be taken to another location—a "secondary crime scene" in police jargon. This move, they explain, provides the felon more privacy and consequently more control. A felon can rob you on the street very quickly and efficiently. If he tries to remove you to another location, whether by car or on foot, it is a certain indication that he has more in mind than robbery. Even if the felon has a gun or knife, your chances are infinitely better running away. If the felon grabs your purse, let him have it. If he grabs your coat, come out of the coat. Hanging onto your money or coat is not worth getting mugged, raped, or murdered.

Another maxim: Never believe anything a felon tells you, even if he's telling you something you desperately want to believe, for example, "I won't hurt you if you come with me." No matter how logical or benign he sounds, assume the worst. Always, always, break off contact as quickly as possible, even if that means running.

In Public Transport   When riding a bus, always take a seat as close to the driver as you can; never ride in the back. Likewise, on the subway, sit near the driver's or attendant's compartment. These people have a phone and can summon help in the event of trouble.

In Cabs   While it is possible to hail a cab on the street in Washington, you are somewhat vulnerable in the process. Particularly after dusk, call a reliable cab company and stay inside while they dispatch a cab to your door. When your cab arrives, check the driver's certificate, which must, by law, be posted on the dashboard. Address the cabbie by his last name (Mr. Jones or whatever) or mention the number of his cab. This alerts the driver to the fact that you are going to remember him and/or his cab. Not only will this contribute to your safety, it will also keep your cabbie from trying to run up the fare.

If you are comfortable reading maps, familiarize yourself with the most direct route to your destination ahead of time. If you can say, "Georgetown via Wisconsin Avenue, please," the driver is less likely to run up your fare by taking a circuitous route so he can charge you for three zones instead of two.

If you need to catch a cab at the train station or at one of the airports, always use the taxi queue. Taxis in the official queue are properly licensed and regulated. Never accept an offer for a cab or limo made by a stranger in the terminal or baggage claim. At best, you will be significantly overcharged for the ride. At worst, you may be abducted.

■ **Personal Attitude** ■

While some areas of every city are more dangerous than others, never assume that any area is completely safe. Never let down your guard. You can be the victim of a crime, and it can happen to you anywhere. If you go to a restaurant or nightspot, use valet parking or park in a well-lighted lot. Women leaving a restaurant or club alone should never be reluctant to ask to be escorted to their car.

Never let your pride or sense of righteousness and indignation imperil your survival. This is especially difficult for many men, particularly for men in the presence of women. It makes no difference whether you are approached by an aggressive drunk, an unbalanced street person, or an actual felon, the rule is the same: Forget your pride and break off contact as quickly as possible. Who cares whether the drunk insulted you, if everyone ends up back at the hotel safe and sound? When you wake up in the hospital with a concussion and your jaw sewn shut, it's too late to decide that the drunk's filthy remark wasn't really all that important.

Felons, druggies, some street people, and even some drunks play for keeps. They can attack with a bloodthirsty hostility and hellish abandon that is beyond the imagination of most people. Believe me, you are not in their league (nor do you want to be).

■ Self-Defense ■

In a situation where it is impossible to run, you'll need to be prepared to defend yourself. Most policemen insist that a gun or knife is not much use to the average person. More often than not, they say, the weapon will be turned against the victim. Additionally, concealed firearms and knives are illegal in most jurisdictions. The best self-defense device for the average person is Mace. Not only is it legal in most states, it is nonlethal and easy to use.

When you shop for Mace, look for two things: It should be able to fire about eight feet, and it should have a protector cap so it won't go off by mistake in your purse or pocket. Carefully read the directions that come with your device, paying particular attention to how it should be carried and stored, and how long the active ingredients will remain potent. Wearing a rubber glove, test-fire your Mace, making sure that you fire downwind.

When you are out about town, make sure your Mace is someplace easily accessible, say, attached to your keychain. If you are a woman and you keep your Mace on a keychain, avoid the habit of dropping your keys (and the Mace) into the bowels of your purse when you leave your hotel room or your car. The Mace will not do you any good if you have to dig around in your purse for it. Keep your keys and your Mace in your hand until you have safely reached your destination.

■ Carjackings ■

With the recent surge in carjackings, drivers also need to take special precautions. "Keep alert when you're driving in D.C. traffic," Officer Ryan warns. "Keep your doors locked, with the windows rolled up and the air conditioning or heat on. In traffic, leave enough space in front of you so that you're not blocked in and can make a U-turn. That way, if someone approaches your car and starts beating on your windshield, you can drive off." Store your purse or briefcase under your knees when you are driving, rather than on the seat beside you.

■ Ripoffs and Scams ■

First-time visitors to the Mall stepping off the escalator at the Smithsonian Metro are often confronted by fast-talking men who try to sell them museum brochures. Don't fall for it; the brochures are free in Smithsonian museums—and the fast-talkers are trying to rip you off.

Another scam that visitors need to watch out for is the well-dressed couple who claim their car broke down and they need $5 for train fare. Refer them to a cop for help and move on.

■ More Things to Avoid ■

When you do go out, walk with a minimum of two people whenever possible. If you have to walk alone, stay in well-lit areas that have plenty of people around. And don't walk down alleys. It also helps not to look like a tourist when venturing away from the Mall. Don't wear a camera around your neck, and don't gawk at buildings and unfold maps on the sidewalk. Be careful about whom you ask for directions. (When in doubt, shopkeepers are a good bet.) Don't count your money in public, and carry as little cash as possible. At public phones, if you must say your calling card number to make a long-distance call, don't say it loud enough for strangers around you to hear. And, with the exception of the Mall, avoid public parks after dark. In particular, don't go to Rock Creek Park at night.

■ Help May Be Nearer Than You Think ■

While walking in Washington, try to be aware of public and federal facilities. If, despite your precautions, you are attacked, head for any federal office building for help. The entrances are all patrolled by armed guards who can offer assistance.

While this litany of warnings and precautions may sound grim, it's really common-sense advice that applies to visitors in any large American city. Keep in mind that Washington's reputation for crime is enhanced by the worldwide media attention the city gets: Local news in Washington is really national news. Finally, remember that 21 million visitors a year still flock to the nation's capital, making it one of the most-visited destinations in the United States. The overwhelming majority encounter no problems with crime during their Washington visit.

Though most police officials offer similar advice when it comes to personal safety on the streets, Detective J. J. Bittenbinder of the Chicago Police Department has consolidated professional opinion on the subject in an instructional audiocassette entitled *Street Smart: How to Avoid Being a Victim*. In this logical and forceful presentation, Bittenbinder offers practical suggestions for safeguarding your body, possessions, and sanity in the city. The cassette can be ordered from the J Marc Group, (800) 888-5176, for about $15 (worth every penny, in our opinion).

■ The Homeless ■

If you're not from a big city or haven't visited one in a while, you're in for a shock when you come to Washington. It seems that every block in the city is filled with shabbily dressed people asking for money. Furthermore, along the Mall, near the national monuments, on downtown sidewalks, and in parks and gardens, you will see people sleeping in blankets and sleeping bags, their possessions piled up next to them. On crowded Georgetown streets filled with opulent shops, homeless women with small children beg for money. Drivers in cars are approached at stoplights by men carrying Magic-Marker-on-cardboard signs reading "Homeless—Will Work for Food." Virtually every Metro exit is choked with clusters of people begging for money.

Who Are These People? "Most are lifelong D.C. residents who are poor," according to Joan Alker, assistant director of the National Coalition for the Homeless, an advocacy group headquartered in Washington. "The people you see on the streets are primarily single men and women. A disproportionate number of them are minorities and people with disabilities—they're either mentally ill, or substance abusers, or have physical disabilities."

Are They a Threat to Visitors? "No," Ms. Alker says. "Studies done in Washington show that homeless men have lower rates of conviction for violent crimes than the population at large. We know that murders aren't being committed by the homeless. I can't make a blanket statement, but most homeless people you see are no more likely to commit a violent crime than other people."

Should You Give the Homeless Money? "That's a personal decision," Ms. Alker says. "But if you can't, at least try to acknowledge their existence by looking them in the eye and saying, 'No, I can't.'" While there's no way to tell if the guy with the Styrofoam cup asking for a handout is really destitute or just a con artist, no one can dispute that most of these people are what they claim to be: homeless.

Ways to Help It's really a matter for your own conscience. We confess to being both moved and annoyed by these unfortunate people: moved by their need and annoyed that we cannot enjoy the nation's capital without running a gauntlet of begging men and women. In the final analysis, we found that it is easier on the conscience and spirit to get a couple of rolls of quarters at the bank and carry an overcoat or jacket pocket full of change at all times. The cost of giving those homeless who approach you a quarter really does not add up to all that much, and it is much better for the psyche to respond to their plight than to deny or ignore their presence.

There is a notion, perhaps valid in some instances, that money given to a homeless person generally goes toward the purchase of alcohol or drugs. If this bothers you excessively, carry granola bars for distribution, or, alternatively, buy some inexpensive gift coupons that can be redeemed at a McDonald's or other fast-food restaurant for coffee or a sandwich.

We have found that a little kindness regarding the homeless goes a long way, and that a few kind words delivered along with your quarter or granola bar brighten the day for both you and your friend in need. We are not suggesting a lengthy conversation or prolonged involvement, just something simple like, "Sure, I can help a little bit. Take care of yourself, fella."

Those moved to get more involved in the nationwide problem of homelessness can send inquiries—or a check—to the National Coalition for the Homeless, 1612 K Street, NW, Suite 1004, Washington, D.C. 20006.

Keep It Brief   Finally, don't play psychologist. All the people you encounter on the street are strangers. They may be harmless, or they may be dangerous. Either way, maintain distance and keep any contacts or encounters brief. Be prepared to handle street people in accordance with your principles, but mostly, just be prepared. If you have a druggie in your face wanting a handout, the last thing you want to do is pull out your wallet and thumb through the twenties looking for a one-dollar bill. As the sergeant on *Hill Street Blues* used to say, be careful out there.

PART FIVE

Getting around Washington

Driving Your Car: A Really Bad Idea

■ Traffic Hot Spots ■

Here's some bad news for anyone considering driving to Our Nation's Capital: Washington is legendary for its traffic congestion. Let's start with the Capital Beltway (I-495 and I-95), which encircles the city through the Virginia and Maryland suburbs: It's guaranteed to be logjammed on weekdays from 7 A.M. to 9:30 A.M. and again from 3 P.M. to 7 P.M. Unremitting suburban growth and geography confound the best efforts of traffic engineers to alleviate the congestion.

Inside the Beltway, the situation only gets worse. The few bridges that connect Washington and Virginia across the Potomac River are rush-hour bottlenecks. Interstates 66 and 395 in Virginia have restricted car-pool lanes inbound in the morning and outbound in the evening. Inside the District, Rock Creek Parkway becomes one-way during rush hour, and major thoroughfares such as Connecticut Avenue switch the direction of center lanes to match the predominant flow of traffic at different times of day. Downtown, the city's traffic circles can trap unwary motorists and reduce drivers to tears or profanity. Pierre L'Enfant's eighteenth-century grand plan of streets and avenues that intersect in traffic circles is a nightmare for twentieth-century motorists.

First-time drivers to Washington should map out their routes in advance, avoid arriving and departing during rush hour, and then leave the car parked throughout their stay. Lunch-hour traffic can be equally ferocious, and don't think that weekends are immune from traffic snarls: Washington's popularity as a tourist mecca slows Beltway traffic to a crawl on Saturdays and Sundays in warm weather. If there's any good news about driving in Washington, it's this: After evening rush hour subsides, getting around town by car is pretty easy.

■ Parking ■

If you ignore our advice about driving in Washington (we repeat: don't) and battle your way downtown by car, you'll find yourself stuck in one of those good news/bad news scenarios. The good news: There are plenty of places to park. The bad news: Virtually all the spaces are in parking garages that charge an arm and a leg. Figure on $12 a day or $5 an hour, minimum.

Think you can beat the system by finding street parking? Go ahead and try, but bring a lot of quarters—and plenty of patience. Most metered parking is restricted to two hours—not a long time if you're intent on exploring a museum or attending a business meeting. And D.C. cops are quick to issue tickets for expired meters. Also, a lot of legal spaces turn illegal during afternoon rush hour.

In popular residential neighborhoods such as Georgetown and Adams-Morgan, parking gets even worse at night. Unless you've got a residential parking permit—not likely if you're from out of town—street parking is limited to from two to three hours, depending on the neighborhood. The parking permits are prominently displayed in the cars of area residents.

If you're tempted to park illegally, be warned: D.C. police are grimly efficient at whisking away cars parked in rush-hour zones, and the fines are hefty. (If your car is towed, call the D.C. Department of Public Works at (202) 727-9200.) Incredibly, there's free parking along the Mall beginning at 10 A.M. weekdays; the limit is three hours. Needless to say, competition for the spaces is fierce.

Riding the Metro:
A Really Good Idea

■ A Clean, Safe Alternative ■

It should be clear by now that visitors who would prefer to spend their time doing something productive rather than sit in traffic jams shouldn't drive in or around Washington. Thanks to the Metro, visitors can park their cars and forget them. Five color-coded subway lines connect downtown Washington to the outer reaches of the city and beyond to the Maryland and Virginia suburbs. It's a clean, safe, and efficient system that saves visitors time, money, and shoe leather as it whisks them around town. Visitors to Washington should use the Metro as their primary mode of transportation.

The trains are well maintained and quiet, with carpeting, cushioned seats, and air conditioning. The stations are modern, well lighted, and usually spotless and are uniformly constructed with high, arching ceilings paneled with sound-absorbing, lozenge-shaped concrete panels. The wide-open look of the stations has been criticized as sterile and monotonous, but the design may explain why the Metro has maintained a crime-free reputation: There's no place for bad guys to hide. In addition, the entire system is monitored by closed-circuit TV cameras, and each car is equipped with passenger-to-operator intercoms, as are rail platforms and elevators. And cars and stations are nearly graffiti-free.

The Metro (nobody calls it Metrorail, its real name) transports more than half a million passengers a day along 92 miles of track and through 75 stations. When the system is completed early in the next century, the Metro will boast 83 stations connected by 103 miles of track. It's a world-class engineering marvel.

Trains operate so frequently that carrying a schedule is unnecessary. During peak hours (weekdays 5:30 A.M. to 9:30 A.M. and 3 P.M. to 8 P.M.), trains enter the stations every three to six minutes. During off-peak hours, the interval increases to an average of 12 minutes; it can go to 15 minutes on weekends. To maintain the intervals throughout the year, the Metro adds and deletes trains to compensate for holidays and peak tourist season. Hours of operation are 5:30 A.M. to midnight weekdays, and 8 A.M. to midnight on weekends and holidays.

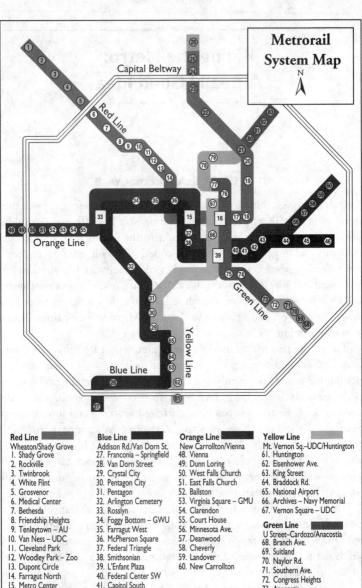

Metrorail System Map

N

Capital Beltway

Red Line

Orange Line

Green Line

Yellow Line

Blue Line

Red Line
Wheaton/Shady Grove
1. Shady Grove
2. Rockville
3. Twinbrook
4. White Flint
5. Grosvenor
6. Medical Center
7. Bethesda
8. Friendship Heights
9. Tenleytown – AU
10. Van Ness – UDC
11. Cleveland Park
12. Woodley Park – Zoo
13. Dupont Circle
14. Farragut North
15. Metro Center
16. Gallery Place, Chinatown
17. Judiciary Square
18. Union Station
19. Rhode Island Ave.
20. Brookland – CUA
21. Fort Totten
22. Takoma
23. Silver Spring
24. Forest Glen
25. Wheaton
26. Glenmont

Blue Line
Addison Rd./Van Dorn St.
27. Franconia – Springfield
28. Van Dorn Street
29. Crystal City
30. Pentagon City
31. Pentagon
32. Arlington Cemetery
33. Rosslyn
34. Foggy Bottom – GWU
35. Farragut West
36. McPherson Square
37. Federal Triangle
38. Smithsonian
39. L'Enfant Plaza
40. Federal Center SW
41. Capitol South
42. Eastern Market
43. Potomac Ave.
44. Stadium – Armory
45. Benning Rd.
46. Capitol Heights
47. Addison Rd.

Orange Line
New Carrollton/Vienna
48. Vienna
49. Dunn Loring
50. West Falls Church
51. East Falls Church
52. Ballston
53. Virginia Square – GMU
54. Clarendon
55. Court House
56. Minnesota Ave.
57. Deanwood
58. Cheverly
59. Landover
60. New Carrollton

Yellow Line
Mt. Vernon Sq.–UDC/Huntington
61. Huntington
62. Eisenhower Ave.
63. King Street
64. Braddock Rd.
65. National Airport
66. Archives – Navy Memorial
67. Vernon Square – UDC

Green Line
U Street–Cardozo/Anacostia
68. Branch Ave.
69. Suitland
70. Naylor Rd.
71. Southern Ave.
72. Congress Heights
73. Anacostia
74. Navy Yard
75. Waterfront
76. Shaw – Howard University
77. U Street – Cardozo
78. Columbia Heights
79. Georgia Ave. Petworth
80. West Hyattsville
81. Prince George's Plaza
82. College Park – U of MD
83. Greenbelt

⬤ **Stations**–all day parking
◯ **Stations**–no all day parking
☐ **Transfer stations**

■ How to Ride the Metro ■

Finding the Stations

Many (but, unfortunately, not all) street signs in Washington indicate the direction and number of blocks to the nearest Metro station. Station entrances are identified by brown columns or pylons with an "M" on all four sides and a combination of colored stripes in red, yellow, orange, green, or blue that indicate the line or lines serving that station. Since most stations are underground, users usually descend on escalators to the mezzanine or ticketing part of the station. At above-ground and elevated stations outside of downtown Washington, the mezzanine is most often on the ground level. At the kiosk located there, pick up a system map with quick directions on how to use the Metro.

Purchasing a Farecard

Next comes the tricky part: You must determine your destination and your fare ahead of time because the ticketing system is automated. Walk up to the backlit, color-coded map located in each mezzanine and locate the station nearest your ultimate destination. Then look on the bottom of the map, where an alphabetized list of stations reveals both the fare (peak and off-peak) and the estimated travel time to each. Peak fares, usually more expensive, are in effect from 5:30 A.M. to 9:30 A.M. and 3 P.M. to 8 P.M. weekdays. Unless you're traveling from a suburban station to downtown, or from one suburb to another, the one-way fare is typically $1.10 (non-rush hour). One last note: Before you walk away from the map, make a mental note of the last station of the train that you plan to board, even though you're probably not traveling that far. The name of your train's final destination is the name of the train, thus the key to locating the right platform—the one whose trains are going in the right direction. (See photographs starting on page 113.)

Farecard Vending Machines

Those big vending machines lining the walls of the mezzanine don't dispense sodas. Instead, they swallow your money and issue farecards with magnetic stripes that get you in and—this is crucial—out of Metro stations. Once you get your card, hang onto it.

Buying a farecard works like this: Walk up to the farecard vending machine and look for the numeral "1" on the left side at eye level. (We'll call this **Step 1.**) This is where you insert bills and/or coins. If your destination is, say, a $1.10 fare, and you're making a round trip, insert $2.20 into the machine. As the money slides in, look at the middle of the machine for the numeral "2" (**Step 2**), where a digital readout registers the amount you've shoved into the contraption.

Machines that accept paper money invariably screw up, and these machines are no exception. They often spit back bills they don't like, so try smoothing wrinkled bills before inserting them and choose new, unfrayed greenbacks over bills that are worn. Inserting coins is nearly foolproof, but not very practical if you're riding the Metro a lot.

Our advice is to cut down on using these infernal machines as much as possible by plugging in $5, $10, or even $20 at once, which means you're buying a ticket that can last several days or longer. The computerized turnstiles print the remaining value on the farecard after each use, which lets you know when it's time to buy a new one. A major drawback, of course, is the possibility of losing the farecard while it's still worth a few bucks. If you value your time at all, take the risk. Below the digital readout at Step 2 are white "plus" and "minus" buttons that let you adjust the readout to the exact fare you wish to purchase. For example, if your round-trip fare is $2.20 and you inserted a $5 bill, toggle the readout from $5 down to $2.20 by repeatedly pushing the "minus" button. (If you overshoot, push the "plus" button to increase the value.) Then look to the right side of the machine and the numeral "3" (**Step 3**), and press the button that reads "Press for Farecard." If all goes well (and, in all fairness, it usually does), out pops your farecard and your change—in this case, $2.80 in change; the machines don't dispense bills. (We *told* you to buy a $5 farecard.)

The farther out you get from downtown, the fewer farecard machines line the walls of the mezzanines—which usually isn't a problem at these less-busy stations. For balky machines that won't take your money, or any problem at all, help is only a few steps away at the kiosk located at each station near the faregate. Inside is a breathing human being who will help. Don't be shy.

One last warning: If the farecard machine accepts $20 bills, keep in mind that the maximum amount of change the machine can spit out is $4.95—which means you're stuck buying a farecard with a minimum value of $15.05.

New Talking Fare Machines

Recently, Metro installed new talking express farecard vending machines at 46 mezzanines in the system's busiest stations; look for the name *Passes/Farecards* across the top. An optional audio button lets you hear a voice guide you through the steps to purchase farecards, which removes much of the confusion and is a real boon to visually impaired riders.

The new machines let you buy up to $200 worth of farecards with a top denomination of $45. You can also purchase the $5 one-day pass, valid for unlimited rides after 9:30 A.M. weekdays and all day on weekends and holidays (a very good deal that we recommend most visitors take advantage of). An upcoming feature will let you charge your farecard purchases to Discover, VISA, Most, and MasterCard credit cards. *Note:* Most users will want to press button two, for a single farecard, to begin the card purchase process.

Entering the Station

With your farecard firmly in hand, you are now authorized to enter the Metro station. Hold the card in your right hand with the brown magnetic stripe facing up and on the right. Walk up to one of the waist-high faregates with the green light and white arrow near the kiosk (not the faregates that read "Do Not Enter"—they are for passengers exiting the station) and insert your card into the slot, where it is slurped into the bowels of the Metro. As the gate opens, walk through and grab your card as it is regurgitated from the slot at the top of the gate. All this happens in less than a second. Place the farecard in a safe place; if you lose it, you must pay the maximum fare when you exit.

Finding the Train Platform

Once you're past the faregate, look for signs with arrows and the name of your intended line's end station that point toward the platform where your train will arrive. At an underground station, you will descend on an escalator or stairs to the train platform; at an above-ground station, you will ascend to the platform. You can reconfirm that you're on the correct side of the platform by reading the list of stations printed on the pylon located there and finding your destination. If your destination is listed, you're on the right track; departing trains go in one direction only. Stand in the red-tiled area to wait for the next train.

Boarding the Train

As a train approaches a station, lights embedded in the floor along the granite edge of the platform begin flashing. As the train comes out of the tunnel, look for a sign over the front windshield that states the train's destination and line (blue, red, green, orange, or yellow). The destination, but not the color, is also shown on the side of the train. Double-check to make sure the approaching train is the one you want.

If it's the right train, approach the doors, but stand clear to let departing passengers exit the train. Then move smartly; the train stops for only a few seconds, then chimes will indicate that the doors are about to close. If you're rushing to catch a train and hear the chimes, don't attempt to board. Unlike elevator doors, the train doors won't pop open if you lean on them—and they exert a lot of pressure. Wait for the next train.

Inside, take a seat or, if you're a first-time Metro user, study the system map located near the doors. The trains all have real operators who announce the next station over a PA system and give information for transferring to other lines (sometimes you can even hear them over the din). It's better to study the map and read the signs mounted on the cavernous station walls at each stop.

Exiting the Station

As the train enters your station, move toward the doors. When you step off the train, look for stairs or escalators on the platform and walk toward them. Some stations have two or more exits, but the signs on the walls of the stations aren't always clear about where each exit goes. If you know which exit you want (for example, at the Smithsonian station most tourists want the Mall exit, not Independence Avenue), look for that sign and follow the arrow.

At the top of the escalator or stairs, walk toward the mezzanine area, get your farecard ready, and repeat the same procedure you used to enter the Metro system (card in right hand, magnetic stripe up and on the right, insert in slot). If you bought exact fare you won't get your card back, but the gate will open and a little sign will flash "Exact Fare." You're on your way. If your farecard still has money left on it, it pops up as the gate opens and the sign flashes "Take Farecard." Do same; exit station.

If your farecard doesn't have enough value to cover your trip, the gate won't open and the card will pop back out. You need to take it to an "Exit-fare" machine somewhere just behind you. (Invariably ten people are lined up behind you when this happens, creating the equivalent of a minor Beltway backup.) The reddish-colored Exitfare machines look like their brothers, the farecard machines. Insert your card and immediately the digital readout displays the exact amount of moolah it needs so you can exit the station. (Don't make my mistake: The machine asked for 40 cents and I stuck a $5 bill into it. I got $4.60 in change back.) Plug in the coins; the farecard reappears; grab it; insert same into the faregate, which swallows it and sets you free.

Changing from One Line to Another

Sooner or later—probably sooner—you will need to transfer from one Metro line to another. Metro Center is the Big Enchilada of the transfer stations, where the red, orange, and blue lines converge in downtown Washington. Other transfer stations that tourists are likely to hit are Gallery

Place–Chinatown (red, yellow, and green); L'Enfant Plaza (yellow, blue, orange, green); Rosslyn (orange and blue); and Pentagon (yellow and blue).

To transfer, you don't use your farecard. Simply exit your train, take the escalator to the correct platform, and reboard. Try to listen to the PA system as your train enters the station: The driver recites where the different lines are located in the approaching station (for example, "Transfer to the red line on the lower level"). If you can't hear the driver's instructions, look for the color-coded pylons with arrows that point toward the platforms, and look for the one with your destination listed on it.

The Gallery Place–Chinatown station is especially complicated. Frequently, you're routed down and up escalators to reach your platform. Keep your eyes up for signs overhead that state reassuring messages such as "Red Line–Wheaton Straight Ahead."

■ Metro Foibles and How to Cope ■

Boarding the Wrong Train

Unless you're concerned about being ten minutes or so late for your meeting with President Clinton, boarding a train going in the wrong direction isn't a big problem. Simply get off at the next station, and if the platform is located between the tracks, go to the other side of the platform to wait for the next train running in the opposite direction, and board it. If both sets of tracks run down the center of the station, take the escalator or stairs and cross the tracks to the other side, where you can catch the next train going the other way.

If you belatedly realize you boarded the wrong *color* train (say, the orange train to Vienna, Virginia, instead of the blue train to Van Dorn Street), just get off at the next station, stay on the same platform, and take the next blue line train.

What to Do with Farecards Worth 50 Cents

After a few days in Washington, you may start accumulating farecards that don't have enough value for even a one-way trip. Don't throw them away! Instead, next time you're using the Metro go up to a farecard vending machine in the mezzanine and insert the old farecard into the slot on the right side of the machine where it says "Trade In Used Farecard." Its value will be displayed on the digital readout at Step 2. Feed the machine money at Step 1, futz with the "plus" and "minus" buttons, and press the white "Push for Farecard" button to get a new card that includes the value on your old card.

If, Like Joe, You're Color Blind

Joe's heart sank the first time he tried to figure out Washington's Metro system: Like gazillions of other men, he is afflicted with red-green color blindness. To his eyes, the Metro's red and green lines look nearly identical in color, and the orange line looks a lot redder than it ought to. The only lines on the system map he could distinguish by color were the blue and yellow ones.

The solution is to fixate on the names of the stations at the ends of the lines. That way, the red line becomes the "Wheaton/Shady Grove" line, while the green line is the "U Street–Cardozo/Anacostia" line. It's harder, at first, but you'll end up with a distinct advantage over those who blindly follow colored signs: Knowing a line's end station is helpful when you've got to make a split-second decision on whether or not to board a train that's almost ready to depart the station. For instance, if you enter the Dupont Circle Metro and want to go to Union Station, you need to board the red line train heading toward Wheaton—not Shady Grove. So, sooner or later, you'll get familiar with the end stations anyway.

■ Discounts and Special Deals ■

Children   Up to two children under age five can ride free when accompanied by a paying passenger.

Senior Citizens and People with Disabilities   Reduced fares are available for qualified senior citizens; call (202) 637-7000 for more information. People with disabilities can call (202) 962-1245 for information on reduced fares. A new service called "Metro Mobility Link" supplies people with disabilities with specialized information about Metro stations, including general features of each station, the location of Braille signs, whether the station has a center or side platform, and other disabled-accessible features. The number is (202) 962-6464.

The Metro is a tourist attraction in its own right, featuring the longest escalator in the Western Hemisphere: the 230-foot, mezzanine-to-platform-level behemoth at the Wheaton Metro in suburban Maryland. If that's a little out of the way, the Dupont Circle Metro's escalator is nearly as long. If escalators terrify you or you are wheelchair-bound, all stations are equipped with elevators. But it's a good idea to check at a station kiosk and confirm that the elevator at your destination station is in operation. To find the elevator, look for the wheelchair symbol near the station entrance.

Fare Discounts   If you plan on using the Metro more than once or twice a day, call Metrorail at (202) 637-7000 to find out what discounts are in

Bronze pylons (*top*) identify Metro stations; colored stripes at top show the
line or lines served by that station.

Metro systems and neighborhood maps (*bottom*) are located in the mezzanine of each station.

Rush hour and non-rush hour fares are listed alphabetically at each station's kiosk (*top*).

Automated Farecard machines (*bottom*) are located in the mezzanine of each station.

Step 1 (*top*): To purchase a farecard, insert bills and/or coins.

Step 2 (*bottom left*): Use toggle switches to add or decrease the farecard's value. Plug in enough cash to buy at least a round-trip ticket (or more, if desired).

Step 3 (*bottom right*): Press the "Push for Farecard" button; the farecard appears at the "Used Farecard Trade-In" slot.

Automated faregates, which control access in and out of spacious Metro stations, are located near the kiosk. The woman pictured here is exiting the station.

When entering or exiting, insert the farecard (face up with the magnetic stripe on the right) into the slot on the front of the faregate (*top*).

The farecard reappears at the top of the faregate (*bottom*); remove it and the faregate opens. On new faregates for disabled people, the farecard reappears at the front of the gate.

Note: Remember to hang on to the farecard—you need it to exit the system.

When the value of a farecard drops below $1, trade
it in for a new one at a farecard machine (*top*).
Emergency intercoms (*bottom*) are located on all station platforms.

effect during your visit. A high-value farecard of $20 or more garners a 10% bonus. A Metrorail One-Day Pass lets you ride from 9:30 A.M. till midnight for $5 weekdays, and all day on weekends and holidays; it's the way to go if you plan to ride the subway to several locations in one day. Commuters can save money by purchasing passes that let them ride anywhere, anytime, for two weeks. Discount passes are available at the Metro Center sales office and from the new talking farecard machines installed in busier Metro Stations. Discount passes are also sold at many Safeway, Giant, and SuperFresh grocery stores.

Free information   For a free visitor information kit that includes a Metro system map, specific information on getting to Smithsonian museums and other attractions, and driving to suburban Metro stations, call this number: (202) 637-7000. The computer literate can get up-to-the-minute information on using the Metro on the World Wide Web at http://www. wmata.com.

■ A Note about Metrobus ■

Washington's extensive bus system, known as Metrobus, serves Georgetown, downtown, and the suburbs. With 400 routes and more than 1,500 buses, Metrobus is also an extremely complicated system to figure out how to use. As a result, we feel that visitors to Washington should leave Metrobus to the commuters and stick to the Metro. For the few places that the Metro doesn't reach—notably Georgetown and Adams-Morgan—we recommend taking a cab.

Bus Transfers

If, despite our advice, you plan to transfer from the Metro to a Metrobus in D.C. or Virginia, get a free transfer before you board the Metro train from the machine located next to the escalator in the mezzanine of the station that you entered. You also need to pick up a bus transfer at the White Flint, Twinbrook, and New Carrollton suburban stations to qualify for reduced parking fees on weekdays; look for signs in the station.

Taxis

Washington taxis are plentiful and relatively cheap. They're also strange. Instead of a metered fare system, fares are figured on a map that splits the city into 5 zones and 27 subzones; the base fare for one zone is $3.70. A zone map and fare chart are posted in all legal cabs but probably won't mean much to first-time visitors—or most residents, for that matter. If you're concerned about getting ripped off, request a receipt before you start the ride. That way the driver knows he's got no defense in an overcharging claim. (*Note:* In late 1998, D.C.'s cabs are scheduled to switch over to meters.)

The cab system has other quirks. Drivers can pick up other fares as long as the original passenger isn't taken more than five blocks out of the way of the original destination. That's good news if you're the second or third rider and it's raining; it's not so hot if you're the original passenger and trying to catch a train.

To eliminate the possibility of a ride in a poorly maintained cab or one driven by a recent immigrant who is as unfamiliar with the city as you are, stick to the major cab companies, which include Yellow Cab, Diamond, and Capitol. Some of the independents are illegal, yet still carry the markings and roof light of a seemingly legit cab. One way to spot a fly-by-night taxi is to check for hubcaps. If there aren't any, pass that one by.

People with Special Needs

Washington is one of the most accessible cities in the world for folks with disabilities. With the equal-opportunity federal government as the major employer in the area, Washington provides a good job market for disabled people. As a result, the service sector—bus drivers, waiters, ticket sellers, retail clerks, cab drivers, tour guides, and so on—are somewhat more attuned to the needs of people with disabilities than service-sector employees in other cities. It doesn't hurt that a number of organizations that lobby for handicapped people are headquartered in Washington.

The Metro, for example, was designed to meet federal standards for accessibility. As a result, the stations and trains provide optimal services to a wide array of people with special requirements. Elevators provide access to the mezzanine or ticketing areas, platform, and street level; call the Metro's 24-hour elevator hot line at (202) 962-1825 to check if the elevators at the stations you plan to use are operating.

The edge of the train platform is built with a 14-inch, smooth, light gray, granite strip that's different in texture from the rest of the platform flooring so that visually impaired passengers can detect the platform edge with a foot or cane. Flashing lights embedded in the granite strip alert hearing-impaired passengers that a train is entering the station. Handicapped-only parking spaces are placed close to station entrances. While purchasing a farecard is a strictly visual process (unless the station is equipped with the new talking vending machines), visually impaired passengers can go to the nearby kiosk for assistance. Priority seating for senior citizens and passengers with disabilities is located next to doors in all cars.

Visitors with disabilities who possess a transit ID from their home city can pick up a courtesy Metro ID that provides substantial fare discounts; the ID is good for a month. Go to Metro Headquarters, 600 5th Stre NW, from 8 A.M. to 4:30 P.M. weekdays to pick one up; call (202) 962-1 for more information. If you want to ride the Metro to get there, th est station is Gallery Place. For a free guide with information on M and bus system for the elderly and physically disabled, call (202) "Metro Mobility Link" is a new help line for people with di (202) 962-6464 for basic as well as more specialized inform stations.

The Smithsonian and the National Park Service, agencies that run the lion's share of popular sights in Washington, offer top-notch services to folks with disabilities. Designated handicapped parking spaces are located along Jefferson Drive on the Mall, and museums are equipped with entrance ramps, barrier-free exhibits, elevator service to all floors, and accessible rest rooms and water fountains. Visually impaired visitors can pick up large-print brochures, cassette tapes and recorders, and raised-line drawings of museum artifacts at many Smithsonian museums. The National Air and Space Museum offers special tours that let visitors touch models and artifacts; call (202) 357-1400 for information.

Hearing-impaired visitors to the National Air and Space Museum can arrange tours with an interpreter by calling (202) 357-1400 (voice) or (202) 357-1729 (TTY). Public telephones in the museum are equipped with amplification, and the briefing room is equipped with audio loop. For a copy of the Smithsonian's "A Guide for Disabled Visitors," call (202) 357-2700 or (202) 357-1729 (TTY).

The Lincoln and Jefferson Memorials and the Washington Monument are equipped to accommodate disabled visitors. Most sight-seeing attractions have elevators for seniors and others who want to avoid a lot of stair climbing. The White House, for example, has a special entrance on Pennsylvania Avenue for visitors arriving in wheelchairs, and White House guides usually allow visually handicapped visitors to touch some of the items described on tours.

Tourmobile offers a special van equipped with a wheelchair and scooter lift for handicapped visitors. The van visits all the regular sites on the tour; in fact, visitors can usually specify what sites they want to see in any order and the van will wait until they are finished touring. The service is the same price as the standard Tourmobile rate, $12 for adults and $6 for children. Call (202) 554-7020 at least a day in advance to reserve a van.

In spite of all the services available to disabled visitors, it's still a good idea to call ahead to any facility you plan to visit and confirm that services are in place and that the particular exhibit or gallery you wish to see is still available.

Foreign visitors to Washington who would like a tour conducted in their native language can contact the Guide Service of Washington. See page 224 in our "Touring" chapter in Part Nine.

PART SIX

Entertainment and Night Life

Washington Night Life
More Than Lit-Up Monuments

Washington after-hours used to be an oxymoron. Public transportation set its clock by the bureaucracy, commuters had too far to go (and come back the next morning) to stay out late, and big expense account money was lavished on restaurants and buddy bars. Besides, Washingtonians suffered from a persistent cultural inferiority complex that had them running to buy tickets to see touring theatrical companies while not-so-benignly neglecting homegrown troupes.

Nowadays, though, the joke about "Washington after-hours" being an oxymoron is just that: a joke. It's not that there's too little night life around, it's that there's too much. Or too many. Washington is a polyglot of big-city bustlers, yuppies, diplomats, immigrants, CEOs, and college students; and every one of these groups is trying to create, and then integrate, their own circles. The fact that many overlap, and others evolve, means you can dabble in a little of everything.

Washington's legitimate theatrical community is underestimated but excellent; ballet, Broadway, and cabaret are almost constant presences, opera less so but increasingly frequent. At least some of th[...] are open year-round; there are major- and minor-league sport[...] season (see the "Spectator Sports" chapter). And nigh[...] flavors as their patrons: discos, live music venues, c[...] try dance halls, specialty bars, sports bars, espress[...] "second scenes" for re-entering singles. There are e[...] around for boys' night sentimentalists and brew[...]

Live entertainment in Washington can be divided into three categories: legitimate theater, comedy, and live rock/pop/jazz/country music. The 30 profiles of clubs that follow focus on live music, comedy clubs, discos/dance clubs, and noteworthy after-hours scenes because they generally require no advance planning. (In some cases, live music venues might sell out particular performances, so call ahead.) Nightly schedules of live music clubs, comedy clubs, and theatrical productions, as well as listings of piano rooms, opera companies, movie showtimes, etc., are printed in the *Washington Post* Friday "Weekend" section and the free *Washington City Paper*.

■ Legitimate Theater ■

Washington boasts six major theatrical venues (ten if you count the Kennedy Center's five stages separately) and more than a half-dozen smaller residential and repertory companies, plus university theaters, small special-interest venues, and itinerant troupes. The Big Six are where national touring companies, classical musicians, and celebrity productions are most apt to show up, and have the most complete facilities for handicapped patrons. They are also likely to be the most expensive.

On any given night at the **Kennedy Center for the Performing Arts,** you might see the resident National Symphony Orchestra under Leonard Slatkin or a visiting philharmonic in the 2,500-seat Concert Hall, a straight drama or classic farce in the 1,100-seat Eisenhower Theater, and a Broadway musical, kabuki spectacular, or premiere cru ballet company in the 2,300-seat Opera House. The two smaller arenas, Terrace Theater and Theater Lab, share the third floor with the restaurant (which has a nice view if you can get it) and archives. Philip Johnson's steeply canted and gracious Terrace, a gift from the nation of Japan, houses experimental or cult-interest productions, specialty concerts, and showcases; in the Theater Lab, designed to accommodate the avant and cabaret, the semi-improvised murder farce "Sheer Madness" has moved into its second decade. The Kennedy Center is at Virginia and New Hampshire Avenues, NW, next to the Watergate; the closest subway station is Foggy Bottom. For tickets and information, call (202) 467-4600. The Kennedy Center also houses the American Film Institute, which nightly screens films, usually double bills, of particular historical and aesthetic value.

The **National Theatre,** which was thoroughly, if a little showily, restored in Miami heat pastels a few years ago, is managed by the Shubert Organization, which not only books its touring Broadway productions but more and more often uses it for pre-Broadway tryouts. The is at 1321 Pennsylvania Avenue, NW, near the Federal Triangle or

Metro Center subway stop; for information call (202) 628-6161; for tickets call (800) 447-7400.

The **Shakespeare Theatre,** which moved in 1992 from its beloved but cramped home at the Folger Shakespeare Library into new digs in the grandly renovated Lansburg Building, now seats about 450. Each season it produces four classic plays, three by Shakespeare, and regularly corrals a few major stage and screen stars to headline. It also puts on free Shakespeare at the Carter-Barron amphitheater every summer. Shakespeare Theater is at 450 Seventh Street, NW, near the Gallery Place subway stop; for information call (202) 393-2700.

Ford's, where the balcony box in which Abraham Lincoln was shot remains draped in black (and spectrally inhabited, according to rumor), is a smallish (750) but comfy venue that hosts primarily family fare such as the annual production of Dickens's *A Christmas Carol* and musicals and revues. Ford's is at 511 10th Street, NW (Metro Center subway); call (202) 347-4833.

The **Warner Theatre,** which survived a two-year restoration marathon, is now a rococo delight, complete with a few special boxes with food service. Although it is emphasizing more legitimate theatrical bookings and musicals, it still occasionally harkens back to the days when it was one of the nicer small-concert venues for popular music. The Warner is at 13th and E Streets, NW, near Federal Triangle or Metro Center; for information call (202) 783-4000.

The tripartite **Arena Stage** is the most prestigious of Washington resident companies and was a prime factor in the rebirth of American regional theater. The Fichandler theater-in-the-round seats a little over 800; the Kreeger holds more than 500, and the tiny, pubbish Old Vat Room, home of the political comedy troupe Gross National Product, seats fewer than 200. Though it likes to show off its versatility (such as a dizzying reenactment of the Marx Brothers' "Coconuts" or the Flying Karamazov Brothers acting in *The Brothers Karamazov*), Arena is dedicated and fearless, producing Athol Fugard as well as Tennessee Williams. The Arena is at Sixth and Maine Avenue, SW—on the waterfront, which is also the subway station; call (202) 488-3300.

Although many of these professional productions can be pricey and often sell out, the Ticket Place office in the Old Post Office Pavilion at 1100 Pennsylvania Avenue, NW (Federal Triangle subway stop), sells half-price tickets (plus a service charge amounting to 10% of the face value) for same-day shows and concerts. Only cash is accepted. Ticket Place is open Tuesday–Friday from noon until 6 P.M. and Saturday from 11 A.M. until 5 P.M., when it also sells tickets for Sunday and Monday shows; call (202) 842-5387 for a list of available tickets. The Kennedy Center also sells a limited number of same-day tickets at half price and offers half-price tickets for students, seniors, and those with permanent disabilities. For information call (202) 467-4600. A limited number of standing-room passes at reduced prices and occasional returned seats may be available as well. (Several other ticket vendors in the area such as Top Centre sell tickets to area concerts and sporting events, but they usually impose a large service charge.)

Washington's "off-Broadway" theaters are clustered along 14th Street, NW, specializing in new and cutting-edge works. Among the most intriguing are **Source Theater Co.** (1835 14th Street, NW; (202) 462-1073), **Woolly Mammoth** (1401 Church Street, NW; (202) 393-3939), and the **Studio Theater** (14th and P Streets, NW; (202) 332-3300).

One of the strongest "small" theaters is **Signature Theatre** in Arlington, which is getting some national reviews, especially of its Sondheim productions (3806 South Four Mile Run Drive; (703) 820-9771). There are a few dinner theaters in the suburbs; if you're interested, check the Guide to the Lively Arts in the *Washington Post* Friday "Weekend" or Sunday "Show" sections, or look for a copy of *Washingtonian* magazine.

In general, Washington audiences have loosened their ties when it comes to theater attire; to some extent, the more "serious" a production is, the dressier the crowd, although jeans have become ubiquitous, particularly at the smaller, avant-garde companies. Opening nights are often black tie (or "creative black tie"), but you can go as you are. And incidentally, many of the nicer restaurants near the big-ticket venues offer pre-theater menus at fixed (and bargain) prices; be sure to inquire.

■ Comedy in Washington ■

Washington is full of jokes—and that's the first one. Capital comedians divide very roughly into three generations and styles: the cabaret performers (those "Washington institutions" whose satires are usually musical and relatively gentle); the sketch and improvisational troupes from the post-Watergate "Saturday Night Live" era; and the stand-up artists who are the anti-establishment baby-busters—in some cases, the urban guerillas. The first two groups are almost unavoidably political; the stand-up comedians range from political podium to locker room.

The most famous of the cabaret comedians is PBS irregular **Mark Russell,** whose residency at the Omni Shoreham lasted about four senatorial terms and who still plays several weeks at a time at Ford's Theatre every year. His slot at the Shoreham is filled these days by star headliner **"Mrs. Foggybottom"** (a.k.a. Joan Cushing), who performs weekends in the Marquee Lounge (above the Woodley Park Metro at 2500 Calvert Street, NW; (202) 745-1023).

The most loyal opposition is offered by the **Capitol Steps,** a group of former and current Hill staffers who roast their own hosts by rewriting familiar songs with pun-ishing lyrics. In addition to entertaining at semi-official functions (which may be one reason why their barbs are a tad blunter than some more outspoken satirists'), the Capitol Steps are a popular tourist attraction (which may be another) and perform every Friday and Saturday at Chelsea's nightclub in Georgetown (1055 Thomas Jefferson Street, NW; (202) 298-8222).

The most successful sketch-humor troupe in Washington is **Gross National Product** (reservations (202) 783-7212), an underground resistance movement that went above-ground after Reagan's election. Politics, especially the executive power structure, is its obsession: It skewers snoops, creeps, and veeps with gusto and, despite its long tenure, a hint of childish glee. Revues have titles like "Clintoons: The First Hundred Daze" and "A Newt World Order." Shows are about 90 minutes long, and since topicality is the name of the game, skits rise and fall with the state of the world. Performances are one-third to one-half improvisation. GNP's Saturday night shows at the Bayou in Georgetown (profiled below) have become required recreation not only for unreconciled rat race victims but the newer, looser White House staff as well. GNP also operates one of Washington's more unique tour services, **Scandal Tours,** which takes sight-seers past such political landmarks as Gary Hart's townhouse; the Jefferson Hotel, where political gun-for-hire Dick Morris simultaneously sucked a prostitute's toes and directed Democratic campaign strategy; and Fanne Fox's impromptu swimming pool, the Tidal Basin—an event retold by sex scandal veteran "Bob Packwood." Scandal Tours depart from the Old Post Office Pavilion Saturdays at 1 P.M. (reservations (800) 758-TOUR).

ComedySportz, which is both improvisational and interactive, is part Rorschach test, part parlor game, part contortionists' convention. Audience members select the topics, the characters, and all the particulars, and troupe members then ad-lib the skits. Actually, it's like a cross between American Gladiators and hockey: archetypes on thin ice. ComedySportz plays Thursday through Saturday at the Fun Factory in Alexandria, VA (3112 Mt. Vernon Avenue; (703) 684-5212).

The overbooking and overbuilding that made comedy shops the fast-food entertainment of the '80s is giving way to more exclusive (or at least better-budgeted) clubs. The most reliable are the downtown franchise of the star-circuit **Evening at the Improv** and the cable-comic showcase's **Headliners** (both profiled below). Hip gay and straight comedians of both

sexes—Kate Clinton, Paula Poundstone, Dennis Miller, Judy Tenuta—
draw so well in Washington that many are regularly booked not into clubs
but into mid-sized theatrical venues and colleges. Many other nightclubs or
restaurants offer comedy one night a week; check newspapers for specific
listings.

In general, all clubs now follow a standard lineup: the opener, usually a
local beginner who patters about ten minutes and also serves as emcee (and
who, especially on open mike night, may mean the difference between a
smooth production and a free-for-all); the "featured act," either an experi-
enced journeyman or perhaps a second-rank national or cable TV per-
former, who does about 30 minutes; and the headliner, usually somebody
with Letterman or Leno credits or at least a cable special, who plays about
an hour.

■ Live Pop/Rock/Jazz ■

Although it isn't widely advertised, for some reason, Washington is a
haven for music lovers of all types, and in the summer especially, an astonishing amount of music is free to the public. From classical to college-radio
rock, from hole-in-the-wall to the Washington Mall, you can hear it all.
Credit for the boom in live-music clubs in the Washington area is split
between the booming third-world community, used to later hours and different music styles; the large college and twentysomething population looking for entertainment, along with the thirtysomethings who started looking
ten years ago; the increasing number of those twenty- and thirty- and even
fortysomethings who live in the suburbs and don't want to go downtown
for a good time; the more assertive gay and faux-prole communities seeking accommodation; and the fair number of stubborn musicians and
underground entrepreneurs who have established venues and support net-
works for themselves and one another.

Jazz, of course, has a long history in Washington—in the '30s and '40s,
the U Street/Howard Theater corridor was known as the "Black Broadway"
and rivaled Harlem. But after years of declining audiences and bankrupted
clubs, jazz is reviving all around the area; and the number of young jazz
musicians, black and white, classical and contemporary, is remarkable. In
fact, the **Lincoln Theater** (1215 U Street, NW; (202) 328-6000), which
used to be one of the most popular stops for nationally ranked performers,
has been restored to its Georgian Revival glory and is beginning to feature
jazz and pop shows again.

Among the best places to hear jazz are **Blues Alley, One Step Down,
Takoma Station Tavern,** and **Cafe Lautrec** (all profiled in the next sec-

tion); **City Blues Cafe** (facing the Woodley Park stop at 2651 Connecticut Avenue, NW; (202) 232-2300); **Twins** (5516 Colorado Avenue, NW; (202) 882-2523); **Busara** (2340 Wisconsin Avenue, NW; (202) 337-2340); **Brewbaker's** (6931 Arlington Road, Bethesda, MD; (301) 907-2602); the **Basin Street Lounge/219 Restaurant** (219 King Street, Alexandria, VA; (703) 549-1141); **The Ice House Cafe** (760 Elden Street, Herndon, VA; (703) 471-4256); and **Normandie Farm Inn** (10710 Falls Road, Potomac, MD; (301) 983-8838). In addition, many hotels have fine jazz pianists in their lounges.

The mega–rock concert venues tend to be sports arenas doing double duty: the 20,000-seat **USAirways Arena** (formerly the **Capital Centre**); the new 20,000-plus-seat MCI Centre downtown, home to the Washington Bullets basketball and Washington Wizards hockey teams; the 50,000-seat RFK **Stadium**, erstwhile home of the Redskins football team (which has the advantage of being accessible by subway to the Stadium/Armory stop); and the all-purpose 10,000-seat **Patriot Center** college arena at George Mason in Fairfax, which also tends to carry the big-name country concerts. Tickets for these shows are usually available by phone from TicketMaster at (202) 432-7328, but beware: "service charges" and handling fees have been known to reach $4.50 per person—not per order.

The most popular outdoor commercial venue is **Wolf Trap Farm Park** off Route 7 in Vienna, VA, which offers almost nightly entertainment—pop, country, jazz and R&B, MOR (middle-of-the-road) rock, and even ballet and Broadway musical tours—and picnicking under the stars during the summer at its Filene Center amphitheater. During the winter season, Wolf Trap shifts to its small but acoustically magnificent Barns, literally two rebuilt barns; among its best concerts are the annual Folk Masters series coordinated with the Smithsonian. Wolf Trap has started its own phone-charge service called ProTix, which charges lower fees than TicketMaster; call (703) 218-6500 for Wolf Trap shows. On summer nights, the Metro operates a $3.50 shuttle service from the West Falls Church station to the Filene Center, but watch your watch: The return shuttle leaves either 20 minutes after the final curtain or 11 P.M., whichever is earlier, in order to ensure that riders don't miss the subway.

Merriweather Post Pavilion in Columbia, MD, has the busiest pop/rock outdoor arena and specializes in old-favorite rock and pop tours; but it is some distance from Washington and can only be reached by car. (It also uses the ProTix network; see newspapers for current listings.) However, it has a new rival around the other side of the Beltway: the **Nissan Pavilion** outside Manassas, VA, which has 10,000 seats under cover and lawn seating for another 15,000 people. Operated by Cellar Door Productions, the largest booking agency on the East Coast (and owners of the Bayou nightclub in Georgetown), Nissan Pavilion is currently booking many of the same acts as MPP but uses the TicketMaster network (phone (202) 432-7328). Like Merriweather Post, however, it can only be reached by car. The more progressive rock acts, which draw strong college and postgrad audiences, tend to be booked into college auditoriums such as George Washington University's **Lisner Auditorium** or **Smith Center**. National acts with limited audiences—R&B, gospel, soul, folk—are often booked into DAR **Constitution Hall** alongside the Ellipse. Check the newspaper listings for entertainers and phone numbers while you're in town. **George Mason University Center for the Arts,** which adjoins the Patriot Center, is a lovely new mid-sized venue for classical and jazz music and drama. Its phone-charge ticket service is (703) 993-8888.

You will also find concerts at many Washington churches, including the **National Cathedral**; check the newspapers.

There are several fine outdoor music venues in the area, including **Freedom Plaza** at 14th and Pennsylvania Avenue near the White House, home to numerous free music and ethnic festivals during the summer, particularly the annual DC World Jazz Fest held during the Fourth of July celebrations. **Carter-Barron Amphitheatre** in Rock Creek Park hosts gospel, soul, jazz, and R&B concerts on summer weekends; and several other smaller city parks, museums, and federal building plazas stage concerts that are listed in the newspapers.

The Mall between the U.S. Capitol and the Washington Monument is the site of many festivals during the year, especially on such holidays as Memorial Day, July 4, and Labor Day, when the National Symphony Orchestra headlines family concerts. The Smithsonian's annual Festival of American Folklife, which features three or four different ethnic groups every year, also has music and dance parties every night; it runs from the weekend before the Fourth of July through the holiday itself.

The most important clubs booking national alternative rock acts are the **9:30** club and the **Black Cat** (both profiled) and the new, edge-of-town **Capitol Ballroom** on Capitol Hill near the Navy Yard Metro (Half and K Streets, SE; (202) 554-1500). The mainstream national and regional rock market belongs to the **Bayou** (profiled). The most interesting techno and progressive bands play **Club Heaven/Hell,** a really split-level club—above and below the Green Island Cafe—in Adams-Morgan (2327 18th Street, NW; (202) 667-4355).

For folk, country, and bluegrass music, the most important venue is the **Birchmere** in Alexandria, VA, which has the Seldom Scene as a house band (Thursdays) and Mary-Chapin Carpenter as favorite daughter. The major old R&B, blues, and rockabilly clubs are **Twist and Shout** in Bethesda, MD, and **Phantasmagoria** in Wheaton, both of which book national Cajun/zydeco and deep-blues acts and front-line local groups. All are profiled below. Piano bars are legion, but the best and most accomplished jazz is played by classically trained Burnett Thompson at the **West End Cafe** in Washington Circle.

The best bets for acoustic, folk-rock, or folk music on just any old night are **Iota** (profiled), which is especially popular with local progressive pop/rock writers, and **Food for Thought,** near the Dupont Circle Metro (1738 Connecticut Avenue, NW; (202) 797-1095). The last of the area's once-plentiful bluegrass spots is the **Tiffany Tavern** in Alexandria (1116 King Street; (703) 836-8844). "Coffeehouses" are flourishing (the folk music variety, not the cappuccino type, though they're booming, too), but many coffeehouse acoustic music events occur only monthly in area churches or schools; check the papers.

Irish bars do a flourishing business in Washington with the help of a resident community of performers. Among the pubs with live music—and almost always at least one fireplace—are the **Dubliner** (profiled below); **Ireland's Four Provinces** (by the Cleveland Park Metro at 3412 Connecticut Avenue, NW; (202) 244-0860), and **Nanny O'Brien's** across the street (3319 Connecticut Avenue, NW; (202) 686-9189); the **Old Brogue** (760-C Walker Road, Great Falls, VA; (703) 759-3309); **Ireland's Own** (132 North Royal Street, Alexandria, VA; (703) 549-4535); and **Flanagan's** (near the Bethesda station at 7637 Old Georgetown Road, Bethesda, MD; (301) 986-1007), which also hosts the semiannual appearances of Irish veterans Tommy Makem and the Furey Brothers.

The local reggae acts generally play the **Grog & Tankard** (2408 Wisconsin Avenue, NW; (202) 333-3114), which is also local Deadhead Central; Dead die-hards can also drop by **LuLu's** on Monday nights.

Washington is also home to one other type of band: the **armed services bands**. From about Memorial Day to Labor Day, ensembles from the four branches perform Monday, Tuesday, Wednesday, and Friday at 8 P.M. at the East Terrace of the Capitol; Tuesday, Thursday, Friday, and Sunday at 8 P.M. at the Sylvan Theatre at the foot of the Washington Monument; and Tuesday at 8 P.M. at the Navy Memorial at Seventh and Pennsylvania Avenue, NW. Programs include patriotic/martial numbers, country, jazz, pop, and some classical music. You're welcome to bring brown bags, but alcohol is not permitted.

■ Swing Your Partner ■

Country and disco dancing have been big for years in Washington, but ethnic and folk dancing—klezmer, polka, contra, Cajun—as well as swing dance and big-band boogie are also popular, especially in the suburbs. They're also nonthreatening and hospitable spots for singles, even novices, since many have predance "workshops" for learning the steps, and all seem well supplied with tolerant and deft "leaders."

For swing dancing, the best bets are the **Washington Swing Dance Committee**, which holds Saturday night dances in all but the coldest weather at the grand deco Spanish Ballroom in the old Glen Echo amusement park in Bethesda, MD (information: (301) 340-9732); and the **Rock Around the Clock Club,** which holds dances twice a month at the Cherry Hill Park clubhouse in College Park, MD (information: (301) 897-8724). Glen Echo also hosts folk, Cajun, and contra dances every weekend; call the **Glen Echo** schedule hotline at (301) 492-6282 or the **Washington Area Folklore Society** hotline at (202) 546-2228. And since many Cajun and zydeco bands double-book in the area to cut traveling costs, they frequently also play at **Tornado Alley** in Wheaton; dance lessons sometimes precede the concerts.

And you can polka (and pile on the bratwurst) to your heart's content any Friday, Saturday, or Sunday at **Blob's Park,** a Bavarian-fantasy beer hall and polka pavilion that holds 1,000 and a five-man oompah band in Jessup, MD; call (410) 799-0155 for information.

For country and western dancing, you may need to hitch a ride; try **The Junction** (1330 East Gude Drive, Rockville, MD; (301) 217-5820); or **Latela's** (Route 175 and the Baltimore-Washington Parkway, Jessup, MD; (410) 799-7110).

For waltzing on a Sunday afternoon, head to **Glen Echo** or call (703) 978-0375. For Latin dancing, try **Coco Loco**, which offers free salsa and merengue lessons on Wednesdays (see the restaurant profiles); and for *Brady Bunch*–style '70s retro, try **Polly Esther's**, a *Saturday Night Fever* revival club for white lipstick lovers (605 12th Street, NW; (202) 737-1970—get it?).

The 20-to-40 crowd into Top 40 disco tends to hang out at **Zei** (profiled below) or the **Fifth Column** and their neighbors; the leading black/buppie disco is the **Ritz** (919 E Street, NW; (202) 638-2582), whose five rooms program house, R&B, techno, and contemporary jazz. **Tracks** (also profiled) is the largest mixed gay/hip disco in town. **The Cellar** (2100 M Street, NW; (202) 457-8180), ideally located between the meat-market West End and Georgetown and across from LuLu's/Déjà Vu, is a disco inferno updated for the '90s: a wall o' video screens, laser lights, three bars, and mega-megawatts of Top 40, rock, progressive rock, and dancehall.

But if you're a real fan of the Big Band era—and the conga line—set your Thursday calendar for the **Ritz-Carlton** in Tysons Corner, where you'll find the Cab Calloway–mustached Doc Scantlin and His Imperial Palms Orchestra, complete with five women singers (head torcher Chou Chou is his missus), black tie, and tails. The 8:30 show includes dinner for $52 (phone (703) 506-4300).

■ Ashes to Ashes ■

Here as in many other urban centers, cigars are the latest show of sophistication manqué. Aside from **Ozio,** profiled below, Washington now has a branch of **Beverly Hills' Havana Club** (1220 19th Street, NW; (202) 293-6848), which deals glamor, food, and prices to match. The Grand Hyatt Hotel has jumped the trend-bar time warp and remodeled its old sports bar into **Butlers Cigar Bar** (10th and H Streets, NW; (202) 637-4765). Not far away is **Shelly's Back Room** (1331 F Street, NW; (202) 737-3003). And the wine bar at **Melrose** restaurant in the Park Hyatt Hotel is mixing its wines by the glass with a cigar menu (21st and M Streets, NW; (202) 955-3899).

■ Espresso and Eight-Ball ■

The two biggest trends in Washington are coffee bars and billiards parlors. At either you can spend not merely hours but whole evenings, and in a few cases, hang out virtually around the clock.

Many of the espresso bars are tiny walk-ins; some are mere service windows. But a couple are among the most interesting after-hours hangouts in the city, even if the patrons are the only "entertainment." The **Pop Stop** (1513 17th Street, NW; (202) 328-0880) is a flamboyantly busy, bustling, and hustling Dupont Circle sidewalk cafe that mixes smarts, gays, and straights with such spur-of-the-moment giggles as bingo and performance art.

The biggest billiards parlors around are **Dave & Buster's** and **Buffalo Billiards** (both profiled); **Georgetown Billiards** (3251 Prospect Street, NW; (202) 965-7665); **Babe's** (near the Tenleytown Metro at 4600 Wisconsin Avenue, NW; (202) 966-0082); **Champion Billiards** (1776 East Jefferson Street, Rockville, MD; (301) 231-4949), which also serves food 24 hours a day; and **CarPool** (4000 Fairfax Drive, Arlington; (703) 532-7665), which has the specific attraction of serving barbecue from Rocklands (see profile in Part Eleven: Dining and Restaurants).

For funkier decor and less formal atmosphere, try **Atomic Billiards**

(3427 Connecticut Avenue, NW at the Cleveland Park Metro; (202) 363-7665), **Bedrock Billiards** (1841 Columbia Road, NW; (202) 667-7665), **Julio's** in Adams-Morgan (16th and U Streets, NW; (202) 483-8500), or **Bardo Rodeo** (see the section below on brewpubs).

■ True Brews ■

Washington has also discovered another fresh brew—beer. In fact, the entire Washington-Baltimore region has gone silly for suds. A boom in brewpubs and microbreweries has made it possible to support your local craft brewers in style and also to taste a huge number of recipes, from pilsners and lagers to stouts, porters, wheat ales, fruit beers, bocks, and seasonals. And most offer at least informal tours of the works, if you're intrigued.

Among the nearer brewpubs are the **Capital City Brewing Co.** branches near the Washington Convention Center (11th and H Streets, NW; (202) 628-2222), the Village at Shirlington (2700 South Quincy Street, Arlington; (703) 578-3888), and in the Postal Museum building (at Massachusetts Avenue and First Street, NW), which are as much singles scenes as beer temples; and **John Harvard's Brewhouse**, a branch of a Cambridge, MA, favorite (13th and Pennsylvania Avenues, NW). In Bethesda, the latest outpost of the Cap City group goes mug to mug with **Rock Bottom Brewery** at Old Georgetown Road and Woodmont Avenue, or keep going: the **Olde Towne Tavern & Brewing Co.** in Gaithersburg, MD (Summit and Diamond Avenues; (301) 948-4200), which is also a popular restaurant with live music; **Old Dominion Brewing Co.** in Ashburn, VA (44633 Guilford Drive; (703) 724-9100), which is also the area's most successful microbrewing company; **Potomac River Brewing Co.** in Chantilly, VA (14141-A Parke Long Court; (703) 631-5430); **Blue-N-Gold Brewing Co.** near the Clarendon station in Arlington, VA (3100 Clarendon Boulevard; (703) 908-4995); and **Bardo Rodeo** near the Courthouse Metro stop in Arlington, VA (2000 Wilson Boulevard; (703) 527-9399). Bardo is a very funky young-Turk hangout named for the Tibetan Buddhist version of Limbo; it's still best known for its disposable street-art decor, oddball sandwiches, and the fact that William Kennedy Smith got into a fistfight here, but its beers are very good and have begun to win prizes in national competitions. In addition to its own brews, Bardo has scores of beers on tap from other craft brewers and houses two dozen pool tables. And, since Blue-N-Gold is within walking distance, you can make a mini–pub crawl of it.

Those interested in trying beers from around the world should also check the profile of the **Brickskeller** or the "Best Beer" special features list at the beginning of the restaurant chapter.

■ The Sex Thing ■

Washington is not the singles capital of the world, but it does have many of the ingredients for a busy meat-market scene: frequent turnovers in power, a dozen colleges and universities, a continual influx of immigrants and corporate hires, and what until recently was considered a "recession-proof" economy.

The singles bars around Washington are relatively benign. Many of them are dance clubs as well, so there's something to do besides discuss astrological incompatibilities. The sports-bar habitués tend to be a little more flagrant in their appraisals of fresh talent, as are those in bars that cater to the fortysomething crowd.

The busiest singles strip in the District is midtown just south and a bit west of Dupont Circle, especially around the intersection of 19th and M Streets, where the **Sign of the Whale, Rumours, Madhatter,** and **Mr. Day's** pack them in starting at happy hour. A few blocks west is the **LuLu's/Déjà Vu** complex (profiled below), and a few more blocks west is Georgetown, so you can have a sort of progressive singles party.

The busiest singles bar for the older and cash-flow-confident crowd is the **Yacht Club of Bethesda** (profiled below).

Suburban singles centers are easy to spot: Anything with a bar will do.

Although the District has been home to a strong gay community for many years, most clubs attract at least a slightly mixed crowd, albeit unobtrusive. However, there are many well-established gay nightspots, especially around Dupont Circle and Capitol Hill. Among the most popular are the Polo-label **JR's** (1519 17th Street, NW; (202) 328-0090) near Dupont Circle; the pointy-toe and big-buckle **Remington's** (near the Eastern Market station at 639 Pennsylvania Avenue, SE; (202) 543-3113), and the softcore leather-with-rhythm **DC Eagle** (near Gallery Place at 639 New York Avenue, NW; (202) 347-6025). **El Faro** is a semi-reticent Adams-Morgan hangout primarily for Latino lovers (2411 18th Street, NW; (202) 387-6554). One of the newest bars is **Green Lantern** near MacPherson Square (1335 Green Court, NW, in the alley off 14th and L; (202) 638-5133).

The hottest dance clubs are **Tracks,** which is a vast and mixed gay and straight disco of long standing (see profile below); **Badlands,** which has semi-steamy videos to go with the marathon mixes (Dupont Circle, 1415 22nd Street, NW; (202) 296-0505); and the predominantly lesbian **Hung Jury** (near Farragut West at 1819 H Street, NW; (202) 785-8181). **Ziegfeld's** is the most flamboyant of the hangouts, featuring uproarious and often astonishingly polished drag shows (1345 Half Street, SE; (202) 554-

5141). Although it's not the safest neighborhood, Ziegfeld's will call you a cab when you're ready to leave.

If you can't dance but hate to eat alone, try the **Paramount Steak House** (1609 17th Street, NW; (202) 232-0395), **Perry's** (1811 Columbia Road, NW; (202) 234-6218), or the **Pop-Stop** coffee bar, which has turned into the busiest yuppie-gay appraisal scene in town.

Finally, although the onetime red-light district around 14th Street was officially eradicated by redistricting and redevelopment, old habits die hard. North and east of the White House, and especially in the blocks around 13th and L, prostitutes not only parade past and proposition pedestrians but take advantage of traffic lights and stop signs to accost drivers. Periodically the police crack down on the scene, which is signalled by the overnight closing of streets in the neighborhood; but it makes only a temporary dent. The business also takes advantage of public transportation: Many of the hotel bars along the subway are hangouts for soliciting singles—and humorously, they seem to prefer the red line, as if in tribute to "red-light" districts.

A few reminders: Although most prostitutes try to protect themselves from disease, both drug use and AIDS are pervasive. Second, many dates are actually bait, fronts for drug dealers who can more immediately endanger your health and safety. Besides, District police are fully familiar with the tricks of the trade, so we don't advise that you get involved. If you must look, don't touch—and keep your car doors locked.

For a somewhat less hands-on experience, there are a couple of relatively sedate strip joints downtown: the new and discreet gentlemen's-special **1720 Club** two blocks from the White House (see profile below) and **Archibald's,** which is on the ground floor of the Comedy Cafe building off MacPherson Square (1520 K Street, NW; (202) 737-2662). And for the safest fantasy trips around, drop by Georgetown's funny/fantasy sex boutiques: the **Pleasure Place** (1063 Wisconsin Avenue, NW; (202) 333-8570), which offers videos, X-rated birthday cards, T-shirts, fishnet stockings, and the like, and its across-the-street-rival **Dream Dresser,** a fancy-silly X-rated Victoria's Secret, which dispenses leather and latex as well as lighter-hearted souvenirs and accoutrements (1042 Wisconsin Avenue, NW; (202) 625-0373).

■ More on the Safety Thing ■

There is only one safety tip to remember: You're never entirely safe. There is no guaranteed neighborhood in the area. In fact, we have left some otherwise deserving and successful clubs off the list because they're in questionable territory, even for savvy residents. The suburbs are generally okay, but even the ostensibly upscale areas of the District, such as Georgetown and Dupont Circle, are not immune to crime. It's best to leave nightclubs, especially after about 10 P.M., in company. Attach yourself to a group or ask the club management for an escort. It's also wiser to call a cab than to walk more than a block or so. (Mace, incidentally, is now legal in Maryland, Virginia, and the District of Columbia.)

And a final tip: If you believe in helping out the homeless (the staggering number of which you may find one of the less inspiring monuments to modern life in Washington), try stashing dollar bills or change in an outside pocket so that you can reach them without opening your wallet or purse.

■ Profiles of Clubs and Nightspots ■

THE BAYOU

Live national and regional pop, rock, reggae, Deadhead, and dinosaur rock bands showcase

Who Goes There: 21–45; locals and tourists; MOR radio addicts, yuppies, nongrads, metal lite dabblers

3135 K Street, NW
  (202) 333-2897   Georgetown, Zone 5

Cover: Varies with act; roughly $5–20
Minimum: None
Mixed drinks: $3.25–5
Wine: $3.75
Beer: $3.25–4.50
Dress: Match the act: jackboots, flannel shirts, jacket and tie, big hats, tie-dye

Specials: Occasional all-ages (18 and up) shows, usually semiheavy metal or arena rockers with area following
Food available: Basket food: pretzels, pizza

Hours: Every day, 8 P.M.–2 A.M.

What goes on: This is the flagship club venue of a national concert promoter, Cellar Door, and serves to break both regional bands the agency has signed and bands on the up- or downturn who can't quite pull the big arena crowds. Local bands work their way from opening act to headliners. Political satirists of Gross National Product play an early show on weekends.

(The Bayou)

Setting & atmosphere: It's not too pretty, but it's powerful. This 400-seat club has, as you'd expect, high-quality sound equipment and even a couple of obstructed-view TVs. A U-shaped balcony overlooks the main floor and elevated stage, with one bar downstairs, one upstairs, and table service. Rest rooms are upstairs.

If you go: Expect the show to start late; the Bayou is notoriously slow to get going (to let bar tabs accumulate a little first). You'll still need to get in line early to get good seats, but remember, front seats aren't necessarily the best seats; there's an informal dance floor just below the stage.

BIRCHMERE

Live folk, new acoustic, newgrass, hip rockabilly/outlaw, light jazz and country, and occasional off-peak pop music

Who Goes There: Gracefully aging boomers and a few recalcitrant rednecks, unreconciled folkies, local musicians

3701 Mt. Vernon Avenue, Alexandria
(703) 549-7500   Virginia suburbs, Zone 11C

Cover: Varies with entertainment; roughly $8–20
Minimum: None
Mixed drinks: $2.50–5
Wine: $4.25
Beer: $3.25–3.75
Dress: A few suits, a lot of flannels, universal jeans, neo-farm country wear and boots of all sorts— cowboy, hiking, motorcycle
Food available: After years of getting by on potato chips, Birchmere patrons can now get serious tavern fare, including barbecue, burgers, and hot nibbles, from the folks at Union Street Pub and King Street Blues.

Hours: Tuesday–Saturday, 7–11:30 P.M. Shows start at 8:30.

What goes on: This is one of the major clubs in town, the biggest for new acoustic and country acts especially, such as Rosanne Cash and hometown heroine Mary-Chapin Carpenter, plus cult regulars Jerry Jeff Walker and Delbert McClinton; old folk Tom Paxton and John Stewart; new femme fronters Kristin Hersh, Christine Lavin, and Maria Muldaur.

Setting & atmosphere: The long-awaited new home for this venerable club has jumped from old-fashioned to new-fangled: not only a much more spacious 500-seat main stage but a cigar-martini bar (for the expected influx of trendy patrons?), a 150-seat side stage/cafe, a microbrewery on site, and "real" pub food.

(The Birchmere)

If you go: Go early: Parking is tight (but free), the line is long, and seating is first-come, closest-in. If you're trying to eat light, eat elsewhere. Remember to take off your big hat so the folks behind you can see. And take thankful note of the sign that asks for quiet during performances: This really is a listening club.

BLUES ALLEY

National-circuit jazz dinner club

Who Goes There: 20–60; locals and tourists; other jazz pros; neo-jazz fans

1073 Wisconsin Avenue, NW (in the alley)
  (202) 337-4141   Georgetown, Zone 5

Cover: Varies with entertainment;
  $13–40
Minimum: Two drinks or $7 food
Mixed drinks: $3.95–7.50
Wine: $3.50–5

Beer: $3–5
Dress: Jacket over jeans, business
  attire, musician chic
Food available: Full menu of semi-
  creole food: gumbo, chicken, steak

Hours: Every day, 6 P.M.–midnight

What goes on: When the big-name jazz performers come to town, this is where they play. And although many customers grumble about ticket prices, they pay anyway—partly because the acts require high guarantees, partly because Georgetown rents are high, and partly because so many other jazz clubs have folded.

Setting & atmosphere: A fairly simple lounge, with exposed brick walls, a platform at one end and the bar at the other, and smallish dinner tables scattered between.

If you go: Get there early; the line often goes around the block, and seating is first-come and squeeze-'em-together, even with reservations. The old and cramped rest rooms that are barely accessible upstairs are one drawback, and the ventilation can be another, but the acoustics are very good.

BRICKSKELLER

Encyclopedic beer rathskeller

Who Goes There: 21–45; students, former students,
home brewers, beer fanatics

1523 22nd Street, NW
(202) 293-1885   Dupont Circle/ Adams-Morgan, Zone 6

Cover: None
Minimum: None
Mixed drinks: $2.75–4.75
Wine: $3.25–4.50
Beer: $2.75–54

Dress: Jackets, jeans, khakis
Specials: Monthly beer tastings, often
with guest speaker
Food available: The house specialty is
buffalo; good pub food in general

Hours: Monday–Thursday, 11:30 A.M.–2 A.M.; Friday, 11:30 A.M.–
3 A.M.; Saturday, 6 P.M.–3 A.M.; Sunday, 6 P.M.–2 A.M.

What goes on: Thirty-five years ago, Maurice Coja put 50 kinds of beer,
mostly bottled, in the basement of the Marifex Hotel and opened for business. Twenty years later, he had to give up kegs because room was so tight,
and now, with 500 beers from all over the world offered at the same time,
including over 100 microbrews, brands and cans are stuffed into every corner. The Brickskeller used to offer live music of the folk-rock variety but
eventually realized the beer was sufficient entertainment. There are dart
boards and a jukebox instead.

Setting & atmosphere: A rabbit warren of rooms, with the main bar in the
front and scuffed and hard-working tables snaking around between the dart
boards. Feel free to strike up a conversation; the Brickskeller is unpreten-
tious, college-bar friendly, and lively.

If you go: Don't be shy; consult the staff. Beer is serious business here—
three-liter bottles of Corsondonk go for $54—and you can learn a lot if
you go slowly. Start light and work your way up to Samiclaus, a potent by-
the-fireside beer of 14% alcohol. Skip the mixed beer cocktails, or beer-tails;
they're more novelty act than revelation.

BUFFALO BILLIARDS

Part biz-whiz pool party, part singles bar (over 21 only)

Who Goes There: Junior associates, postgrads, and bar pros

1330 19th Street, NW
  (202) 331-7665   Dupont Circle/ Adams-Morgan, Zone 6

Cover: None
Minimum: None for bars or people-watching; to play, $5 per player per hour
Mixed drinks: $3.25–6
Wine: $3.50–4
Beer: $3.25–6.50
Dress: A mix of officewear and jock chic, with as many lace-ups as high-rises

Specials: Happy hour 4–8 P.M. weekdays, 1–7 P.M. weekends, with beer specials and wine and rail drinks for $2.50
Food available: Mostly small plates—nachos, buffalo wings (of course), sandwiches—but also some fairly serious entrees such as tuna steak and trout

Hours: Monday–Thursday, 4 P.M.–2 A.M.; Friday, 4 P.M.–3 A.M.; Saturday, 1 P.M.–3 A.M.; Sunday, 1 P.M.–1 A.M.

What goes on: Parties circulate, singles practice their shots, and couriers wait for assignments.

Setting & atmosphere: This is just one of a half-dozen upscale, all-the-modern-indulgences pool halls all over the area (see the section "Espresso and Eight-Ball" above), but it's one of the busiest and largest, the flagship of its owners' half-dozen parlors, with two entire rooms (one smoking, one nonsmoking) and vibrators to alert waiting customers to their tables. It's woodyish—Buffalo Bill-iards, get it?—but not too gadget-happy. And it's one level down from the street, which gives a sort of old-fashioned speakeasy quality.

If you go: Don't worry about your pool skills particularly, unless you're hoping to shark someone; a lot of the patrons are pleasure-seekers, not pros, and they won't be looking over your shoulder. The main thing is to watch where you're going: Don't knock someone else's cue or back into the player at the next table, and if that player lines up a shot first, it's his/her right of way, so to speak.

CAFE LAUTREC

Neo-Boho bistro and jazz bar

Who Goes There: 23–50; neighborhood jazz fans, postgrads, artistes

2431 18th Street, NW
(202) 265-6436   Dupont Circle/ Adams-Morgan, Zone 6

Cover: None
Minimum: $6
Mixed drinks: $3.25–6
Wine: $4–5
Beer: $3.25–5.75
Dress: Jacket and jeans; black on black, a touch of grunge, a bit of cafe society leotard
Food available: Old-style bistro fare: pasta, salads, trout meunière, lamb shanks, maybe sweetbreads

Hours: Sunday–Thursday, 5 P.M.–2 A.M.; Friday and Saturday, 5 P.M.–3 A.M.

What goes on: As the night progresses, Lautrec evolves from early-offhours bar for neighborhood vegans to old-favorite cafe to Rive Gauche stage set, with live jazz nightly and old-style tap-dancing on the bar Thursdays through Sundays.

Setting & atmosphere: This comfortably careless wood and brick shoebox turns its age to atmospheric advantage, picking up the decadent posture along with the Moulin Rouge reproductions, which include a 20-foot Lautrec reproduction painted over the facade. Study the wait staff and their black leggings and you'll suddenly catch the kinship between Bohemian Paris soul and post-punk flat soles.

If you go: Go late and get the whole show. Sundays, when longtime jazz grace Mary Jefferson sings, the trio plays, and dapper tapper Johne Forges croons a little, you get the full Folies. Don't bother to dress to impress this crowd: Cafe Lautrec's lack of attitude about your attitude is its most valuable asset. If you're a guy with a shy bladder, you may have to concentrate; the men's room is truly a water closet under the stairs.

CHAMPIONS

Sports-memorabilia gallery and jock-groupie audition spot

Who Goes There: TV-game regulars; local pro-team fans, faded glory boys, B-ball boys, and big-eyed businessmen

1206 Wisconsin Avenue, NW
(202) 965-4005   Georgetown, Zone 5

Cover: None
Minimum: Weekends after 10:00, one drink
Mixed drinks: $3.25–5.50
Wine: $3.50–3.85
Beer: $2.75–4.50

Dress: Casual
Specials: Friday 5–10 P.M., $1.75 drafts, $2.25 rail drinks
Food available: Ballpark franks, burgers, and also larger portioned pub fare for old athletic appetites

Hours: Monday–Thursday, 5 P.M.–1:30 A.M.; Friday, 5 P.M.–2:30 A.M.; Saturday, 11:30 A.M.–2:30 A.M.; Sunday, 11:30 A.M.–2 A.M.

What goes on: Redskins fans and the braver adherents of other teams break bread, and often beer mugs, together over multiscreen satellite TV games; real pros from area teams and former pros-turned–sports announcers are common sightings. On any given night, some sort of promotion or "contest" may be going on, from wet T-shirt parades to faked-orgasm competitions.

Setting & atmosphere: Part sports bar, part meat market, this is simultaneously a sports trivia master class and competitive escort parade—thanks to the guiding example of founder and professional bachelor Mike O'Harro, who never saw a beauty pageant contestant he didn't like. This is the flagship club of a coast-to-coast franchise, with $250,000 worth of sports memorabilia, autographed photos, uniform shirts, etc.

If you go: Have a valid ID; O'Harro, having had plenty of opponents—business rivals and area residents—looking for reasons to shut down his bar, is very strict on legal drinking ages. He has even started requiring his dates to be 21. Don't expect to talk business unless you bring your client with you; this is major playtime. Do not peer into the tinted windows of limos; these guys are paying for privacy so they can make a public spectacle. A safe bet for protective camouflage is either a Redskins or Georgetown U. sweatshirt, available on the streets. This is not a sanctuary for solo (or sensitive) women.

DAVE & BUSTER'S

Adult entertainment a la Spielberg—part high tech, part retro-regressive

Who Goes There: Late-20s couples bored with disco, traveling salesmen nostalgic for Vegas, some computer geeks and groups of mixed-sex hangers looking for postmovie action

White Flint Mall, Bethesda
(301) 230-5151   Maryland suburbs, Zone 10B

Cover: $5 weekends after 10 P.M.
Minimum: None
Mixed drinks: $5–7
Wine: $3.50–5.75
Beer: $2.75–4
Dress: Upper shopping mall quality: casual, but no tank tops, cutoffs, etc.

Specials: Half-price rail drinks and beer specials at happy hour
Food available: A full range of familiar '90s, upscale suburban fare: from artichoke dip and stuffed jalapeños to pastas, grilled salmon, and Sante Fe chicken pizza to ribs and rib-eyes

Hours: Monday– Saturday, 11 A.M.–1 A.M.; Sunday, 11:30 A.M.–midnight

What goes on: This is a carnival of the business animals: a half-dozen pocket billiard tables, pinball and video games, a couple of simulated "19th hole" golf games, shuffleboard, and four full-size virtual-reality pods, interlinked for games and sports simulation; plus casino games, with fully trained blackjack dealers and tables—but the poker chips are "on loan" only. No actual gambling is allowed. Everything is played by token, in fact, except the virtual-reality pods. On Fridays and Saturdays, it's murder mystery dinner theater.

Setting & atmosphere: This is unabashedly a bar as well as a playroom, with two sidelines bars; the double-sided, 40-foot bar that partners the "midway" (a stretch of interactive video and carny attractions); and the elevated, square "Viewpoint" bar (not to mention the private "showroom" with its own stage, bar, dining tables, and even audio-visual equipment, which is bound to become the status CEO party room of D.C.).

If you go: This is Dave & Buster's ninth such complex around the country, and they've got it down smooth. Besides offering nearly every sort of game, it has polished service, fairly strict rules about drinking and dressing, and even stricter rules about under-21-year-olds being with an adult. Even better in this cigar-crazed era, smoking is extremely limited (and even cigarettes only where it's allowed).

DUBLINER

Classic Irish pub

Who Goes There: Hill workers, both upwardly mobile (staffers) and established (senators and lobbyists)

520 North Capitol Street, NW
  (202) 737-3773   Capitol Hill, Zone 2

Cover: None
Minimum: None
Mixed drinks: $3.25–6. Dubliner
  coffee is an Irish coffee with
  Bailey's added.
Wine: $3.50–4
Beer: $3–4
Dress: No cutoffs or tank tops
  allowed

Specials: Reduced light-fare prices,
  11 P.M.–1 A.M.; daily specials
  Monday–Friday for lunch and
  dinner
Food available: Irish pub classics, from
  stew to hot sandwiches

Hours: Monday–Thursday, 7 A.M.–2 A.M.; Friday, 7 A.M.–3 A.M.; Saturday, 9 A.M.–3 A.M.; Sunday, 9 A.M.–2 A.M.

What goes on: This is not the oldest Irish bar in town, but it has become the clan leader—centrally located, pol-connected, and providing the training ground for founders of a half-dozen other bars, including the semi-sibling-rival Irish Times next door. Fittingly, the Dubliner also has one of the most colorful histories, filled with romantic intrigue, boom-and-bust bank troubles, and riotous St. Patrick's week parties.

Setting & atmosphere: Now part of the pricey and hunt-country gracious Phoenix Hotel complex, the Dubliner is filled with antiques, such as the 1810 hand-carved walnut bar in the back room. The front bar is louder and livelier, often populated by the surviving members of the Dubliner's Irish football and soccer teams; the snug is a discreet heads-together, take-no-names hideaway in the finest tradition; and the parlor is where the tweeds gather.

If you go: Be sure to have at least one Guinness on draft: The Dubliner pours an estimated quarter-million pints a year. Then brave the Gaelic Triangle, where many a fine stout imbiber has lost, if not his life, then several hours of unexplained time. If you're dressed nicely, slip upstairs to the Powerscourt restaurant and sip a wee one while gauging the Jesuit/politico connection. Drop by the Irish Times for a breather (the high ceilings carry smoke away) and the Finnegans Wake crazy quilt of literary and political conversation. Then call a cab. Please.

FAIRFAX BAR

A rich romantic piano bar with political connections

Who Goes There: 30–60; old Washington money and power and new-administration wannabes

Ritz-Carlton Hotel, 2100 Massachusetts Avenue, NW
(202) 736-1414   Dupont Circle/ Adams-Morgan, Zone 6

Cover: None
Minimum: None
Mixed drinks: $6.75
Wine: $6.50–9
Beer: $4.25–4.75
Dress: Casual, but "informal" is relative here—suggests resort hopping at best; jackets for men in the evening
Food available: Light fare, primarily sandwiches and dessert

Hours: Sunday–Thursday, 11:30 A.M.–1:30 A.M.; Friday and Saturday, 11:30 A.M.–2:30 A.M.

What goes on: Cocktail party chatter of the rich or famous (it's déclassé to be both, unless you're hereditarily obliged to serve your country).

Setting & atmosphere: The aristocrats' hideaway of your dreams: oriental rugs, gleaming wood, real fireplaces, and a pianist. It's like some grand racing stable that's been hand-polished in and out; you see the other tables as if over stall doors. One's almost surprised it doesn't smell of saddle soap. (The rest rooms, on the other hand, are strictly Big House.) Make sure to tour the astonishing series of scene boxes, meticulous miniature rooms of behind-the-scenes 19th-century life.

If you go: Enjoy the history. This is an old pols' networking cradle, literally: Al Gore spent a lot of time here as a child when it belonged to the Republican side of his family. Besides, like any other vanishing breed, armchair clubs have a sentimental attraction.

HARD ROCK CAFE

Souvenir shop disguised as barbecue bar

Who Goes There: 12–55; tourists and locals; Hard Rock memorabilia collectors; air-guitar experts

999 E Street, NW
(202) 737-7625   The Mall, Zone 1

Cover: None
Minimum: None
Mixed drinks: $6–15
Wine: $6–15
Beer: $3–7
Dress: To be seen: pony-print leather, denim, sports or rock and roll tour jackets, business attire, creative black tie, Bermuda shorts (on tourists)
Specials: None
Food available: Surprisingly good barbecue, burgers, nachos

Hours: Sunday–Thursday, 10:30 A.M.–midnight; Friday and Saturday, 10:30 A.M.–1 A.M.

What goes on: One of perhaps 30 Hard Rocks around the world, each of which takes its nickname from the site, this is the "Embassy" and sometimes the "Smithsonian of Rock 'n' Roll," taking its turn rotating the nearly 7,000 pieces of music history in the HRC collection. The souvenir shop, with its signature T-shirts, is as busy as the bar, which is often stand-in-line packed—a doorman passes inspection on the hopeful.

Setting & atmosphere: This is ersatz nostalgia for the second Rolling Stone generation—a bar designed like a piano, half of a pink Cadillac (sort of a franchise signature) hanging from the ceiling, and a lot of fed suits from nearby buildings trying to look cool. Hard Rock also makes a point of being Lollapalooza-era PC, supporting the Walden Project and nuclear freezes and hosting radio-chic benefits and postconcert VIP receptions, usually without the star.

If you go: Pick up the guidebook, formally known as the "Hard Rock Cafe Self-Motivating Non-Nuclear-Powered Memorabilia Tour of the World's Foremost Rock 'n' Roll Museum" and start circling the balcony. Look for such treasures as Bo Diddley's first jerry-rigged electric guitar, Michael Jackson's glittering kneepad, and a stained-glass triptych featuring Elvis, Jerry Lee Lewis, and Little Richard.

HEADLINERS

Pro-circuit comedy club

Who Goes There: 18–50; suburban singles, young marrieds, comedy groupies, unbooked businessmen

Holiday Inn, 2160 Eisenhower Avenue, Alexandria
  (703) 379-4242   Virginia suburbs, Zone 11C
Holiday Inn, 8120 Wisconsin Avenue, Bethesda
  (301) 942-4242   Maryland suburbs, Zone 10A

Cover: $9.95 Friday and Saturday	Beer: $2.25–4
Minimum: Two items	Dress: Anything goes
Mixed drinks: $3–6	Food available: Full hotel menus,
Wine: $3–6	burgers to prime rib to seafood

Hours: Show times Friday and Saturday, 8:30 and 10:30 P.M.

What goes on: One of the better regional performers and comic writers, Chip Franklin, books these clubs as well as doing feature duty; he brings in not only cable-friendly names but sharp, cutting-edge "smart" comics. (Franklin's good connections and good taste are one reason he's stayed in business while so many other post-comedy-boom types have busted.) Like the Improv, Headliners largely eschews novices for full-time pros, although unlike the Improv, Headliners sticks to rotating performers every couple of nights.

Setting & atmosphere: Nice but fairly simple rooms, with stages, brick backdrops, etc.

If you go: You can expect three performers, the opener/emcee, a brief second banana, and the featured act. The hotel affiliation means that occasionally you may have a few over-cocktailed hecklers or loud talkers to overcome, but most of the time it's a good audience.

THE IMPROVISATION

National-circuit comedy club

Who Goes There: Visiting business types, 30ish suburbanites, 25–45 midlevel managers

1140 Connecticut Avenue, NW
(202) 296-7008   Downtown, Zone 3

Cover: $12 Sunday–Thursday, $15 Friday and Saturday
Minimum: Two items
Mixed drinks: $4–6
Wine: $3.50–5
Beer: $3–4
Dress: T-shirts with jackets, suits, casual yup attire
Specials: Tuesday free admission to anyone wearing an Improv T-shirt ($12 in the lobby)
Food available: Full menu described as being available before the 8:30 P.M. show, but light fare available whenever; standard one-size-fits-all menu with chicken cordon bleu, prime rib, catch of the day, Caesar salad, etc.

Hours: Sunday–Thursday, 7–10:30 P.M.; Friday and Saturday, 7 P.M.–12:30 A.M. Shows at 8:30 (every day) and 10:30 (Friday and Saturday)

What goes on: Standard Improv franchise fare: A short opening act, often local; a semiestablished feature act; and a headliner from the national club/cable showcase circuit. Monday and Tuesday are "best of Washington" nights, i.e., minor-league tryouts. However, like many comedy clubs, the Improv is increasingly depending on extended bookings of more theatrical comics such as Rob "The Caveman" Becker or Jack Gallagher, who perform alone for 90 minutes or so.

Setting & atmosphere: Again, this goes with the franchise—a "brick wall" stage sentimentally recalling the original no-frills Improvisation, and the black-and-white checkerboard floor and trim that is practically a logo design. TV screens hang overhead for those with obscured views, but they're not big enough to be terribly useful. The wait staff wear tux-material Bermuda shorts.

If you go: Don't bother to come early, at least on weeknights, when being seated in order of arrival isn't apt to be a problem. Since latecomers are usually seated amongst the diners, you have no real reason to seek early reservations. Besides, nibbling through the appetizers list is a more satisfying experience than sitting down to dinner and then sitting through the show. The Improv, though below sidewalk level, has wheelchair access via the elevator in the building lobby. Check your check before tipping; a 15% gratuity is figured in automatically.

IOTA

Neighborhood tavern joint with smart conversation
and live new-pop roots rock

Who Goes There: Messengers, students, thirtysomething T-shirts,
microbrew-savvy beer buddies, and other musicians

2832 Wilson Boulevard, Arlington
(703) 522-8340   Virginia suburbs, Zone 11B

Cover: $4–10, some shows free
Minimum: None
Mixed drinks: $3.20–9.75
Wine: $3.50–4.50
Beer: $2.80–8.50
Dress: Jeans, with or without bolo;
  motorcycle leathers; baggy athletic
  wear, and frayed button-down
  collars

Specials: Happy hour 5–7 P.M.,
  $1 off rail and draft prices
Food available: Freestyle, eclectic pub
  food but far better than most:
  spicy lentil dip, quesadillas,
  spinach-stuffed chicken breasts,
  veggie burgers with basil and
  roasted peppers, etc.

Hours: Monday–Friday, 5 P.M.–2 A.M.; Saturday, 2:30 P.M.–2 A.M.

What goes on: On a regular basis, this has the best lineup of acoustic rock, neo-roots, and eclectic melodic rock in town, and it's the quality of the people who run the shows, both before and behind the scenes, that makes it so. Steve Hagedorn holds the open mike on Wednesdays. When he's in town, this is where you're likely to find hometown favorite Kevin Johnson hosting songwriters' nights.

Setting & atmosphere: In a time when a lot of Washington bars have an intentionally mismatched rec-room random look, Iota's decor is unusual but intelligent—murals, geometric eyecatchers chiseled into the exposed brick walls, and beams that show the age of the neighborhood (especially nice, since there's so little of it left otherwise). The room used to be only half this size, but giving the performers some extra elbow room has not made either the musicians or their audiences self-conscious.

If you go: This is a good place to strike up a conversation at the bar before the music gets loud: You run into crossword puzzle freaks, novelists, doctoral candidates, musicians, roadies, and ponytails of the friendly sort. It's the sort of bar that makes hanging out a pleasure.

LULU'S/DÉJÀ VU

Mardi Gras singles bar/semioldies disco

Who Goes There: 25–45; office fugitives, knit collars, former college jocks

2121 M Street, NW (on the corner of 22nd and M Streets)
(202) 861-5858   Dupont Circle/ Adams-Morgan, Zone 6

Cover: $3 Friday and Saturday after 9 P.M.
Minimum: None
Mixed drinks: $3.75–5.50
Wine: $3.50
Beer: $3.50–4.50
Dress: Georgetown prep, after–office hours, Cajun cowpunk
Specials: Sunday brunch includes complimentary beignets and champagne; happy hour with half-price wine, rail drinks, and domestic drafts, 4–7 P.M. weekdays
Food available: Gumbo, étouffée, po'boys, sometimes crawfish and half-shells

Hours: Monday–Thursday, 11:30 A.M.–10 P.M.; Friday, 11:30 A.M.–11 P.M.; Saturday, 5 P.M.–11 P.M.; Sunday, 11 A.M.–3 P.M. (brunch), 5–10 P.M. (dinner)

What goes on: This is a pack-'em-in lunch spot, catering to nearby office workers, but beginning at 4 P.M., when the Dixieland band "promenades" and the appetizer baskets begin to fry, it becomes a permanent party. In the DJ areas, the music is '60s to '80s; for the early boomers who used to patronize the bar nearly 20 years ago when it was called Déjà Vu, dancing here is really Déjà Vu all over again.

Setting & atmosphere: A re-created corner of Bourbon Street, with the restaurant area authentically accessorized with a wrought-iron balcony and the glittering carnival queen gown that the owner's mother, Lulu, wore in the 1962 Mardi Gras procession. There's a garden-style dining room reminiscent of Brennan's conservatory, and the multiple bar and informal dance rooms form a warren of exposed-brick walls, bare-board floors, and mahogany bars.

If you go: Try arriving at happy hour—a 22-ounce beer in a souvenir plastic cup is $1.75.

9:30

National-name live alternative, progressive, semipunk rock music club

Who Goes There: 18–35; new music hopefuls, postgrads, young media and political types, couriers, and cowpunks

815 V Street, NW
(202) 393-0930   Downtown, Zone 3

Cover: Varies with entertainment, from $3 to as much as $20
Minimum: None
Mixed drinks: $4–5.25
Wine: $4.50
Beer: $3.25–4.25
Dress: Grunge, imitation grunge, rhinestone cowboy, leftover businesswear, knife-customized athletic wear, black jersey, black spandex, black denim, and black baggies
Food available: Tex-Mex and barbecue fare

Hours: Sunday–Thursday, 7:30 P.M.–?; Friday and Saturday, 9 P.M.–?

What goes on: "9:30" is the name, it used to be the address (before the former club moved into an old gospel music hall and radio broadcast site), and it used to be the showtime, but thanks to workday hangovers, midweek music now starts at 8:30. This is one of Washington's most important clubs, the loss-leader indulgence of major concert promoter Seth Hurwitz, who, with daring and eclectic booking of breaking acts, fosters loyalty from new bands as their reputations rise. Promising local bands fight to get work as first acts here; a headliner contract is a real prize.

Setting & atmosphere: A slightly trendy mix of leftover cornices, pilasters, virtue-of-necessity exposed steel trusses, and dropped lighting—but still theatrically dark, with great sight lines. The balconies are fine, and there are several bars, including one "quiet room" and a nostalgic, grungier one downstairs.

If you go: Find out who's playing: The crowd that pays up for Ice T isn't the same as the one for Marshall Crenshaw or Happy Mondays. But most are serious music lovers, not just hangovers.

ONE STEP DOWN

Live national and local jazz club

Who Goes There: 18–65; students, novices,
professional musicians, locals, jazz pilgrims

2517 Pennsylvania Avenue, NW
(202) 331-8863   Georgetown, Zone 5

Cover: Varies with act, roughly
$5–13.50
Minimum: Two drinks
Mixed drinks: $3.75–4
Wine: $5.50
Beer: $2.25–4.25
Dress: Casual

Specials: Happy hour 3–7 P.M.
weekdays, with $2.25 rail drinks
and $1.50 drafts
Food available: Touch-all-bases
lunchspot/bar menu, sandwiches
to steak

Hours: Every day, 3 P.M.–1 A.M.

What goes on: Less famous than Blues Alley but more purist, One Step Down books the sort of jazz performers described as musicians' musicians, as well as the more experimental artists. Imported headliners play Friday and Saturday. Sunday afternoon is the live jam session, which draws local pros as well as journeymen and students; Sunday night is a regular set by vibist Lenny Cuje.

Setting & atmosphere: This dark little shoebox pays homage to the old jazz faith, and it shows; most of the seats aren't seats—they're pews, salvaged from an old Sunday school in coal town, Cumberland, Maryland, along with the stained glass. The other tables are old-style booths with scratched-up tops and mini-flip jukebox controls (jazz standards, of course). Access is very tight; the rest rooms are at the far end of the squeezehall past the bar.

If you go: Wear comfortable clothes; after all, pews get hard. Seats fill up fast, and One Step Down doesn't take reservations. If you don't mind stools, sitting at the bar gives you both a good view of the performers and access to a great bartending staff; they know and can make almost any drink, and tell good stories, too. *Note:* Drink prices may increase during performances, since they're part of the cover.

OZIO

Trend-happy, neocon martini and cigar lounge

Who Goes There: Ash-kissing Standard & Poor's wannabes, but with only standard pickup lines and a limited grasp of the inside-the-Beltway gossip they dish; nouveau riche-makers

1835 K Street, NW
(202) 822-6000   Foggy Bottom, Zone 4

Cover: None
Minimum: None
Mixed drinks: $5–8
Wine: $5–9
Beer: $3.50–4
Dress: European-cut jackets and Nicole Miller ties (especially the ones with martini glasses); imitation menswear or Eurotrash skinny-fits for women
Food available: "American tapas" that are more like Middle Eastern crostini, but interesting; and a short menu of entrees, primarily steaks

Hours: Monday–Thursday, 11 A.M.–2 A.M.; Friday, 11 A.M.–3 A.M.; Saturday, 6 P.M.–3 A.M.

What goes on: Posturing for fun and profit. The name is Italian slang for "the act of doing nothing"—hanging, in other words.

Setting & atmosphere: This is actually what a cigar and martini lounge ought to look like: Tuscan red sponged walls; a sleek, glass-walled, walk-in cigar vault; lots of low, row cocktail tables for noshing and ashing set off with recycled wrought-iron fencing and Deco-ish light fixtures designed to suggest the French Metro. It is, in fact, downstairs from the sidewalk, which makes even more atmospheric sense.

If you go: Bring your gold and platinum cards: The martinis are long and strong and cost between $7.25 and $8.50, while the cigars run up to $15.50. And carry a lot of business cards, too: This is turning into a network center for up-and-coming lobbyists and credit card sharks.

PHANTASMAGORIA

Live alternative, rockabilly, rock noir and horror flick spoof bands, and a bit of reggae, world beat, and space cowboy music as well

Who Goes There: Mixed boots (pointy-toed, motorcycle, and steel-cap), black leather, bluejeans, spliffers, Deadheads, and space cadets—the friendly type

11319 Elkins Avenue, Wheaton
(301) 949-8886   Maryland suburbs, Zone 10C

Cover: Varies with entertainment, roughly $6–12
Minimum: None
Mixed drinks: $3.25–4
Wine: $2–3.50
Beer: $2.25–3.50
Dress: Anything goes, and although the crowd somewhat fits the band, this is really one size fits all

Specials: Occasional no-cover shows midweek
Food available: A limited menu, mostly Tex-Mex and Southwestern—quesadillas, burritos, chicken salad, etc.—but with a few Cajun touches such as oyster and shrimp po' boys.

Hours: Tuesday–Thursday, Sunday, 6–11 P.M.; Friday and Saturday, 6 P.M.–1 A.M.; Monday, closed.

What goes on: Phantasmagoria bills itself as "the record store with a stage," and that's what it is: The original Phantas was just around the corner, a first-rate used CD, cassette, and, most importantly, vinyl store dealing in almost every sort of music except possibly disco. For several years it was the site of the Twist & Shout club, which has moved back to Bethesda; and while it still plays some roots-rock, it's definitely second generation, not founding fathers. (Just check the website: www.phantasmagoria.com.) But it has been experimenting with Cajun dance lessons, so who knows?

Setting & atmosphere: This is a carpet warehouse turned Louisiana roadhouse turned rock corral—big, open, and frankly cinderblock, with the bar at one end, the stage at the other, and a handful of booths circling the tables. The four ceiling fans make fair headway against the smoke, and the sound system was a sound investment.

If you go: Come early if you want to browse the record bins, because the store closes at 8:00 (6:00 on Sundays).

THE RITZ-CARLTON HOTEL, TYSONS CORNER

Retro-sophisticated dining room–cum-nightspot

Who Goes There: Visiting business types, 40ish corporate card second-time-around singles, radio-free suburbanites, and big band sentimentalists

1700 Tysons Boulevard, McLean
   (703) 506-4300   Virginia suburbs, Zone 11A

Cover: $8 Sunday–Thursday, $10 Friday and Saturday
Minimum: None
Mixed drinks: $5–20
Wine: $5–21
Beer: $3.50–5

Dress: Business or nice informal; retro splashy on Thursdays
Food available: Classic continental fare, but carefully presented. On Friday evenings, it sets out a pretty stunning seafood buffet.

Hours: Sunday–Thursday, 6 P.M.–2 A.M.; Friday and Saturday, 6 P.M.–3 A.M.

What goes on: It's a little of everything old-fashioned here: in the lobby lounge, cabaret singing Tuesdays and Wednesdays; local favorite jazz/standards pianist Peter Robinson on the weekends; and on Thursdays at The Restaurant, the incomparable Big Band nostalgia of Doc Scantlin and His Imperial Palms Orchestra—pencil-thin mustache and Cab Calloway moves to match, torch singers, dinner jackets, and even a conga line. (This is a dinner show, however, with a fixed price of $52 for a four-course meal.)

Setting & atmosphere: Ritz-Carlton standard style, which is to say old gentlemen's club sheen and low-key elegance. Although this Ritz has gotten much less attention than its fellows in Washington and Pentagon City, it has the same good manners and perhaps a little more fun.

THE 1720 CLUB

A combination white-collar lunch spot and uptown strip club

Who Goes There: 24–60; professionals, students, bankers, tourists, younger federal types, and a few power women

1720 H Street, NW
  (202) 338-1774   Downtown, Zone 3

Cover: None
Minimum: None
Mixed drinks: $5.95–6.95
Wine: $5.95
Beer: $5–5.50
Dress: A mix of pinstripes, jeans and khakis, and after-work; no hats or tank tops allowed
Food available: Full menu from smoked salmon to burgers to sandwiches

Hours: Monday–Thursday, 11 A.M.–2 A.M.; Friday, 11 A.M.–3 A.M.; Saturday, 4 P.M.–3 A.M.; Sunday, 4 P.M.–2 A.M.

What goes on: Exotic dancers entertain on two levels, the apparently less practiced ones downstairs, where the platform is between the door and the bar; and the senior "headliners" upstairs, in camera view and televised to the group downstairs. Most of the dancers are young and quite sweet and may even ask permission of apparent dates or wives to approach men for the traditional tips. The styles vary from romantic to athletic to go-go; and in general, the raunch quotient is kept to a minimum until at least after dinner.

Setting & atmosphere: Outside, it's a subtle nod to Bourbon Street, whitewashed brick and wrought-iron ivy. Inside, atmosphere is not at a premium, but the bar is nice enough, and the exposed brick very Fed City.

If you go: Don't go to jeer; if you enter, expect to see what you're seeing. (Women need not stare, but they shouldn't grimace or sneer.) Bring a supply of dollar bills, even higher denominations, to offer better dancers; they will circle the tables after their shift is over, so if you don't have the nerve to tuck it in somewhere while they're working, you may either slip it into their garters or merely hand it over, which is considered more polite for women patrons. And bring a sense of humor: Watching puffed-up young congressional types getting caught by the credentials chain around their necks or having their beeper slipped out of their belts is pretty funny—and obviously deflating. Remember, too, that the waitresses need separate tips.

STUDEBAKER'S

Golden-oldies disco and sync tank

Who Goes There: 25–50; jitterbug jocks, office partiers, off-duty waiters

8028 Leesburg Pike, Tysons Corner
  (703) 356-9334   Virginia suburbs, Zone 11A

1750 Rockville Pike (Doubletree Hotel), Rockville
  (301) 881–7340   Maryland suburbs, Zone 10B

Cover: Tysons Corner: $2 weekdays and before 9 P.M.; $5 Friday and Saturday, free Tuesday and Wednesday; Rockville: $1, $4 after 8 P.M. Friday and Saturday
Minimum: None
Mixed drinks: $3.50–6
Wine: $4
Beer: $3.25–3.75
Dress: Department-store prep and workday stuff, nothing much hipper than Gap; Spandex is a poor advertisement here, unless you're really advertising

Specials: All-you-can-eat buffet, 4:30–7 P.M. Wednesday–Friday; ladies' night Thursday (Tysons Corner), Wednesday (Rockville) with $1.50 rail drinks (Rockville only) or beer specials (Tysons Corner)

Food available: '50s diner updated; alcoholic ice cream sodas (Rockville)

Hours: Tysons Corner: Sunday and Monday, closed; Tuesday–Friday, 4:30 P.M.–2 A.M.; Saturday, 7 P.M.–2 A.M. Rockville: Tuesday–Thursday, 4:30 P.M.–1 A.M.; Friday, 4:30 P.M.–2 A.M.; Saturday, 7 P.M.–2 A.M.; closed Sunday and Monday.

What goes on: A staff of costumed, lip-synching, and choreographed (on the counters) sock-hoppers alternate performance with the DJ spinning music from the '60s to '80s and customers jiving and synchin'. Tuesdays in Rockville, boogie piano boss Daryl Davis swings for '50s and even '40s revivals.

Setting & atmosphere: American Graffiti comes to chrome-edged life, with glass bricks, red vinyl–topped soda counter stools, waitresses in poodle skirts, and round-bumpered service tables like car grilles. In Tysons Corner, a rock and roll "wall of fame" salutes 20 of the late greats, from Elvis to Otis, but with plaques, not Hard Rock–style memorabilia. In Rockville, the secondary theme is sports souvenirs. Rockville also has an outdoor "patio" in warm weather.

If you go: Prepare for some jostling. The music is fun, if not fresh; and some of the dancers are really good. Don't cut in here, just wait for a break in the music—unless you're really good, then you grab a solo spotlight.

TAKOMA STATION TAVERN

Classically minded buppie jazz bar

Who Goes There: 25–55; mixed media types, yuppies, buppies, other musicians

6914 4th Street, NW
(202) 829-1937   Upper Northwest, Zone 7

Cover: $5
Minimum: None
Mixed drinks: $4–8.50; their Long Island Iced Tea is strong enough to make you confuse your geography
Wine: $3.50–7
Beer: $3–5

Dress: Suits and nice dresses; jeans, but with a jacket; no cutoffs; no tennis shoes
Specials: Happy hour 4–8 P.M. weekdays
Food available: Southern-style fried chicken, greens, meatloaf, ribs

Hours: Sunday–Thursday, 4 P.M.–1:30 A.M.; Friday and Saturday, 4 P.M.–2 A.M.

What goes on: Cocktail conversation here is loud, but once the performers—high-profile area pros and often national-rank musicians passing through who drop in to jam—begin, the attention level is pretty good. A true neighborhood joint owned by the taciturn Bobby Boyd, this bar was one of the nightspots that helped revitalize the untrendy side of Takoma Park without changing its character.

Setting & atmosphere: This building, a former boxing gym, wears its age gracefully, with exposed brick, see-through room dividers that make the bar an integral part of the stage area, and just a handful of hanging plants.

If you go: Don't be demonstrative, especially if you arrive early; the Boyds live on the nightside schedule and like to start mellow. Don't gawk at the media types who come in after production hours. Sunday is change-up night, with live reggae and a slightly younger crowd.

TWIST AND SHOUT

Live blues, zydeco, R&B, and rockabilly dance club

Who Goes There: 20–50; locals, swing and Cajun dancers, electric-blues revival fans

4800 Auburn Avenue, Bethesda
(301) 652-3383   Maryland suburbs, Zone 10A

Cover: Varies with entertainment, roughly $7–15
Minimum: None
Mixed drinks: $3.50–4.25
Wine: $3–3.50
Beer: $3–4
Dress: Anything goes for listeners; dancers tend toward Western swing with shiny boots and calico on rockabilly nights, sea o' denim for blues and R&B, after-hours workboots and flannel shirts with leather vests for longneck-sipping spectating

Specials: Occasional no-cover shows midweek

Food available: Ribs and barbecue-grilled chicken; andouille po'boys, pulled pork, Cajun pizza and shrimp creole

Hours: Wednesday–Thursday and Sunday, 5 P.M.–1 A.M.; Friday and Saturday, 5 P.M.–2 A.M.; Monday and Tuesday, closed.

What goes on: This is Yasgur's farm for children of the '50s and the very same "Twist & Shout" that inspired the Mary-Chapin Carpenter hit. Owner Marc Gretschel has an old blues habit that jumped him to the front of the Delta revival and gave him an early in on booking acts that blues labels are "rediscovering." Gretschel alternates lean, mean Chicago blues with flashy Cajun barnstorming, hot (and getting hotter) zydeco, and six-cylinder rockabilly, drawing both a mom-and-pop crowd and a roots-rock second generation.

Setting & atmosphere: This is a minimally redecorated American Legion Hall—big, open, and roadhouse-y, with the bar at one end, the stage at the other, and a couple of pool tables in the back. The only decorations are old blues and Texabilly concert posters. The sound system was a sound investment.

If you go: Wear washable clothes; the squeaky-polystyrene plates provide slippery chicken parts with a launch pad. After 9, the room gets crowded, and chairs and tables get shoved together as the dance crowd expands beyond the floor inset.

TRACKS 2000

Mixed gay/straight, black/white/Asian disco

Who Goes There: 21–50; heterogeneous if not heterosexual; strong postgrad and dance-addicted elements

1111 1st Street, SE
(202) 488-3320   Southeast, Zone 9

Cover: Usually none early in the evening, then progressively increasing from 9:00 to about midnight; between about $5 and $9, higher for under-21s whose drink tabs are lower
Minimum: None
Mixed drinks: $3.50–6.75
Wine: $3.75

Beer: $1.75–3.75
Dress: Discreet, drag, denim, grunge, sleek, Eurotrash, body-bar exercisewear
Specials: Ladies' Night on last Tuesday of the month; most nights, free drinks 9–10 P.M.; country-western dance, Sunday 4–9:30 P.M.

Hours: Thursday, 9 P.M.–4 A.M.; Friday, 9 P.M.–6 A.M.; Saturday, 8 P.M.–6 A.M.; Sunday, 8 P.M.–4 A.M.; closed Monday.

What goes on: This is one of the greatest, most free-spirited dance clubs in town, having survived the periodic antigay upsurges with a becoming poise. It's also popular with some wheelchair athletes, as it has wide-open spaces. The mix is harder hip, house, and industrial on weekends, a slightly softer soul mix midweek. The closest thing to Tracks-for-beginners—that is, a less flagrant and somewhat safer setting—is Planet Fred (1221 Connecticut Avenue, NW; (202) 466-2336), which caters to both area twentysomethings and storefront hipsters, including a few budding poets, and which dabbles in drag freak bingo Wednesdays, Monday night salsa, and, in general, world-beat rock disco.

Setting & atmosphere: When we say wide-open spaces, we mean 20,000 square feet: indoor-outdoor disco, volleyball court, and a half-dozen full bars. This is still The Place to dance, unless by dancing you mean ballet. It is frequently where the post-post-party party is, after which the post-post-post-party munchie attack packs head off in cabs.

If you go: Take cash, but tuck it away; this is a rough part of town. Cabbing is best, and company is even better, if possible (at Tracks, anything is possible).

WHITEY'S

Old redneck tavern/good-eats joint with live blues

Who Goes There: Old-timers, yuppie couples with blues joneses, frathouse beer buddies

2761 North Washington Boulevard, Arlington
(703) 525-9825   Virginia suburbs, Zone 11B

Cover: None
Minimum: None
Mixed drinks: $3.15–4.20
Wine: $3–4
Beer: $2.65–3.50
Dress: Jeans, with or without bolo; motorcycle leathers; athletic uniforms

Specials: Happy hour 4–7 P.M. (weekdays), noon–4 P.M. (Saturday and Sunday) with reduced prices
Food available: Legendary "broasted" chicken; home-style dinners, sandwiches, bar food

Hours: Monday and Tuesday, 9 A.M.–1 A.M.; Wednesday–Friday, 9 A.M.–2 A.M.; Saturday, 8 A.M.–2 A.M.; Sunday, 8 A.M.–midnight

What goes on: Although Whitey's was for many years the best bar–blues roadhouse in the region—Sunday night jams were bywords and drew national-rank performers passing through town—neighborhood complaints about noise and parking (and overindulged patrons) gutted their live-music permit, so now Whitey's is limited to karaoke on Thursdays, open mike (usually led by an area pro) on Tuesdays, and top local bands on Saturdays. Pee Wee, the Wednesday-night DJ, has been spinning golden oldies for nearly 15 years.

Setting & atmosphere: This is a real neighborhood tavern, whose neighborhood has upscaled around and past it, at least in some eyes. As neighbor and harmonica godfather Mark Wenner of the Nighthawks says, "We plant one bike outside and one official biker at the bar for atmosphere." It's a plain old wood and beer-sign bar with booths, a game room in the rear with dart board, pinball, shufflebowl, etc., and longneck regulars talking politics.

If you go: Don't go by appearances; if you strike up a conversation, you'll discover this draws one of the most eclectic and politically opinionated crowds around. If you like the Dallas Cowboys, don't admit it. Tip well; since the kitchen keeps costs down, the waitresses don't always make what those at pricier nightspots do. Park legally—after 7 at the Country Club Cleaners and the law firm around the corner—and don't litter; Whitey's doesn't need your help in alienating more neighbors.

YACHT CLUB OF BETHESDA

Second-chance singles bar and retro disco

Who Goes There: 28–55; platinum cards and platinum blondes, the monied and the alimonied

8111 Woodmont Avenue, Bethesda
(301) 654-2396   Maryland suburbs, Zone 10A

Cover: $4 Wednesday, $6 Friday and Saturday
Minimum: None
Mixed drinks: $3.95–4.50
Wine: $3.65
Beer: $3.65–4.25

Dress: Dress as class advertisement; big earrings, gold chains—for women, too; jacket and tie required for men
Food available: Entrees, appetizers, and sandwiches

Hours: Tuesday–Thursday, 5 P.M.–1 A.M.; Friday, 5 P.M.–2 A.M.; Saturday, 8 P.M.–2 A.M. Closed Sunday and Monday.

What goes on: Upper, upper-middle, and upper-ambitious ring candidates in recession denial eye their conjugal options; more than 80 marital matches have been made here. This astonishingly successful mating pen is the brain-child of longtime singles-bar spinmaster, flatter-patter DJ, and trend-shift sacrificial lamb Tom Curtis.

Setting & atmosphere: A classy woodgrain, gray, and burgundy deco style that in fact does suggest the master suite of a luxury cruiser. The name, and Curtis's use of the title "commodore," are metaphors for preferred rather than actual lifestyle, like wearing Polo sportswear. Or maybe it suggests the amount of booze that nightly goes down the hatch.

If you go: Either line up before 8:00 or wait till about 11:00. This is the sort of place that confuses Gloria Vanderbilt with Coco Chanel; you can be rich and thin enough, but your dress can never be too little or too black. The Yacht Club boasts the only black-tie waiting line in Bethesda, which is sort of a self-fulfilling prophecy. If you don't dance (and many who do, shouldn't), get in line at the pool table. Or just plunk yourself down at the bar with a drink; the soft-hearted Curtis, an inveterate yenta, will have a candidate for your company in a flash.

ZANZIBAR

Worldbeat disco

Who Goes There: 23–45; trade law, embassy, and import reps; buppies, West African entrepreneurs, and Latin chic-sters

1714 G Street, NW
   (202) 842-4488   Foggy Bottom, Zone 4

Cover: $10 after 7:00 on Friday and after 10:00 on Saturday
Minimum: None
Mixed drinks: $4.25–8.50
Wine: $4.75
Beer: $4.25–4.75
Dress: Dress to impress or advertise success: European lapels, dresses with hip flounces, aerobic wear disguised as cocktail spandex; no T-shirts, jeans, or sneakers allowed
Specials: Free admission and hors d'oeuvres at happy hour, 5–7 P.M. Fridays and 9–10 P.M. Saturdays
Food available: Appetizers

Hours: Friday, 5 P.M.–3 A.M.; Saturday, 9 P.M.–3 A.M.; Sunday–Thursday, closed

What goes on: Salsa, soca, soukous, samba salsa, and so on circulate under a disco inferno mirror ball. This is an expansively, expensively stylish singles bar, with potentially valuable networking as the undertone. The serious action starts after midnight; the visiting amateurs tend to turn pumpkin at 12.

Setting & atmosphere: A sometime bureaucrats' business lunchspot, this is a long, underground wood and brick conference setup divided into larger and smaller areas, with a mahogany bar facing both and a lighted patio fountain outside the window.

If you go: Be prepared to dance if you want to meet people; there's very little chatter at the bar unless you prove yourself (or are extremely well dressed). To go with the flow, move up and down both sides of the room; there is an unspoken tidal wave of unattached partners. Note that to simplify life, the tips are built into the drink prices, which makes them something more of a bargain.

ZEI

State-of-the-techno disco

Who Goes There: 22–35; Manhattan wannabes, fashion-mag victims, drug-and-power pretenders

1415 Zei Alley, NW (half-block south of I Street between 14th and 15th)   (202) 842-2445   Downtown, Zone 3

Cover: $10
Minimum: None
Mixed drinks: $4.25–6.25
Wine: $4.25–5.25
Beer: $3.75–4.75

Dress: Alphabet soup, no sneakers or athletic wear
Specials: Varying specials; call for info
Food available: Sushi

Hours: Thursday, 10 P.M.–2 A.M.; Friday and Saturday, 10 P.M.–3 A.M.; closed Sunday–Wednesday.

What goes on: The trendiest resident techno-rave in town, Zei manages to play up to the remnants of Republican class consciousness (by offering $750 private memberships and restricted access to the third floor) and also to neoliberals through a meritocracy of fashion and physical fitness. Actually, under-21s are allowed in, but they tend to overcompensate and look too, too old.

Setting & atmosphere: This $1.55 million re-creation of a floating warehouse club turns the thrift-shop ethic on its head: Oversized Mad Tea Party furniture with shoulder-pad silhouettes (on the elite third-floor area), a 24-screen video-mix wall, aerobically correct house dancers, and a burnished steel mirror above the bar that turns the whole dance floor into a living video. The DJ, often a visiting dance-hall celeb from New York, works from an overhead catwalk like a starship bridge. There's an artsy steel "curtain" gathered to one side that's almost as heavy as the smoke screen from the cigarettes.

If you go: Polish up a shorthand version of cocktail conversation, because even in the "quiet zones," the 22-speaker sound system will reduce you to body language. Zei has particularly good wheelchair access. If for some reason the action here is a little too loud and attitudinal, step across the alley to the less frenetic, more landed-class Spy Club, a morning-in-America-singles-bar-cum-disco that draws late boomers, BMW tailgate partiers, and the prematurely jaded plastic riche.

PART SEVEN

Exercise and Recreation

Working Out

Most of the folks on our *Unofficial Guide* research team work out routinely. Some bike, some run, some lift weights or do aerobics. While visiting Washington during the hot summer months, it didn't take long to figure out that exercising in the city's fearsome heat and humidity presented some problems.

The best months for outdoor exercise are March through June and October through December. In July and August, you must get up very early to beat the heat. January and February can bring very cold weather, although snow isn't usually a problem. During the summer months, unless you get up very early, we recommend working out indoors.

■ Walking ■

With its wide-open spaces, Washington is made for walking. Security is very good along the Mall and Potomac Park, making for a safe walking environment at all hours of the day and night.

A long walk down the Mall and through East and West Potomac Parks offers grand views of the Lincoln, Jefferson, and FDR Memorials and the Washington Monument, as well as the Tidal Basin and the Potomac River. For a really long excursion, cross Arlington Memorial Bridge and explore Arlington National Cemetery. You can also walk north along the river past the Kennedy Center and the Thompson Boat Center and into Georgetown.

North of the Mall, downtown is not particularly interesting or aesthetically pleasing—and not too safe above New York Avenue. North of the

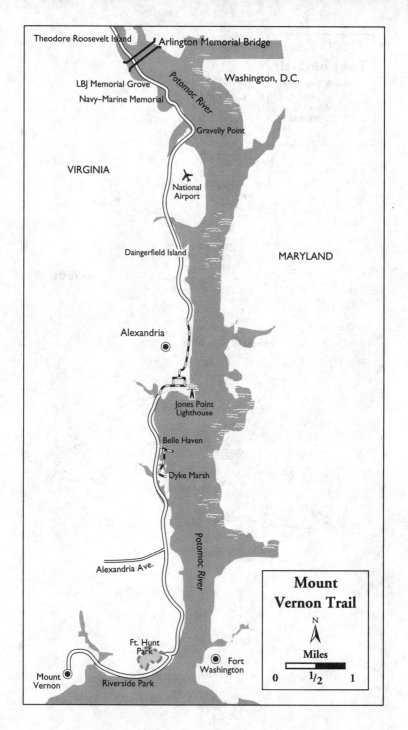

Theodore Roosevelt Island

Arlington Memorial Bridge

Washington, D.C.

Potomac River

LBJ Memorial Grove

Navy–Marine Memorial

Gravelly Point

VIRGINIA

National
Airport

Daingerfield Island

MARYLAND

Alexandria

Jones Point
Lighthouse

Belle Haven

Dyke Marsh

Alexandria Ave.

Potomac River

Ft. Hunt
Park

Fort
Washington

Mount
Vernon

Riverside Park

**Mount
Vernon Trail**

N

Miles

0   1/2   1

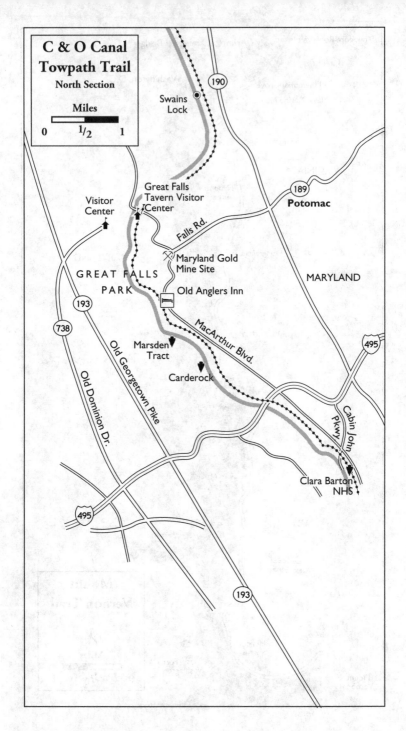

C & O Canal
Towpath Trail
North Section

Miles

0   1/2   1

190

Swains
Lock

Great Falls
Tavern Visitor
Center

189

Potomac

Visitor
Center

Falls Rd.

Maryland Gold
Mine Site

MARYLAND

GREAT FALLS

PARK

Old Anglers Inn

193

738

Marsden
Tract

MacArthur Blvd.

495

Carderock

Old Georgetown Pike

Old Dominion Dr.

Cabin John Pkwy.

Clara Barton
NHS

495

193

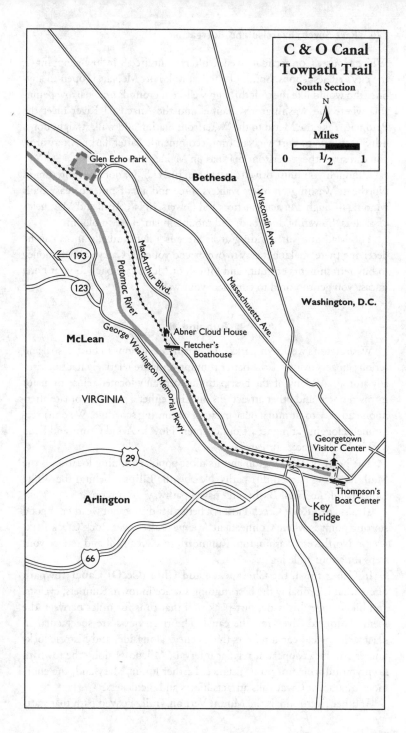

**C & O Canal
Towpath Trail**

South Section

N

Miles

0   1/2   1

Glen Echo Park

Bethesda

Wisconsin Ave.

193

123

Potomac River

MacArthur Blvd.

Massachusetts Ave.

Washington, D.C.

McLean

George Washington Memorial Pkwy.

Abner Cloud House

Fletcher's
Boathouse

VIRGINIA

Georgetown
Visitor Center

29

Arlington

Thompson's
Boat Center

Key
Bridge

66

White House, Connecticut Avenue offers unlimited window-shopping at the city's ritziest shops. South of the Capitol, Fort McNair is open to anyone who would like to stroll through well-kept grounds on a narrow peninsula where the Washington Channel and the Anacostia River meet the Potomac: Take the Metro to the Waterfront Station and walk straight down 4th Street, SW, to Fort McNair (not recommended after dark). Afterwards, you can stroll the waterfront marinas on Maine Avenue.

Although you must drive to get there, the U.S. National Arboretum in Northeast Washington offers walkers three and a half miles of easy trails winding through 444 acres of trees and flowers. In late April and May, fields of azaleas, flowering dogwood, and mountain laurel are in bloom.

The Mall and surrounding areas are fairly flat, and distances can be deceiving there, making it easy to overextend yourself. Carry enough money to buy refreshments en route and for cab or Metro fare back to your hotel in case you get too tired to complete your walk.

■ **Running** ■

Washington's wealth of parks offers plenty of options to both casual and serious joggers. Most of the better running areas are relatively flat but visually stunning. Many of the best paths are centrally located, close to major in-town hotels and other attractions, making either a morning or late afternoon run easy to fit into a busy business or touring schedule. We don't recommend jogging at night; see our chapter "How to Avoid Crime and Keep Safe in Public Places" in Part Four.

The heart of Washington and its most popular running location is the **Mall**, featuring packed-dirt paths. Nearby, the **Ellipse** (behind the White House) and the **Tidal Basin** offer paved pathways to run on.

Tree-shaded **Rock Creek Park** is a better bet during hot weather. A good starting point is where Connecticut Avenue crosses over Rock Creek Parkway in Northwest Washington. Run north to Pierce Mill and retrace your steps for a four-mile jog.

In Georgetown, the **Chesapeake and Ohio (C&O) Canal Towpath** offers what is probably the best running surface in town. Runners, cyclists, and hikers love this wide, dirt-pack trail that runs for miles between the scenic Potomac River and the canal. The river views are spectacular in places, the placid canal reflects the greenery alongside, and historic lockhouses and locks appear at regular intervals. Mileposts along the towpath keep you informed of your distance. Farther up, in Maryland, the enormous cataract at Great Falls attracts hikers and picnickers.

Another river route is the **Mount Vernon Trail**, a paved path that starts near the Lincoln Memorial, crosses Arlington Memorial Bridge, and goes downriver on the Virginia side of the Potomac for about 16 miles to Mount Vernon. Unless you're a marathoner, cut this run in half: Run to the airport and back, about seven and a half miles. In blustery fall, winter, and early spring weather, runners and cyclists will find that the better-protected C&O Canal Towpath offers more protection from strong winds coming off the river. **West Potomac Park** is the best route in the spring, when the Japanese cherry trees are blooming around the Tidal Basin. Start near the Jefferson Memorial, head down Ohio Drive, and make the loop at the end of the park; if you've got any energy left, continue past the Jefferson Memorial and loop around the Tidal Basin. Go early in the morning to beat the crowds.

Getting to the Track

If your hotel is downtown, the Mall is the closest option you have without driving or taking the Metro. If you're staying along the Connecticut Avenue corridor, Rock Creek Park and the C&O Canal Towpath are your best bets. In Alexandria or Rosslyn, the Mount Vernon Trail and the Washington and Old Dominion Regional Park are popular paved running paths. In suburban Maryland, Greenbelt Park offers both paved and unpaved surfaces to run on, as well as a one-mile fitness trail outfitted with 20 exercise stations.

■ Swimming ■

Local waters are polluted to one degree or another, so stick to your hotel swimming pool. The closest saltwater beach is **Sandy Point State Park** in Maryland, about an hour's drive east on US 50 on the shores of the Chesapeake Bay. Atlantic Ocean beaches are a minimum three-hour drive; traffic tie-ups on summer weekends are horrendous as beachgoers funnel into the twin Chesapeake Bay bridges, where multihour backups are routine.

■ Free Weights and Nautilus ■

Almost all of the major hotels have a spa or fitness room with weightlifting equipment. For an aerobic workout, most of the fitness rooms offer a Lifecycle, a Stairmaster, or a rowing machine.

■ Fitness Centers and Aerobics ■

Many Washington fitness centers are members-only and don't offer daily or short-term memberships. The few exceptions are all coed. **Sport Fit,** located on Vermont Avenue, NW, between 14th and 15th Streets downtown, features free weights, fixed weights, a full range of aerobic exercise equipment including a StairMaster, rowing and cycling machines, and a full schedule of aerobics classes. Visitors can take advantage of the facilities for $10 a day. Call (202) 638-3539 for more information.

Washington Sports Club, at 1835 Connecticut Avenue, NW (across from the Hilton near Dupont Circle), offers much the same activities and services as Sport Fit. The daily rate is $20, and a month costs $120. For more information, call (202) 332-0100.

On Capitol Hill, the **Washington Office Center Fitness Club** offers a full range of services, including free weights, fixed weights, aerobics classes, and cardiovascular workout equipment. The club, located at 409 3rd Street, SW, charges $5 a day. Call (202) 488-2822.

■ Tennis ■

Washington's two public tennis clubs are popular, making it difficult to get a court during peak hours without a reservation. The **Washington Tennis Center,** located at 16th and Kennedy Streets in Upper Northwest, offers 15 clay courts and 10 hard courts (5 lighted) during the warm weather months. In winter, 5 indoor courts are available in addition to the 10 hard courts. The club accepts reservations up to a week in advance. The club is open from 7 A.M. to 11 P.M. and indoor rates begin at $20.40 an hour; outdoor rates begin at $3.25 an hour. A $25 deposit is required. Call (202) 722-5949 for more information.

The **East Potomac Tennis Club,** located on Ohio Drive in East Potomac Park, features 5 indoor and 19 outdoor courts. Reservations for prime-time hours go fast, and you need to make reservations a week in advance. Players have a good chance of getting a court without reservations weekdays between 10 A.M. and 3 P.M. Rates range from $20 to $27 an hour (indoor) and $3.25 to $7.50 an hour (outdoor). A credit card deposit is required. Call (202) 554-5962 for more information.

Recreational Sports:
Biking, Hiking, Kayaking, and So On

■ Bicycling ■

Washington offers both on- and off-road cyclists a wide variety of bicycling, from flat and easy cruises along paved bike paths and the C&O Canal Towpath, to challenging terrain in the rolling countryside of nearby Virginia and Maryland.

In early spring and late fall, cyclists should wear riding tights and arm warmers to keep the chill off. From May through October, the temperatures range from comfortable to scorching—predictably the latter on summer afternoons. Listen to weather forecasts for predictions of afternoon thunderstorms in the late summer; they can be fearsome. Fall is the best season for cycling around Washington, with cool, crisp weather and a riot of color as the leaves turn in mid- to late October. Even in winter, Washington's mild climate offers at least a few days a month that are warm enough to induce cyclists to jump on their bikes.

A variety of bicycles are available for rent at **Thompson Boat Center** (phone (202) 333-4861), located between the Kennedy Center and Georgetown on the Potomac, and **Fletcher's Boathouse** (phone (202) 244-0461), above Georgetown on Canal Road. **City Bikes** in Adams-Morgan (phone (202) 265-1564) rents mountain and hybrid ("city") bikes for $10 an hour and $25 a day.

Road Biking

In downtown Washington, bicycling is better left to couriers. Unrelenting traffic congestion, combined with absent-minded tourists preoccupied with monuments and finding a cheap parking space, makes riding a bike on Washington's streets a brutal experience for all but the most hardened urban cyclists. Luckily, Washington is blessed with a network of bike paths that takes the terror out of riding a skinny-tired bike in—and out of—the city.

In terms of great scenery and enough distance to really get a workout, the **Mount Vernon Trail** is Washington's premier bike path. In addition to pedaling the 16 paved miles to Mount Vernon, cyclists can make side trips to Dyke Marsh wildlife habitat, explore fortifications at Fort Hunt, and see a 19th-century lighthouse at Jones Point Park.

Another good out-and-back ride is the **Washington and Old Dominion Railroad Regional Park** (W&OD), a 45-mile-long, paved linear bikeway that connects with the Mount Vernon Trail upriver of Arlington Memorial Bridge on the Virginia side of the Potomac. The trail intersects with a series of "bubble" parks in urban Northern Virginia and provides access to the rural Virginia countryside beyond the Capital Beltway. Both the Mount Vernon Trail and the W&OD trail are easily reached from Washington by bicycle by riding across the Arlington Memorial Bridge, at the Lincoln Memorial.

Road riders itching to see beautiful countryside outside the Washington metropolitan area (but within a day's drive) should go to either Middleburg, Virginia, or Frederick, Maryland. **Middleburg,** about 30 miles west of D.C., is in the heart of Virginia's horse country. Beautiful rolling countryside in the foothills of the Blue Ridge Mountains and low-traffic roads bordering thoroughbred horse farms make this area a fantastic place to spin the cranks.

Frederick, Maryland, is about an hour's drive north of Washington. North of town along US 15, covered bridges, narrow back roads, fish hatcheries, and mountain vistas evoke images of Vermont. To the south of Frederick, a 25-mile loop around Sugar Loaf Mountain is a favorite with local road cyclists.

Mountain Biking

Fat-tired cyclists can ride 184 miles one-way on the **Chesapeake and Ohio Canal Towpath,** beginning in Georgetown and following the Potomac River upstream to Cumberland, Maryland. The hardpacked dirt surface gives the illusion of being flat all the way; actually, the trip upriver is slightly uphill. Because of floods in the winter and spring, it's a good idea to call the National Park Service at (301) 739-4200 to make sure the section you're planning to ride is open to cyclists.

Hammerheads looking for challenging singletrack and some steep climbing have to do some driving to find it, but it's worth it. The **Frederick Municipal Watershed** offers the best technical singletrack this side of West Virginia—and it's a lot closer. Located an hour's drive from Washington near Frederick, Maryland, the 6,000-acre, mountaintop forest is riddled with narrow trails and well-maintained dirt roads. Since there are hardly any signs or trail markers, the Catoctin Furnace Quadrangle topographic map and a compass are a must. Local knowledge helps, too; call the Wheel Base, Frederick's pro bike shop, at (301) 663-9288 for maps and advice.

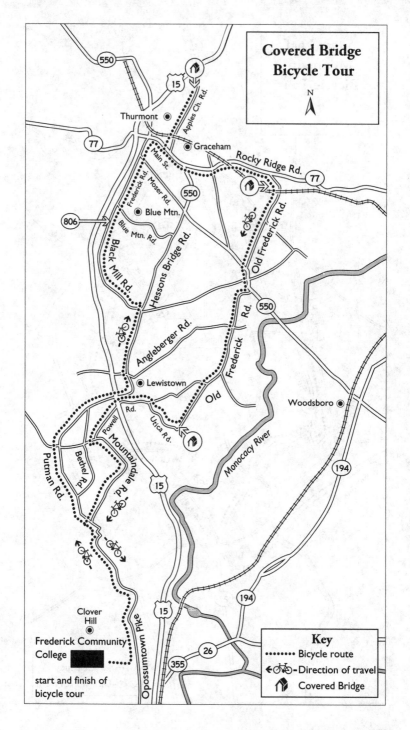

Covered Bridge Bicycle Tour

N

Thurmont

Graceham

Rocky Ridge Rd.

Apples Ch. Rd.

Main St.

Frederick Rd.

Moser Rd.

Blue Mtn.

Blue Mtn. Rd.

Black Mill Rd.

Hessons Bridge Rd.

Old Frederick Rd.

Angleberger Rd.

Lewistown

Frederick Rd.

Old

Woodsboro

Powell Rd.

Utica Rd.

Bethel Rd.

Mountaindale Rd.

Putman Rd.

Monocacy River

Clover Hill

Frederick Community College

start and finish of bicycle tour

Opossumtown Pike

Key

•••••• Bicycle route

←🚲– Direction of travel

🏠 Covered Bridge

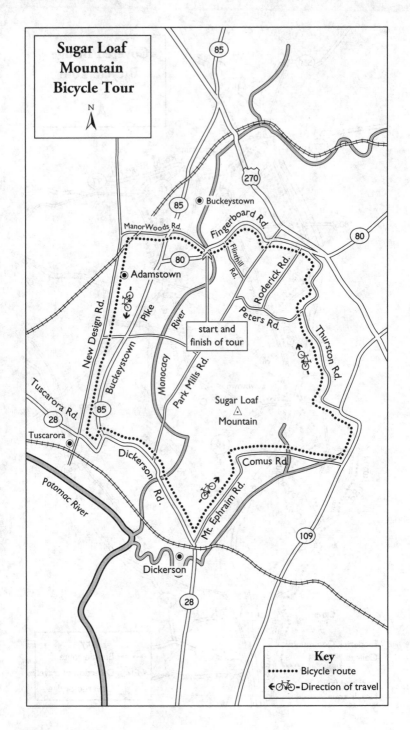

Sugar Loaf Mountain Bicycle Tour

N

Buckeystown

ManorWoods Rd.

Fingerboard Rd.

85

270

80

Flinthill Rd.

Roderick Rd.

Adamstown

80

Peters Rd.

Thurston Rd.

start and finish of tour

New Design Rd.

Buckeystown Pike

Monocacy River

Park Mills Rd.

Tuscarora Rd.

28

85

Sugar Loaf
△
Mountain

Tuscarora

Dickerson Rd.

Comus Rd.

Potomac River

Mt. Ephraim Rd.

109

Dickerson

28

Key

••••••• Bicycle route

←🚲→ Direction of travel

■ Hiking ■

While only about 15 minutes from downtown, **Theodore Roosevelt Island** is a wilderness oasis offering hikers a little over three miles of wide, flat paths through forests, swampy marshes, and rocky beaches. The park is located in the Potomac River across from the Kennedy Center and can be reached by car. Park in the area off the northbound lanes of the George Washington Memorial Parkway on the Virginia side of the river. A footbridge connects the Virginia shore to the island. Another alternative is Washington Water Bus, which stops at the island every 20 minutes from 11 A.M. to 6 P.M. daily, May through October. Call (800) 288-7925 for more information.

The C&O Canal, which begins in Georgetown, features a hardpacked dirt path that follows the Potomac River north for 184 miles. Along the way are river views, forest, and wildlife. At **Great Falls Park,** north of Washington on the Virginia side of the river, the Potomac roars over a series of steep, jagged rocks and flows through a narrow gorge. It's a dramatic scene and worth the trip. Hiking trails follow the river and offer views of Mather Gorge. Rock Creek Park in Northwest Washington offers 15 miles of hiking trails, plus bridle trails you can hike. Maps are available at the park headquarters, 5200 Glover Road, NW (phone (202) 426-6829).

■ Canoeing and Kayaking ■

Canoes and rowboats are available for rent on the C&O Canal and the Potomac River at **Thompson Boat Center,** located between the Kennedy Center and Georgetown (phone (202) 333-4861), **Fletcher's Boat House** at Canal and Reservoir Roads above Georgetown (phone (202) 244-0461), and **Jack's Boats** on K Street in Georgetown (phone (202) 337-9642). Pedal boats for two can be rented at the Tidal Basin (phone (202) 484-0206).

Whitewater enthusiasts need go only a few miles north of the Capital Beltway to find excellent Class I through Class VI rapids year-round on the **Potomac.** Local boaters boast that it's the best urban whitewater experience in the United States, featuring a very remote, wilderness feel. One of the most popular trips is the Class II Seneca rapids section. The put-in is at Violets Lock, located on River Road (MD 190), north of Potomac, Maryland. Violets Lock is also the take-out, meaning you don't have to run a shuttle: It's a round trip that lets you return to your starting point by paddling up the C&O Canal, about one and a half miles below Violets Lock. Below the Seneca Rapids, the river is very scenic, featuring many islands and no rapids.

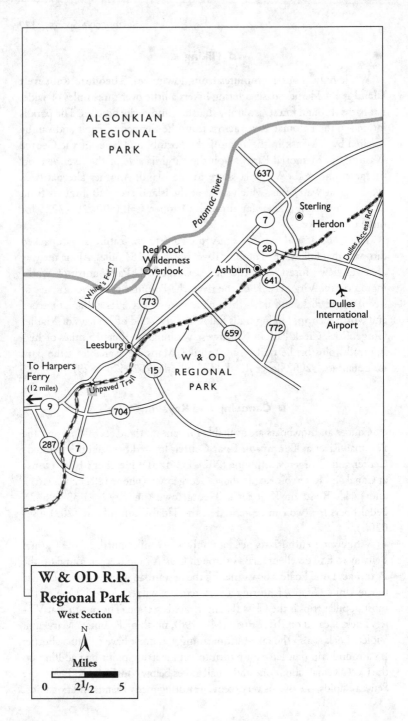

ALGONKIAN
REGIONAL
PARK

Potomac River

637

Sterling

7

Herdon

28

Dulles Access Rd

Red Rock
Wilderness
Overlook

Ashburn

641

White's Ferry

773

Dulles
International
Airport

Leesburg

659

772

W & OD
REGIONAL
PARK

To Harpers
Ferry
(12 miles)

15

Unpaved Trail

9

704

287

7

W & OD R.R.
Regional Park
West Section

N

Miles

0   2½   5

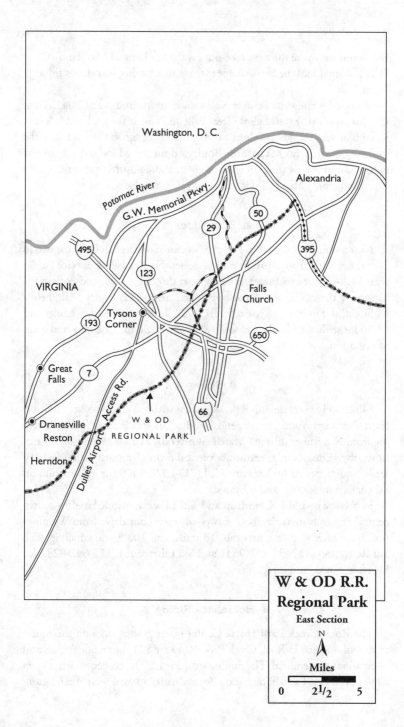

Washington, D. C.

Potomac River

G.W. Memorial Pkwy.

Alexandria

(50)

(29)

(495)

(395)

(123)

VIRGINIA

Falls
Church

(193)

Tysons
Corner

(650)

Great
Falls

(7)

Dulles Airport Access Rd.

Dranesville
Reston

W & OD

REGIONAL PARK

(66)

Herndon

**W & OD R.R.
Regional Park**

East Section

N

Miles

0   2 1/2   5

But you must make the next take-out on the left bank at Maryland's Great Falls National Park or become another statistic as the river drops through Great Falls.

Seasoned whitewater boaters may want to try running the Class II/Class III-plus rapids that start below Great Falls and end at the Old Angler's Inn. As with Seneca Rapids, no shuttle is required: Park across the road from the Old Angler's Inn on MacArthur Boulevard on the Maryland side of the Potomac and follow the trail to the put-in. Paddle upstream on the C&O Canal to below Great Falls (at least 100 yards) for the return leg.

■ Boat Rides ■

Ninety-minute excursions leave Georgetown on the C&O Canal two to four times daily from April to mid-October. National Park Service guides wear 19th-century costumes, take the boat through a lock, and explain the history of the canal. Board and buy tickets near the Foundry Mall, below M Street at Thomas Jefferson Street, NW. Tickets are $4 for adults and $3.50 for seniors and children. Call (202) 653-5190 for schedules and more information.

■ Skiing ■

Moderately good downhill ski slopes are within a couple of hours' drive from Washington and offer dependable, machine-made snow and night skiing from November through March. **Whitetail,** a new $25-million ski area in nearby Pennsylvania, features a vertical drop of almost 1,000 feet, 14 trails, and plenty of lift capacity. Call (717) 328-9400 for information on ski packages, lodging, and lift rates.

Jointly owned **Ski Roundtop** and **Ski Liberty,** also located in south-central Pennsylvania, are about a two- to three-hour drive from Washington. Both offer 600-foot verticals, 13 trails, and 100% snowmaking. Call Ski Roundtop at (717) 432-9631 and Ski Liberty at (717) 642-8282 for lift rates, hours, and directions.

■ Horseback Riding ■

The **Rock Creek Park Horse Center** offers guided rides on the equestrian trails located in Rock Creek Park. Rates are $21 for an hour's ride, and reservations are required. The minimum age is 12. The center, which is open all year, is located at Military and Glover Roads in Northwest Washington.

Hours: Tuesday–Friday, 2–8 P.M.; Saturday and Sunday, 10 A.M.–5 P.M. Call (202) 362–0118 for more information.

■ Golf ■

Washington has three public golf courses operated on National Park Service land and open from dawn to dusk. Fees are $9 for 9 holes and $15 for 18 holes weekdays; weekends, the rates are $12.25 and $19. Reservations are not accepted. All three courses feature snack bars, pro shops, rental clubs, and gas cars ($11.50 for 9 holes, $18 for 18 holes).

East Potomac Golf Course, located in East Potomac Park across from Washington's waterfront area, offers one 18-hole course, two 9-hole courses, and an 18-hole miniature golf course. It's the busiest of the three courses; plan to arrive at dawn on weekends if you don't want to wait. East Potomac has wide-open fairways, well-kept greens, and great views of surrounding monuments. Call (202) 554-7660 for more information.

Langston Golf Course, at 26th Street and Benning Road, NE (near RFK Stadium), features an 18-hole course and driving range. Langston, the only public course with water holes, is located along the Anacostia River. For more information, call (202) 397-8638.

Rock Creek Golf Course is located at 16th and Rittenhouse Streets, NW, four and a half miles north of the White House on 16th Street. It offers duffers a hilly and challenging 18-hole course through rolling hills and wooded terrain. Call (202) 882-7332 for more information.

Spectator Sports

Alas, America's national pastime, baseball, is not played professionally in the nation's capital anymore. But Washingtonians have developed a fierce devotion to the **Baltimore Orioles,** only an hour away. Visitors to D.C. can make the trek by train and catch the Birds in their new digs, Oriole Park at Camden Yards, near Baltimore's downtown Inner Harbor. Check the sports section of the *Washington Post* for information on home games and tickets.

However, if you're one of the growing number of fans of minor-league baseball, Washington is worth a minitour. The Class A **Frederick Keys** (named in honor of Francis Scott Key, a rural Maryland native) play in the historic town of Frederick, Maryland, about an hour to the northeast. The Class A **Prince William Cannons,** a farm team for the Chicago White Sox, play just outside Fairfax County; call (703) 730-2640.

The closest option for baseball is Prince George's County Stadium, where the **Bowie Baysox,** a Class AA team belonging to the same group as the Keys, have been steadily building a crowd. Both teams are associated with the Orioles, so they're sentimental favorites. Baysox tickets are only $9 for box seats, $6 for adults, and $3 for children. Call (301) 805-6000 for information.

For professional basketball, the **Washington Bullets,** former NBA champs, play out of the USAir Arena (formerly the Capital Centre) in suburban Landover, Maryland. Call the USAir Arena box office for ticket information: (301) 773-2255. Take the Beltway to either of two exits, 32 or 33. *Note:* The Bullets are scheduled to move to new digs in late 1997: the new, 20,600-seat MCI Center, located downtown near Gallery Place.

The University of Maryland offers topflight **college basketball** at Cole Field House on its campus in suburban College Park. Call (301) 314-7064 for information. Georgetown University plays its home games at the USAir Arena; call (301) 350-3400 for ticket and schedule information.

Lots of luck getting tickets to see **professional football** in Washington: The Redskins have sold out RFK Stadium for years, and the team holds the reputation as the hardest ticket to acquire in pro sports. Still interested? Scalpers in front of RFK before game time regularly charge three and four times the correct ticket price—and higher, if the 'Skins are playing Dallas.

The Redskins are hoping to be in new digs in Landover by the 1997 season, but the schedule is uncertain. The new stadium will have nearly 80,000 seats, so maybe tickets will become easier to obtain.

Meanwhile, a football stadium is also being built in Baltimore for the Ravens, née Cleveland Browns, who are in the Orioles' *old* Memorial Stadium for now.

College football is another matter. The Maryland Terrapins play in Byrd Stadium at College Park; call (301) 314-7064. The Naval Academy in Annapolis, Maryland, and Howard University in Washington also field teams; check the *Post* for home game information.

Washington's **professional hockey** team, the Washington Wizards, plays at the USAir Arena in Landover, Maryland. Call (301) 386-7000 for information. *Note:* The Wizards are slated to move to the new MCI Center, located downtown, in late 1997.

Pro soccer comes to Washington as D.C. United plays 18 home games each season (April through September) at RFK Stadium. Tickets for evening and Sunday afternoon games range from $12 to $32; call TicketMaster at (202) 432-SEAT to reserve individual game tickets.

Horse racing is available at a number of tracks around Washington; check the *Washington Post* to see which track is in season during your visit. Bus service from the city is usually available.

Harness:

Rosecroft Raceway—Oxen Hill, MD (301) 567-4000.

Thoroughbred:

Bowie Race Course—Bowie, MD (301) 262-8111;
Laurel Race Course—Laurel, MD (301) 725-0400;
Pimlico Race Course—Baltimore, MD (410) 542-9400;
Charles Town Raceways—Charlestown, WV (304) 725-7001.

PART EIGHT

Shopping in Washington

Mall Shopping

It should come as no surprise that Washington—where residents earn the highest median household income in the nation—offers a lot of shopping. You can quite literally shop until you drop—virtually malled to death. On Saturday afternoons, roads leading to the shopping centers are as congested as commuter routes during rush hour. The stretch of I-95 south of Washington around the Potomac Mills factory outlet complex in Woodbridge—which has now surpassed even Colonial Williamsburg as the number one tourist attraction in Virginia—is nearly always backed up (see "Bargains" in the "Specialty Shops" chapter below). And Tysons Corner, just west of the Beltway, is so large it helped inspire one of the catch phrases of '90s development, the "edge city." Tysons is a Siamese twin mall now, the original Tysons and the Galleria at Tysons II, and now has its own brewpub, appropriately named the Edge City Brewery.

■ Suburban Malls ■

Most of the smaller suburban malls are probably similar to what you have back home, with a few notable exceptions. One is **The Fashion Centre** at Pentagon City in Arlington, Virginia, a beautiful conservatory-style building filled with high-end retailers: *Crate and Barrel*, the *Museum Company*, the *Nature Company*, *Macy's*, and *Nordstrom*, the Seattle-based clothing retailer renowned for its service and selection. It also opens onto the Ritz-Carlton Hotel, where you can have a very refreshing, elegant meal or high tea. The Pentagon City Metro stop, on the blue line, deposits shoppers right into the mall. The **Chevy Chase Pavilion,** at the very north end of the District of Columbia on the border of Maryland, has a somewhat similar look and such new "chain-boutique" stores as *Country Road Australia, Joan Vass, Gazelle* (wearable art), and *Everett Hall.* Like most malls, it has a food court, but it also has the Southwestern chic Canyon Cafe, a Cheesecake Factory, California Pizza Kitchen, and Mozzarella's. It is also directly accessible by the Metro (the Friendship Heights station).

Catty-corner from the Pavilion is **Mazza Gallerie,** a slightly quieter mall with *Neiman-Marcus, Williams-Sonoma, Ann Taylor,* and a branch of the famed Boston discounter *Filene's Basement.* For emergencies, there is an American Express office on site.

White Flint Mall, north of Washington, also has a subway stop, although it's a block or so away; shuttle bus service is continuous. It houses *Bloomingdale's, Ann Taylor, Lord & Taylor,* a Cheesecake Factory restaurant (which hands out silent "beepers" so you can keep shopping while waiting for a table), and a Bertollini's, both with elaborate decors, as well as a better-than-average food court and a huge three-story *Borders Books & Music. Dave & Buster's,* a vast virtual-reality sports/billiard parlor/bar/casino/restaurant complex, dominates the top floor (see profile in Part Six: Entertainment and Night Life). There is also a European-style day spa, *Roxanne,* which offers everything from hairstyling to ornately painted (real or false) nails, mud baths, massages, and all-natural facials.

Tysons Corner, although it does not have subway access, offers nearly 400 shops in two large arcades including *Nordstrom, Lord & Taylor, Bloomingdale's,* and a branch of Legal Seafood with a stunning glass-wall view. (The "Corner" fills up the neighborhood between Routes 7 and 123.) Just up the way is **Fairfax Square,** a sort of mini-mall of super-label shops (see "Designer Clothing" in the "Specialty Shops" chapter) that whet your appetite for the platinum-card eateries such as Morton's of Chicago and the old-guard white linen Ritz-Carlton Hotel.

■ Malls in D.C. ■

There are fewer malls within city limits. Georgetown Park, near the intersection of M Street and Wisconsin Avenue, is the most extravagant, featuring a lush Victorian design and some even fancier retailers: *FAO Schwarz, Ralph Lauren Polo, Ferragamo, Liberty of London, Tommy Hilfiger, Sharper Image,* and the *White House,* which stocks only cream, white, or ecru clothes and accessories. It also includes several full-service restaurants, one Tex-Mex, one Japanese steak house with sushi bar, and the original Clyde's of Georgetown, as well as a food court.

Two Washington landmarks have lately been reborn as shopping centers: the **Old Post Office Pavilion** and **Union Station.** The Pavilion, on Pennsylvania Avenue just north of the Smithsonian, is the place for stocking up on souvenirs; it also has a tower with a view that rivals the Washington Monument but with a fraction of the waiting line. Union Station, the city's restored train station on Massachusetts Avenue, is a grand beaux arts building whose glory is undiminished by its two-story arcade of shops. Be sure to wander into the East Hall, which has kiosks selling one-of-a-kind jewelry, Russian ethnic and Afrocentric crafts, and other merchandise. The lowest level is a bustling food court, and there's more just outside the train track waiting areas. It also has a branch of the New York neo–soul food restaurant B. Smith's, a Pizzeria Uno, Coco Pazzo, America (a restaurant that claims to have dishes from all 50 states), a couple of elevated-view bars, and a multiplex cinema. The Pavilion is very near the Federal Triangle subway stop; Union Station's Metro stop is an escalator ride down.

And although it's a couple of blocks from the Metro Center subway, most tourists will want to look into the **Shops at National Place** (F Street, SW, between 13th and 14th Streets), which has a *Sharper Image, Banana Republic, Victoria's Secret,* and a couple of cafes. For free, you get to watch for political and media celebrities while you window shop; the building also houses the National Press Club.

Great Neighborhoods
for Window-Shopping

If malls make you crazy, Washington has a number of neighborhoods made for window-shopping.

■ Georgetown ■

In Georgetown, the city's largest walk-and-shop district, most of the clothing stores, both franchise and boutique, are right along the two main drags, M Street and Wisconsin Avenue. You'll find a preponderance of stores selling teen fashions—notably, *Commander Salamander* (1420 Wisconsin Avenue, NW; (202) 337-2265); *Betsey Johnson* (1319 Wisconsin Avenue, NW; (202) 338-4090); and *Urban Outfitters* (3111 M Street, NW; (202) 342-1012). These are also the two main restaurant strips. Shops for antiques, both formal and more offbeat, stretch up Wisconsin past R Street, interspersed with collections of artworks, books, and shoes.

Georgetown also has more than a few shops specializing in one-of-a-kind crafts—including art glass at *Maurine Littleton* (1667 Wisconsin Avenue, NW; (202) 333-9307); ceramics at *American Hand/Plus* (2906 M Street, NW; (202) 965-3273); jewelry and wooden crafts at *Appalachian Spring* (1415 Wisconsin Avenue, NW; (202) 337-5780); and Southwestern imports from *Santa Fe Style* (1413 Wisconsin Avenue, NW; (202) 333-3747). For more traditional gifts, old-line Georgetowners prefer *Little Caledonia* (1419 Wisconsin Avenue, NW; (202) 333-4700); and *Martin's* (1304 Wisconsin Avenue, NW; (202) 338-6144). Author Larry McMurtry operates a fine second-hand store for collectors and real bookworms called *Booked Up* (1204 31st Street, NW; (202) 965-3244), and the gentleman himself is frequently on the premises. But the specialty collector fascinated by late-19th- and early-20th-century decorative arts will find a paradise on M Street; see "Decorative Arts" in the "Specialty Shops" chapter.

■ Adams-Morgan ■

Amid all the ethnic eateries, this is the neighborhood to look for African and Hispanic ethnic clothing and crafts (see "Ethnic Goods," under "Specialty Shops").

Also, be sure to check out the architectural remnants—mantels, stained and leaded glass windows, chandeliers, and door handles—at the *Brass Knob* (2311 18th Street, NW; (202) 332-3370); and the innovative furnishings at *Skynear & Co.* (2122 18th Street, NW; (202) 797-7160), which stocks hand-painted fabric pillows, whimsical wrought iron, etc.

■ Dupont Circle ■

Dupont Circle is for shoppers looking to enrich the mind—it's full of art galleries, espresso bars, and bookstores (see "Specialty Shops"). Most of these are on the north side of the circle: The art galleries are generally clustered along R Street in the two blocks just west of Connecticut Avenue (leading you gently over toward the *Phillips Collection*). The *Chao Phraya Gallery* (2009 Columbia Road, a half-block east of Connecticut Avenue; (202) 745-1111), showing Chinese and Southeast Asian art and antiques, is a few blocks north.

Across the street is *Circa 1940* (1608 18th Street, NW, upstairs; (202) 265-2270), which adorns gentlemen of taste in pleated trousers, three-button suits, smoking jackets, embroidered tuxedo pumps, and even spats; they also provide hat cleaning and reblocking and, in the rear, antique wedding gowns. Just up the street, above one of the several Starbucks in the Circle, is *Secondi,* a contemporary consignment clothing store that savvy Washington women make a regular part of their shopping routines (1702 Connecticut Avenue, NW; (202) 667-1122).

West of the circle near the Phillips Collection is the *Geoffrey Diner Gallery* (1730 21st Street, NW; (202) 483-5005), which specializes in American and English arts and crafts furniture, including Stickley and Mission, and Deco and Nouveau pieces.

South of the circle, on Connecticut Avenue, NW, between N and K Streets, are high-end retailers such as *Ralph Lauren Polo, Burberry's, Hugo Boss, Zoran, Betsey Fisher, Rizik's,* a prominent local women's shop, and a Cartier boutique called *CdeCarat* in the Mayflower Hotel. There is also a fine estate jewelry shop called the *Tiny Jewel Box,* and even a branch of Boston's landmark discount retailer, *Filene's Basement.*

■ Chevy Chase ■

At the northwest edge of D.C., where it blends into Montgomery County, Maryland, well-heeled shoppers love the stretch of Wisconsin Avenue from about Jenifer Street to Park Avenue. With two malls—**Mazza Gallerie** and **Chevy Chase Pavilion**—and lots of freestanding boutiques, there is much browsing and spending to do. Among the shops: *Neiman-Marcus, Jackie Chalkley,* and *Gazelle,* which is a great spot for wearable art, *Joan and David, Pottery Barn, Lord & Taylor, Saks Fifth Avenue, Saks-Jandel* and *Rosendorf-Evans* furriers, *Gucci,* and other couture clothiers (see "Designer Clothing" under "Specialty Shops"). There are also jewelry and antique shops.

■ Bethesda ■

Bethesda, Maryland, which is just beyond Chevy Chase, has become not only one of the major restaurant centers in the Washington area but also a magnet area for fine rugs, art and antiques, books, tobacconists, vintage and consignment clothing (which, in an area as prosperous as this, means everything from faux pearls to furs), and trendy home furnishings. *Urban Country* (7801 Woodmont Avenue; (301) 654-0500) is crammed with painted and gilded furniture, desktop accessories, ceramics, linens, glass, and flatware; they also custom-upholster. *Ancient Rhythms,* about two blocks away (7920 Woodmont; (301) 652-2669) specializes in Southeast Asian and African-style furniture, jewelry, tapestry, and accessories of wood, art paper, and metalwork; similarly opulent and/or "primitive" furnishings from Turkey, Nepal, the Balkans, India, and China fill the nearby *Material Culture* (7920 Norfolk Avenue; (301) 907-3055). And *Bartley Tile Concepts* (6931 Arlington Road; (301) 913-9113) sells hand-painted tiles, marble, and slate, both new and salvaged. The *Washington Antiques Center* Bethesda gallery (6708 Wisconsin Avenue; (301) 654-3798) is a drop-off for more than 40 dealers of European and Asian as well as American fine art, furniture, and jewelry.

Among art galleries are *Allyson Louis* (7200 Wisconsin Avenue; (301) 656-2877); *Capricorn Galleries* (4849 Rugby Avenue; (301) 657-3477); *Marin-Price* (7022 Wisconsin Avenue; (301) 718-0622); and *Turtle Island Gallery* (4901 Auburn Avenue; (301) 986-1992). Particularly fine art glass is available—one might almost say on exhibit—at the *Glass Gallery* (4720 Hampden Lane; (301) 657-3478). *ZYZYX* mix-and-matches art glass and ceramics with better production pieces (10301-A Old Georgetown Road; (301) 493-0297).

■ Capitol Hill ■

On Capitol Hill, most shops are in the vicinity of Eastern Market—an actual market where vendors set up tables selling produce, baked goods, and flea market bric-a-brac—located on 7th Street between Pennsylvania and Independence Avenues, SE. There, amid the restaurants and bars, are secondhand clothing shops and first-rate crafts stores. Around the old Eastern Market building on Eighth just north of Pennsylvania Avenue, you can browse through a variety of antique stores and boutiques, as well as farmers' produce and fresh poultry. There's a pottery co-op upstairs at the Market itself. Closer to the Capitol, *Moon, Blossoms and Snow* stocks unusual gifts such as glass salt-and-pepper shakers shaped like cacti or handpainted dog dishes (225 Pennsylvania Avenue, SE; (202) 543-8181).

■ Old Town Alexandria ■

Old Town Alexandria, Virginia, is a walker's delight, too, with shops clustered up, down, and around King Street, most of them selling antiques, crafts, and home furnishings. Wayne Fisher's *American Design* (114 South Royal Street; (703) 836-6043) specializes in charming old toys, pottery, tools, and painted wood ornaments as well as furniture. *Vanech Interiors* (624-B North Washington Street; (703) 836-4033) sells hand-painted cachepots and vases, wooden screens, and canvas flooring. *Art F/X* (1219 King Street; (703) 519-9412) gilds the lily, so to speak, painting, brushing, and otherwise customizing strong, one-of-a-kind neoclassical furniture and accents.

Other good poking-around spots include *Random Harvest* (1117 King Street; (703) 548-8820), the *Old Colony Shop* (222-B South Washington Street; (703) 548-8008), and *Robert Bentley Adams* (405 South Washington Street; (703) 549-0650).

Specialty Shops

Antiques   Serious antique-seekers get out of town—driving an hour or more to the countryside of Maryland, Virginia, West Virginia, or Pennsylvania for the bargains. Frederick, Maryland, about an hour north of Washington, is particularly popular with area antiquers. The biggest single group is at the 125-dealer **Emporium Antiques** (112 East Patrick Street, Frederick; (301) 662-7099), but walking the Main Street neighborhood and the streets just off it will turn up plenty of others. But you will find treasures—though few bargains—in and around Washington. The largest concentration of such shops is on **"Antique Row"** in Kensington, Maryland, about four miles from the D.C. line. There are more than 50 antique dealers on **Howard Avenue,** with smaller shops east of Connecticut Avenue and larger warehouses west of Connecticut. *Sparrows* (4115 Howard Avenue; (301) 530-0175) specializes in late-eighteenth- to early nineteenth-century French pieces, including fine Deco and Nouveau. *Jantiques* in "Antique Row" (10429 Fawcett Street; (301) 942-0936) offers silver flatware and filigree, fine estate jewelry, and Limoges.

In Georgetown and Alexandria, you'll find a variety of shops selling eighteenth-, nineteenth-, and twentieth-century collectibles. One Georgetown favorite is *Christ Child Opportunity Shop* (1427 Wisconsin Avenue, NW; (202) 333-6635), where, on the second floor, you'll find silver, china, paintings, and other cherishables on consignment from the best Georgetown homes. (See the neighborhood profiles above.)

The best antiques in Alexandria are in **Old Town** along Washington Street and between 4000 King Street; but the **Thieves' Market** in Alexandria (8101 Richmond Highway; (703) 360-4200) has scores of booths with good used rugs, antique furniture, and jewelry.

Art   The city's best selection of art for sale—traditional, modern, and ethnic—can be found around **Dupont Circle.** Your best bet, besides looking along Connecticut Avenue, is to head west off Connecticut onto R Street, where there are a dozen galleries within two blocks.

However, a renaissance of independent artists and co-ops has made the Seventh Street area just north of Pennsylvania Avenue the SoHo of D.C. Among the important stops are the *Zenith Gallery* (413 Seventh Street,

NW; (202) 783-2963), which specializes in photography, new art, and neon; and the *Lansburg Building* (406 Seventh Street, NW), a former department store that has been transformed into a three-story assortment of art and photography spaces.

Another popular source for art is the *Torpedo Factory Art Center* in Old Town Alexandria (105 N. Union Street; (703) 838-4565), where 150 artists in a range of media—painting, sculpture, jewelry, and more—have set up studios. You can buy their work, or simply watch them create.

Bargains Washington may have its million-dollar houses, expense-account restaurants, and pricey private schools, but it also has a surprising number of discount outlets. Savvy shoppers never pay full price for their Coach bags, their Lancôme cosmetics, or their Polo dress shirts.

Some of the best buys are in warehouses buried in industrial parks—not worth a drive unless you know where you're going and you know what you're after. What is worth a trip is **Potomac Mills Mall** in Dale City, VA—one of the world's largest outlet malls. Just 45 minutes south of D.C., off I-95, this 250-store mall (phone (800) VA-MILLS) gets more visitors each year than any other Virginia tourist attraction—more than Colonial Williamsburg. It's nearly impossible to hit all of the stores, which include the popular *IKEA* (Swedish furniture store) and outlets for *Nordstrom, Eddie Bauer, Athlete's Foot, Laura Ashley,* and *Benetton.* And even if you do see them all, it's a short-lived victory; another huge retail center across the highway is in the planning stages.

If you can't make it to Potomac Mills, Washington now has its first inside-the-Beltway off-price mall, **City Place** in Silver Spring, MD (phone (301) 589-1091). At the intersection of Colesville Road (Route 29) and Fenton Street, three blocks north of the Silver Spring Metro (red line), City Place's best assets are *Nordstrom Rack, Marshalls,* and its shoe outlets.

Bookstores It's little wonder Washingtonians are well-read: Almost everywhere you look, there is a bookstore. There are general-interest chains like *B. Dalton* and *Borders,* but the majority are small independents, many with narrow specialties such as art, travel, Russian literature, or mystery.

If you're in a book-browsing mood, you might take the red line to Dupont Circle or the orange line to Farragut West. Between these two Metro stops, along and just off Connecticut Avenue between S and I Streets, are some of the city's best bookstores.

Walking south from S Street, NW, toward Dupont Circle, you'll hit the *Newsroom,* with an exhaustive stock of foreign-language periodicals (1753 Connecticut Avenue, NW; (202) 332-1489); *Mystery Books* (1715 Connecticut Avenue, NW; (202) 483-1600); *Lambda Rising,* a gay/lesbian bookshop (1625 Connecticut Avenue, NW; (202) 462-6969); and *Kramerbooks,* a bookstore and cafe that's quite the scene on weekends, when it's open 24 hours (1517 Connecticut Avenue, NW; (202) 387-1400). Right off the circle on P Street you'll find *Second Story Books,* a terrific source for used books where, for $3, they'll search for any out-of-print edition (2000 P Street, NW; (202) 659-8884); and *Backstage,* which sells scripts and performing arts books (2101 P Street, NW; (202) 775-1488). Down side streets you can seek out *Lammas,* devoted to feminist/gay concerns (1426 21st Street, NW; (202) 775-8218); and *Olsson's Books and Records,* the city's most beloved general-interest book source, with a selective but broad inventory (1307 19th Street, NW; (202) 785-1133). One of the Crown Books' *Supercrown* stores is also on Dupont Circle between New Hampshire Avenue and P Street at about one o'clock (phone (202) 319-1374); it puts the current *New York Times* bestsellers on 40% sale.

Over by Farragut West, you'll find political and business books in *Sidney Kramer* (1825 I Street, NW; (202) 293-2685); volumes on the visual arts at *Franz Bader* (1911 I Street, NW; (202) 337-5440); travel guides at *The Map Store* (1636 I Street, NW; (202) 628-2608); and literary criticism, biography, poetry, and a good general stock, as well as frequent Saturday-afternoon readings at *Chapters* (1512 K Street, NW; (202) 347-5495). There is a fairly large *Borders* on L Street, at 19th, though not as overwhelming as the flagship store in White Flint Mall; and a three-decker *Barnes and Noble* store, one of several recently opened in the Washington area, in Georgetown at M and 21st Streets.

And even Washingtonians tend to overlook the *Government Printing Office Bookstore,* which carries more than 15,000 books and pamphlets as well as books of photographs, and sometimes the real things, from the Library of Congress (710 North Capitol Street; (202) 512-0132).

Two other special bookstores are farther north on Connecticut Avenue, in the neighborhood known as Chevy Chase. *Politics & Prose* specializes in psychology, politics, and the works of local authors—and hosts many of their book-signing parties (5015 Connecticut Avenue, NW; (202) 364-1919). A few blocks away is *Cheshire Cat Children's Bookstore,* a treasure trove for kids and parents, complete with a play area (5512 Connecticut Avenue, NW; (202) 244-3956).

Decorative Arts The south side of M Street between 28th and 30th streets, NW, in Georgetown offers a staggering array of antiques and decorative arts, particularly rich in Art Deco, Art Nouveau, and Moderne pieces. *The Galerie Lareuse* (2820 M Street, NW; (202) 333-5704) is a fine art gallery that specializes in twentieth-century prints and lithographs by Picasso, Miró, etc. At *Justine Mehlman* (2824 M Street, NW; (202) 337-0613), you'll find silver, pewter and glass, and ceramic vases, the majority of them attributed, from Liberty arts and crafts and Nouveau artists; plus fine Victorian rings and earrings, enamel, intaglio, and even Bakelite.

Janis Aldridge, Inc. swings around the corner of 29th and M (2900 M Street, NW; (202) 338-7710), displaying floral paintings and still-lifes, handpainted furniture, tapestry cushions, and folk art as well as fine furniture. *Grafix* (2904 M Street, NW; (202) 342-0610) sells vintage posters—including Art Nouveau and Deco examples, antique hand-tinted maps, and collectible prints and illustration plates. A sort of mini-mall—really just a divided-up townhouse—called the *Georgetown Antique Center* (2918 M Street, NW) features *Michael Getz* (phone (202) 338-3811) and *Cherub Antiques* (phone (202) 337-2224) and gathers a collection of works by such artists and studios as Tiffany, Lalique, Daum, and Icart. Here you can find heavy wrought andirons, ivory-handled fish services and magnifying glasses, cream pitchers and perfume bottles, elegant cocktail shakers, nymphic candelabra, and ornate photo frames. In the back room is the largest collection of silver napkin rings outside a melting pot. *Keith Lipert* (2922 M Street, NW; (202) 965-9736) also displays arts, glass, and silver, but its emphasis is on enamelware, ceramics, and heavier pieces.

Designer Clothing

Maryland Border. In the free-spending '80s, couture clothiers couldn't open shops fast enough in Washington. While the '80s may be gone, most of the boutiques remain. And most are in "Gucci Gulch"—a row of chic shops extending from the 5200 to 5500 blocks of Wisconsin Avenue, from the upper edge of the District of Columbia right into Montgomery County, Maryland. Among the boutiques: *Saks Jandel, Gucci, Hugo Boss, Jaeger, Georgette Klinger, Elizabeth Arden, Cartier, Saks Fifth Avenue, Joan and David,* and *Gianfranco Ferre.*

Virginia. Here, the gold-card crowd heads to **Fairfax Square,** a mall on Leesburg Pike in Tysons Corner that is home to *Tiffany & Company, Gucci, Fendi, Hermes,* and *Louis Vuitton.*

Washington, D.C. In the District, the grand old Willard Hotel on Pennsylvania Avenue, NW, houses a set of shops that includes *Chanel* and *Jackie Chalkley,* good for crafty clothing and art jewelry.

Ethnic goods   Whether it's a dashiki or a Rasta hat you're after, you'll find it in Adams-Morgan. Along 18th Street and Columbia Road, NW, are a number of shops selling clothing and gifts from Africa, South America, Asia, and other foreign lands. Also in Adams-Morgan are numerous mom-and-pops selling the foods of Africa and Latin America.

Insider Shops Although the White House, the House of Representatives, and even Camp David have monogrammed and souvenir merchandise, it's available only to special staff. Outsiders who want to look like Washington insiders do have a few options, however.

The *Tobacco Shop* in the Dirksen Senate office building (1st and C Streets, NE; (202) 224-4416) is open to the public and sells souvenirs emblazoned with the Senate seal. The *NASA Exchange* gift shop (300 E Street, SW; (202) 358-0162) is for astronaut wannabes. It is open 8:15 A.M. to 4 P.M., Monday to Friday (closed during lunch, 1–2 P.M.).

Museum Shops Some of Washington's greatest finds are in its museum gift shops. A museum's orientation is a good guide to its shop's merchandise—prints and art books fill the *National Gallery of Art* shop, model airplanes and other toys of flight are on sale at *Air and Space*.

Some good museum shops are often overlooked by tourists: The *National Building Museum* shop, which sells design-related books, jewelry, and gadgets; the *Arts and Industries* shop, a pretty, Victorian setting stocked with Smithsonian reproductions; the *Department of the Interior Museum's Indian Craft Shop,* which sells one-of-a-kind creations at the museum and in Georgetown Park Mall; the *National Museum of African Art* shop, a bazaar filled with colorful cloth and wooden ceremonial instruments such as hand drums and tambourines; the *Arthur M. Sackler Gallery* shop, with cases full of brass Buddhas, Chinese lacquerware, jade and jasper jewelry, and porcelain; the *Renwick* shop, which stocks unusual art jewelry; and the newly expanded shop at the *John F. Kennedy Center for the Performing Arts,* stocked with videos, opera glasses, and other gifts for performing arts lovers.

Political Memorabilia If you're a serious collector, no doubt you already know about stores selling political buttons and ribbons, autographed letters and photos, commemorative plates and pens. If you're not a collector, these shops can be as fun to browse through as museums, except that you can touch things, buy them, and take them home. Two such shops, within walking distance of one another, are *Capitol Coin and Stamp* (1701 L Street, NW; (202) 296-0400) and *Political Americana* (685 15th Street, NW; (202) 547-1871), which also has a branch inside Union Station. The feminist and liberal outlook is more broadly represented at the *NOW Store* (1615 K Street, NW; (202) 467-6980), which stocks scores of T-shirts with political and socially conscious slogans, many of them quite funny, along with buttons and bumper stickers. A more somber annex salutes the Names Project, which is an AIDS memorial, and has some shirts and buttons of its own.

Oriental Rugs Washington, D.C., offers the broadest selection of handmade oriental rugs available in the United States. In fact, there is so much competition here that prices are forced below what you would expect to pay for comparable quality in other American cities. Though shops are sprinkled all around the greater Washington area, the greatest concentration of stores is located on Wisconsin Avenue from Friendship Heights to Bethesda.

Salon Products EFX in Georgetown (3059 M Street, NW; (202) 965-1300) is a Merle Norman for the '90s, stocked with custom creams, exotic oils, and lipsticks named for film stars. Even more "now" is *Better Botanicals* (3066 M Street, NW; (202) 625-2440), the Aveda of D.C. *BB* offers body products from toners to massage oils, all made of only plant products—no artificial scents or coloring and no animal testing, either—and scented by the likes of rosemary, cinnamon, sesame and almond oils, coconut, and coriander. The staff can even help you customize your purchases. Soaps, bath salts, facial steams, and oils are available by the ounce as well as the bottle.

Wine and Gourmet Foods *Mayflower Wines* joined forces with the *Sutton Place Gourmet* shops in 1992 to provide one-stop, fine-food shops in the greater Washington area. Each shop offers an excellent selection of wines and an impressive variety of gourmet and ethnic foods. The wine buyers travel abroad each year to select the stores' wine inventory and are particularly tuned in to Italian reds. Visitors to the stores from outside the District, Virginia, and Maryland can buy wine and have it shipped home. If you do not have time to shop in person, the Sutton Place Gourmet publishes a newsletter describing highly touted (and reasonably priced) wines. The newsletter also includes recipes. To receive the free newsletter call (202) 363-5800.

Another fine wine store, which invests in wine futures and offers a strong catalog, is *MacArthur Liquors* (4877 MacArthur Boulevard, NW; (202) 338-1433) in the Palisades neighborhood west of Georgetown. It's worth remembering that because of tax laws, wine for consumption is less expensive in stores like this within the District than in stores just over the border in Maryland or Virginia. Originally owned by the well-liked purveyor, Addy Bassin's *MacArthur* is still often called "Bassin's" by Washington natives.

The family that brought you Crown Books and Trak Auto also owns a mega-wine and liquor warehouse line called *Total Beverage,* which has three Virginia stores, including one at the already bargain-heavy Potomac Mills. However, unless you plan to purchase in real bulk, you may do just as well in town.

Writing Implements *Fahrney's* (1430 G Street, NW; (202) 628-9525) has all the write stuff: For more than 70 years Fahrney's has sold nothing but beautiful pens, including Watermans and Montblancs. White Flint Mall has a smaller shop but one well-versed in the instant unblocking of recalcitrant fountain pens, *Bertram's Inkwell.*

PART NINE

Sight-Seeing Tips and Tours

Plan before You Leave Home

There are several good reasons why you should take the time to do some planning before coming to Washington to tour its sights. First of all, Washington is a big, sprawling city that covers a lot of real estate. The National Mall, for example, is two miles long—and there's more to Washington beyond that long expanse of green. Spending a poorly planned day traipsing back and forth from monument to museum to federal building to monument can waste a lot of time, energy, and shoe leather.

But it's not only Washington's physical size that makes planning a must: It's the mind-boggling number of tourist attractions that are available. Even if your vacation is a week long, be prepared to make some hard choices about how many sights you can fit into your itinerary. If your visit is shorter, say only two or three days, it's even more imperative that you have a firm idea of what you want to see. Attempting to see too much during your allotted time is exhausting: Your visit becomes a blur of marble monuments and big rooms. As with most large-scale projects, a little research can go a long way in making your trip more pleasurable.

Our recommendation is to do some soul-searching and try to reach some decisions about what your interests are before you leave for Washington. Are you curious about how the government spends all your tax money? Have you always wanted to gaze up at the solemn figure of Lincoln in his marble memorial? Do you love antiques? Are you a military buff? Does technology fascinate you? Do you love exploring art museums? Gardens? Historical houses? Washington offers places to explore for people with all these interests. Yet neither this guide nor any other can tell you what your interests are. You gotta do your homework.

D.C. Information Services	
Washington, D.C., Convention and Visitors Association	(202) 789-7000
Washington, D.C., Accommodations	(202) 289-2220 or toll-free (800) 503-3338
International Visitor Information Center	(202) 939-5566
American Express Travel Service	(202) 457-1300
Smithsonian activities	(202) 357-2020

Some more advice: To help winnow your choices, get as much written information as you can before you leave—and read it. To supplement this guide, you can get information concerning Washington tourist attractions, hotels, and recreation at the public library and travel agencies, or by calling or writing any of the sources listed in the box.

Web surfers and the computer literate will be glad to know that Washington now has its own Website. It offers a comprehensive guide to D.C. hotels that's searchable by location and price, restaurants searchable by neighborhood, tour information, and a quarterly calendar of special events and festivals. The Internet address is http://www.washington.org.

■ Thinking in Categories ■

Visitors to Washington are often thrown into large groups of tourists as they visit famous and popular edifices such as the U.S. Capitol, the Washington Monument, and the White House. Unless you've made prior arrangements for a VIP tour or Uncle Milt is a congressional staffer, you'll be craning your neck under the Capitol dome with 49 other tourists as you listen to your tour guide's spiel. Our advice: Go with the flow, relax, and enjoy the tour. But not everything you do while in Washington has to turn into a group traipse.

Question: How do you avoid the big crowds that clog the major tourist attractions?

Answer: By organizing your visit around things that interest you.

By charting your own course, you get off the beaten track and visit places that offer higher-quality tours than the canned presentations given in the better-known attractions. Often, you find yourself visiting places with small groups of people who share your interests. In short, you have more fun.

By following your own interests, you can make some intriguing discoveries as you visit Washington:

- a collection of miniature Revolutionary soldiers fighting a mock battle (Anderson House)

- a four-sided, colonial-era mousetrap that guillotines rodents (Daughters of the American Revolution building);

- a tropical rain forest located just off the Mall (Organization of American States building);

- a space capsule you can climb into (Navy Museum);

- Fabergé eggs encrusted with diamonds (Hillwood Museum);

- the tomb of the only president buried in Washington (National Cathedral);

- a garden filled with flowers mentioned in the plays of William Shakespeare (the Folger Shakespeare Library);

- a building where scientists and engineers track satellites orbiting the earth (Goddard Space Flight Center); and

- a pub that shows how typical colonial-era Americans lived (Gadsby's Tavern).

As you travel around Washington, you'll discover sights like these and many others that most visitors miss. To help you on your way, we've selected major categories and listed the best destinations for visitors to explore. As you read the list, keep in mind that many attractions overlap. For example, the National Air and Space Museum appeals to both technology and military buffs, while the Woodrow Wilson House is interesting to history fans, lovers of the decorative arts, and folks curious about how the high and mighty conducted their day-to-day lives in the 1920s.

Government

Bureau of Engraving and Printing	U.S. Department of the Treasury
Federal Bureau of Investigation	U.S. Supreme Court
Old Executive Office Building	Voice of America
U.S. Capitol	White House

Monuments and Memorials

Arlington Cemetery
Black Revolutionary War
    Patriots Memorial
Franklin Delano Roosevelt
    Memorial
U.S. Holocaust Memorial
    Museum
Freedom Park (Rosslyn, Virginia)
Iwo Jima Memorial
Kennedy Center

Korean War Veterans Memorial
Lincoln and Jefferson Memorials
National Law Enforcement
    Officers Memorial
Navy Memorial
Vietnam Veterans
    Memorial
Washington Monument
Women in Vietnam
    Memorial

Historic Places

Arlington House
Chesapeake and Ohio Canal
Decatur House
Ford's Theatre
Frederick Douglass House
Georgetown
Mount Vernon

Old Stone House
Old Town Alexandria
The Octagon
U.S. Capitol
White House
Woodrow Wilson House

Art Museums

Art Museum of the Americas (at
    the Organization of American
    States)
Corcoran Gallery of Art
Dumbarton Oaks
Freer Gallery of Art
Hirshhorn Museum and Sculpture
    Garden
National Gallery of Art

National Museum of African
    Art
National Museum of Women
    in the Arts
National Portrait Gallery
Phillips Collection
Renwick Gallery
Sackler Gallery

History

Anacostia Museum
Arlington House
Bethune Museum and Archives
Chesapeake and Ohio Canal
Decatur House
Folger Shakespeare Library
Georgetown

Lincoln Museum (in Ford's
    Theatre)
Mount Vernon
National Air and Space
    Museum
National Archives
National Cryptologic Museum

National Museum of American
  History
National Portrait Gallery
Newseum (Rosslyn, Virginia)

Old Town Alexandria
Pentagon
U.S. Holocaust Memorial
  Museum

Technology

Arts and Industry Building
Goddard Space Flight Center
National Air and Space Museum
National Building Museum
National Cryptologic Museum
National Museum of American
  History

National Museum of Health
  and Medicine
National Postal Museum
Newseum (Rosslyn, Virginia)
Washington Navy Yard

Children

Bureau of Engraving and Printing
Capital Children's Museum
Federal Bureau of Investigation
Museum of Natural History
National Air and Space Museum
National Aquarium
National Geographic Society's
  Explorers Hall
National Museum of
  American History

National Postal Museum
National Wildlife Visitor
  Center
National Zoological Park
Old Post Office Pavilion
Washington Monument
Washington Navy Yard

Decorative Arts and Antiques

Anderson House
Christian Heurich Mansion
Daughters of the American
  Revolution Museum and
  Period Rooms
Decatur House
Dumbarton Oaks
Hillwood Museum
Mount Vernon
The Octagon

Old Town Alexandria
Textile Museum
Tudor Place
U.S. Department of State
  Diplomatic Reception
  Rooms
U.S. Department of the
  Treasury
White House

Gardens

Bishops Garden at Washington
  National Cathedral

Constitution Gardens
Dumbarton Oaks

Enid A. Haupt Garden (behind the Castle on the Mall)
Folger Shakespeare Library
Franciscan Monastery
Hillwood Museum
Kenilworth Aquatic Gardens

Meridian International Center
Mount Vernon
National Arboretum
Tudor Place
U.S. Botanic Garden

Military

Anderson House
Arlington National Cemetery
Black Revolutionary War Patriots Memorial
Iwo Jima Memorial
National Air and Space Museum
National Cryptologic Museum

Pentagon
Smithsonian's Garber Facility*
U.S. Navy Memorial
Vietnam Veterans Memorial
Washington Navy Yard
Women in Vietnam Memorial

Science

Arts and Industries Building
NASA/Goddard Space Flight Visitor Center
National Academy of Sciences
National Air and Space Museum
National Aquarium
National Cryptologic Museum
National Geographic Society's Explorers Hall

National Museum of American History
National Museum of Health and Medicine
National Museum of Natural History
National Wildlife Visitor Center
U.S. Naval Observatory

Architecture

Constitution Hall
Daughters of the American Revolution Museum
Hirshhorn Museum
House of the Temple
Kennedy Center
Library of Congress (Jefferson Building)
Meridian International Center
National Archives

National Building Museum
National Gallery of Art (East Building)
National Postal Museum
Old Executive Office Building
Old Post Office Pavilion
Pentagon
U.S. Capitol
U.S. Department of the Treasury

*A storehouse for the National Air and Space Museum that houses aircraft from both World Wars.

U.S. Supreme Court
Union Station
Washington Monument

Washington National
   Cathedral

Places of Worship

Adas Israel Synagogue at the
   Lillian and Albert Small
   Jewish Museum
Franciscan Monastery
National Shrine of the
   Immaculate Conception

St. John's Episcopal Church
   (across from the White
   House)
Islamic Center
Washington National
   Cathedral

African-Americans

Anacostia Museum
Arts and Industries Building
   (Smithsonian)
Bethune Museum and Archives
Black Revolutionary War Patriots
   Memorial
Frederick Douglass House (Cedar
   Hill)

Lincoln Memorial
National Museum of
   African Art
National Museum of
   American Art

Great Views

Arlington House (Arlington
   National Cemetery)
Iwo Jima Memorial
Kennedy Center
Lincoln and Jefferson Memorials

Mount Vernon
Old Post Office Pavilion
Washington Monument
Washington National
   Cathedral

Outdoors

Chesapeake and Ohio Canal
Great Falls Park
Mount Vernon Trail
National Wildlife Visitor Center

Potomac Park
Rock Creek Park
Roosevelt Island

Great Places to Walk When You're Sick of Museums

Cathedral Avenue between
   Connecticut Avenue and
   Washington National Cathedral
anywhere along Connecticut
   Avenue

Dupont Circle
Embassy Row (Massachusetts
   Avenue northwest of
   Dupont Circle)
Fort McNair and the Southwest

waterfront
Georgetown
Kenilworth Aquatic Gardens
The Mall
National Arboretum

National Zoo
the bike path along the
 Potomac from the Kennedy
 Center to Georgetown

■ Putting Your Congressperson to Work ■

A letter to a representative or senator well in advance of your trip (six months is not too early) can bring a cornucopia of free goodies your way: reservations on VIP tours of the White House, the Supreme Court, the FBI, and the Bureau of Engraving and Printing that can save you hours of time waiting in line, as well as getting you on longer, more informative tours. In addition, your eager-to-please congressperson (he or she wants your vote) can provide timely information about hotels, restaurants, shopping, and special events. It's all free. Just be sure to include the exact dates of your visit.

Here's why you must send off your letter as soon as you know the dates that you'll be in Washington: Senators and House members are limited in the number of spaces on VIP tours they can provide to constituents. Since all the legislators get the same number of passes, reason dictates that the farther away your state is from Washington, D.C., the better chance you have of getting on a coveted VIP tour. For example, Maryland legislators, some of whose constituents can literally jump on the Metro to reach D.C., are often booked five and six months in advance for the popular White House VIP tours. But if you're from South Dakota, chances are your congressperson will be able to get you reservations during your visit.

There is a downside to the VIP tours: Some of them take place very early, usually before the regular, nonreserved tours begin. For example, VIP White House tours are scheduled at 8 A.M., 8:15 A.M., and 8:45 A.M.; Bureau of Engraving and Printing VIP tours depart at 8 A.M. Monday through Friday. The upside: If you're touring in the spring and summer, you've already resigned yourself to early starts to beat the worst of the crowds anyway. Another myth shattered: The VIP tour of the White House still requires waiting in line. But the tour is longer and, unlike the unreserved version, guided.

How do you reserve a VIP tour? Write a letter to your senator or representative at his or her home office or the one in Washington. For senators, the Washington address is U.S. Senate, Washington, D.C. 20510. For House members, address your letter to the U.S. House of Representatives, Washington, D.C. 20515. Again, don't forget to include the dates you'll be visiting Washington.

A Sample Letter

25 October 1997

The Honorable (your congressperson or senator's name)
U.S. House of Representatives (or U.S. Senate)
Washington, D.C. 20515 (or 20510 for the Senate)

Dear Mr. or Ms. Congressperson,

During the week of [fill in your vacation date] my family and I will be visiting Washington to tour the major attractions on the Mall, Capitol Hill, and downtown. I understand your office can make reservations on VIP tours for constituents.

Specifically, I would like tours for the White House, the Bureau of Engraving and Printing, and the FBI during that week. I'll need four reservations for each tour. If at all possible, please schedule our tours in the middle of our week.

In addition, I'd appreciate any other touring information on Washington you can send me. Thanks in advance for your help.

Yours truly,
[Your name]

■ Operating Hours ■

By and large, Washington's major attractions keep liberal operating hours, making it easy for visitors to plan their itineraries without worrying about odd opening and closing times. There are, however, a few exceptions. Of all the major tourist attractions, the Bureau of Engraving and Printing and the White House keep the weirdest hours: both close in the afternoon (the White House at noon), and neither is open seven days a week.

Smithsonian museums are open every day from 10 A.M. to 5:30 P.M. During the summer, hours may be extended into the evening if operating budgets allow. The U.S. Capitol is open from 9 A.M. to 4:30 P.M. daily (with longer evening hours during the summer, budgets allowing); the Bureau of Engraving and Printing allows visitors to view its money-printing operation Monday through Friday from 9 A.M. to 2 P.M. and again from 5 P.M. to 7:30 P.M. in the summer (a free time-ticket system is in effect in the spring and summer); and the White House is open from Tuesday through Saturday from 10 A.M. to noon. (You need to arrive at the new White House Visitors Center before 7:30 A.M. to get a free time ticket.)

Most monuments, on the other hand, are open 24 hours a day. Our recommendation is to visit the Lincoln and Jefferson Memorials after dark. Lit up by floodlights, the marble edifices appear to float in the darkness, and the Reflecting Pool and Tidal Basin dramatically reflect the light. It's much more impressive than by day—and a lot less crowded. The Washington Monument now has a time-ticket system that eliminates long lines; during the spring and summer, when the monument remains open until midnight, the ticket system is scrapped after 8 P.M.

While many sights are open every day, a lot of Washington attractions close on federal holidays: January 1, Martin Luther King Day (the third Monday in January), Presidents' Day, Memorial Day, Independence Day, Labor Day (the first Monday in September), Columbus Day (the second Monday in October), Veterans Day, Thanksgiving, and Christmas Day (when virtually everything except outdoor monuments and Mount Vernon is closed).

■ **Rhythms of the City** ■

Although it's impossible to be specific, the ebb and flow of crowds follows a pattern throughout the day and the week at major tourist attractions. By being aware of the general patterns, you can sometimes avoid the worst of the crowds, traffic congestion, and long lines.

Mornings are slow, and the quietest time to visit most museums and sights is when they open. As lunchtime approaches, the number of people visiting a popular attraction begins to pick up, peaking around 3 P.M. Then the crowds begin to thin, and after 4 P.M. things start to get quiet again. It follows that the best times to visit a wildly popular place like the National Air and Space Museum is just after it opens and just before it closes. Conversely, when the crowds are jamming the Museum of Natural History during the middle of the day, expand your cultural horizons with a visit to the Sackler and Freer Galleries, or the National Museum of African Art. They are rarely, if ever, crowded.

Among days of the week, Monday, Tuesday, and Wednesday see the lowest number of visitors. If you must visit the Washington Monument, the Bureau of Engraving and Printing, the National Air and Space Museum, the National Museum of American History, and the National Museum of Natural History, try to do so early in the week. Attempt to structure your week so that Thursday, Friday, and the weekend are spent visiting sights that are away from the Mall.

■ **If You Visit during Peak Tourist Season** ■

The key to missing the worst of the crowds in spring and summer is to get a hotel close to a Metro station, park the car, and leave it. Then decide what is most important for you to see, and get to those places early.

An example: You've miraculously secured a convenient D.C. hotel room in early April. From your in-town window, Washington is laid out before you—and for most of the day, it's a view of gridlocked motor coaches, school buses, families in cars, angry commuters, and jammed sidewalks. Everybody but the commuters is drawn by the Japanese cherry trees in bloom along the Tidal Basin and the Reflecting Pool on the Mall.

But don't rush out the door and join the throngs on their way to see the trees. Because it's early (say, 7 A.M.), your plan is to hit the sights that you want to see before the crowds arrive. So walk to the nearby Metro station and take the train to the Smithsonian station. From there, it's a 10-minute stroll to the Washington Monument—and at 7:30, you're near the front of the line when the kiosk that distributes time tickets opens. By 9 A.M., you're out of the marble obelisk and on your way to the nearby Bureau of Engraving and Printing. At the ticket office on Raoul Wallenberg Place, pick up a time ticket for a tour of the money-printing facility that begins at 1:30 P.M. From there, it's a short walk to the Jefferson Memorial and those famous trees.

At 10 A.M, you stroll toward the Mall for a visit to the National Air and Space Museum as it opens. At 10:15, you join a free, guided tour. At 11 A.M., you're back on your own again to explore some corners of the museum that interest you.

By noon, the crowds are starting to fill the museum, so you leave Air and Space in search of a bite to eat. If it's a weekday, L'Enfant Plaza, only one subway stop away from the Smithsonian station, has a wide array of eateries. Then it's an easy walk to the Bureau of Engraving and Printing to see the stacks of money.

By 2 P.M., you have already visited three of the world's most popular attractions during peak season with almost no waiting in line. Now, you can spend the afternoon exploring a wide range of attractions that never get crowded, even when Washington is besieged by tourists in the spring: the Freer Gallery, the Hirshhorn Museum, the Vietnam Veterans Memorial, the Corcoran Gallery, or the DAR Museum, just to name a few.

■ Intragroup Touring Incompatibility: ■
What It Is and How to Avoid It

The incidence of "Intragroup Touring Incompatibility" (members of the same group having strongly conflicting interests or touring objectives) is high in Washington, thanks to the city's wide variety of touring attractions. An example: Some people would be happy never to leave the National Air and Space Museum; a lot of other folks find that, after an hour or two of staring at old airplanes and spacecraft, it's time to move on.

Children, at the other extreme, haven't the patience or inclination for all the reading required by the exhibits and fizzle out after a couple of hours of touring D.C. museums. In fact, even grown-ups should consider a touring plan that puts reading-intensive attractions such as self-guided museum tours at the beginning of the day, and take guided tours in the afternoon, where you're spoon-fed information by a guide and you can put your brain on autopilot.

A touring plan made up before your arrival in Washington can help your group avoid the worst manifestations of intragroup incompatibility. If your group contains, for example, a real "Rocket George," let him linger at the National Air and Space Museum while the rest of you move on to another Mall attraction. Arrange a meeting place later in the day where you can all regroup; both you and Rocket George will be happier.

Washington with Children

Most adult visitors to Washington experience a rush of thrill and pride on viewing the U.S. Capitol, the Washington Monument, and the White House. And, for most of us, those are feelings that hold up well over repeat visits to the nation's capital. In fact, a fascination for the city often begins on a first visit to Washington in grade or high school and can continue through adulthood.

So it follows that Washington is one of the most interesting, beautiful, and stimulating cities in the world for children and young people. Where else can kids visit the president's house, touch a moon rock, feed a tarantula, and view a city from the top of a 555-foot marble obelisk?

Luckily, most popular Washington tourist destinations for kids offer a lot to hold an adult's attention, too—which means you don't have to worry about parking the kids someplace while you tour a museum. For example, as your kids marvel at the dinosaur skeletons in the Museum of Natural History or feed that giant spider, you can be fantasizing over the Hope Diamond. Even so, on a Washington vacation with small children, anticipation is the name of the game. Here are some things you need to consider:

Age   Although the big buildings, spaciousness, and excitement of Washington excite children of all ages, and while there are specific sights that delight toddlers and preschoolers, Washington's attractions are generally oriented to older kids and adults. We believe that children should be a fairly mature nine years old to get the most out of popular attractions such as the National Museum of Natural History, the U.S. Capitol, and the White House, and a year or two older to get much out of the art galleries, monuments, and other federal buildings around town.

Time of Year to Visit   If there is any way to swing it, avoid the hot, crowded summer months. Try to go in late September through November or mid-April through mid-June. If you have children of varying ages and your school-age kids are good students, consider taking the older ones out of school so you can visit during the cooler, less-congested off-season. Arrange special study assignments relating to the many educational aspects of Washington. If your school-age children are not great students and cannot afford to miss any school, take your vacation as soon as the school year ends in late May or early June. Nothing, repeat, nothing will enhance your Washington vacation as much as avoiding the early spring and summer months.

Building Naps and Rest into Your Itinerary   Washington is huge and offers more attractions than you can possibly see in a week, so don't try to see everything in one day. Tour in the early morning and return to your hotel midday for a swim (if your hotel has a pool; see below) and a nice nap. Even during the fall and winter, when the crowds are smaller and the temperature more pleasant, the sheer size of D.C. will exhaust most children under eight by lunchtime. Go back and visit more attractions in the late afternoon and early evening.

Where to Stay   The time and hassle involved in commuting to and from downtown Washington and its surrounding neighborhoods will be lessened if you can afford to stay inside the District and near a Metro station. But even if, for financial or other reasons, you lodge outside of Washington, it remains imperative that you get small children off of the Mall for a few hours to rest and recuperate. Neglecting to relax and unwind is the best way we know to get the whole family in a snit and ruin the day (or the entire vacation).

With small children, there is simply no excuse for not planning ahead. Make sure you get a hotel, in or out of Washington, within a few minutes' walk to a Metro station. Naps and relief from the frenetic pace of touring Washington, even in the off-season, are indispensable. While it's true that you can gain some measure of peace by finding a quiet spot near the Tidal Basin to relax, there is no substitute for returning to the familiarity and security of your own hotel. Regardless of what you have heard or read, children too large to sleep in a stroller will not relax and revive unless you get them back to your room.

Another factor in choosing a hotel is whether or not it has a swimming pool. A lot of visitors to D.C. assume that, like those in most destinations, Washington hotels automatically come with a pool. Alas, it ain't necessarily so. A swimming pool, especially in warmer weather, can be a lifesaver for both you and your kids. So if a refreshing dip is important to your family, be sure to ask before making hotel reservations.

Be in Touch with Your Feelings   While we acknowledge that a Washington vacation can be a capital investment (pardon the pun), remember that having fun is not necessarily the same as seeing everything. When you and your children start getting tired and irritable, call time out and regroup. Trust your instincts. What would really feel best right now? Another museum, a rest break with some ice cream, going back to the room for a nap? *The way to protect your investment is to stay happy and have a good time, whatever that takes.* You do not have to meet a quota for experiencing every museum on the Mall, seeing every branch of government, walking through every monument, or anything else. It's your vacation; you can do what you want.

Least Common Denominators   Remember the old saying about a chain being only as strong as its weakest link? The same logic applies to a family touring Washington. Somebody is going to run out of steam first; when they do, the whole family will be affected. Sometimes a cold Coke and a rest break will get the flagging member back into gear. Sometimes, however, as Marshall Dillon would say, "You just need to get out of Dodge." Pushing the tired or discontented beyond their capacity is like driving on a flat tire: It may get you a few more miles down the road but you will be sorry in the long run. Accept that energy levels vary among individuals and be prepared to respond to small children or other members of your group who poop out. *Hint:* "After we've driven a thousand miles to take you to Washington, you're going to ruin everything!" is not the right thing to say.

Setting Limits and Making Plans   The best way to avoid arguments and disappointments is to develop a game plan before you go. Establish some general guidelines for the day and get everybody committed in advance. Be sure to include:

1. Wake-up time and breakfast plans.

2. What time you need to depart for the part of Washington you plan to explore.

3. What you need to take with you.

4. A policy for splitting the group up or for staying together.

5. A plan for what to do if the group gets separated or someone is lost.

6. How long you intend to tour in the morning and what you want to see, including fall-back plans in the event an attraction is too crowded.

7. A policy on what you can afford for snacks, lunch, and refreshments.

8. A target time for returning to your hotel for a rest.

9. What time you will return to touring D.C. and how late you will stay.

10. Plans for dinner.

11. A policy for shopping and buying souvenirs, including who pays: Mom and Dad or the kids.

Be Flexible   Having a game plan does not mean forgoing spontaneity or sticking rigidly to the itinerary. Once again, listen to your intuition. Alter the plan if the situation warrants. Be prepared to roll with the punches.

Overheating, Sunburn, and Dehydration   In the worst of Washington's hot and humid summers, the most common problems of smaller children are overheating, sunburn, and dehydration. A small bottle of sunscreen carried in a pocket or fanny pack will help you take precautions against overexposure to the sun. Be sure to put some on children in strollers, even if the stroller has a canopy. Some of the worst cases of sunburn we have seen were on the exposed foreheads and feet of toddlers and infants in strollers. To avoid overheating, rest at regular intervals in the shade or in an air-conditioned museum, hotel lobby, or federal building.

Do not count on keeping small children properly hydrated with soft drinks and water fountain stops. Long lines often make buying refreshments problematic, and water fountains are not always handy. What's more, excited children may not inform you or even realize that they're thirsty or overheated. We recommend renting a stroller for children six years old and under, and carrying plastic water bottles.

Blisters   Blisters and sore feet are common for visitors of all ages, so wear comfortable, well-broken-in shoes and two pairs of thin socks (preferable to one pair of thick socks). If you or your children are unusually susceptible to blisters, carry some precut Moleskin bandages; they offer the best possible protection, stick great, and won't sweat off. When you feel a hot spot, stop, air out your foot, and place a Moleskin over the area before a blister forms. Moleskin is available by name at all drugstores. Sometimes small children won't tell their parents about a developing blister until it's too late. We recommend inspecting the feet of preschoolers two or more times a day.

Health and Medical Care   If you have a child who requires medication, pack plenty, and bring it in a carry-on bag if you're flying to Washington. A bottle of liquid Dramamine will come in handy to fight off car sickness

Major D.C. Hospitals
George Washington University Medical Center 901 23rd Street, NW (202) 994-1000   Georgetown University Medical Center 3800 Reservoir Road, NW (202) 784-2000 Children's National Medical Center 111 Michigan Avenue, NW (202) 745-5000

or motion sickness, which can affect kids who are normally fine in a car but may get sick in a plane, train, or boat.

A small first-aid kit, available at most pharmacies, will handle most minor cuts, scrapes, and splinters and is easy to pack. Grown-up and children's strength aspirin or Tylenol, a thermometer, cough syrup, baby wipes, a plastic spoon, a night light, and pacifiers will round out a small kit of health-related items for people traveling with children or infants.

Be sure to carry proof of insurance and policy numbers with you. Check with friends or relatives before you leave for Washington to get the name of a pediatrician who practices locally; it could save a lot of time thumbing through the yellow pages if a youngster should fall ill. For emergency treatment, dial 911 or go to the emergency room of the nearest hospital.

Sunglasses If you want your smaller children to wear sunglasses, it's a good idea to affix a strap or string to the frames so the glasses won't get lost and can hang from the child's neck while indoors.

If You Become Separated Before venturing out of your hotel room, sit down with your kids and discuss what they should do if they get separated from you while touring a museum, monument, or federal building. Tell them to find a uniformed guard and ask for help. Point out that the main entrance of most Washington attractions has an information desk where they should go if they temporarily get separated.

We suggest that children under age eight be color-coded by dressing them in purple T-shirts or equally distinctive attire. It is also a good idea to sew a label into each child's shirt that states his or her name, your name, and the name of your hotel. The same thing can be accomplished less elegantly by writing the information on a strip of masking tape: Hotel security professionals suggest that the information be printed in small letters and that

The Ten Most Popular Sights for Children
1. National Air and Space Museum
2. National Zoo
3. The Capital Children's Museum
4. National Museum of Natural History
5. Bureau of Engraving and Printing
6. Federal Bureau of Investigation
7. National Museum of American History
8. National Geographic Society's Explorers Hall
9. Washington Navy Yard
10. Washington Monument

the tape be affixed to the outside of the child's shirt five inches or so below the armpit.

Rainy Days Rainy days and Mondays can get you down—even while on vacation—and cooped-up children suffer even worse. Museums and galleries are obvious choices during inclement weather (as you can tell from the crowds), but don't rule out some other options to keep children entertained when the sun doesn't shine or if you're museumed-out. Catch a movie at Union Station's nine-screen cinema complex or take the Metro to Alexandria's Torpedo Factory, where 150 craftsmen work and sell their creations Tuesday through Sunday. And don't forget that age-old panacea for boredom—shopping. Union Station, the Old Post Office Pavilion, the Shops at National Place, and Georgetown Park are all indoor shopping centers with interesting specialty stores. If you run out of ideas, check the *Washington Post* "Weekend" section for inspiration.

The Ten Least Popular Sights for Children
1. National Gallery of Art–West Building
2. Library of Congress
3. U.S. Supreme Court
4. Pentagon
5. Kennedy Center
6. Dumbarton Oaks museum
7. National Portrait Gallery
8. Folger Shakespeare Library
9. Textile Museum
10. Renwick Gallery

Of course, some attractions can bore active kids to tears—even if it's raining outside. An entire afternoon in the National Gallery of Art can be deadly to eight-year-olds. The best plan is to reward your youngsters for their patience with a trip to someplace really special when the weather clears. The National Zoo should top the list. And you'll enjoy it, too.

A final tip that can help you and your kids weather a storm: Stay in a hotel with a pool; on rainy days, kids love getting wet indoors.

Touring

With only a few exceptions (such as the FBI), it isn't absolutely necessary to join a group tour while visiting Washington's attractions. Simply explore on your own, letting your curiosity and interests be your guide. This strategy works well in a large museum such as the National Museum of Natural History—dinosaur skeletons? an insect zoo? the Hope Diamond? Take your pick. At selected locations, though, it can be a nice change of pace to have an expert lead you by the hand and—who knows?—even enlighten you. What follows is a highly arbitrary list of guided tours that the authors of the *Unofficial Guide* think do a splendid job at introducing visitors to their respective attractions. For more addresses and phone numbers for the following attractions, see the listings in Part Ten.

1. U.S. Department of State Diplomatic Reception Rooms   One of the advantages of taking tours that require advance reservations is that the tour guides are top-notch. The guide we encountered on this tour of the $90 million rooms housed on the eighth floor of this otherwise humdrum building really knows her stuff, from the art on the walls to the historical significance of the impressive furniture that fills these spectacular, ornate rooms.

2. U.S. Capitol   While the "introductory" tour offered every 10 minutes to groups of 50 may not be the best way to get a feel for this magnificent building, it's a good start. Stick close to your guide so you can hear his or her comments about the artwork on display and the history of the building. Afterwards, you can go back on your own and visit the rooms and chambers you missed on the tour. *Warning:* This is a confusing building, and most people manage to get lost.

3. Washington National Cathedral   While this is an easy place to just wander around in, don't: Take the free tour. The docent (or museum guide) who led my group of out-of-towners showed enthusiasm, a real concern for her charges, and a deep knowledge of the cathedral. She also mentioned the free organ demonstration that followed the tour, which I stayed for. It turned out to be the highlight of my day.

4. Library of Congress   This tour is led by a knowledgeable tour guide who takes your group to the Jefferson Building's magnificent Main Reading Room, one of the most beautiful interiors in D.C. And don't miss the 12-minute video that explains the mission of the world's largest library.

5. Daughters of the American Revolution (DAR) Museum and Period Rooms   My tour of the period rooms (there are 33, but no one sees them all on one tour) was led by a poised young woman who really knew her history—and her decorative arts. She also was well informed on the handsome building that serves as DAR headquarters: A special railroad spur was built to bring the massive, solid-marble columns on the front of the building to the site. For antique lovers, this tour is about two hours of bliss.

6. The Phillips Collection   The 45-minute tour highlights the best items in the modern art collection and puts them in the context of the wealthy collector who founded the museum. The guides know their art and manage to tie together different art periods as they talk about the paintings. The comfortable Phillips is a welcome contrast to Mall megamuseums. Guided tours are free and offered on Wednesdays and Saturdays.

7. Hillwood Museum   My only complaint about this reservation-only tour was its length—two hours. But it will fascinate anyone interested in the decorative arts, antiques, jewelry, porcelains, paintings, furniture . . . the list goes on. It's a breathtaking collection, and you'll tour in small groups led by knowledgeable guides. *Note:* Hillwood closes in December 1997 for renovations, and re-opens in late 1999.

8. Old Executive Office Building   Here's another reservation-only tour that gives visitors that "insider" feel. The exterior of this huge, nineteenth-century palace is considered a monstrosity by many, but its recently renovated interior is magnificent. The elevators still need work, though—nervous types may not enjoy the part where you jump up and down to get the doors to close.

9. U.S. Department of the Treasury   This reservation-only, behind-the-scenes tour lets visitors feel like they're really seeing something special. The interior of the building was recently renovated: The tour takes you through sumptuous offices and corridors restored to their mid-nineteenth-century opulence.

10. The Voice of America (VOA)   I liked this small, off-the-beaten-track tour. Most of the visitors who go are from foreign countries and listen to Voice of America broadcasts at home. (Listening to the VOA in the United States requires a shortwave radio.) You'll also see a four-panel mural painted by noted artist Ben Shahn in the early 1940s. And the broadcast studios are really neat.

11. Arlington National Cemetery   Tourmobile does a good job of transporting visitors around 612-acre Arlington National Cemetery. The thought of trying to see all the sights in the cemetery on foot makes my feet hurt. The bus stops at the Kennedy gravesite, the Tomb of the Unknowns, and Arlington House, where you can linger as long as you like, since you have unlimited boarding privileges to the buses that come about every 15 minutes.

12. The Kennedy Center   This leisurely tour of the sumptuous performing arts center and JFK memorial gives visitors a behind-the-scenes look at Washington's cultural life, as well as a chance to linger over some of the artwork donated to the center from countries from around the world. The 360° view of Washington from the center's roof terrace is a knockout.

13. The National Portrait Gallery   What would have been an aimless ramble through this downtown art museum turned into an informative tour. On a whim, I asked the guard at the information desk when the next guided tour left. The answer: "Whenever you're ready." So I got a one-on-one tour from a docent who's the wife of an admiral and really knows her history. The moral: Don't be afraid to ask for the free tour, which is available by request between 10 A.M. and 3 P.M. weekdays and from 11 A.M. to 1:30 P.M. weekends. Scheduled tours are also offered on weekends at 11:15 A.M. and 1 P.M.

14. Decatur House   A half-hour tour of the Federalist home brings early Washington to life as the tour guide explains what life was like when Stephen Decatur lived here in 1819. Upstairs, visitors get a glimpse of how upper-crust Washington society, including President and Mrs. Kennedy, were entertained by later owners of the house.

15. Woodrow Wilson House   A video narrated by Walter Cronkite primes you for a detailed tour of the house where President Wilson retired after leaving the White House. He was the only president to live in Washington after leaving office. The house preserves elements of Wilson's day-to-day life, including an ancient movie projector he used and his meticulously kept basement kitchen.

16. Cedar Hill   The 19th-century home of abolitionist Frederick Douglass is a find. Our well-informed guide provided a detailed commentary on Douglass's life and times, including pointing out intimate details such as Douglass's barbells on the floor next to his bed. A late afternoon visit is almost like stepping back into the 19th century because the house is preserved as it was when Douglass died in 1895: There's no electricity, and the gathering shadows in the house evoke the past. Be sure to see "The Growlery," a small, one-room structure behind the main house Douglass declared off-limits to the household so that he could work alone. Bad news: Due to staff cutbacks, advance reservations are required to get on the 30-minute guided tour.

17. The Franciscan Monastery   The 45-minute tour includes a beautiful, recently restored church and replicas of shrines in the Holy Land. But the real treat is hair-raising stories of Christian martyrs told by your guide as you wind your way through a replica of Roman catacombs.

18. The *Washington Post*   This is a great tour for anyone who's never seen the insides of a big-city newspaper. On the 45-minute tour, you visit the newsroom, the composition rooms, a small museum showing how it was all done before computers took over, and the big presses.

19. Gadsby's Tavern   After seeing nothing but sumptuousness and 20-foot ceilings in Washington's magnificent edifices, it's a relief to make the short trek to Alexandria and see how average Americans lived and worked in the 18th century. The tour of this tavern gives a glimpse of how most people traveled, ate, and slept during the period when Alexandria was a major port—and Washington didn't exist.

20. FBI Headquarters   This popular tour follows a rigid formula executed with military precision and features lots of static displays. But is it good? The young women leading the tour recited a series of canned presentations that sounded memorized. Most of the exhibits are inert displays of guns, drug paraphernalia, fingerprinting methods, and old "most wanted" posters. I suspect it's the demonstration of automatic weapons fire at the end of the tour—and the chance to hear a real FBI special agent talk and answer questions—that makes this tour so popular.

■ Taking an Orientation Tour ■

First-time visitors to Washington can't help but notice the regular procession of open-air, multicar tour buses—"motorized trolleys" is probably a more accurate term—that prowl the streets along the Mall, the major monuments, Arlington Cemetery, downtown, Georgetown, and Upper Northwest Washington. These regularly scheduled shuttle buses drop off and pick up paying customers along a route that includes the town's most popular attractions. Between stops, passengers listen to a tour guide talk about the city's monuments, museums, and famous buildings. The guides also suggest good places to eat and drop tidbits of interesting—and often humorous—Washington trivia. Our advice: If this is your first trip to Washington, take one of the tours early in your visit.

Here's why: Geographically, Washington is a spread-out city. Attempting to hoof it to Capitol Hill, the Washington Monument, and the Lincoln and Jefferson Memorials in one day amounts to cruel and unusual punishment to the body—especially your feet. Throw in a hot and humid Washington afternoon and a few cranky kids, and it's a recipe for vacation meltdown.

Think of the narrated shuttle-bus tours that cruise Washington as a special transportation system that not only gets you to the most popular sights, but also provides a timely education on the city's size and scope. The money you pay for your ticket allows unlimited reboarding privileges for that day, so you can get off at any scheduled stop and reboard a later bus (they run at 20- to 30-minute intervals).

The three guided tours that operate on a regular route in the city, Tourmobile, Old Town Trolley, and Gray Line's Li'l Red Trolley, are good values.

Tourmobile has the National Park Service franchise and shuttles its open-air, articulated buses to 18 sights around the Mall, Capitol Hill, and Arlington Cemetery from 9 A.M. to 6:30 P.M. between June 15 and Labor Day and from 9:30 A.M. to 5 P.M. the rest of the year. For tour information, call (202) 554-5100. Ticket booths are located at Arlington Cemetery, the Lincoln Memorial, and the Washington Monument, but you can board at any red-and-white Tourmobile stop sign on the route and pay the driver ($12 adults, $6 children). The company also runs narrated tours to Mount Vernon (four hours; $20 adults, $10 for children ages 3 to 11; fee includes admission to the estate) and to the Frederick Douglass Historical Site in Anacostia (two-and-a-half hours; $6 adults, $3 for children ages 3 to 11), mid-June through Labor Day and in February, Black History Month.

Gray Line's Li'l Red Trolley features "hop on–hop off" service at the Mall, Capitol Hill, Chinatown, Dupont Circle, Adams-Morgan, Embassy Row, Georgetown, Foggy Bottom, Arlington Cemetery, and the Waterfront. The two-hour circuit operates on a half-hour schedule (hourly December through February); the adult fare is $18 and $9 for children ages 3 to 11. Hotels on the 18-stop route include the Holiday Inn Capitol Hill, Renaissance Hotel, Willard Hotel, Mayflower Hotel, Washington Hilton, Sheraton Washington, Holiday Inn on the Hill, and the Marriott at Metro Center. For more information, call (800) 862-1400 or (202) 289-1995.

Old Town Trolley takes visitors to the Mall, downtown Washington, Dupont Circle, posh Northwest Washington, Embassy Row, and George-

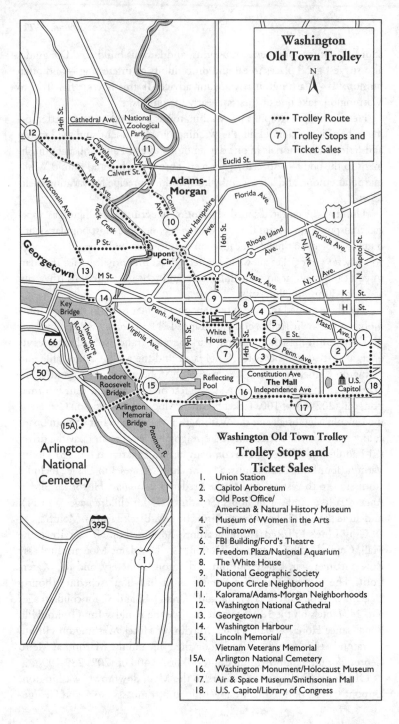

Washington Old Town Trolley

N

•••••• Trolley Route

⑦ Trolley Stops and Ticket Sales

34th St.

Cathedral Ave.

National Zoological Park

⑫

Cleveland Ave.

⑪

Calvert St.

Euclid St.

Wisconsin Ave.

Mass. Ave.

Rock Creek

Adams-Morgan

Conn. Ave.

Florida Ave.

①

Georgetown

P St.

⑩

New Hampshire Ave.

16th St.

Rhode Island Ave.

Florida Ave.

N.J. Ave.

N. Capitol St.

⑬

M St.

Dupont Cir.

Mass. Ave.

N.Y. Ave.

⑭

Penn. Ave.

⑨

K St.

H St.

Key Bridge

Theodore Roosevelt Is.

⑧

④

Mass. Ave.

66

Virginia Ave.

19th St.

White House

⑤

E St.

①

50

⑦

14th St.

⑥

Penn. Ave.

②

③

Theodore Roosevelt Bridge

⑮

Reflecting Pool

Constitution Ave.

The Mall

Independence Ave.

🏛 U.S. Capitol

⑱

Arlington Memorial Bridge

⑯

15A

Potomac R.

⑰

Arlington National Cemetery

395

①

Washington Old Town Trolley
Trolley Stops and Ticket Sales

1.   Union Station
2.   Capitol Arboretum
3.   Old Post Office/
     American & Natural History Museum
4.   Museum of Women in the Arts
5.   Chinatown
6.   FBI Building/Ford's Theatre
7.   Freedom Plaza/National Aquarium
8.   The White House
9.   National Geographic Society
10. Dupont Circle Neighborhood
11. Kalorama/Adams-Morgan Neighborhoods
12. Washington National Cathedral
13. Georgetown
14. Washington Harbour
15. Lincoln Memorial/
     Vietnam Veterans Memorial
15A. Arlington National Cemetery
16. Washington Monument/Holocaust Museum
17. Air & Space Museum/Smithsonian Mall
18. U.S. Capitol/Library of Congress

town. If you're staying at one of the following hotels, you can hop on board and be dropped at your door: Hyatt Regency, Grand Hyatt, Marriott Metro Center, J. W. Marriott, Hotel Washington, Capitol Hilton, Holiday Inn Capitol Hill, and the Washington Hilton. Tickets ($18 adults, $9 for children ages 4 to 12) can be purchased from the driver or at ticket booths located at most of the stops. The tours begin at 9 A.M. and run on the half-hour till 4 P.M. (till 5 P.M. Memorial Day through Labor Day). For more information, call (202) 832-9800.

Hint: If you didn't drive to Washington and don't have a car, take advantage of Old Town Trolley or the Li'l Red Trolley to visit Washington National Cathedral and Georgetown; neither is close to a Metro station, and getting off now can save on cab fare or shoe leather later. Old Town Trolley also offers a "Washington After Hours" tour, which visits illuminated monuments and memorials while tour guides tell ghost stories. Tours begin at 7:30 P.M. at Union Station (6:30 P.M. November and December) and last about two-and-a-half hours. The cost is $22 for adults and $11 for children ages 4 to 12. The tour does not operate in January or February.

■ Other Commercial Guided Tours ■

While Tourmobile, Old Town Trolley, and Li'l Red Trolley do a good job at shuttling visitors around Washington's major tourist attractions, a number of other local companies offer more specialized tours. Here's a rundown of some tours that are a little different.

Gray Line offers a wide variety of narrated bus tours in and around Washington. Half-day, all-day, and overnight tours take visitors to Washington's most popular sights, including the Mall museums, government buildings, Embassy Row, and Mount Vernon and Alexandria in Virginia. Gray Line also offers a "Washington After Dark" tour to see monuments and federal buildings flooded in lights, a black heritage tour, trips to Harpers Ferry and the Gettysburg battlefield, multilingual tours of Washington, and tours of Monticello and Williamsburg. Tours depart from Union Station; call (202) 289-1995 for more information.

Spirit Cruises, located at Pier 4, 6th and Water Streets, SW, takes visitors on boat tours of the Potomac River spring through fall. The star attraction is the half-day cruise to Mount Vernon, where the boat docks and you can tour the mansion and grounds. Call (202) 554-8000 for information and rates on lunch, dinner, and moonlight dance party cruises aboard an air-conditioned luxury ship.

Odyssey III cruises the Potomac River year-round, offering Sunday jazz brunches, lunch and dinner cruises, and midnight cruises. Two-hour and three-hour trips feature live music, entrees and desserts prepared on board by a four-star chef, and views of Washington from outside decks and through the ship's glass ceilings. Prices range from $30 to $78 per person; prices for children under age 11 are half the adult rates. Jackets are recommended for gentlemen on dinner cruises. *Odyssey* departs from the Gangplank Marina, 6th and Water Streets, SW, near the Waterfront Metro Station on the Green Line. For more information and reservations, call (800) 946-7245 or (202) 488-6000.

The Cruise Ship *Dandy* departs Old Town Alexandria for dinner cruises that feature after-dinner dancing. Sights along the way include the floodlit Capitol dome. Dinner cruises start at $50 per person. Call (703) 683-6090 for information and schedules.

GNP's **Scandal Tours** will reinforce every evil thought you ever had about Washington and those who rule. It's a comedy review on wheels— not a sight-seeing tour—and makes stops at, predictably enough, the Watergate complex, the White House (where 494 of Bill's close personal friends spent the night in the Lincoln Bedroom), and the Tidal Basin, where a powerful member of Congress once went skinny-dipping with a stripper. Seventy-five-minute public tours depart Saturdays at 1 P.M., April through Labor Day, from 12th Street and Pennsylvania Avenue, NW. Tickets are $27 and reservations are required; call (800) 758-TOUR for more information. Private charters are available year-round.

Washington Water Bus's electric boats cruise the Potomac River and make four stops at presidential memorials from May through October. The "buses" run approximately every 20 minutes from 11 A.M. to 6 P.M. daily and stop at the waterfront near the Jefferson Memorial and 14th Street Bridge, the Lincoln and FDR memorials, Washington Harbour in Georgetown, and Theodore Roosevelt Island. All-day tickets with unlimited boarding and reboarding are $12 for adults and $6 for children ages 3 to 12; one-way tickets are $7. For more information, call (800) 288-7925.

Bike the Sites offers a new and calorie-burning way to see D.C.'s history and architecture: by bicycle. Two licensed guides lead daily tours ranging in length from one to four hours. Bicycles, helmets, and all necessary equipment are provided on the rides. Tours include the Early Bird Fun Ride ($25), the Capital Sites Ride ($35), and the Mount Vernon Ride ($45). For more information, call (202) 966-8662.

The Guide Service of Washington, the oldest and largest in D.C., offers private, customized VIP tours led by licensed guides. For foreign visitors, guides are available who speak your native tongue. Four-hour tours start at $122, plus transportation, regardless of the size of your group. Tours must be paid for three weeks in advance. Call (202) 628-2842 for more information.

Optimum Adult Touring Plan

An Optimum Touring Plan in Washington, D.C., requires a good itinerary, a minimum of five days in town (i.e., not including travel time), a surprisingly modest amount of money (most attractions are free), and a comfortable pair of walking shoes. It also requires a fairly prodigious appetite for marble edifices, huge museums, and historical trivia. We will provide an itinerary; the rest is up to you.

With an Optimum Touring Plan, you can see the various attractions in and around Washington without facing huge crowds on the Mall, sitting in restaurants and shops that are jammed to capacity, or trudging through heat and humidity during sweltering afternoons.

Since an Optimum Touring Plan calls for seeing a lot of different parts of D.C., it makes for easier logistics if you stay at a hotel that's in the city and close to a Metro station. But even if your hotel is in the suburbs, you can still use the day-by-day plan as long as you can walk to the Metro. You'll lose some time commuting, but you may save some money on hotel rates. You'll lose even more time if you have to drive to a Metro station and park (see pages 235–36). Once you get in your car and start driving around in D.C., you're defeating the purpose of the Optimum Touring Plan, and you'll know it. We repeat: Don't drive in the city.

If you plan to visit Washington during the busiest months (see pages 20–23), you need to get up early to beat the crowds. Getting free "time tickets" for the Washington Monument and the White House is basically incompatible with sleeping in. If you want to sleep late and enjoy your touring experience, visit Washington in the fall or winter, when crowds are smaller. The Optimum Touring Plan assumes your visit is during the busy season.

We do not believe there is one ideal itinerary. Tastes, levels of energy, and basic perspectives on what is interesting or edifying vary. This understood, what follows is our personal version of an optimum Washington vacation week.

Before You Go

1. Write your congressperson as far in advance as possible for VIP tour reservations and a packet of free information on visiting Washington.

2. Review our list of other D.C. attractions that require advance reservations, select one or two that interest you, and make them for the afternoon of Day 3 at the same time you write your congressperson.

3. Read through all your information and make an informal list of sights that you and your family want to see during your Washington stay.

4. Break in a pair of thick-soled walking shoes.

On Site

Day 0 — Travel Day

1. Arrive and get settled. Explore the features and amenities of your hotel.

2. If you get checked in by 3 P.M., go to the Mall and visit the Castle, the Smithsonian's visitor center. (If you're not within walking distance, this is an opportunity to get familiar with the Metro. Read our chapter on how it works and take the red line to the Smithsonian station.) Since crowds start to thin in the late afternoon, you may have time to duck into the National Air and Space Museum or the National Museum of Natural History after viewing the orientation film in the Castle.

3. Take the Metro to Dupont Circle for dinner at the Thai, Japanese, or Greek restaurant of your choice. When you get back to your hotel, check with the desk to find the nearest stop for boarding either the Li'l Red Trolley or Tourmobile sight-seeing tours. This will save you time in the morning.

Day 1

1. After breakfast at your hotel, board one of the sight-seeing buses for an orientation tour of Washington. The driver sells tickets.

2. Stay on the bus for a complete circuit, which takes about an hour and a half (two hours for Li'l Red Trolley; Old Town Trolley tickets are only good for one complete tour). You'll gain a good overview of Washington's huge number of attractions that will help you decide what sights you want to see this trip—and which ones can wait for another visit.

3. For lunch, get off the tour bus at Union Station, an architectural masterpiece, and head for the lower-level food court. Over lunch,

decide what stops you want to make from the tour bus this afternoon.

4. Reboard your tour bus at Union Station. In deciding where to get off next, consider an attraction that's not convenient to your hotel. On Li'l Red Trolley, both Georgetown and Washington National Cathedral are good choices. On Tourmobile, consider the Arlington National Cemetery tour. Another hint: Some of the guides on the buses really know their stuff regarding sights, restaurants, and strategies on how to tour D.C. Ask them for suggestions. Tour until dinnertime.

5. Return to your hotel. For dinner, take a cab to Georgetown. After dinner, take in a stroll and some night life.

Day 2

1. An early start: Get to the Mall by 7 A.M. and pick up "time tickets" to the White House, the Washington Monument, and the Bureau of Engraving and Printing. (See page 229 for a detailed itinerary.)

2. After lunch, return to your hotel for a nap or a dip in the pool.

3. Around 3 P.M. take the Metro to Dupont Circle, where you can window-shop, stroll down Embassy Row, and stop in Anderson House, a sumptuous mansion and museum. Then have dinner in one of the many restaurants nearby. After dinner, take the Metro to the Mall for a spectacular night view of the city from the top of the Washington Monument (summer only).

Day 3

1. Get in line for the FBI tour by 8 A.M. Then hit one of the popular Mall museums right away, before the crowds show up: Air and Space, American History, or Natural History.

2. After lunch, concentrate on some of the best art galleries in the world—the National Gallery of Art and the Hirshhorn Museum and Sculpture Garden. Or take the tour of the U.S. Department of State's Diplomatic Reception Rooms or one of the other reservation-only tours that you set up before the trip. If a few hours off your feet sounds attractive, consider taking in the five-story IMAX movie at the Air and Space Museum.

3. Take the Metro to Gallery Place for dinner in Chinatown. Then take the Metro to the Federal Triangle station and go to the Old Post Office Pavilion for dessert and a spectacular night view of Washington from the 315-foot-high clock tower. Afterwards, go to a jazz or blues club.

Day 4

1. Sleep in from your night on the town. In the morning tour Capitol Hill: the U.S. Capitol, the Supreme Court, and the Library of Congress. Eat lunch at a Capitol Hill cafe.

2. If it's a scorching summer day, consider one of these options after lunch: downtown's National Museum of American Art/National Portrait Gallery or the DAR Museum. Around 4 P.M., take the Metro to Woodley Park and walk or take a cab to the National Zoo. For dinner, pick from the many restaurants in Woodley Park. Hit the sack early: You'll be tired.

Day 5

1. Either drive or take the 8:30 A.M. Gray Line bus or the 10 A.M. Tourmobile to Mount Vernon, George Washington's estate on the Potomac River. If you drive, leave before 7:30 A.M. or after 9:30 A.M. to avoid the worst rush-hour traffic.

2. Visit Old Town Alexandria for lunch and more 18th-century Americana. Stop in the Torpedo Factory to shop for unique arts and crafts.

3. If you're visiting in the summer, start your evening with a free military band concert. These are held on a rotating basis at 8 P.M. at either the U.S. Navy Memorial (Archives/Navy Memorial Metro), the steps of the U.S. Capitol (Capitol South Metro), or the Sylvan Theatre, located on the grounds of the Washington Monument (Smithsonian Metro). Afterwards take the Metro to the Waterfront station and walk to a Maine Avenue seafood restaurant for dinner.

The Mall Touring Plan

Adults and children touring Washington on a Tuesday, Wednesday, Thursday, or Friday during spring or summer, who want a peak-season, whirlwind tour of the White House, the Washington Monument, and the Bureau of Engraving and Printing with a minimum of standing in line, will want to try the following itinerary:

1. Arrive at the new White House Visitors Center at 6:30 A.M. This will get you in line early enough that you'll have your tickets for a 10 A.M. tour shortly after the office opens at 7:30 A.M.

2. Walk to the Mall and the kiosk on 15th Street that hands out "time tickets" to the Washington Monument. Since it's only a little after 8 A.M., you should be able to get a ticket that will admit you to the Big Guy before your White House tour. Then go up 15th Street a little farther to the Bureau of Engraving and Printing's ticket booth to get tickets for a tour early in the afternoon (you can specify your time, up to 1:50 P.M.). Pick a time late enough to give you time to tour the White House.

3. After riding to the top of the Washington Monument, you may have time for a quick late breakfast or early lunch at the Commerce Department cafeteria on 15th Street, NW, before the White House opens at 10 A.M. Other nearby options include the Shops at National Place on F Street between 12th and 13th Streets, NW, and the Old Ebbitt Grill on 15th Street across from the U.S. Treasury Department.

4. Arrive at the Ellipse Visitor Pavilion 10 minutes before your tour is scheduled to leave.

5. After you leave the White House, you may have time for lunch. Consider the options listed above or the Old Post Office Pavilion on New York Avenue.

6. After lunch, walk back to the Bureau of Engraving and Printing on 15th Street for the tour of the money-printing facility.

7. Now you have the rest of the day to explore. Our suggestion is to get off the Mall and visit places off the beaten tourist path: the National Postal Museum, the National Museum of American Art and the National Portrait Gallery, or attractions near Dupont Circle.

The Red Line Tour

When things are really hectic down on the Mall—we especially have in mind spring and summer weekends when the crowds are at their worst—consider exploring a wide range of tourist attractions along the Metro's red line. You'll avoid the worst of the throngs packing the city, yet still see some of the best sights in Washington. Here's a list of sights you can see, station by station:

1. Union Station: Capital Children's Museum, National Postal Museum, U.S. Supreme Court, U.S. Capitol, Folger Shakespeare Library, Library of Congress

2. Judiciary Square: National Building Museum, National Law Enforcement Officers Memorial

3. Gallery Place/Chinatown: National Museum of American Art, National Portrait Gallery, Ford's Theatre, Chinatown

4. Metro Center: National Museum of Women in the Arts

5. Farragut North: National Geographic Society's Explorers Hall

6. Dupont Circle: Phillips Collection, Anderson House, Islamic Center, Woodrow Wilson House, Textile Museum

7. Woodley Park/Zoo or Cleveland Park: National Zoo, Washington National Cathedral (both require some walking, however)

Touring Strategies

■ Attractions Grouped by Metro Station ■

With the exception of the Red Line Tour (see above), we don't recommend structuring your visit around attractions located near Metro stations. But we do think a list of tourist attractions located within walking distance of Metro stations can help make a last-minute touring selection to fill in part of a morning or afternoon—and maybe save you a buck or two in Metro fares. A warning: Although this list shows what attractions are closest to a Metro station, some sights could be as far as 20 minutes away by foot. An example: While the Foggy Bottom/GWU Metro is the closest to the Lincoln Memorial, it's still about a three-quarter-mile hike.

Red Line

Brookland/CUA   The National Shrine of the Immaculate Conception, the Franciscan Monastery (10-minute and 20-minute walks, respectively)

Union Station   Capital Children's Museum, National Postal Museum, the U.S. Supreme Court, the U.S. Capitol, Senate office buildings, Folger Shakespeare Library

Judiciary Square   National Building Museum, National Law Enforcement Officers Memorial, the Lillian and Albert Small Jewish Museum

Gallery Place/Chinatown   National Portrait Gallery, National Museum of American Art, Chinatown, National Building Museum, Washington Convention Center, Ford's Theatre, the FBI

Metro Center   National Museum of Women in the Arts, U.S. Department of the Treasury, the Washington Convention Center, the Shops at National Place

Farragut North   Swank shops on Connecticut Avenue, National Geographic Society's Explorers Hall, the *Washington Post* building

Dupont Circle   Shops and restaurants, Embassy Row, the Phillips Collection, Anderson House, the Islamic Center, Woodrow Wilson House, the Textile Museum, House of the Temple

Woodley Park/National Zoo National Zoo, Washington National Cathedral, Adams-Morgan (Note: The Zoo is about a 10-minute walk, Adams-Morgan is about 15 minutes away on foot, and the Cathedral is a half-hour stroll.)

Van Ness/UDC Intelsat, Hillwood Museum (20-minute walk)

Blue and Orange Lines

Capitol South Library of Congress, House office buildings, Capitol Hill restaurants, the U.S. Capitol, Folger Shakespeare Library, the U.S. Supreme Court

Federal Center, SW U.S. Botanic Garden, the National Air and Space Museum

L'Enfant Plaza Shops and restaurants, the National Air and Space Museum, the Hirshhorn Museum and Sculpture Garden, the Arts and Industries Building

Smithsonian The National Mall, the Freer and Sackler Galleries, the National Museum of African Art, the Bureau of Engraving and Printing, the National Museum of Natural History, the National Museum of American History, the Washington Monument, the Smithsonian Castle visitor center, the Tidal Basin, the Jefferson Memorial (20-minute walk), FDR Memorial (20-minute walk), the U.S. Holocaust Memorial Museum

Federal Triangle The Old Post Office Pavilion, the National Aquarium, the FBI, Pennsylvania Avenue, National Museum of American History, National Museum of Natural History, the White House Visitors Center

McPherson Square The White House, the *Washington Post* building, Lafayette Park

Farragut West Decatur House, Renwick Gallery, the Old Executive Office Building, the White House, the Corcoran Gallery of Art, the DAR Museum, the Ellipse, the Octagon

Foggy Bottom/GWU The Kennedy Center, the U.S. Department of State's Diplomatic Reception Rooms, Vietnam Veterans Memorial, Korean War Veterans Memorial, the Reflecting Pool, the Lincoln Memorial, the FDR Memorial, Georgetown (20- to 30-minute walk)

Rosslyn Freedom Park, Newseum

Arlington National Cemetery   Arlington National Cemetery, the Lincoln and FDR Memorials (across Memorial Bridge)

Pentagon   The Pentagon

National Airport   National Airport

King Street   Old Town Alexandria (15-minute walk), shops and restaurants, the Torpedo Factory (20-minute walk), the George Washington National Masonic Memorial

Yellow Line

Gallery Place/Chinatown   National Portrait Gallery, National Museum of American Art, Chinatown, National Building Museum, Washington Convention Center, Ford's Theatre, the FBI

Archives/Navy Memorial   The National Archives, the U.S. Navy Memorial, the National Gallery of Art, the National Museum of Natural History

Green Line

Waterfront   Washington's Potomac River waterfront area (restaurants, marinas, and river cruises), Fort McNair, Arena Stage

■ Seeing Washington on a Tight Schedule ■

Many visitors do not have five days to devote to visiting Washington. They may be en route to other destinations, or may live within a day's drive, making later visits practical. Either way, efficient, time-effective touring is a must. Such visitors cannot afford long waits in line to see attractions or spend hours trying to find a place to park the family car.

Even the most efficient touring plan will not allow the visitor to visit the Mall, Capitol Hill, and Georgetown in one day, so plan on allocating at least an entire day to the Mall (but not just museums), and splitting your remaining days to other parts of Washington that appeal to you.

■ One-Day Touring ■

A comprehensive tour of Washington is literally impossible in a day. But a day trip to Washington can be a fun, rewarding experience. Pulling it off hinges on following some basic rules.

A. Determine in Advance What You Really Want to See

What are the categories that appeal to you most? If it's government, spend your day on Capitol Hill. If it's exploring museums, visit the Mall. If you like trendy shops and a sophisticated ambience, go to Georgetown or Dupont Circle.

B. Select an Area to Visit

For example, if visiting the U.S. Capitol is your goal, look at what other nearby attractions on Capitol Hill or the east end of the Mall interest you. That way you won't waste time and steps.

C. Arrive Early! Arrive Early! Arrive Early!

This is the single most important key to efficient touring and avoiding big crowds. First thing in the morning, lines are short at the White House Visitors Center and the Washington Monument's ticket kiosk. You can visit three famous Washington attractions in one or two hours that would take an entire afternoon if you arrived at noon. Eat breakfast before you arrive so you will not have to waste your prime touring time sitting in a cowded restaurant.

D. Avoid Bottlenecks

Helping you avoid bottlenecks and big crowds is what this guide is all about. Bottlenecks occur as a result of crowd concentrations in the absence of crowd management. Concentrations of hungry people create bottlenecks at restaurants during the lunch and dinner hours; concentrations of visitors heading toward the best-known monuments, memorials, museums, and government buildings create elbow-to-elbow crowds during afternoons. Avoiding bottlenecks involves knowing when and where large concentrations of visitors begin to occur. That's why we provide a Touring Plan for a lightning-quick visit to the White House, the Bureau of Engraving and Printing, and the Washington Monument (see page 227).

In addition, daytrippers need to avoid the agony of driving in D.C. traffic if they expect to have any fun and see enough Washington attractions to make the trip worthwhile. There are two ways to do it:

1. Park Your Car in the Suburbs

In suburban Maryland and Virginia, the Metro extends to the Beltway and beyond, eliminating the need for you to battle Washington traffic, as well as saving you time, money, and stomach acid. On weekends, Metro users park for free at any suburban station. During the week, unless you arrive before 7 A.M., your choice of suburban Metro stations is limited to five: Vienna (on I-66 in Virginia, which fills by 8 A.M.); New Carrollton (on the Beltway in Maryland); Greenbelt (also on the Beltway in Maryland); Shady Grove (off I-270 in Maryland); and Silver Spring (inside the Beltway in Maryland). We recommend that you park at a Maryland station, unless you can make it to a Virginia station very early. From the outermost suburbs, it's about a 20-minute, stress-free train ride to the Mall.

New Carrollton has plenty of parking, plus a parking garage for overflow. Take Beltway exit 19B (US 50 west) and follow the signs to the Metro. Go to the second parking lot, where you can park all day for $1.75 (free on weekends). If it's filled, park in the five-level garage for $6 all day. On weekdays, make sure to pick up a bus transfer in the station on your return trip to qualify for the low parking rate.

Greenbelt is an easy Metro station to reach for daytrippers from Baltimore and other points north. Take I-95 or the Baltimore-Washington Parkway south to the Capital Beltway, go south about two miles and get off at exit 24, which goes to the Greenbelt Metro station. All-day parking is $1.75 during the week, free on weekends. Take the train to the Fort Totten station (which is temporarily the end of the line) and transfer to the red line train to Shady Grove, which takes you downtown.

Shady Grove also has plenty of parking for daytrippers. From I-270 near Gaithersburg, take exit 9 (marked "Sam Eig Highway/Metro Station") to I-370 East, which takes you directly to the station. Metro parking is $1 for the day (free on weekends); if the Metro lots are filled, park in the nearby garage for $2.50.

Silver Spring is a somewhat less convenient option for daytrippers because it means a short drive inside the Beltway. But there's plenty of commercial parking close by. Take US 29/Colesville Road south from the Beltway and turn left onto Georgia Avenue in downtown Silver Spring; follow the signs to the Metro, loop past it, and park in one of the big parking garages. Parking is around $4 for the day.

2. Take the Train

Taking the train to Washington is a snap for day visitors who live along the Eastern Seaboard from Richmond to Philadelphia. Amtrak, Maryland commuter (MARC), and Virginia Railway Express trains arrive at gleaming Union Station, located on the Metro's red line. You can be on the Mall minutes after getting off your train. From Union Station, visitors are only a few blocks' walk from the U.S. Capitol, the U.S. Supreme Court, the Library of Congress, the Folger Shakespeare Library, and the newest Smithsonian facility, the National Postal Museum.

From Virginia, Virginia Railway Express operates two commuter lines connecting Fredericksburg (to the south) and Manassas (to the west) with Union Station in downtown Washington. The 18-station system offers inbound service in the mornings and outbound service in the afternoons, Monday through Friday. For more information, call (703) 658-6200 or (800) RIDE VRE (743-3873).

MARC train service operates three lines connecting Washington with the Maryland suburbs: one to BWI airport, another to downtown Baltimore, and the third goes northwest along the Potomac River into Western Maryland. For more information on the weekday-only service, call (800) 325-7245. For information and schedules for Amtrak, the national passenger train service, call (800) 872-7245. For express Metroliner information, call (800) 523-8720. By the way, Amtrak also provides weekend and holiday service along several of the lines used by MARC and Virginia Railway Express (but at a higher cost than the commuter services).

Excursions beyond the Beltway

If you've got the time or if your visit to Washington is a repeat trip, consider exploring some places outside the city. From the mountains to the west and the Chesapeake Bay to the east, there's plenty to see. Furthermore, a look at something that's not made of marble or granite can be a welcome relief to eyes wearied by the constant onslaught of Washington edifices and office buildings. Here are a few suggestions for day trips that Washington visitors can make beyond the Beltway.

Annapolis

Maryland's capital for more than 300 years, Annapolis is more than a quaint little town on the Chesapeake Bay—it's one of the biggest yachting centers in the United States. Acres and acres of sailboats fill its marinas. A steady parade of sailboats moves past the City Dock during the sailing season, April through late fall. You'll see oyster and crab boats that work the bay, in addition to pleasure boats, cruise ships, and old sailing ships.

Annapolis has been discovered and is now a major bedroom community for well-off Washingtonians. The town boasts fancy shops, fine restaurants, bars, and jazz clubs. On weekends during the summer, Annapolis is packed with visitors. The town is about a one-hour drive from Washington on US 50.

Baltimore

Steamed crabs, H. L. Mencken, the Orioles, and the National Aquarium are just a few of the reasons Washingtonians trek north one hour on a regular basis to this industrial city on the Chesapeake Bay. Washington's visitors have good reason to detour and discover the charms of Baltimore.

Daytrippers can explore the Inner Harbor, dominated by a bilevel shopping mall that's heavy on restaurants and boutiques. The National Aquarium features a tropical rain forest and a sea mammal pavilion—and it's a much larger attraction than the National Aquarium in Washington. Kids will love the Maryland Science Center and nearby Fort McHenry, where Francis Scott Key wrote the national anthem from a ship anchored offshore. If you've got the time, explore some other Baltimore attractions: the B&O Railroad Museum, the Edgar Allan Poe House, and the Babe Ruth House.

Shenandoah National Park

Although it makes for a long day, a drive to Shenandoah National Park in Virginia is a treat for outdoors-lovers, featuring some of the prettiest mountain scenery in the East. A drive along a portion of the 105-mile-long Skyline Drive takes visitors to a nearly endless series of mountain overlooks where you can get out of the car and walk on well-maintained trails. In early June, the mountain laurel blooms in the higher elevations, and in the fall, it's bumper-to-bumper as hordes of Washingtonians rush to see the magnificent fall foliage. It's about a two-hour drive from Washington, one-way.

Harpers Ferry National Historical Park

This restored nineteenth-century town at the confluence of the Shenandoah and the Potomac rivers in West Virginia offers visitors history and natural beauty in equal doses. At the park's visitor center you can see a film about radical abolitionist John Brown's 1859 raid on a U.S. armory here, an event that was a precursor to the Civil War. Then you can tour a renovated blacksmith's shop, ready-made clothing store, and general store. A short hike to Jefferson Rock is rewarded with a spectacular mountain view of three states (Maryland, Virginia, and West Virginia) and two rivers (the Potomac and the Shenandoah). Thomas Jefferson said the view was "worth a voyage across the Atlantic." Luckily, the trip by car from Washington is only about 90 minutes.

A Tour of Civil War Battlefields

From the number of battlefield sites there, it would seem that the entire Civil War was fought in nearby Virginia, Maryland, and Pennsylvania—which is nearly the truth. Visitors with an interest in history and beautiful countryside can tour a number of Civil War sites within a day's drive of Washington.

Gettysburg, where the Union turned the tide against the South, is about two hours north of D.C. While the overdeveloped town is a testament to tourist schlock gone wild, the National Battlefield Park features a museum, a tower that gives sight-seers an aerial view of the battlefield, and many acres of rolling countryside dotted with monuments, memorials, and stone fences. It's a popular tourist destination and worth the drive.

The first battle of the Civil War took place at Bull Run near Manassas, on the fringe of today's Virginia suburbs. The **Manassas National Battlefield Park** features a visitor center, a museum, and miles of trails on the grounds.

The Confederate victory set the stage for the next major battle, at Antietam, across the Potomac River in Maryland. **Antietam National Battlefield**, near Sharpsburg, is the site of the bloodiest day of the Civil War: On September 17, 1862, there were 12,410 Union and 10,700 Confederate casualties in General Robert E. Lee's failed attempt to penetrate the North. The battlefield, about a 90-minute drive from Washington, is 15 miles west of Frederick, Maryland.

A number of later Union campaigns are commemorated at Fredericksburg and **Spotsylvania National Military Park** in Virginia, halfway between Washington and Richmond. Included in the park are the battlefields of Fredericksburg, Chancellorsville, the Wilderness, and Spotsylvania. The park is about an hour's drive south of D.C.

Helpful Hints

■ **A Worst-Case Touring Scenario** ■

Here's how *not* to visit Washington: On a weekday, load the kids in the family car, and arrive around 8 A.M.—the worst part of rush hour. Then battle your way downtown through bumper-to-bumper traffic, arriving at the Mall about 9:30, your nerves thoroughly frayed. Waste a half-hour looking for a parking space before giving up and shelling out $12 for a space in a parking garage. Next, troop over to the Washington Monument, where a sign in the window of the time-ticket kiosk informs you that the day's allotment of tickets have already been given out. Then go to the National Air and Space Museum, where it's packed shoulder-to-shoulder around the most popular exhibits.

Later, at the National Museum of Natural History, little Jimmy disappears into the bowels of the paleontological exhibits, and since you didn't agree on a designated meeting place, it takes 45 minutes to track him down. At 5 P.M., you and your family stagger back to the car, just in time to join the afternoon rush hour.

Amazingly, people do this all the time. But it doesn't have to be this way. Instead of hitting Beltway traffic at 8 A.M., leave a half-hour earlier and go to any suburban Metro station and park. Then it's a 20-minute trip by train downtown. You can be at the Washington Monument by 8 A.M. and pick up a time ticket while the line is short. Then pick up tickets for a tour of the Bureau of Engraving and Printing later in the morning at the ticket booth on Raoul Wallenberg Place. Next, visit the National Air and Space Museum.

After watching money being printed, eat lunch at the Old Post Office Pavilion, then take the Metro to Dupont Circle. There, you can visit the Phillips Collection, a really classy art gallery, and tour Anderson House, a sumptuous mansion. Next, go to the National Zoo in the late afternoon or early evening, when the temperature begins to drop and the animals get more active. Eat dinner at a restaurant near the Woodley Park Metro on Connecticut Avenue and then take the Metro back to your car.

The second scenario takes advantage of two things: an early start and no time wasted in traffic or searching for a parking space. It lets you visit at a leisurely pace and gives you the freedom to explore out-of-the-way and unusual sights you normally wouldn't take the time to see. It's the smart way to visit Washington.

■ Travel Tips for Tourists ■

The idea behind visiting any major tourist attraction is to have fun, and you can't do that if you're getting fatigued or crabby. Here are some touring tips you should review before your visit. They're really no more than commonsense rules for any type of outing:

1. *Drink Water.* You'll need to drink plenty, especially on hot, humid, sunny Washington afternoons. Dehydration can sneak up and cause physical problems which might ruin your vacation plans. So don't hesitate to drink more water than you think you'll need.

2. *Avoid Sunburn.* Protect sun-sensitive areas of your body. Shade your head and eyes with a hat. Wear sunglasses. Treat exposed skin with a sunscreen lotion—especially your face. And if you're wearing sandals, don't forget your feet. You don't have to go to the beach to get a really nasty burn on the tops of your feet!

3. *Pace Yourself.* Washington is filled with good places to sit in the shade and rest, and people-watching is part of the fun. Hunger, overheating, tension from fighting the crowds for hours, fatigue —each of these realities of touring and all of them together can combine to produce fussy kids and grumpy adults. You'll notice if someone else in your party is getting unpleasant to be around, but you may not recognize the symptoms in yourself unless you periodically make an effort to run a little self-check and think about your behavior. If you and your party can't salvage things with a rest and a food break, cut your day short and go back to your hotel for a swim, a nap—or a drink in the bar. Visiting Washington is not meant to be a test of your temper and patience, after all. You're here to have fun.

4. *Wear Comfortable Clothes.* This especially goes for shoes—shoes that cushion, shoes that are broken in, shoes that won't make your feet too hot. Wear clothing that protects you from the sun and permits the air to circulate around your skin and doesn't bind or chafe.

5. *Food Strategies.* Keep on good terms with your stomach, but don't let it dictate your trip. Eat a good breakfast before you set out for

the day, then snack a lot while touring. Avoid lunch lines, especially those at overpriced museum cafeterias.

6. *Traveling with Teens.* Do yourself and them a favor: Send them off on their own for at least part of a day during your D.C. visit. Arrange to meet them at a specific time and place, and elicit a very firm and definite understanding about this meeting time and place. Give them a watch if they don't have one, a map, and the hotel number for emergencies.

Designated Meeting Places

Families and groups touring together should designate a meeting spot in case members get separated. On the Mall, good places to link up are in front of the Castle (the Smithsonian visitor center) or in front of the domed National Museum of Natural History. The information desks located in most main museum lobbies are logical meeting places if the group separates. Downtown, it's easy to lose your sense of direction due to a scarcity of landmarks. A good designated meeting place would be a hotel lobby, a department store entrance, or a Metro station.

A Money-Saving Tip for Lunch

Where *not* to have lunch: The sidewalk food vendors on the Mall, the kiosk in front of the National Museum of Natural History, and the small restaurant down the hill from the Washington Monument charge about a dollar more for a hot dog than the street vendors you see everywhere off the Mall. Unless you're dying of hunger, walk to either Constitution or Independence Avenue, find a street vendor, and save yourself some dough. The hot dogs, by the way, are pretty good.

Another Money-Saving Tip

The Commerce Department, located on 14th Street, NW, across from the Ellipse, has a pleasant basement cafeteria that offers good, cheap fare: a soup and salad bar, pizza and pasta, a grill, deli, and hot entrees. You can get a whole pizza that will feed a family of four for less than $10. It's open Monday through Friday, 9 A.M. to 2 P.M.

Where's the Smithsonian?

It's a common question fielded by the folks who staff the information desk in the Castle, the main visitor center for the Smithsonian Institution. The query is posed by first-time visitors who have the mistaken notion the renowned museum complex is located in one building somewhere along the Mall. In reality, the Smithsonian is a complex of 14 museums and a world-class zoo, scattered around the city. In addition, the Institution operates the Cooper-Hewitt National Design Museum and the National Museum of the American Indian, both located in New York City. (Some folks are also surprised when they learn that the National Gallery of Art and the Holocaust Memorial Museum are not part of the Smithsonian complex.) In the box is an alphabetical rundown of the Smithsonian's Washington facilities by location.

Get Off the Mall!

A full day of traipsing from museum to museum along the Mall is exhausting and, for most folks, a pretty one-dimensional experience. After a while, it starts to feel like a grade-school field trip—and, later, there's going to be a quiz. Is that a vacation? Snap out of it by breaking up the day and taking the Metro to any number of other fascinating destinations, including Dupont Circle, the waterfront, and the National Zoo. Or grab a cab and visit Georgetown, Adams-Morgan, or the Washington National Cathedral.

A Photography Tip

Washington, D.C., with its impressive memorials and federal buildings, is a photographer's mecca. But for a really spectacular shot of downtown Washington, go across the Potomac River to the Iwo Jima Memorial in

---

The Smithsonian's Facilities

The Mall
African Art Museum
Air and Space Museum
American History Museum
Arts and Industries Building
Freer Gallery
Hirshhorn Museum and
   Sculpture Garden
Natural History Museum
Postal Museum
Sackler Gallery
Smithsonian Institution Building
   Information Center

Downtown
American Art Museum
National Portrait Gallery
Renwick Gallery
Upper Northwest
National Zoo

Arlington, Virginia. Stand on the hill near the Netherlands Carillon and look toward the Lincoln Memorial. At dawn, the sun rises almost directly behind the U.S. Capitol. At dusk, the panorama of twinkling lights includes the Jefferson and Lincoln Memorials, the Washington Monument and, more than two miles away, the U.S. Capitol.

How to Sneak on a Reservation-Only Tour at the National Archives

For the behind-the-scenes tour of the National Archives, most people call weeks in advance for reservations. If you didn't, however, take a chance and show up at the Pennsylvania Avenue entrance (across from 8th Street) at tour time. If there's a cancellation or a no-show, you're in. The free reserved tours begin at 10:15 A.M. and 1:15 P.M. daily and last about an hour and a half. On the reserved tour, you'll explore the building, including the stacks, the microfilm viewing rooms, and the exhibits and models that show how researchers preserve documents. The tour ends in the magnificent Rotunda, where the great documents are on display.

Getting a Free Pass to a National Gallery of Art Show

Most people call or stop by weeks in advance to get free "time tickets" that admit them to the wildly popular art exhibits regularly held in the National Gallery of Art's East Building. What most of them don't know is that hundreds of tickets per half-hour are reserved for folks like you. Tickets can be picked up any day a show is in progress. Just show up by noon on weekends or by 2 P.M. on weekdays at the ticket counter in the main lobby and come back later in the day to see the show.

An Informal Georgetown Tour of JFK Residences

Structure an informal walking tour around Georgetown by viewing—from the outside only, please—a few places where a great American statesman once lived. As a congressman and senator, John F. Kennedy lived in four different houses in Georgetown: 1528 31st Street, NW; 1400 34th Street, NW; 3271 P Street, NW; and 3307 N Street, NW. The last address is where the Kennedys lived just before moving to 1600 Pennsylvania Avenue, NW.

D.C. on the Air

Aside from the usual babble of format rock, talk, easy listening, and country music radio stations, Washington is home to a few radio stations that really stand out for high-quality broadcasting. Tune in to what hip Washingtonians listen to, as listed below:

Format	Frequency	Station
Classical	570/103.5	WGMS-AM/FM
Progressive rock	99.1	WHFS-FM
Classical, NPR	91	WETA-FM
Bluegrass, folk, talk	88.5	WAMU-FM
Jazz	89.3	WPFW-FM
All news	1500	WTOP-AM
Jazz/information	90.1	WDCU-FM
Progressive rock	103.1	WRNR-FM

How to Tell if the President Is Home

A flag flies over the White House when the president is in Washington. At night, one of the facades on the White House stays lit for the benefit of trench coat–clad TV news reporters who intone to the camera, "Live, from the White House . . ."

How to Tell if the House or Senate Is in Session

Look for a flag flying over the respective chamber of the U.S. Capitol to determine which, if either, house of Congress is in session. From the Mall, the Senate is to the left of the dome; the House of Representatives is on the right. At night, a light burns on top of the Capitol dome if Congress is in session.

The Best Time of Day to Visit the Washington Monument in Summer

Avoid the hassle of picking up time tickets (that make you come back to the monument at a specified time) by visiting the monument after 8 P.M. While you may have to wait in line, lots of people say the view from the marble obelisk is better at night. If you must get a bird's-eye view of Washington in daylight but want to avoid the crowds besieging the Big Guy on the Mall, try the Old Post Office Pavilion's clock tower: It's not quite as high, but at least you don't have to squint through tiny windows. And there's rarely a long line.

Avoiding the Heat on a Sweltering Afternoon

On hot, humid D.C. afternoons, it's imperative to avoid long walks between sights; in fact, you shouldn't leave an air-conditioned building at all, if you can help it. On the Mall, one solution to touring on a hot day is to visit this trio of museums: the National Museum of African Art, the Arthur M. Sackler Gallery, and the Freer Gallery. The first two museums are built underground, so they're probably cool even during a power failure (dark, too). The three museums are connected by tunnels, eliminating the need to venture outside.

More good choices that will reduce the possibility of heat stroke include the Corcoran Gallery of Art, the Phillips Collection, and the National Gallery of Art. Another strategy is to visit museums next to each other (say, the National Museum of Natural History and the National Museum of American History). And don't plan any ambitious treks like a walk to the Jefferson Memorial from the Capitol, or from one end of the Mall to the other, when it's scorchingly hot outside.

D.C. after Dark

Touring Washington's monuments and memorials after dark offers dramatic views of both famous marble edifices and Washington itself. At night, the Jefferson and Lincoln Memorials float in pools of light; from the steps of the Lincoln Memorial, the Eternal Flame at the John F. Kennedy grave site shimmers across the river in Arlington National Cemetery. The scene at the Vietnam Veterans Memorial is a moving experience as people hold flickering matches up to the reflective black marble surface, searching for names.

Capitol Hill: A Family Affair

Rather than just getting in line to tour the U.S. Capitol, give yourself and your kids a real civics lesson you'll all remember: Visit your congressperson or senator.

"Go to your member's office and get a pass to see the House and Senate in session," suggests one of the Capitol guards. "It's a real experience—and the kids will love it. And while you're there, ask for a special tour of the Capitol given by a member's staff person." House office buildings are across Independence Avenue from the Capitol building; Senate office buildings are across Constitution Avenue. Offices are open weekdays during normal business hours, and you don't need an appointment. If you don't know the name of your representative, go to either one of your senators' offices.

Where the Real Work of Congress Is Done

Most visitors who obtain gallery passes to the House or Senate in session are mildly disappointed: The scene is usually one member giving a speech to a nearly empty chamber, unless you happen to stumble in during a vote. Everyone else is at committee meetings, where the real work is done. Check the *Washington Post* "A" section for a list of legislative hearings open to the public, along with their time and location (always in one of the buildings near the Capitol).

Another Photo Tip

Across from the Mall near the Lincoln Memorial is the stately National Academy of Sciences on Constitution Avenue. Outside, Albert Einstein's statue is waiting for you to crawl into its lap so you can have your picture taken; it's a D.C. tradition.

Speeding through the Ubiquitous Metal Detectors

Walk-through metal detectors staffed by no-nonsense guards are standard equipment in virtually every federal building in Washington, including the White House, the U.S. Capitol, the Supreme Court, all Senate and House office buildings, and the National Archives. Men: To speed your way through, you should get in the habit of carrying all your change and keys in one place. When your turn comes to pass through the metal detector, dump it all into one of the bowls provided, and you'll avoid the tedious drill of passing through the door-sized detector a half-dozen times. (You'll also find out which metal-buckled belt not to wear when visiting government buildings.) Women have it easier: Just place your purse on the conveyor that shoots it through the X-ray machine, then walk through the detector.

PART TEN

Washington's Attractions

Where to Go

Visitors come to Washington from all over the world—and for a lot of different reasons. Some want to see how the U.S. government works (or, as some cynics say, *doesn't* work), others want to see the places where history happened, and many are drawn by the city's magnificent monuments and museums.

It's tough for a guidebook to decree to such a diverse group where they should spend their time. Is the National Gallery of Art better than the Air and Space Museum? The answer is yes—if your interests and tastes range more toward Van Gogh than von Braun.

Because we can't read your mind and tell *you* the top places you should visit on your trip to Washington, we'll do the next best thing: give you enough information so that you can quickly choose the places you want to see—with enough detail that you can plan your visit logically—without spending a lot of time (and shoe leather) retracing your steps and standing in line.

Armed with enough information that will allow you to make informed choices about how you spend your valuable time, you can avoid a common mistake a lot of visitors to D.C. make: hitting the Mall for a death march through a blur of Smithsonian museums, federal buildings, and monuments.

Zone 1: The Mall

Arlington National Cemetery

Type of Attraction: The largest military cemetery in the United States. Guided and self-guided tours.

Location: Across the Potomac from Washington via Arlington Memorial Bridge, which crosses the river near the Lincoln Memorial.

Nearest Metro Station: Arlington Cemetery

Admission: Free

Hours: April through September, 8 A.M. to 7 P.M.; October through March, closes at 5 P.M.

Phone: (703) 607-8052

When to Go: Before 9 A.M. in spring and summer

Special Comments: Don't underestimate the ferocity of Washington summer afternoons; in hot weather, get here early.

Overall Appeal by Age Group:

Pre-school	Grade School	Teens	Young Adults	Over 30	Senior Citizens
★	★★	★★★	★★★★	★★★★	★★★★

Author's Rating: Beyond tourism. ★★★★

How Much Time to Allow: Two hours

Description and Comments It's not fair to call a visit to Arlington National Cemetery mere sight-seeing; as Americans, our lives are too intimately attached to the 200,000 men and women buried here. They include the famous, the obscure, and the unknown: John F. Kennedy, General George C. Marshall, Joe Louis, Abner Doubleday, and Oliver Wendell Holmes are among them. Sights located in the cemetery's 612 rolling acres include the Tomb of the Unknown Soldier (guarded 24 hours a day; witness the changing of the guard on the hour from October to March, and on the half-hour the rest of the year), memorials to the crew of the space shuttle *Challenger*, the Iran Rescue Mission Memorial, and Arlington House, built in 1802. With the ease of touring provided by Tourmobile, Arlington Cemetery should be on every first-time visitor's list of things to see.

Touring Tips To avoid the worst of Washington's brutal summer heat and humidity, plan to arrive as early as possible. Private cars are not allowed inside, but there's plenty of parking near the visitor center at $1 an hour for the first three hours, then $2 an hour. Take the Metro instead. Although you can wander around the cemetery on your own, the narrated Tourmobile tour is informative and saves wear and tear on your feet—and at $4 for adults and $2 for children under age 12, it's a good deal. The ticket allows you to get off at all the major sites and reboard at your leisure. The shuttle tours leave the visitor center (where tickets are sold) about every 15 to 20 minutes. If you're touring the Mall by Tourmobile, transferring to the cemetery tour is free for that day only. If you want to tour the cemetery by shuttle bus on a different day, don't pay $12 for another full-circuit ticket. Just take the Metro to the Arlington Cemetery station, walk the short distance to the visitor center, buy the cemetery-only ticket, and save a few bucks. Finally, bathrooms are located in the visitor center. But don't come to Arlington Cemetery when you're hungry: There's no place to eat.

Other Things to Do Nearby   The Pentagon is the next stop on the Metro. The Iwo Jima Memorial and the Netherlands Carillon are about a 20-minute walk from Arlington House (down Custis Walk and through Weitzel Gate). Two new attractions are an easy two-block walk from the Rosslyn Metro (one station away on the Metro): Freedom Park is a 1.6-acre park that features a memorial to nearly 1,000 journalists who died or were murdered on the job and a big chunk of the Berlin Wall; Newseum is a $50 million, 72,000-square-foot journalism museum. The nearest restaurants via the Metro are in Rosslyn and Pentagon City.

Arts and Industries Building (a Smithsonian museum)

Type of Attraction: A museum highlighting nineteenth-century American technology and temporary exhibitions. A self-guided tour.

Location: 900 Jefferson Drive, SW, on the Mall.

Nearest Metro Station: Smithsonian

Admission: Free

Hours: 10 A.M. to 5:30 P.M.; closed Christmas Day.

Phone: (202) 357-2700 (voice); (202) 357-1729 (TTY)

When to Go: Anytime

Special Comments: All the exhibits are on one level.

Overall Appeal by Age Group:

Pre-school	Grade School	Teens	Young Adults	Over 30	Senior Citizens
★★	★★★	★★	★★	★★½	★★★

Author's Rating: Fun stuff, but gets tiring fast. ★★

How Much Time to Allow: 30 minutes to an hour

Description and Comments The Arts and Industries Building was the original home of the Smithsonian after it was built in 1879–81. Formerly it housed the anthropological and scientific specimens now in the National Museum of Natural History across the Mall, industrial arts and technology items now in the National Museum of American History, artworks now in the National Museum of American Art and the National Portrait Gallery (both downtown), and aircraft exhibits currently displayed in the National Air and Space Museum. Today the east and west halls of this venerable museum hold some items from Philadelphia's 1876 Centennial Exhibition: steam engines, printing presses, nineteenth-century products, a steam locomotive and generators—a collection of Victorian and Gilded Age engineering might. The south hall features changing exhibits from the Center for African American History and Culture, while the north hall contains other temporary exhibitions.

Touring Tips It's a fun museum to visit, full of polished wood and cast iron, and the exhibits are close enough to touch. Some people call this a great "warm up" museum that gets you ready for the larger Smithsonian institutions; it's friendly and not overpowering.

Other Things to Do Nearby The Hirshhorn and the Air and Space Museum are next door. The Museum of Natural History (the one with the dome) is directly across the Mall. Tired of museums? Jump on the Metro, get off at Capitol South, and explore Capitol Hill. The Metro is also the fastest way to reach two good restaurant locales: L'Enfant Plaza (on weekdays) and the Old Post Office Pavilion (any time).

Bureau of Engraving and Printing

Type of Attraction: The presses that print all U.S. currency and stamps. A guided tour.

Location: Raoul Wallenberg Place (formerly 15th Street) and C Street, SW (two blocks south of the Mall).

Nearest Metro Station: Smithsonian

Admission: Free

Hours: Monday through Friday, 9 A.M. to 2 P.M. Closed on federal holidays and weekends. From April through September a "time ticket" system is in effect. The ticket office, located on Raoul Wallenberg Place, opens at 8 A.M. From June through August, evening tours are available from 5 P.M. to 7:30 P.M.; the ticket booth reopens at 3:30 to distribute free tour tickets for the evening hours on that day only—but only if any tickets are remaining.

Phone: (202) 874-3019, (202) 874-3188 for a recording

When to Go: The earlier, the better. During peak season, try to arrive on Monday by 8 A.M. (or earlier) and pick up tickets for a tour later that day or any time that week. *Note:* Once all tickets for the week are distributed, the ticket office will remain closed until the following Monday. In the fall and winter, a line forms at the long, enclosed entrance on 14th Street; on balmy fall and winter days, waits can last several hours.

Special Comments: Small children may have trouble looking over the ledge and down into the press rooms below.

Overall Appeal by Age Group:

Pre-school	Grade School	Teens	Young Adults	Over 30	Senior Citizens
★★	★★★★	★★★★	★★★★	★★★★	★★★★

Author's Rating: After the novelty of seeing all that cash fades, it's just a printing plant. ★★

How Much Time to Allow: About an hour when the ticket system is in effect. In the early fall, when the line snakes out the front door and up 14th Street, figure on at least two hours.

Average Wait in Line per 100 People in Line ahead of You: 15 minutes (fall and winter only).

Description and Comments This is a 35- to 45-minute guided tour through the rather cramped and elevated glass-lined corridors that go over the government's immense money and stamp printing plant. Visitors look down and gape at the printing presses that crank out the dough and at pallets of greenbacks in various stages of completion. The sign some wag hung on a press, however, says it all: "You have never been so close yet so far away." Kids love this place, so it's a tourist site families should plan on hitting, even if you're only in town for a short period.

Touring Tips Arrive early—this is one of D.C.'s most popular attractions. In early spring and summer, get to the ticket booth before 8 A.M. on Monday to avoid disappointment. The ticket office distributes about 80 tickets for every tour starting at 10-minute intervals between 9 A.M. and 1:50 P.M. When all tickets for the week are gone, the ticket office closes until the following Monday at 8 A.M. After picking up your tickets, come back for your tour and meet near the ticket office on Raoul Wallenberg Place, where you will be escorted into the building. You have about a 30-minute grace period if you're running late. For a unique souvenir, check out the bags of shredded money for sale in the visitor center at the end of the tour. For a VIP guided tour, contact your congressperson's office at least two months before your trip. The VIP tours are conducted at 8 A.M., Monday through Friday. Bathrooms are located inside the building where the tour begins.

Other Things to Do Nearby As you exit the building on Raoul Wallenberg Place, the Tidal Basin is a short walk to the left: Benches, tables, a lot of greenery, and the calming effect of water make it a great spot to unwind or eat lunch—or rent a paddleboat. And there's a great view of the Jefferson Memorial. Other sights close at hand are the Holocaust Memorial Museum, the Washington Monument, and the new seven-and-a-half-acre memorial to President Franklin D. Roosevelt. The $52 million series of gardens, sculptures, and granite walls are located between the Lincoln and Jefferson Memorials along the Potomac River and the Tidal Basin. There aren't a lot of places to eat that are close, however.

Corcoran Gallery of Art

Type of Attraction: A museum that primarily features American art from the colonial period to the present. A self-guided tour.

Location: 17th and E Streets, NW, a half-block west of the White House.

Nearest Metro Station: Farragut West

Admission: Suggested donations for adults, $3; students and seniors, $1; family groups of any size, $5; children under age 12 free.

Hours: Wednesday through Monday, 10 A.M. to 5 P.M.; Thursday, till 9 P.M.; closed Tuesdays, Christmas Day, and New Year's Day.

Phone: (202) 639-1700

When to Go: Anytime

Special Comments: Free 45-minute tours are offered at noon and at 7:30 P.M. Thursdays.

Overall Appeal by Age Group:

Pre-school	Grade School	Teens	Young Adults	Over 30	Senior Citizens
—	★	★★	★★½	★★★	★★★

Author's Rating: Art snobs will feel at home. ★★½

How Much Time to Allow: Two hours

Description and Comments Frank Lloyd Wright called this beaux arts museum "the best designed building in Washington." Inside are works by John Singer Sargent, Mary Cassatt, and Winslow Homer, among others. There's also an abundance of cutting-edge contemporary art. It's a big place with a wide range of periods and styles, so you're bound to see something you like.

Touring Tips   Maybe it's because of the art school next door, but this museum has a distinctly serious atmosphere. It's not a place to drag little Johnny and Sally, who would rather be looking at dinosaur bones in the National Museum of Natural History. For a delightful Sunday museum excursion, take this Smithsonian staffer's suggestion: Begin with brunch in the Corcoran's stunning cafe. Afterwards, take a leisurely tour of the art museum and then stroll over to the Renwick Gallery for more first-class art—and, perhaps, some shopping in the Renwick's excellent museum shop. It's a great, laid-back way to spend the day . . . and you won't be battling the crowds besieging the mega-museums on the Mall. The Corcoran cafe's hours are 11 A.M. to 3 P.M. Reservations are suggested; call (202) 639-1786.

Other Things to Do Nearby   Duck into the Organization of American States and enter a rain forest: A courtyard filled with palm trees and the sound of falling water awaits you. Walk up the staircase and peek into the opulent Hall of the Americas. The Octagon, one of the earliest Federal-period houses in the U.S., is a block to the east; Dolley Madison entertained there after the Brits burned the White House in 1814. For lunch, stroll up 17th Street toward Pennsylvania Avenue. Le Sorbet, around the corner on G Street, can supply a sandwich and drink for less than $5. Another block north is McDonald's.

Daughters of the American Revolution (DAR) Museum

Type of Attraction: The 33 period rooms are a cornucopia of decorative arts and antiques. A self-guided museum tour and a guided tour.

Location: 1776 D Street, NW, across from the Ellipse.

Nearest Metro Station: Farragut West

Admission: Free

Hours: Monday through Friday, 8:30 A.M. to 4 P.M.; Sundays, 1 P.M. to 5 P.M. Guided tours of the period rooms are available Monday through Friday, from 10 A.M. to 2:30 P.M., and Sundays, from 1 P.M. to 5 P.M. Tours leave approximately every 30 minutes.

Phone: (202) 879-3241

When to Go: Anytime

Special Comments: Expect to do a lot of stair climbing on the tour; you can't enter the rooms, and only two or three visitors at a time can squeeze into doorways to peer inside.

Overall Appeal by Age Group:

Pre-school	Grade School	Teens	Young Adults	Over 30	Senior Citizens
—	★	★½	★★	★★★½	★★★★½

Author's Rating: A must-see for lovers of antiques and decorative arts.
★★★½

How Much Time to Allow: Two hours

Description and Comments This beaux arts building, completed in 1910, is a knockout. The huge columns that grace the front of the building are solid marble; a special railroad spur was built to transport them to the building site. The DAR Museum, predictably enough, emphasizes the role of women throughout American history and includes fine examples of furniture, ceramics, glass, paintings, silver, costumes, and textiles. It's a small museum filled with everyday items out of America's past. From the interior of a California adobe parlor of 1850, to a replica of a 1775 bedchamber in Lexington, Massachusetts, to the kitchen of a 19th-century Oklahoma farm family, the period rooms place objects in a context of both time and place. Kids will get a kick out of the four-sided mousetrap that guillotines rodents, the foot-controlled toaster, and the sausage stuffer that looks like an early-19th-century version of a NordicTrack machine.

To make the museum more attractive to children accompanying parents on the period-rooms tour, docents drop kids off at the Touch Area on the third floor. While their parents tour nearby period rooms, kids can play with authentic 18th- and 19th-century toys and objects, including miniature Chippendale tables and chairs, real powder horns, butter molds, candle snuffers, and flags. The museum and period rooms are sleepers that a lot of visitors to Washington overlook. But for lovers of antiques and decorative arts, the rooms provide visitors an opportunity to view beautiful objects in authentic period settings.

Touring Tips Finding the entrance is a bit tough, although the DAR building itself is easy enough to find. At D and 17th (across from the Ellipse), walk about half a block down D Street; the museum and tour entrance is on the side of the building. During the busy spring and summer, the period room tours can get crowded, especially on weekends, so try to arrive before noon.

Other Things to Do Nearby Walk up the marble steps and into the American Red Cross building to see the Memorial Windows, reputed to be the largest suite of Tiffany windows still in their original location (except for in churches). Their theme is ministry to the sick and wounded. Next door to

DAR, the lobby of the Organization of American States building is a bit of a tropical paradise; around back is the Art Museum of the Americas, a small gallery featuring art from Latin America and the Caribbean (open Tuesday through Saturday, 10 A.M. to 5 P.M.; admission is free). Head up 17th Street toward Pennsylvania Avenue to find a large selection of restaurants.

Decatur House

Type of Attraction: One of Washington's earliest surviving important residences. A guided tour.

Location: 748 Jackson Place, NW, across from Lafayette Park.

Nearest Metro Stations: Farragut West, Farragut North

Admission: $4; $2.50 for seniors and students, children under 12 free.

Hours: Tuesday through Friday, 10 A.M. to 3 P.M.; weekends, noon to 4 P.M. Closed Mondays and Thanksgiving and Christmas days.

Phone: (202) 842-0920

When to Go: Anytime

Special Comments: The tour involves descending a steep, curving staircase.

Overall Appeal by Age Group:

Pre-school	Grade School	Teens	Young Adults	Over 30	Senior Citizens
★	★	★	★★	★★	★★½

Author's Rating: An interesting yet narrow slice of early Americana. ★★½

How Much Time to Allow: 30 minutes

Description and Comments Stephen Decatur was a naval war hero who defeated the Barbary pirates off the shores of Tripoli (ring a bell?) during the War of 1812. If he hadn't been killed in a duel, some say he might have been president. No doubt he built this house in 1819 with presidential aspirations in mind: It's close to the White House. The first floor is decorated in authentic Federalist style and displays Decatur's furnishings and sword. The formal parlors on the second floor reflect a later Victorian restyling. Famous statesmen who resided in the building include Henry Clay, Martin Van Buren, and Edward Livingston.

Touring Tips If you're on a tight schedule, this isn't the place to be blowing your time. But it's an okay rainy-afternoon alternative that gives insight into the early days of Washington.

Other Things to Do Nearby The Renwick Gallery is around the corner on Pennsylvania Avenue; next to it is Blair House, where foreign dignitaries stay. Decatur House faces Lafayette Park, frequent site of political demonstrations, once home to many homeless, and predictably filled with statues. Across the street is the White House.

Freer Gallery of Art (a Smithsonian museum)

Type of Attraction: A museum featuring Asian and American art. A self-guided tour.

Location: Jefferson Drive at 12th Street, SW, on the Mall.

Nearest Metro Station: Smithsonian

Admission: Free

Hours: Daily, 10 A.M. to 5:30 P.M.; closed Christmas Day.

Phone: (202) 357-2700 (voice); (202) 357-1729 (TTY)

When to Go: Anytime

Special Comments: This 70-year-old gallery reopened in 1993 after a four-and-a-half-year, $26 million renovation.

Overall Appeal by Age Group:

Pre-school	Grade School	Teens	Young Adults	Over 30	Senior Citizens
★	★★	★★½	★★★	★★★½	★★★★

Author's Rating: Gorgeous art on a human scale in a setting that's not overwhelming. ★★★★

How Much Time to Allow: One to two hours

Description and Comments Well-proportioned spaces, galleries illuminated by natural light, and quiet serenity are the hallmarks of this newly renovated landmark on the Mall. And the art? It's an unusual blend of American paintings (including the world's most important collection of works by James McNeill Whistler), and Asian paintings, sculpture, porcelains, scrolls, and richly embellished household items. Charles Lang Freer, the wealthy nineteenth-century industrialist who bequeathed this collection to the Smithsonian, saw similarities of color and surface texture in the diverse assemblage. Surrender to the gallery's tranquility and you may, too.

Touring Tips An underground link to the nearby Arthur M. Sackler Gallery creates a public exhibition space, as well as convenient passage between the two museums. Don't miss the Peacock Room, designed by James McNeill Whistler; it's widely considered to be the most important nineteenth-century interior in an American museum. Once the dining room of a Liverpool shipping magnate, it was installed in the Freer Gallery after Freer's death. The ornate room was painted by Whistler to house a collection of blue and white Chinese porcelains. Following a restoration that removed decades of dirt and grime, the room has been restored to its original splendor.

Other Things to Do Nearby The Sackler Gallery, the National Museum of African Art, and the Enid A. Haupt Garden are within a few steps of the Freer Gallery. Directly across the Mall are the National Museum of American History and the National Museum of Natural History. Walk up the Mall toward the Capitol to reach the Arts and Industries Building, the Hirshhorn Museum, and the National Air and Space Museum. For lunch, take the Metro to either L'Enfant Plaza (if it's a weekday) or the Old Post Office Pavilion (anytime).

Hirshhorn Museum and Sculpture Garden (a Smithsonian museum)

Type of Attraction: A museum of modern art. A self-guided tour.
Location: 7th Street and Independence Avenue, SW, on the Mall.
Nearest Metro Stations: Smithsonian, L'Enfant Plaza
Admission: Free
Hours: Daily, 10 A.M. to dusk; closed Christmas Day.
Phone: (202) 357-2700 (voice); (202) 357-1729 (TTY)
When to Go: Anytime
Special Comments: The Hirshhorn is a lot of people's favorite art museum on the Mall.
Overall Appeal by Age Group:

Pre-school	Grade School	Teens	Young Adults	Over 30	Senior Citizens
★	★★	★★★	★★★★	★★★★★	★★★★★

Author's Rating: An outrageous collection of 20th-century art; don't miss it. ★★★★★

How Much Time to Allow: Two hours

Description and Comments The art found inside is often as bizarre as the circular building that houses it. Works by modern masters such as Rodin, Winslow Homer, Mary Cassatt, and Henry Moore line the easy-to-walk galleries. The outdoor sculpture garden (set below Mall level) contains works by Rodin, Giacometti, and Alexander Calder, among many others. The sculpture offers a refreshing contrast to the marble palaces that line the Mall. If you only visit one modern art gallery on your visit, make it the Hirshhorn.

Touring Tips   Guided tours of the Hirshhorn are offered at noon, Monday through Friday, and at noon and 2 P.M. on weekends. During the summer months, additional docent-led tours are sometimes added.

Other Things to Do Nearby   Two nearby museums, Arts and Industries and Air and Space, offer startling contrasts to the Hirshhorn's treasures. A less jarring experience may be the National Gallery of Art's East Wing, also featuring modern art. The best bets for lunch are L'Enfant Plaza (on weekdays) and the Old Post Office Pavilion (any time). In the summer, the Hirshhorn has an outdoor self-service cafe featuring sandwiches, salads, and great sculpture.

Jefferson Memorial

Type of Attraction: A classical-style monument to the author of the Declaration of Independence and the third U.S. president. A self-guided tour.

Location: Across the Tidal Basin from the Washington Monument.

Nearest Metro Stations: L'Enfant Plaza, Smithsonian

Admission: Free

Hours: Always open; staffed from 8 A.M. to midnight, except on Christmas Day.

Phone: (202) 426-6841

When to Go: For the best views, go at night or when the cherry trees along the Tidal Basin are in bloom.

Special Comments: The view from the steps and across the Tidal Basin is one of the best in Washington.

Overall Appeal by Age Group:

Pre-school	Grade School	Teens	Young Adults	Over 30	Senior Citizens
★	★★	★★★	★★★	★★★	★★★

Author's Rating: A favorite at night, but not convenient. ★★½

How Much Time to Allow: 30 minutes

Description and Comments   The neoclassical, open-air design of this monument reflects Jefferson's taste in architecture. Because it's somewhat off the tourist path, it's usually less crowded than the monuments on the Mall.

Touring Tips   Park interpreters staffing the monument frequently give talks and can answer questions about Jefferson and the monument. Visitors can walk to the memorial along the rim of the Tidal Basin from Independence Avenue or along 14th Street, SW.

Other Things to Do Nearby   The Bureau of Engraving and Printing and the Holocaust Memorial Museum are both on 14th Street. In 1997, a $52 million memorial to President Franklin D. Roosevelt opened on a seven-and-a-half-acre site located between the Lincoln and Jefferson Memorials. The Tidal Basin is great for paddleboating. L'Enfant Plaza has an underground shopping mall with many places to eat (but not on weekends, when most of the restaurants are closed).

Lincoln Memorial

Type of Attraction: A classical-style memorial to the 16th American president. A self-guided tour.

Location: At the west end of the Mall.

Nearest Metro Stations: Smithsonian, Foggy Bottom/GWU

Admission: Free

Hours: Always open. Rangers on duty from 8 A.M. to midnight, except Christmas Day.

Phone: (202) 426-6841

When to Go: For the best views, visit in the early morning, at sunset, or at night.

Special Comments: At night, facing west across the Potomac River, you can see the eternal flame at John Kennedy's grave.

Overall Appeal by Age Group:

Pre-school	Grade School	Teens	Young Adults	Over 30	Senior Citizens
★★	★★	★★★	★★★	★★★	★★★

Author's Rating: Both solemn and scenic. ★★★

How Much Time to Allow: 30 minutes

Description and Comments   To see what the Lincoln Memorial looks like, just pull out a penny. Yet a visit to this marble monument inspires awe. Historic events took place on the steps: Black soprano Marian Anderson sang here in 1939 after being barred from Constitution Hall; Martin Luther King, Jr., gave his "I Have a Dream" speech here in 1963. The Lincoln Memorial anchors the Mall and should be on anyone's must-see list.

Touring Tips   The new Legacy of Lincoln museum in the memorial's basement is worth a peek. You'll find exhibits about demonstrations held at the memorial and a video recounting the building's history. The Lincoln Memorial's location at the west end of the Mall near the river, however, puts this marble edifice at a distance from any lunch spots except for overpriced

Mall hot dog vendors, so eat first. Bathrooms are located on the memorial's ground level.

Other Things to Do Nearby   The Vietnam Veterans Memorial and the Reflecting Pool are directly across from the Lincoln Memorial. The National Academy of Sciences on Constitution Avenue features science exhibits (open Monday through Friday, 9 A.M. to 5 P.M.; free). Outside, tourists can crawl into the lap of an Albert Einstein statue to have their picture taken; it's a D.C. tradition. A $52 million memorial to President Franklin D. Roosevelt opened in 1997 on a seven-and-a-half-acre site located on the Tidal Basin between the Lincoln and Jefferson Memorials. If you hike a few blocks up 23rd Street or 17th Street, you'll find an alternative to those hot dog vendors.

National Air and Space Museum
(a Smithsonian museum)

Type of Attraction: A museum that chronicles the history of manned flight. A self-guided tour.

Location: On the south side of the Mall near the U.S. Capitol.

Nearest Metro Stations: Smithsonian, L'Enfant Plaza

Admission: Free

Hours: 10 A.M. to 5:30 P.M.; closed Christmas Day. Depending on the shape of the federal budget, hours may be extended during the summer.

Phone: (202) 357-2700 (voice); (202) 357-1729 (TTY)

When to Go: Before noon or after 4 P.M.

Special Comments: If you want to get tickets for the five-story-high IMAX theater, make the box office on the main floor your first stop. Some special exhibits require passes; check with the information desk in the main lobby.

Overall Appeal by Age Group:

Pre-school	Grade School	Teens	Young Adults	Over 30	Senior Citizens
★★★★	★★★★★	★★★★★	★★★★★	★★★★★	★★★★

Author's Rating: Absolutely not to be missed. ★★★★★

How Much Time to Allow: Two hours minimum—and you still won't see it all. If possible, try to spread your tour of the museum over two or more visits.

Description and Comments   This museum is the most visited in the world, drawing about seven million visitors a year. Entering from the Mall, visitors can touch a moon rock, gaze up at the Wright Brothers' plane, the *Enola Gay*, and the *Spirit of St. Louis*, which Lindbergh flew across the Atlantic in 1927. Everywhere you look is another full-size wonder. The only drawback to this museum is its size—going to every exhibit becomes numbing after a while. If your length of stay allows it, try to split your time here into at least two visits. But it's a must-see for virtually anyone—not just airplane buffs and space cadets.

Touring Tips   If you don't have an unlimited amount of time to wander around, try this strategy: After leaving the main lobby, work your way over to Space Hall, where you can tour Skylab and check out the Apollo-Soyuz spacecraft. For more insight into the exhibits, take one of the free, one-hour guided tours starting at 10:15 A.M. and 1 P.M. daily, beginning at the information desk in the main lobby. While you'll never have to stand in line to get into the National Air and Space Museum, you can avoid a few major bottlenecks by staying away from Skylab, the moon rock, and the cafeteria around lunchtime. Four exhibits also worth hitting early to avoid lines: "How Things Fly" (an interactive gallery that teaches the basic principles of flight), "Where Next, Columbus?" (future space travel), "Space Race" (a new exhibit examining the Cold War competition for outer space between the United States and the former Soviet Union), and "Beyond the Limits" (computers in aviation and space).

Other Things to Do Nearby   To escape the worst of the crowds, try a stroll through the fragrant U.S. Botanic Garden, located a block east of the National Air and Space Museum. For lunch, the on-site cafeteria and restaurant feature a great view of the Capitol and expensive, run-of-the-mill dining. Best bet on weekdays: L'Enfant Plaza, where you can dine elbow-to-elbow with Washington bureaucrats in an underground mall with a wide range of eateries. The entrance is south of the Mall on 10th Street, SW, between D and E Streets. On weekends and holidays, Capitol Hill (with its wide array of restaurants, bars, and cafes) and the Old Post Office Pavilion are good bets. In the summer, check out the Hirshhorn Museum's self-service cafe, where you can dine al fresco with great art.

National Aquarium

Type of Attraction: The oldest aquarium in the United States. A self-guided tour.

Location: In the basement of the Department of Commerce building on 14th Street, NW.

Nearest Metro Station: Federal Triangle

Admission: Adults $2; children ages 2–10 years 75 cents

Hours: Daily, 9 A.M. to 5 P.M.; closed Christmas Day.

Phone: (202) 482-2825 (recording); (202) 482-2826

When to Go: Anytime

Special Comments: A cool, dark oasis on a sweltering summer afternoon.

Overall Appeal by Age Group:

Pre-school	Grade School	Teens	Young Adults	Over 30	Senior Citizens
★★★★	★★★★	★★★	★★	★★	★★

Author's Rating: A basement full of fish tanks. ★½

How Much Time to Allow: One hour

Description and Comments   Essentially a long room lined with big fish tanks in the basement of an office building, this aquarium is not in the same league with other, newer fish and dolphin emporiums that are springing up all over (such as the one in Baltimore). But children will love it. Small and lacking crowd-pleasing sea mammals, the aquarium figures as a minor exhibit for filling in the odd hour or to escape from a sweltering afternoon. Otherwise, spend your valuable touring time elsewhere.

Touring Tips   Sharks get fed at 2 P.M. on Monday, Wednesday, and Saturday; the piranhas get their meals at 2 P.M. on Tuesday, Thursday, and Sunday.

Other Things to Do Nearby   The Washington Monument, the National Museum of American History, and the Old Post Office Pavilion are within a few minutes' walk. The Commerce Department cafeteria, open Monday through Friday from 9 A.M. to 2 P.M., offers good, cheap fare: a soup and salad bar, pizza and pasta, a grill, a deli, and hot entrees. You can get a whole pizza that will feed a family of four for less than $10.

National Archives

Type of Attraction: The magnificent rotunda where the Declaration of Independence and U.S. Constitution are displayed. A self-guided tour.

Location: 7th Street and Constitution Avenue, NW, on the Mall.

Nearest Metro Station: Archives

Admission: Free

Hours: April 1 through Labor Day, Exhibition Hall open every day, 10 A.M. to 9 P.M.; September through March 31, 10 A.M. to 5:30 P.M.; closed Christmas Day.

Phone: (202) 501-5205

When to Go: Before noon or after 4 P.M. during spring and summer.

Special Comments: Small children may need a lift to see the documents; skip it if the line is long.

Overall Appeal by Age Group:

Pre-school	Grade School	Teens	Young Adults	Over 30	Senior Citizens
★	★★	★★½	★★★	★★★	★★★

Author's Rating: A letdown. ★½

How Much Time to Allow: 30 minutes

Average Wait in Line per 100 People in Line ahead of You: 20 minutes

Description and Comments   In addition to trying to decipher the faint and flowing script on the sheets of parchment mounted in bronze and glass cases, visitors can stroll through a temporary exhibit of photos and documents covering some aspect of Americana. Most visitors seem as fascinated by the written description of the elaborate security system that lowers the sacred documents into a deep, nuclear-explosion-proof vault each night as they are by seeing the charters themselves—and you can't even see the contraption. While the 75-foot-high rotunda is impressive, most people are surprised at how little there is to see inside this huge building. In fact, there *is* a lot more to see—but you've got to call in advance to arrange a tour. If the line to get in is long, skip it and come back later. It's really not worth the wait.

Touring Tips   Some visitors say the documents on display in the exhibition areas outside the rotunda are more interesting—and certainly easier to read—than the better-known parchments under the big dome. For a behind-the-scenes view of the workings of the National Archives, arrange to take a reserved tour. During spring and summer, four weeks' notice is recommended. Or take a chance and show up at the Pennsylvania Avenue entrance (across from 8th Street, NW) at tour time. If there's a cancellation or a no-show, you're in. The reserved tours begin at 10:15 A.M. and 1:15 P.M. Monday through Friday and last about an hour and a half. On the reserved tour, visitors take a tour of the building, including the stacks, microfilm viewing rooms, and exhibits and models that show how researchers preserve documents. The tour ends at the Rotunda. Oh, and don't miss the gift shop, where the best-selling item is a photograph of President Nixon and Elvis Presley embracing. It's a scream.

Other Things to Do Nearby   Pick a Smithsonian museum you haven't seen yet and dive in. Several good restaurants popular with folks who work in the museums along the Mall are located across Pennsylvania Avenue from the National Archives on Indiana Avenue, NW.

National Gallery of Art: East Building

Type of Attraction: A museum housing 20th-century art and special exhibitions. A self-guided tour.

Location: 4th Street and Constitution Avenue, NW, on the Mall.

Nearest Metro Stations: Archives, Judiciary Square, Smithsonian

Admission: Free

Hours: Monday through Saturday, 10 A.M. to 5 P.M.; Sundays, 11 A.M. to 6 P.M., closed Christmas and New Year's days.

Phone: (202) 737-4215

When to Go: Anytime

Special Comments: Usually referred to as the "East Wing" of the National Gallery. Visitors with disabilities may park in available spaces in front of the building. Introductory tours are offered daily and last about an hour; for times, call (202) 842-6247.

Overall Appeal by Age Group:

Pre-school	Grade School	Teens	Young Adults	Over 30	Senior Citizens
★	★★	★★★	★★★★★	★★★★★	★★★★★

Author's Rating: Even the building is a great work of art. ★★★★★

How Much Time to Allow: Two hours

Description and Comments   Both the interior and exterior of this I. M. Pei–designed building are spectacular, so it's worth a visit even if you hate modern art. Outside, the popular 1978 building consists of unadorned vertical planes. Inside, it's bright, airy, and spacious. Look for art by modern masters such as Picasso, Matisse, Mondrian, Miró, Magritte, Warhol, Lichtenstein, and Rauschenberg. The exhibits change constantly, so there's no telling which of these is on display.

Touring Tips   Occasionally, temporary exhibits (such as a recent Picasso show) are extremely popular and may require a free "time ticket" that admits you on a certain day at a specific hour. You may pick up such tickets in advance; tickets are available as much as a month before a show opens. If you don't have a ticket on the day you visit the East Wing, you're not completely out of luck: a number of tickets are set aside every day for distribution that day only. If you want one, arrive at the ticket counter on the main floor by noon (or 2 P.M. during the week). Then come back later to see the exhibit. When you exit the museum, turn left and check out the high, knife-edge exterior corner wall of the gallery, near the Mall—it's almost worn away from people touching their noses to it.

Other Things to Do Nearby The West Wing, with its more traditional European art, is connected to the East Building by an underground concourse. The Capitol and the U.S. Botanic Garden are close by, as is the National Archives. The Cascade Cafe/Buffet, a cafeteria along the concourse, may be the best official Mall eatery, featuring a classy selection of food and an espresso bar. Otherwise, the Old Post Office Pavilion and L'Enfant Plaza (weekdays only) offer the best food choices nearby.

National Gallery of Art: West Building

Type of Attraction: Museum featuring European and American art from the 13th through the 19th centuries. Self-guided and guided tours.

Location: 6th Street and Constitution Avenue, NW, on the Mall.

Nearest Metro Station: Archives

Admission: Free

Hours: Monday through Saturday, 10 A.M. to 5 P.M.; Sundays, 11 A.M. to 6 P.M. Closed Christmas and New Year's days.

Phone: (202) 737-4215

When to Go: Anytime

Special Comments: Introductory tours are offered daily and last about an hour. For times, call (202) 842-6247. Some galleries may be closed on your visit due to an ongoing skylight replacement project. Usually referred to as the "West Wing" of the National Gallery.

Overall Appeal by Age Group:

Pre-school	Grade School	Teens	Young Adults	Over 30	Senior Citizens
★	★★½	★★★	★★★★	★★★★★	★★★★★

Author's Rating: Art with a capital "A." ★★★★★

How Much Time to Allow: Two hours for a light skimming, but you could spend a week.

Description and Comments This is where you find the heavy hitters: Dutch masters such as Rembrandt and Vermeer, plus Raphael, Monet, and Jacques-Louis David, just to name a few. And it's all housed in an elegant neoclassical building designed by John Russell Pope. It's a world-class art museum; first-time visitors should make at least one stop.

The new Micro Gallery, 13 computer stations featuring high-tech computers and 20-inch touchscreen color monitors, provides visitors with images and information on about 1,700 paintings, sculptures, and decorative arts; 650 artists; and more than 530 art-related subjects. Modeled after a similar system at the National Gallery in London, the Micro Gallery lets visitors with little or no computer experience expand their appreciation of the Gallery's permanent collection. You can even create a personal tour of the museum and print a map showing the locations of works of art you've selected. The Micro Gallery is located on the Main Floor near the Mall entrance.

Touring Tips Most of the museum's paintings are hung in many small rooms, instead of a few big ones, so don't try to speed through the building or you'll miss most of them. When museum fatigue begins to set in, rest your feet in one of the atriums located between the museum's many galleries. If you plan on dragging kids through this massive place, try bribing them with a later trip to the National Zoo.

Some temporary exhibits require a free time ticket that admits you on a certain day at a specific hour. You may pick up such tickets in advance; tickets are available as much as a month before a show opens. If you don't have a ticket on the day you want to visit the West Wing, you're not completely out of luck: a number of tickets are set aside every day for distribution that day only. If you want one, arrive at the ticket counter on the main floor by noon (or 2 P.M. during the week). Then come back later to see the exhibit.

Other Things to Do Nearby Take the connecting corridor (an underground concourse) to the Gallery's East Building. The Air and Space Museum is directly across the Mall, while the National Archives is in the other direction, across Constitution Avenue. Probably the best museum cafeteria on the Mall is located along the concourse. Otherwise, L'Enfant Plaza (an underground shopping mall loaded with restaurants and fast food places; weekdays only) and the Old Post Office Pavilion are your best bets for lunch (anytime).

National Museum of African Art
(a Smithsonian museum)

Type of Attraction: A museum specializing in the traditional arts of Africa. A self-guided tour.

Location: 950 Independence Avenue, SW, on the Mall near the Castle (the Smithsonian Institution building).

Nearest Metro Station: Smithsonian

Admission: Free

Hours: Daily, 10 A.M. to 5:30 P.M.; closed Christmas Day.

Phone: (202) 357-2700 (voice); (202) 357-1729 (TTY)

When to Go: Anytime

Special Comments: Provides a quiet respite when other Mall attractions are jammed; an excellent museum shop.

Overall Appeal by Age Group:

Pre-school	Grade School	Teens	Young Adults	Over 30	Senior Citizens
★	★★	★★	★★½	★★½	★★½

Author's Rating: Exquisite sculpture and fascinating household items. ★★

How Much Time to Allow: One hour

Description and Comments   This relatively new subterranean museum, which opened in 1987, is paired with its mate, the Sackler Gallery, a museum of Asian art, and separated by an above-ground garden. Inside is an extensive collection of African art in a wide range of media, including sculpture, masks, household and personal items, and religious objects. Intellectually, this museum transports museum-goers far away from the Mall. It's an okay destination for older children, teens, and adults looking for some non-European cultural history and art. This museum is a great alternative on hot or crowded days in Washington.

Touring Tips   One-hour guided tours are given at 1:30 P.M. Monday through Thursday and at 11 A.M. and 1 P.M. on weekends. And don't miss the excellent museum shop, where you'll find textiles, jewelry, scarves and sashes, wood carvings, and a wide selection of African music on tape, CD, and video.

Other Things to Do Nearby   This museum is twinned with the Arthur M. Sackler Gallery, and even connects with it below ground—a nice feature on a sweltering Washington afternoon. If the weather's mild, stroll the Enid A. Haupt Garden, which separates the two museums at ground level. Neither museum has a cafeteria; the closest places featuring good selections and reasonable prices are L'Enfant Plaza (weekdays) and the Old Post Office Pavilion (anytime).

National Museum of American History (a Smithsonian museum)

Type of Attraction: An extensive collection of artifacts reflecting the American experience—historical, social, and technological. A self-guided tour.

Location: 14th Street and Constitution Avenue, NW, on the Mall.

Nearest Metro Stations: Smithsonian, Federal Triangle

Admission: Free

Hours: Daily, 10 A.M. to 5:30 P.M.; extended summer hours depend on budget restraints. Closed Christmas Day.

Phone: (202) 357-2700 (voice); (202) 357-1729 (TTY)

When to Go: To avoid the worst crowds, visit before noon and after 3 P.M.

Special Comments: The immensity of this museum almost demands that visitors try to see it in more than one visit.

Overall Appeal by Age Group:

Pre-school	Grade School	Teens	Young Adults	Over 30	Senior Citizens
★★★	★★★★★	★★★★★	★★★★★	★★★★★	★★★★★

Author's Rating: A collection of national treasures; don't miss it. ★★★★★

How Much Time to Allow: Two hours on a first pass; it would take a week to see it all.

Description and Comments   Three exhibit-packed floors feature such treasures as the original Star-Spangled Banner, steam locomotives, a Model T Ford, a pendulum three stories high that shows how the earth rotates, a collection of ball gowns worn by First Ladies, and Archie Bunker's chair. If you can't find something of interest here, you may need mouth-to-mouth resuscitation. For a lot of people, this ranks as their favorite Mall museum. No wonder: It offers viewers a dizzying array of history, nostalgia, technology, and culture. And kids love it. It's a must-see for virtually all visitors.

Touring Tips   At most museums, you look at *stuff,* but a lot of the collection at American History is arranged so that viewers can learn about *people* in the context of their times. To see what we mean—and to help you organize yourself in this bewilderingly large museum—make it a point to see these exhibits: the First Ladies' Exhibition, Field to Factory (about the migration of Southern rural African-Americans to northern cities), and a collection of objects about television that includes Archie Bunker's chair, Fonzie's jacket, one of Mr. Rogers' sweaters, Oscar the Grouch (of *Sesame Street* fame), and for baby boomers, some items from the *Howdy Doody Show.* Check at the information desk for a schedule of tours (usually at 10 A.M. and 1 P.M. daily), demonstrations, concerts, lectures, films, and other activities put on by the museum staff. Some final hints: A lot of people touring the museum on their own overlook the Hall of Transportation in the museum's east wing, which features an excellent collection of cars, trains, and motorcycles. Car aficionados will love it. Kids (and most adults) enjoy the Science in American Life exhibit, the Hands-on Science Center, and the Hands-On History Room.

Other Things to Do Nearby Within a short walk are the Washington Monument, the National Aquarium, the Old Post Office Pavilion, and the National Museum of Natural History. Almost directly across the Mall are the Freer and Sackler Galleries and the National Museum of African Art. And, yes, the American History Museum has a cafeteria and an ice cream parlor.

National Museum of Natural History
(a Smithsonian museum)

Type of Attraction: America's treasure chest of the natural sciences and human culture. A self-guided tour.

Location: On the Mall at 10th Street, NW, and Constitution Avenue.

Nearest Metro Stations: Smithsonian, Archives, Federal Triangle

Admission: Free

Hours: 10 A.M. to 5:30 P.M.; closed Christmas Day.

Phone: (202) 357-2700 (voice); (202) 357-1729 (TTY)

When to Go: Before noon and after 4 P.M.

Special Comments: In the Discovery Room, kids ages 4 years and up can touch nearly everything. Hours are Tuesday through Friday, noon to 2:30 P.M. and weekends, 10:30 A.M. to 3:30 P.M. Make the popular Discovery Room your first stop and pick up free time tickets; tour the rest of the museum and return at the time stamped on your ticket. Free guided tours of museum highlights are offered at 10:30 A.M. and 1:30 P.M. daily.

Overall Appeal by Age Group:

Pre-school	Grade School	Teens	Young Adults	Over 30	Senior Citizens
★★★★	★★★★★	★★★★½	★★★★★	★★★★★	★★★★★

Author's Rating: The displays of huge dinosaur fossils and the world's best-known gem make this museum a classic. ★★★★½

How Much Time to Allow: Two hours is enough time to see the really cool stuff, but you could easily spend an entire day here.

Description and Comments Distinguished by its golden dome and the towering bull elephant in the rotunda, the Museum of Natural History is a Washington landmark. It's also a bit old-fashioned, with long halls filled with dioramas, display cases, and hanging specimens that reflect the Victorian obsession with collecting things. This museum, along with Air and Space across the Mall, is immensely popular with families, and for a good reason—folks of all ages and tastes will find fascinating things to see here.

In September 1997, the Janet Annenberg Hooker Hall of Geology, Gems, and Minerals opened, showcasing the museum's world-class gem and mineral collection. It's part of an ongoing $8.5 million museum renovation. The new gem hall features interactive computers, animated graphics, film and video presentations, and hands-on exhibits. In addition to the 45.52-carat Hope Diamond, the new space features meteorites, emeralds, a 23,000-carat topaz gem, crystals, a walk-through mine, a re-creation of a cave, and a plate tectonics gallery showing how the earth's surface shifts.

Touring Tips After entering through the big doors at the Mall entrance, bear right to see the dinosaur skeletons. Then ascend to the second floor to gaze upon the supposedly cursed Hope Diamond and to explore the new Geology, Gem, and Mineral Hall. If you're not put off by crawling critters, stop by the Insect Zoo, which features a wide array of (live) bugs. Special exhibits are located on the ground level (Constitution Avenue entrance).

Other Things to Do Nearby The National Museum of American History is next door; across the Mall is the Hirshhorn Museum, the Arts & Industries Building, the Museum of African Art, and the Sackler and Freer Galleries; the National Archives is across Constitution Avenue. A convenient choice for lunch is the Old Post Office Pavilion, about a block away on 12th Street, NW. The fast-food kiosk in front of the museum on the Mall is overpriced: If you crave a hot dog, walk over to Constitution Avenue, find a street vendor, and save a buck.

The Octagon

Type of Attraction: One of the first great homes built in Washington; a museum showcasing American architecture and historic preservation. A guided tour.

Location: 1799 New York Avenue, NW.

Nearest Metro Station: Farragut West

Admission: $3 for adults, $1.50 for students and seniors.

Hours: Tuesday through Sunday, 10 A.M. to 4 P.M.; closed Mondays and Christmas and New Year's days.

Phone: (202) 638-3221

When to Go: Anytime

Special Comments: One long staircase leads to the second-floor exhibition galleries.

Overall Appeal by Age Group:

Pre-school	Grade School	Teens	Young Adults	Over 30	Senior Citizens
★	★½	★★	★★½	★★½	★★½

Author's Rating: Another interesting, yet narrow, slice of early Washington history. ★★½

How Much Time to Allow: One hour

Description and Comments   This elegant building is where President James Madison and First Lady Dolley Madison took up temporary residence after the British burned the White House during the War of 1812. Built in 1801 (when Washington was mostly swamp), this early Federalist building recently underwent a $5 million, six-year renovation; it's owned by the American Architectural Foundation. Period rooms on the first floor offer visitors a glimpse of how the upper crust lived in the early days of Washington; the coal stoves in the entrance hall are original. The former bedrooms upstairs are now galleries displaying temporary exhibits on architecture and design.

Touring Tips   Interpreters give half-hour tours of the building that provide additional glimpses into the past—and tell fascinating anecdotes about the building and the city's early days. For example, President Madison signed the Treaty of Ghent, which ended the war that had driven him from the White House, in the upstairs parlor. Later the building served as a girls' school and was subdivided into ten apartments before it was acquired by the American Architectural Foundation in 1899.

Other Things to Do Nearby   The Corcoran Gallery of Art is a block away. The Renwick Gallery and the White House are also close by. Walk up 17th Street for a selection of fast-food places and restaurants.

Old Executive Office Building

Type of Attraction: The ornate building that houses many agencies that are part of the Executive Office of the President. A guided tour.

Location: Next to the White House on Pennsylvania Avenue; use the visitors entrance on 17th Street, NW.

Nearest Metro Station: Farragut West

Admission: Free

Hours: Saturdays from 9 A.M. to 12 noon by reservation only.

Phone: (202) 395-5895. Call Tuesday through Friday, 9 A.M. to noon, for reservations.

Special Comments: The recent overhaul of the building skimped on elevators: They're tiny and require visitors to jump up and down to close the doors. Nervous types, beware. Call for reservations a month in advance of your visit to Washington during the spring and summer. And leave the camera in your hotel: No photography is permitted on the tour.

Overall Appeal by Age Group:

Pre-school	Grade School	Teens	Young Adults	Over 30	Senior Citizens
★	★	★½	★★	★★½	★★½

Author's Rating: For those who can't get their fill of ornate buildings.
★★½

How Much Time to Allow: One hour and a half

Description and Comments   The Old Executive Office Building's baroque, Second Empire exterior falls into the "love it or hate it" category. President Harry S Truman, for example, called it "the greatest monstrosity in America." Yet its recently renovated interior is more like a palace than an assembly of government offices—even if they are the offices of the president's minions. The massive building boasts four-and-a-half-foot-thick granite walls, 16-foot ceilings, and nearly two miles of corridors. Grand staircases, bronze stair balusters, four skylight domes, and two stained-glass rotundas grace the interior. Other marvels include the four-story Executive Office of the President Library (constructed of cast iron), the Indian Treaty Room (featuring rich marble wall panelings and gold-leaf ornamentation), and the opulent office of the vice president. This tour offers more than stunning interiors: Pay close attention to the windows and you'll get an overhead view of the White House that's usually reserved for government honchos. This is another "behind-the-scenes" tour that lets visitors get a glimpse of a part of Washington that few people ever see. First-time visitors should pass on it, but for those on a second or third trip, it's an interesting Saturday morning diversion.

Touring Tips   By guided tour only; advance reservations required. Tours leave between 9 A.M. and 12 noon on Saturdays only. To make a reservation, call (202) 395-5895 Tuesday through Friday, between 9 A.M. and 12 noon. Make reservations several weeks before your visit; you'll have to give each visitor's correct name, date of birth, and social security number. Bring a photo ID when you come; parents can vouch for kids. The 90-minute tour is long on walking and short on places to sit. Bathrooms are available once the tour guide gets you out of the waiting area and past the metal detectors.

Other Things to Do Nearby   A lot: The White House, the Renwick Gallery, the Corcoran Gallery of Art, the DAR Museum, the Washington Monument, and the National Aquarium are all within a few blocks. The Octagon, where President Madison and First Lady Dolley Madison lived after the British burned the White House in 1814, is two blocks south and one block east on New York Avenue.

Old Post Office Tower and Pavilion

Type of Attraction: A multi-ethnic food court in a spectacular architectural setting; home of the second-best view in Washington; trendy shops. A guided tour (of the tower).

Location: 12th Street and Pennsylvania Avenue, NW.

Nearest Metro Station: Federal Triangle

Admission: Free

Hours: During the summer, retail stores are open Monday through Saturday, 10 A.M. to 9 P.M., and Sundays, noon to 6 p.m; in the winter, Monday through Saturday, 10 A.M. to 7 P.M., and Sundays, noon to 6 P.M. Summer food court hours are Monday through Saturday, 10 A.M. to 9 P.M., and Sundays, noon to 8 P.M.; the food court closes an hour earlier the rest of the year. From Easter Sunday through Labor Day, the tower is open from 8 A.M. to 10:45 P.M.; the rest of the year it's open from 10 A.M. to 5:45 P.M.

Phone: (202) 289-4224; (202) 606-8691 for the tower

When to Go: Anytime to take the glass elevator up the clock tower; beat the worst of the crowds in the food court after 1 P.M.

Special Comments: This is the place to come when they run out of time tickets at the Washington Monument. The food court is a favorite stop for tour buses, making it difficult at times to find a table.

Overall Appeal by Age Group:

Pre-school	Grade School	Teens	Young Adults	Over 30	Senior Citizens
★★★★	★★★★	★★★★	★★★	★★★	★★★

Author's Rating: A great view and a lifesaver for tourists who hate the overpriced, crummy food served in most museums. ★★★½

How Much Time to Allow: One hour for the clock tower.

Description and Comments   This fine old building, a Pennsylvania Avenue landmark, was slated for demolition, but preservationist groups intervened to save it. Today, the 315-foot clock tower offers a spectacular view of Washington, while the multi-ethnic food court occupies a stunning, glass-roofed architectural space ten stories high. It offers a complete tourist experience for people of all ages: a view to kill for (through large plate glass windows, not tiny windows like at the Monument), great food, and a shopping mall. And with its proximity to the Mall and White House, the Pavilion is a convenient place to visit for a quick lunch or snack.

Touring Tips   It's elbow to elbow in the small elevator to the observation deck. Beware of groups of screaming teenagers in the food court—it's a popular destination for school groups. To reach the glass-enclosed elevators to the observation deck, go to the patio area in the food court. The National Park Service rangers on duty in the tower are a great source of advice about D.C. touring. Ask one to show you the lay of the land from the observation deck.

Other Things to Do Nearby   Make faces at the groupers in the National Aquarium, see an agent rip off some rounds of automatic weapons fire at the FBI, or visit Ford's Theatre. If you can't find anything good to eat in the food court, it's time to go home.

The Pentagon

Type of Attraction: The world's largest office building, and headquarters for the Department of Defense. A guided tour.

Location: Across the Potomac River in Arlington, Virginia.

Nearest Metro Station: Pentagon (the tour office is at the top of the Metro escalator)

Admission: Free

Hours: Monday through Friday, 9:30 A.M. to 3:30 P.M.; tours leave every 30 minutes. Closed weekends and federal holidays.

Phone: (703) 695-1776

When to Go: By 9 A.M. during peak tourist season (May through August).

Special Comments: Valid photo ID such as a driver's license, passport, or student ID is required for visitors over age 16; children under age 16 must be accompanied by an adult. Small children and senior citizens may find the brisk pace of this 75-minute tour exhausting. Ramp access is available for disabled folks.

Overall Appeal by Age Group:

Pre-school	Grade School	Teens	Young Adults	Over 30	Senior Citizens
—	★	★	★½	★½	★★

Author's Rating: Boring. ★

How Much Time to Allow: One hour and 15 minutes

Description and Comments This tour is a furiously paced run through a mile of the Pentagon's 17.5 miles of corridors. Along the way you get to see General MacArthur's West Point uniform, a blur of military paintings, and an exhibit featuring the names of every Medal of Honor winner. Between flashes of art, keep your eyes peeled for two things: your guide, who walks backwards the entire time to keep an eye on his charges; and brief glimpses of Pentagon top brass. On my tour I saw Admiral Frank B. Kelso, then Chief of Naval Operations. He didn't stop to chat. The tour is best suited for retired military personnel and their dependents—I mean, families.

Touring Tips Eat and go to the bathroom before arriving: Incredibly, the Department of Defense provides neither eating facilities nor rest rooms for visitors to use. For lunch, you must reboard the Metro; the nearest place to eat is Pentagon City.

Other Things to Do Nearby Arlington Cemetery is one Metro station away. The Newseum, D.C.'s newest museum, is an homage to journalism located near the Rosslyn station, two Metro stops away. It's free and open Wednesday through Sunday.

Renwick Gallery (a Smithsonian museum)

Type of Attraction: A museum dedicated to American crafts and decorative arts. A self-guided tour.

Location: 17th and Pennsylvania Avenue, NW (diagonally across from the White House).

Nearest Metro Station: Farragut West

Admission: Free

Hours: Daily, 10 A.M. to 5:30 P.M.; closed Christmas Day.

Phone: (202) 357-2700 (voice); (202) 357-1729 (TTY)

When to Go: Anytime

Special Comments: Don't expect an exhibition of hand-woven baskets: The museum features a wide array of mixed-media sculptures, tapestries, and constructions by major contemporary artists.

Overall Appeal by Age Group:

Pre-school	Grade School	Teens	Young Adults	Over 30	Senior Citizens
★	★★	★★	★★	★★½	★★½

Author's Rating: An elegant setting, yet a bit dull. ★★

How Much Time to Allow: One hour

Description and Comments   Both the art and the Second Empire architecture of the mansion make this Smithsonian museum worth a stop when you're near the White House. Works on display are constructed in glass, ceramics, wood, fiber, and metal. But folks on a first-time visit to Washington or with children should skip it.

Touring Tips   Glide up the Grand Staircase to enter the elegant Grand Salon, now an art gallery featuring floor-to-ceiling oil paintings, velvet curtains, and traditional furniture. On the same floor is the elegant Octagon Room, which faces the street and is used as exhibition space. The first floor hosts temporary exhibits.

Other Things to Do Nearby   Next door is Blair House, where visiting foreign dignitaries stay; you can't get in, but look for Secret Service agents and diplomatic limos. A plaque on the wrought-iron gates honors a guard who saved President Truman from a would-be assassin. Around the corner on 17th Street is the closest McDonald's to the White House. Arrive early in the morning and maybe you'll catch a glimpse of President Clinton in jogging togs.

Franklin Delano Roosevelt Memorial

Type of Attraction: A 7.5-acre, open-air memorial to the 32nd president of the United States. A self-guided tour.

Location: West Potomac Park, between the Tidal Basin and the Potomac River.

Nearest Metro Station: The Smithsonian (Independence Avenue exit) is about a brisk, 30-minute walk away. Other Metro stations even less convenient are Foggy Bottom and Arlington Cemetery (across Memorial Bridge in Virginia).

Admission: Free

Hours: Daily, 8 A.M. to midnight; closed Christmas Day.

Phone: (202) 426-6841

When to Go: Anytime, except during inclement weather; the FDR Memorial is unenclosed.

Special Comments: Folks old enough to have voted for FDR and disabled people may find it difficult to visit the memorial; nearby parking is scarce and the walk from the nearest Metro station is about a mile. One hundred and sixty unmetered parking spaces are located along Ohio Drive, SW, eastbound, and three lots with a total of 247 spaces are in East Potomac Park under the 14th Street bridges. Five handi-capped spaces and one van space are located at the main entrance to the memorial on West Basin Drive. Except at off-peak times (before noon on weekdays and evenings), competition for the spaces is fierce. Other options for reaching the memorial include cabs and a water taxi.

Overall Appeal by Age Group:

Pre-school	Grade School	Teens	Young Adults	Over 30	Senior Citizens
★★½	★★★	★★½	★★★	★★★½	★★★★

Author's Rating: Washington's newest presidential memorial successfully blends history, texture, drama, nostalgia, landscaping, and flowing water. The result is a dramatic and inspiring memorial to America's best-loved 20th-century leader. ★★★½

How Much Time to Allow: 30 minutes to an hour

Description and Comments Unlike the nearby imposing marble edifices to Lincoln and Jefferson, the FDR Memorial on the Tidal Basin tells a story: In four open-air, interconnected "rooms" ("enclaves" or "tableaus" might be better words) that represent each of Roosevelt's four terms, his words are carved on granite walls, bronze images depict the alphabet-soup of pro-grams and agencies he created to help millions of Americans devastated by the Depression, and statues depict the average citizens whose lives he touched. One shows a man listening intently to a radio, evoking the days before television—and a time when FDR's strong and vibrant voice gave hope to Americans in his "fireside chats."

Roosevelt himself is represented in the third room in a larger-than-life bronze statue. The president is seated, his body wrapped in a cape, his face lined with weariness as he approaches the final year of his life. His Scottish terrier Fala is at his feet. The fourth room features a statue of Eleanor Roo-sevelt, widely regarded as America's greatest First Lady for her services as a delegate to the United Nations and as a champion for human rights. This is the first presidential memorial to honor a presidential wife.

Many elements work in harmony to make the memorial a success. Tex-tures of South Dakota granite, brick, rough wood, and falling water com-bine with ornamental plantings and shade trees to create the ambience of a secluded garden rather than an imposing structure. Nor is this a "hands off" memorial: The slightly-larger-than-life figures of FDR and Mrs. Roosevelt, as well as statues of five men in an urban bread line and a rural couple outside a barn door, are placed at ground level. Visitors can easily drape an arm around the First Lady, sit in Franklin's lap as he delivers a fireside chat, or join the men in line for a souvenir snapshot. The memorial's many waterfalls (FDR considered himself a Navy man) attract splashers with stepping stones while kids enjoy climbing on giant, toppled granite blocks inscribed with the words "I hate war." As a result, visitors to the new memorial, both young and old, seem to enjoy themselves.

Yet irony abounds in this $52 million monument to the president who gave the nation a New Deal and expanded the role of federal government: Many of today's legislators at the other end of the Mall are striving to dismantle FDR's legacy of an activist government.

Touring Tips   While you can enter the new memorial (dedicated in May 1997) from either end, try to start your tour at the official entrance so you can stroll through the outside rooms in chronological order. That's not a problem if you're walking to the memorial from the Lincoln Memorial. But folks trekking from 14th Street and the Jefferson Memorial should resist the temptation to enter the memorial by continuing along the Tidal Basin and entering at the information center and bookstore. Rest rooms are located at both entrances.

Other Things to Do Nearby   The Lincoln, Korean War, and Jefferson Memorials are relatively close; just wear comfortable walking shoes and keep in mind that distances along the Tidal Basin and Mall are deceiving. The Bureau of Engraving and Printing and the Holocaust Memorial Museum are located on Raoul Wallenberg Place, on the east side of the Tidal Basin just beyond the Jefferson Memorial; both require picking up time tickets during the spring and summer (year-round at the Holocaust Museum). Hungry? Pack a lunch. The Holocaust Museum has a small cafe with a limited selection and is the closest place to grab something to eat. During warm weather, paddleboats are available for rent on the east side of the Tidal Basin, and a water taxi service shuttles tourists along the Potomac River from 11 A.M. to 6 P.M. daily.

The Arthur M. Sackler Gallery (a Smithsonian museum)

Type of Attraction: A museum dedicated to Asian art from ancient times to the present. A self-guided tour.

Location: 1050 Independence Avenue, SW, on the Mall near the Castle (the Smithsonian Institution building).

Nearest Metro Station: Smithsonian

Admission: Free

Hours: Daily, 10 A.M. to 5:30 P.M.; closed Christmas Day.

Phone: (202) 357-2700 (voice); (202) 357-1729 (TTY)

When to Go: Anytime

Special Comments: A quiet respite when other Mall attractions are jammed with visitors.

Overall Appeal by Age Group:

Pre-school	Grade School	Teens	Young Adults	Over 30	Senior Citizens
★	★★	★★	★★½	★★½	★★½

Author's Rating: Fabulous and exotic art. ★★½

How Much Time to Allow: One hour

Description and Comments   Descend through a granite-and-glass pavilion to view a collection of Asian (mostly Chinese) treasures, many of them made of gold and encrusted with jewels. The Sackler is full of exotic stuff that will catch the eye of older children, teens, and adults. Barring a strong interest in the Orient, however, first-time visitors on a tight schedule should visit the Sackler another time.

Touring Tips   Stop at the information desk and ask about the guided tours offered throughout the day. The gift shop is an exotic bazaar, featuring paintings, textiles, ancient games, Zen rock garden kits, and plenty of other Asian-influenced items.

Other Things to Do Nearby   The Sackler is connected with its twin, the Museum of African Art, below ground, so that's the logical next stop—especially if it's rainy or blazingly hot outside. In the spring of 1993, the Freer Gallery reopened after a four-and-a-half-year, $26 million renovation. A new underground corridor connects it to the Sackler. None of these museums offers a cafeteria, but that's okay: Try either L'Enfant Plaza (weekdays) or the Old Post Office Pavilion (anytime). The only remaining problem is deciding what to eat.

Smithsonian Institution Building (the Castle)

Type of Attraction: Information desks and displays, and a continuously running movie that introduces visitors to the vast number of Smithsonian museums.

Location: 1000 Jefferson Drive, SW, on the Mall.

Nearest Metro Station: Smithsonian

Admission: Free

Hours: Daily, 9 A.M. to 5:30 P.M.; closed Christmas Day.

Phone: (202) 357-2700 (voice); (202) 357-1729 (TTY)

When to Go: Anytime

Author's Rating: A must for first-time Mall visitors. ★★★★

How Much Time to Allow: 30 minutes

Description and Comments   This red brick building—you can't miss it—contains no exhibits. The Castle serves as an information center that will help you save time and trouble and reduce the frustration that comes from visiting the Smithsonian's large and perplexing museum complex. Step into one of the two theaters to see the 20-minute film. It's a bit long but gives a good idea of what each museum has to offer. Then you can talk to someone at the information desk for specific directions and advice (including multilingual assistance). A nifty map exhibit on the east wall lights up the location of each of the museums on the Mall, as well as other popular D.C. sights, when you press the corresponding button.

U.S. Department of the Treasury

Type of Attraction: Recently restored, this oldest federal office building in Washington houses the offices of the national treasury. A guided tour.

Location: Next to the White House at 15th and Pennsylvania Avenue, NW. Visitors enter at the appointment center doors on 15th Street.

Nearest Metro Station: Metro Center

Admission: Free

Hours: Because this is a working office building, guided tours are offered on Saturday mornings only at 10 A.M., 10:20 A.M., 10:40 A.M., and 11 A.M. Reservations are required.

Phone: (202) 622-0896; (202) 622-0692 (TDD)

Special Comments: The name and date of birth of each person in your group is required when you make reservations; a photo ID is required for each adult on the day of the tour. The tour lasts about 90 minutes, and you'll be standing and walking the whole time.

Overall Appeal by Age Group:

Pre-school	Grade School	Teens	Young Adults	Over 30	Senior Citizens
—	★	★½	★★	★★½	★★½

Author's Rating: Austere and cold, like a big bank. ★★

How Much Time to Allow: 90 minutes

Description and Comments Recent renovations to the interior of this imposing building next to the White House restored its 1860s atmosphere. For example, the Secretary's Conference and Reception Rooms were reconstructed into the American Renaissance Revival style of the 1860–80 period. A recently discovered burglar-proof vault that had been hidden by plasterboard now serves, appropriately enough, as part of the U.S. Treasurer's Office. The tour ends in the marble-walled Cash Room, heralded as the most expensive room in the world when it opened in 1869. This tour is for the person who's been to Washington before and wants to see something unique. First-time visitors, unless they have a strong interest in decorative art or banks, should save it for their next visit.

Touring Tips Advance reservations are required; during spring and summer, call at least a month in advance. Kids would be bored silly by this one.

Other Things to Do Nearby The National Aquarium is in the basement of the Commerce Department; enter on 14th Street, NW. Both F and G Streets offer plenty of eating opportunities, including the three-level Shops at National Place. The food court in the Old Post Office Pavilion is about three blocks away on Pennsylvania Avenue. The White House is next door.

U.S. Holocaust Memorial Museum

Type of Attraction: A museum and memorial presenting the history of the persecution and murder of six million Jews and others by Nazi Germany during World War II. A self-guided tour.

Location: 100 Raoul Wallenberg Place, SW (formerly 15th Street), near the Mall between the Washington Monument and the Bureau of Engraving and Printing. Entrances are on Raoul Wallenberg Place and 14th Street.

Nearest Metro Station: Smithsonian (Independence Avenue exit)

Admission: Free

Hours: Daily, 10 A.M. to 5:30 P.M.; closed Christmas Day and Yom Kippur.

Phone: (202) 488-0400

When to Go: After favorable publicity generated large crowds following its opening in the spring of 1993, the Holocaust Museum went to a "time ticket" system to eliminate long lines at its permanent exhibits. While the ticket office opens at 10 A.M., plan on getting in line no later than 9 A.M. to be sure of getting a ticket (which are given out for that day only). If you want to be sure of getting on a morning tour during the busy spring and summer months, get in line by 8:30 A.M.

Special Comments: According to Holocaust Museum officials, the main exhibit is inappropriate for children under age 11—and we agree. However, a special exhibit on the museum's first floor, "Daniel's Story: Remember the Children," is designed for visitors age 8 years and older. It gives a child's perspective on the Holocaust, but without the shocking graphics of the permanent exhibit. No tickets are required for the special, nonpermanent exhibitions. Tickets can also be ordered in advance through ProTix; call (800) 400-9373.

Overall Appeal by Age Group:

Pre-school	Grade School	Teens	Young Adults	Over 30	Senior Citizens
—	★½	★★	★★★	★★★½	★★★★

Author's Rating: As its designers intended, the Holocaust Museum is ugly, forbidding, and grim—and delivers a stern message about the evils of racial persecution. It also packs an emotional punch that may not fit some folks' vacation plans. ★★½

How Much Time to Allow: One and a half to two hours

Description and Comments   This new $168 million museum utilizes stunning, high-tech audiovisual displays, advanced computer technology, and a model of a Nazi death camp to deliver a message about one of the darkest periods in human history. But that's not all. As part of the museum experience, museum-goers are cast as "victims" of Nazi brutality. Visitors receive an identity card of a real Holocaust victim matched to their sex and age—a demographic double. The building attacks the emotions of visitors in other, more subtle, ways. The interior of the museum, while spotless, is relentlessly industrial and forbidding—pipes are exposed and rough surfaces of brick and concrete are cold and unwelcoming. Diagonal walls in the exhibition areas create a disorienting effect. Ghostly shapes pass overhead on glass-bottomed walkways, suggesting anonymous prison guards patrolling a camp. (Actually, they are visitors walking on footbridges linking the permanent exhibit spaces.) Every moment spent inside the museum is orchestrated to impart the horror of Nazi persecution.

While many exhibits focus on Jewish life prior to the Holocaust and the political and military events surrounding World War II, the most disturbing displays are graphic depictions of Nazi atrocities. Large TV screens scattered throughout the exhibits present still and motion pictures of Nazi leaders, storm troopers rounding up victims, and life inside Jewish ghettoes.

Some of the TV screens are located behind concrete barriers to prevent younger (and, inadvertently, shorter) visitors from seeing them. They show executions, medical experiments on Jewish prisoners, and suicide victims. It's very strong, grim stuff.

Touring Tips   Given the unrelenting horror of its subject matter, the Holocaust Museum is at best sobering and, at worst, depressing. There's no bright gloss to put on a museum chronicling the systematic murder of six million people . . . and anyone visiting the Holocaust Museum during a vacation should keep that in mind before placing it on his or her touring agenda, especially if traveling with small children.

Other Things to Do Nearby   The Holocaust Memorial Museum occupies some prime real estate near the Mall, the Bureau of Engraving and Printing, the Washington Monument, the Tidal Basin, the new FDR Memorial, and the Jefferson Memorial, so finding things to do before or after a tour of the museum is easy. The Museum Annex on Raoul Wallenberg Place has a small deli/cafe that's expensive but convenient.

Vietnam Veterans Memorial

Type of Attraction: A memorial to U.S. soldiers who died in Vietnam.
Location: On the west end of the Mall near the Lincoln Memorial.
Nearest Metro Station: Foggy Bottom/GWU
Admission: Free
Hours: This outdoor monument is always open.
When to Go: Anytime
Special Comments: At night this memorial is especially moving as people light matches to search for names inscribed on the wall.
Overall Appeal by Age Group:

Pre-school	Grade School	Teens	Young Adults	Over 30	Senior Citizens
★	★★	★★	★★★	★★★★	★★★★

Author's Rating: Deeply moving. ★★★½
How Much Time to Allow: 30 minutes

Description and Comments   This long, narrow wall of polished black stone is inscribed with the names of the more than 58,000 Americans who died in Vietnam. Many visitors to the memorial make rubbings of loved ones' names, while others leave flowers, military medals, letters, and gifts along the base of the wall. The wall, a black rift in the earth, packs an emotional wallop.

Touring Tips   At both ends of the wall visitors will find books that list the inscribed names and the panel number to help them locate an inscription.

Other Things to Do Nearby   The Lincoln Memorial, the Reflecting Pool, and Constitution Gardens are close by. Across from the Mall, the National Academy of Sciences features science exhibits and a statue of Albert Einstein with a lap that's large enough to sit in for picture-taking. For food, walk up 23rd Street toward Foggy Bottom and an assortment of restaurants and carryouts.

Voice of America

Type of Attraction: The U.S. Government's overseas radio broadcasting studios. A guided tour.

Location: Tours meet at the C Street entrance between 3rd and 4th Streets, SW.

Nearest Metro Station: Federal Center SW

Admission: Free

Hours: The 45-minute tours begin at 10:40 A.M., 1:40 P.M., and 2:40 P.M., Monday through Friday, except holidays.

Phone: (202) 619-3919

Special Comments: A "must" for news junkies.

Overall Appeal by Age Group:

Pre-school	Grade School	Teens	Young Adults	Over 30	Senior Citizens
—	★	★	★★	★★	★★

Author's Rating: Fascinating and informative. ★★½

How Much Time to Allow: 45 minutes

Description and Comments   After a short video about the VOA, the knowledgeable tour guide walks you through some of the agency's 34 studios, where you see and hear radio announcers reading newscasts in languages such as Arabic, Estonian, and Urdu. Worldwide, the VOA operates more than 100 shortwave radio transmitters, and all broadcasts originate in this building. You'll also see some murals painted by noted artist Ben Shahn in the 1940s. But mostly this is a tour for people interested in media and world events; it would bore most children silly.

Touring Tips   You can call to reserve a place on a tour, but individuals and small groups won't have trouble joining a tour by just showing up a few minutes before a scheduled departure.

Other Things to Do Nearby The U.S. Botanic Garden is around the corner on Maryland Avenue, SW, and the Mall is two blocks away. For lunch, try the L'Enfant Plaza underground shopping mall, which on weekdays is usually jammed with bureaucrats looking for good, cheap food—and finding it. But don't go on weekends: Most restaurants are closed and the place is dead. Capitol Hill has a wide assortment of restaurants and cafes; another good choice for off-the-Mall eating is the Old Post Office Pavilion.

Washington Monument

Type of Attraction: A monument to the first U.S. president.

Location: On the Mall between 15th and 17th Streets, NW.

Nearest Metro Station: Smithsonian

Admission: Free

Hours: In the spring and summer, 8 A.M. to midnight; September through March, 9 A.M. to 5 P.M. The monument may be closed in thunderstorms and during periods of sustained high winds (not out of fear that the giant obelisk will tumble, but to protect visitors waiting in line on this exposed hilltop).

Phone: (202) 426-6841

When to Go: At 8 A.M. to pick up a time ticket or after 8 P.M. (April through August), when no tickets are required. *Note:* Extensive interior and exterior renovations will begin in October 1997, closing the monument for about six months.

Special Comments: Skip this one in bad weather—the view can be lousy. The Park Service operates a "time ticket" system to eliminate the long lines that used to wrap three times around the base of the monument. Pick up the free tickets (a maximum of six per person) at the kiosk located on 15th Street on the edge of the monument grounds. Then return at the time stamped on your ticket for the trip up the elevator later that day; kiosk hours are 7:30 A.M. until tickets run out. Show up five minutes before the time printed on your ticket. With only 150 tickets given out per half hour, all the tickets are usually gone by 10 A.M. on busy days and by 1:30 P.M. on slow days; early morning tickets go first. Tickets can be reserved in advance for a fee by calling TicketMaster at (800) 505-5040. Another way to get tickets the day before your visit is to purchase advance tickets at the Warner Theatre box office (at 13th and E Streets, NW), Hecht's department store (12th and G Streets, NW), or Tower Records (20th Street and Pennsylvania Avenue, NW). There's a $1.50 service charge per ticket

. . . and if it's raining or the view's socked in by clouds the next day, too bad. Refunds are given only if the monument is closed.

The stairs are now closed, except for special, guided walk-down-only tours given on weekends at 10 A.M. and 2 P.M. Come to the base of the monument a half hour before the tours; no tickets are required. The tours last from one to one and a half hours. *Note:* You won't be visiting the observation deck on the walk-down-only tour, so you'll still need to get a time ticket to check out the view.

Overall Appeal by Age Group:

Pre-school	Grade School	Teens	Young Adults	Over 30	Senior Citizens
★★★★	★★★★★	★★★★★	★★★★★	★★★★★	★★★★★

Author's Rating: Obligatory for first-time visitors. ★★★★★

How Much Time to Allow: Once you make it to the top, 30 minutes on the cramped observation deck can seem like an eternity.

Average Wait in Line per 100 People in Line ahead of You: 20 minutes (summer evenings after 8 P.M. only; otherwise you must get a time ticket, which eliminates long lines).

Description and Comments   At the top you're 500 feet up, and D.C.'s absence of other tall buildings (it's a law) guarantees a glorious, unobstructed view of Washington—if it's not raining. For most people, a first-time trip to Washington isn't complete without an ascent of this famous landmark. Yet most of them are surprised when they reach the cramped observation deck: You almost have to elbow your way to the tiny windows to see anything. The view, however, is great. Nobody's ever disappointed once they see it.

Touring Tips   The new, year-round "time ticket" system eliminates three-hour waits in line for the elevator trip to the top of the monument. (The wait in line is now reduced to about half an hour for most visitors.) But if you want to avoid the hassle of getting a ticket that requires a return to the monument later in day, come after 8 P.M. and see Washington at night (summer only). But the wait in line can be as long as two hours on busy summer evenings. Bathrooms are located behind the outdoor amphitheater on the Monument grounds, but use them only in desperate situations: They are usually dirty. A nearby snack bar is overpriced; during the week, try the cafeteria in the basement of the Commerce Department or the food court in the Old Post Office Pavilion. *Note:* Visiting the monument at night is an option only in the summer.

Other Things to Do Nearby   You're at the heart of tourist Washington: At hand are the Bureau of Engraving and Printing, the Holocaust Memorial Museum, the National Museum of American History, and the National Aquarium. At one end of the Mall is the Lincoln Memorial; the U.S. Capitol is at the other. If it's a nice day and you're museumed-out, explore the stretch of the Mall between the Washington Monument and the Lincoln Memorial. Much of it is tree-lined, tranquil, and not nearly as crowded as the east end of the Mall (toward the U.S. Capitol).

The White House

Type of Attraction: The official residence of the president of the United States. A self-guided tour.

Location: 1600 Pennsylvania Avenue, NW.

Nearest Metro Stations: McPherson Square, Vermont Avenue exit (closed on weekends), Farragut West

Admission: Free

Hours: Fifteen- to 20-minute walk-through tours are available Tuesday through Saturday, 10 A.M. to 12 P.M.; you must first pick up a "time ticket" *for that day only* from the ticket counter in the new White House Visitors Center located in the Department of Commerce building at 1450 Pennsylvania Avenue, NW (a block southeast of the White House). Your ticket will be stamped with a time and tour number; meet across 15th Street at the Ellipse Visitor Pavilion 10 minutes before your tour is scheduled to leave. Guided VIP tours are also available through your congressperson. The busiest period is late May through mid-August.

Phone: (202) 456-7041

When to Go: Very early. Get in line at the ticket counter in the White House Visitor Center no later than 7 A.M. (6:30 A.M. if you want to be absolutely sure of getting a ticket). The center opens at 7:30 A.M.; it typically takes about 50 minutes to distribute the day's allotment of tickets; a maximum of four tickets are available per person.

Special Comments: With very little notice and no explanation, public tours are occasionally canceled for the day by the White House, so it's a good idea to call the day before you plan to visit. Also, there are no public rest rooms or phones in the White House; the closest ones are in the Ellipse Visitor Pavilion (where tours assemble) and the White House Visitor Center across 15th Street. The visitor center is open from 7:30 A.M. to 4:30 P.M. daily.

Overall Appeal by Age Group:

Pre-school	Grade School	Teens	Young Adults	Over 30	Senior Citizens
★★	★★★	★★★½	★★★★	★★★★	★★★★

Author's Rating: During high tourist season, the tour requires too much time and effort for this 15-minute experience. ★★

How Much Time to Allow: Block out an entire morning, even though there's time to do something else (like eat breakfast) before your scheduled tour.

Description and Comments First things first: You have absolutely zero chance of seeing the president on this tour of the White House. The all too quick tour passes through the ubiquitous metal detectors and into the East Wing lobby; look out the window into the Rose Garden. Then it's up the stairs to the East Room, the Green Room, the Blue Room, the Red Room, and the State Dining Room—and you're done! It's hard to dispute the emotional pull of the presidential residence or its sumptuous beauty, but if you're on a first-time visit to Washington and on a limited schedule, consider visiting the White House on another trip, preferably in the fall or winter.

The new visitor center is large and attractive, featuring lots of carpeting, places to sit, nice rest rooms, static displays on the White House, a gift shop, and a video tour of the mansion for those who didn't crawl out of bed before dawn to get in line for a ticket.

Touring Tips The good news: Once you have a ticket, you now are free to do other things until your reserved tour assembles later that morning. The bad news: When you show up for your scheduled tour, it may still be an hour before you actually get in the White House. The other tour alternative is to write your congressperson or senator for free tickets to a VIP tour. While you'll still have to get up early (tours are at 8:15, 8:30, and 8:45 A.M.), the VIP tours are longer (between 30 and 45 minutes) and are guided by Secret Service agents who discuss White House history, art, and furnishings. And you'll have to stand in line to get into the Executive Mansion.

Other Things to Do Nearby After picking up your ticket, you'll probably want to get breakfast. Two nearby choices are the Commerce Department cafeteria (the entrance is on 15th Street, NW, across from the Ellipse; weekdays from 9 A.M. to 2 P.M.; cheap) and the Old Ebbitt Grill (675 15th Street, NW; not cheap). The Ellipse Visitor Pavilion sells muffins, hot dogs, snacks, and beverages. Across from the White House on Lafayette Square is St. John's Episcopal Church, known as "The Church of the Presidents," because every president since Madison has attended services here. Step inside the small church to view its simple design; on most Wednesdays at noon there's an organ recital. Behind the White House stands the Washington Monument, another D.C. edifice that requires time tickets. Pick them up at the kiosk on 15th Street.

Capitol Hill

N

1. United States Capitol Building
2. Russell Senate Office Building
3. Dirksen Senate Office Building
4. Hart Senate Office Building
5. United States Supreme Court
6. Library of Congress-Jefferson Building
7. Library of Congress-Madison Building
8. Cannon House Office Building
9. Longworth House Office Building
10. Rayburn House Office Building
11. United States Botanic Garden

2nd Street

3rd Street

Constitution Ave.

Independence Ave.

Zone 2: Capitol Hill

Capital Children's Museum

Type of Attraction: A touchy-feely museum for kids. A self-guided tour.

Location: 800 3rd Street, NE (behind the Union Station parking garage)

Nearest Metro Station: Union Station

Admission: $6; free for children ages two and under.

Hours: Memorial Day through Labor Day, 10 A.M. to 6 P.M. daily; 10 A.M. to 5 P.M. daily the rest of the year; closed New Year's, Thanksgiving, and Christmas days.

Phone: (202) 675-4120, (202) 675-4125 for a recording

When to Go: Anytime

Special Comments: The museum is located in a borderline neighborhood. Either drive or take the Metro to Union Station, where you can grab a cab for the short ride.

Overall Appeal by Age Group:

Pre-school	Grade School	Teens	Young Adults	Over 30	Senior Citizens
★★★★★	★★★★	★★	★½	★	★

Author's Rating: Poor location and a bit shabby. ★½

How Much Time to Allow: To justify the rather steep admission fee, plan on staying at least three or four hours. You'll still have to drag the kids away.

Description and Comments   On the outside it looks like a large school, but the inside is loaded with interactive exhibits that will keep youngsters fascinated for hours. Neato attractions include a cave you can walk through (complete with dripping noises); TV, radio, and animation studios; voice synthesizers; a maze built for ankle biters; and computers that quiz kids. Alas, this museum is a bit shabby around the edges. On my visit, a lot of the exhibits were closed or not working, and some of the equipment (such as personal computers) was outdated. But smaller children probably won't notice. A great place to reward tots dragged through boring Mall museums.

Touring Tips   Plan your visit around lunch at nearby Union Station, since there's nothing else close by. Again, the neighborhood is marginal, so walk in a group, take a cab, or drive. Combine a visit to the Capital Children's Museum with a stop by the National Postal Museum and be a real hero to your kids.

Other Things to Do Nearby   Union Station is a combination transportation hub, shopping mall, theater complex, and food emporium. The food court is pricey but casual, and you're sure to find something you like.

Folger Shakespeare Library

Type of Attraction: A museum and library dedicated to the Bard. A self-guided tour.

Location: 201 East Capitol Street, SE

Nearest Metro Stations: Union Station, Capitol South

Admission: Free

Hours: Monday through Saturday, 10 A.M. to 4 P.M.; tours at 11 A.M. daily and at 10 A.M. and 11 A.M. on Tuesdays; closed on federal holidays.

Phone: (202) 544-7077

When to Go: Anytime

Special Comments: The library is available only to accredited scholars.

Overall Appeal by Age Group:

Pre-school	Grade School	Teens	Young Adults	Over 30	Senior Citizens
—	★	★½	★★	★★	★★

Author's Rating: Dull. ★★

How Much Time to Allow: One hour

Description and Comments   The Folger House is the world's largest collection of Shakespeare's printed works, as well as a vast array of other rare Renaissance books and manuscripts. But unless you're a scholar doing research, you can't see any of it. Instead, stroll the Great Hall, featuring hand-carved, oak-paneled walls and priceless displays from the museum's collection. You may also visit the three-tiered Elizabethan theater, with walls of timber and plaster and carved oak columns. The Folger is an incongruous attraction that holds appeal only for people with a love of language, Merrie Olde England, and the theater. But it's worth a peek on a second or third trip to Capitol Hill.

Touring Tips   Guided tours of the building, exhibits, and the Elizabethan garden are conducted daily at 11 A.M. Special tours of the garden, featuring herbs and flowers grown in Shakespeare's time, are held every third Saturday from April through October at 10 A.M. and 11 A.M. At the west end of the building, a statue of Puck from *A Midsummer Night's Dream* presides over a fountain and pool. The Folger doesn't have much of interest for kids, unless yours have a fondness for gardens or exhibits on Elizabethan England.

Other Things to Do Nearby The Folger is directly behind the Library of Congress, which sits in front of the U.S. Capitol. The Supreme Court is less than a block away. Walk south on 2nd Street, SE, to find a wide array of restaurants and cafes. The sixth-floor cafeteria in the Library of Congress's Madison Building is a cheap lunch option.

Library of Congress

Type of Attraction: The world's largest library. Guided and self-guided tours.

Location: 1st Street, SE, on Capitol Hill

Nearest Metro Station: Capitol South

Admission: Free

Hours: Exhibition areas in the newly restored Jefferson Building are open Monday through Saturday, 10 A.M. to 5 P.M.; the library is closed Sundays, federal holidays, and Christmas and New Year's days. The Visitors Theater in the Madison Building shows a free 12-minute film on the library's mission. Free guided tours are offered Monday through Saturday, at 11:30 A.M., 1 P.M., 2:30 P.M., and 4 P.M. Groups are limited to 40 people; sign up for any tour (for that day only) at the Information Desk located in the visitor center (on the ground floor on the west side of the Jefferson Building). Pick up your tickets 10 minutes before the tour begins.

Phone: (202) 707-8000

When to Go: Anytime

Special Comments: A trip to the library might not be on most folks' vacation itinerary, but consider making an exception in this case.

Overall Appeal by Age Group:

Pre-school	Grade School	Teens	Young Adults	Over 30	Senior Citizens
—	★	★★	★★★	★★★½	★★★★

Author's Rating: Impressive and informative. ★★★★

How Much Time to Allow: One hour for the guided tour and another hour to browse the exhibits.

Description and Comments   Three huge structures make up the Library of Congress: the Jefferson, Madison, and Adams Buildings. For an understanding of what goes on here, take one of the guided tours. (To get the most out of the tour, first see the 12-minute video about the varied workings of the library.) After the tour, which lasts about an hour, you can look at other exhibits in the Jefferson and Madison Buildings on your own. Who should go? The Library of Congress holds strong appeal for folks interested in books, academic research, American history, and antiquities. On the other hand, it won't interest many kids, and most first-time visitors on a tight schedule shouldn't waste their valuable touring time here.

In the spring of 1997 a permanent exhibit called "American Treasures of the Library of Congress" marked the reopening of the Thomas Jefferson Building, under renovation since 1984. The rotating exhibition in the Great Hall features 200 of the library's rarest and most significant items, such as Thomas Jefferson's rough draft of the Declaration of Independence, Lincoln's first and second drafts of the Gettysburg Address, Wilbur Wright's telegram to his father announcing the first heavier-than-air flight, and Bernard Hermann's manuscript score for the film classic *Citizen Kane*.

Touring Tips   Although the Library consists of three buildings, visitors enter at the newly restored Jefferson Building on 1st Street. The tour, with its well-informed guide, is the way to go if you have the time and interest. *Note:* The tours are extremely popular, and it's a good idea to arrive early during the spring and summer to sign up for a tour later in the day. Tickets are available for that day only.

A permanent exhibit on copyright located on the fourth floor of the Madison Building features the original Barbie and Ken dolls, Dr. Martin Luther King's "I Have A Dream" speech, and the statue of the "Maltese falcon" used in the famous film of the same name. More temporary exhibits are located on the sixth floor. Library materials available here go way beyond books. For instance, the Library of Congress has an extensive collection of recorded music, broadcast material, and films. While ostensibly these research materials are for "serious" researchers only, almost anyone with a strong interest in, say, the recordings of Jimmy Durante can find valuable information and hear rare recordings. For musical material, go to the Recorded Sound Reference Center, located on the first floor of the Madison Building, where helpful librarians are ready to assist.

Other Things to Do Nearby   The U.S. Capitol, Supreme Court, and Folger Library are all within a block or two. Capitol Hill abounds with nearby lunch spots, not the least of which is right here. The sixth-floor cafeteria in the Madison Building is popular with congressional staffers, and it's a good deal for visitors, who can grab a bite to eat here from 12:30 P.M. to 3:00 P.M.

National Postal Museum (a Smithsonian museum)

Type of Attraction: Displays from the largest philatelic collection in the world and exhibits about the social, historical, and technological impact of the U.S. postal system. A self-guided tour.

Location: Washington City Post Office building, 2 Massachusetts Avenue, NE, next to Union Station.

Nearest Metro Station: Union Station

Admission: Free

Hours: Daily, 10 A.M. to 5:30 P.M.; closed Christmas Day.

Phone: (202) 357-2700 (voice); (202) 357-1729 (TTY)

When to Go: Anytime

Special Comments: The Smithsonian's newest museum (opened summer 1993).

Overall Appeal by Age Group:

Pre-school	Grade School	Teens	Young Adults	Over 30	Senior Citizens
★½	★★★	★★	★★	★★½	★★½

Author's Rating: Nifty and new. And the building that houses the museum is stunning. ★★★

How Much Time to Allow: One to two hours

Description and Comments   It's more interesting than it sounds—even if you're not one of America's 20 million stamp collectors. Kids will love the real airplanes hanging from the ceiling in the atrium, plus hands-on fun like the chance to sort mail on a train and track a letter from Kansas to Nairobi. Exhibits are arranged so that children and adults are entertained while they're in relative proximity to each other. Themes focus on the history of mail service, how the mail is moved, the social importance of letters, and the beauty and lore of stamps. Serious collectors can call in advance for appointments to see any stamp in the museum's world-class collection or to use the extensive library.

Touring Tips   Due to its small size (at least when compared to museums on the Mall), it's easy to whiz through it in a half-hour or so. And because it's right across the street from Union Station, many folks will find it convenient to drop in while waiting for a train.

Other Things to Do Nearby   The Capital Children's Museum is only a few blocks away, making a full day of kid-oriented museum-hopping a distinct possibility—without going near the Mall. Union Station's food hall can satisfy any food craving.

The U.S. Supreme Court

Type of Attraction: The nation's highest court. A self-guided tour.

Location: One 1st Street, NE, across from the east front of the U.S. Capitol.

Nearest Metro Stations: Union Station, Capitol South

Admission: Free

Hours: 9 A.M. to 4:30 P.M. Free lectures are offered between 9:30 A.M. and 3:30 P.M. when the court isn't in session.

Phone: (202) 479-3000

When to Go: Anytime to tour the building. To see the Court in session, the public may attend oral arguments held Mondays, Tuesdays, and Wednesdays, 10 A.M. to 2 P.M., in two-week intervals from October through April; check the "A" section of the *Washington Post*.

Special Comments: Seeing an oral argument here is probably your best chance of witnessing one of the three major branches of the government in operation while in D.C.

Overall Appeal by Age Group:

Pre-school	Grade School	Teens	Young Adults	Over 30	Senior Citizens
—	★	★★	★★★	★★★½	★★★★

Author's Rating: Extremely interesting and enlightening. ★★★★

How Much Time to Allow: One hour to tour the building; plan on at least two hours total to see an oral argument.

Description and Comments   This magnificent faux Greek temple is where the nine-member Supreme Court makes final interpretations of the U.S. Constitution and laws passed by Congress. When the Court's not in session, visitors may enter the stunning courtroom and hear a short lecture on its workings. An excellent 20-minute film explains the workings of the Supreme Court in more detail. On the ground floor is a small museum, a gift shop, a cafeteria, and a snack bar. A visit to the Supreme Court is a must for anyone interested in how the federal government works, or how the law works in general. Others should pass it up, although the building itself is impressive.

Touring Tips To see an oral argument, plan on arriving no later than 9 A.M. to get in line. Two lines form: a regular line, for those wishing to hear an entire argument (an hour), and a three-minute line, for folks who just want to slip in for a few moments. Bring quarters: You will have to place personal belongings like backpacks and cameras in coin-operated (quarters only) lockers. Security here is no-nonsense: Visitors pass through *two* X-ray machines before entering the courtroom, where very serious-looking security people patrol the aisles. Small children are not allowed in the courtroom during oral arguments.

Other Things to Do Nearby The U.S. Capitol, the Library of Congress, the National Postal Museum, and the Folger Shakespeare Library are all close by. The comfortable cafeteria on the ground level of the Supreme Court is one of the better government eateries. It's open for breakfast from 7:30 A.M. to 10:30 A.M. and for lunch from 11:30 A.M. to 2 P.M. except for 15-minute periods when only Court employees may enter. Capitol Hill is renowned for its many bars and cafes, many of which are a short walk up 2nd Street, SE.

Union Station

Type of Attraction: A spectacular interior space housing a transportation hub, upscale shops, a theater complex, and a food court.

Location: Massachusetts Avenue and North Capitol Street, NE.

Nearest Metro Station: Union Station

Admission: Free

Hours: Shops open Monday through Saturday, 10 A.M. to 9 P.M.; Sundays, noon to 6 P.M.

Phone: (202) 371-9441

When to Go: Anytime

Special Comments: The food court's fare is on the expensive side, but the vast selection justifies the extra cost.

Overall Appeal by Age Group:

Pre-school	Grade School	Teens	Young Adults	Over 30	Senior Citizens
★	★★	★★★	★★★½	★★★½	★★★½

Author's Rating: A beaux arts palace and a great lunch stop. ★★★½

How Much Time to Allow: One hour to wander; longer for shopping or eating.

Description and Comments   The Main Hall, with a 90-foot barrel-vaulted ceiling, is breathtaking. Shops run the gamut: chic clothing stores, The Great Train Store, bookstores, Brookstone, the Nature Company—more than 100 altogether. In the food court you'll find everything from sushi to ribs, while a nine-screen cinema complex offers solace on a rainy day. First-time visitors to D.C. shouldn't miss this magnificent structure. With more than seven million visitors a year, Union Station is the most-visited tourist attraction in Washington (the National Air and Space Museum is number two).

Touring Tips   Union Station is a great jumping-off point for touring Washington. Capitol Hill is a few blocks away (step out the front and walk toward the big dome), and Tourmobile, Gray Line, and Old Town trolley tours stop in front. Monday through Friday, Maryland commuter trains (called MARC) regularly shuttle between D.C. and Baltimore, stopping at points between (round-trip from Baltimore is $10.25). Virginia Railway Express shuttles commuters and daytrippers from Fredericksburg, Manassas, and points in between to Union Station weekdays. To top it off, there's a Metro station in the basement. It's hard to believe that Washington functioned before Union Station's rebirth (at a cost of more than $100 million) in 1988.

Other Things to Do Nearby   The Capital Children's Museum is only a few blocks away. Kids will love it, but either walk in a group or take a cab; the neighborhood is marginal. The Postal Museum is next door to Union Station, and the U.S. Capitol, the Supreme Court, and the Library of Congress are close.

U.S. Botanic Garden

Type of Attraction: A permanent collection of tropical, subtropical, and desert plants housed in a stunning, 38,000-square-foot greenhouse. A self-guided tour.

Location: 1st Street and Maryland Avenue, SW, near the U.S. Capitol.

Nearest Metro Station: Federal Center, SW

Admission: Free

Hours: Daily, 9 A.M. to 5 P.M. Closed Inauguration Day (once every four years).

Phone: (202) 225-8333

When to Go: Anytime

Special Comments: Skip it on a sweltering summer afternoon.

Overall Appeal by Age Group:

Pre-school	Grade School	Teens	Young Adults	Over 30	Senior Citizens
★	★½	★★	★★½	★★★½	★★★★

Author's Rating: An excellent and comprehensive collection of plant life.
★★★

How Much Time to Allow: 30 minutes

Description and Comments The Conservatory, a building that reflects the grand manner of Victorian architecture (even though it was constructed in the 1930s), houses a living museum on the Mall. The central palm house is complete with a flowing stream, while other sections display orchids, ferns, cacti, and other types of plants in naturalistic settings. While people with green thumbs will want to put these gardens on their first-visit itinerary, most folks will just want to know it's nearby for a quiet break from more hectic sights along the Mall. You can sit down here, relax, read a book—or just do nothing in a magnificent setting.

Touring Tips Before or after strolling through this giant greenhouse, visit Frederic Bartholdi Park, located across Independence Avenue from the Conservatory and named for the designer of the Statue of Liberty. The park features displays of bulbs, annuals, and perennials. The focal point is Bartholdi Fountain, originally exhibited at the 1876 Centennial Exposition in Philadelphia.

Other Things to Do Nearby The National Air and Space Museum and the Hirshhorn Museum and Sculpture Garden are close, as is the U.S. Capitol. L'Enfant Plaza, about five blocks away, has a shopping mall loaded with restaurants and fast-food outlets. But most are open only on weekdays. On weekends and holidays, try the Old Post Office Pavilion or Capitol Hill, with its wide array of restaurants and cafes.

U.S. Capitol

Type of Attraction: The building where Congress meets. Self-guided and guided tours.

Location: East end of the Mall.

Nearest Metro Stations: Capitol South, Union Station

Admission: Free

Hours: The building is open from 9 A.M. to 8 P.M. daily, March through August; 9 A.M. to 4:30 P.M. the rest of the year. Free 30-minute guided tours begin approximately every 10 minutes in the Rotunda from 9:30 A.M. to about 7 P.M. Monday through Friday (spring and summer) and from 9:30 A.M. to 4 P.M. on Saturdays and on weekdays the rest of the year. Guides are stationed in the building from 1 P.M. to 4:30 P.M. on Sundays to answer questions, but no guided tours are offered. Closed Thanksgiving, Christmas, and New Year's days.

Phone: (202) 225-6827 for a recording. Call 225-3121 to reach the Capitol switchboard.

When to Go: Go in the late afternoon, evening (summer only), or at lunchtime to beat the crowds. The public entrance is on the east front, the side opposite the Mall. (The Capitol has an east front and a west front, but no "rear.")

Special Comments: The Capitol hosts about 25,000 visitors a day, and most get lost—the building is both large and confusing. Make sure to pick up a map at the tour desk in the Rotunda, and don't be shy about asking one of the many guards on duty for directions.

Overall Appeal by Age Group:

Pre-school	Grade School	Teens	Young Adults	Over 30	Senior Citizens
★	★★½	★★★	★★★★	★★★★½	★★★★★

Author's Rating: Interesting and beautiful. ★★★★½

How Much Time to Allow: One to two hours

Average Wait in Line per 100 People in Line ahead of You: 20 minutes. Groups of 50 leave every 10 minutes for the "introductory" tour. Lines for the free tours can vary considerably in length; waits during peak season can be up to two hours in the mornings, but only a few minutes in the evenings or at lunchtime.

Description and Comments   The U.S. Capitol manages to be two things at once: an awesome monument to democracy and one of the most important places in the world, as the frequent presence of reporters and film crews outside attests. The rather brief (typically 30 minutes) public tour, however, takes visitors through only a small part of the Capitol: the Rotunda and a few other rooms, which may include Statuary Hall, the House or Senate chambers (when they're not in session), and the low-ceilinged crypt. Usually, tours get shorter as the crowds get bigger. From the soaring Rotunda to the opulent rooms where the House and Senate meet, the Capitol is both physically beautiful and packed with historical significance. For first-time visitors, the tour is both awe-inspiring and relatively quick.

Touring Tips   If your plans include viewing a session of Congress, don't make the time-consuming mistake thousands of other visitors make: coming to the Capitol without a gallery pass. Go first to the office of your senator or representative to pick one up. (Don't forget to ask for maps and other helpful touring goodies while you're there.) Don't know the name of your representative or of your senators? Then call (202) 224-3121 for help locating an office. The free tour is heavy on the history of the building, but if your group makes it to either the House or Senate chambers, you'll get a good run-down on how Congress operates. (Stick close to the guide if you expect to hear the entire spiel.) As a visitor, however, you're not restricted to the tour: If there's an area you would like to see but didn't on the tour, your guide can give directions on how to find it.

Other Things to Do Nearby   Explore the rest of Capitol Hill: The Supreme Court and Library of Congress face the Capitol's east front. On the other side, the east end of the Mall features the U.S. Botanic Garden and the East Wing of the National Gallery of Art. The Senate Refectory, a small sit-down cafeteria, is famous for its bean soup. Your best bet, however, is to go to a cafeteria in one of the House or Senate office buildings. Capitol Hill is famous for its bars and restaurants. To find them, walk toward Constitution Avenue and past the Library of Congress's Madison Building, located between Independence Avenue and C Street, NE.

Zone 3: Downtown

B'nai B'rith Klutznick Museum

Type of Attraction: A museum featuring Jewish folk and ceremonial art. A self-guided tour.

Location: 1640 Rhode Island Avenue, NW.

Nearest Metro Stations: Farragut North, Dupont Circle

Admission: Suggested donation $2; seniors and children $1.

Hours: Sunday through Friday, 10 A.M. to 5 P.M., except Jewish holidays.

Phone: (202) 857-6583

When to Go: Anytime

Overall Appeal by Age Group:

Pre-school	Grade School	Teens	Young Adults	Over 30	Senior Citizens
★	★½	★½	★★	★★½	★★½

Author's Rating: Small and tasteful, but inconveniently located. ★★½

How Much Time to Allow: One hour

Description and Comments   Although it's small, the Klutznick Museum features a wide variety of items, from 1,000-year-old coins to modern art. You'll also find the 1790 letter from President George Washington to a Newport, Rhode Island, synagogue. While you don't have to be Jewish to appreciate this attractive museum, for most folks it's not a main attraction.

Other Things to Do Nearby   The National Geographic Society's Explorers Hall, a must-see for kids, is at 17th and M Streets, NW. For a limitless selection of eateries, just walk toward Connecticut Avenue.

Federal Bureau of Investigation

Type of Attraction: FBI headquarters. A guided tour.

Location: 10th Street, NW, at Pennsylvania Avenue. Visitor's entrance is at 9th and E streets, NW.

Admission: Free

Hours: Monday through Friday, 8:45 to 4:15 P.M. Closed weekends and federal holidays. Be sure to call first; due to staff cutbacks, morning public tours are sometimes canceled and tours don't begin until 1 P.M.

Phone: (202) 324-3447

Nearest Metro Stations: Federal Triangle, Archives, Gallery, and Metro Center

When to Go: To beat the crowds, arrive either by 8 A.M. or around lunch hour (if morning tours haven't been canceled during your visit; call the day before).

Special Comments: Children should try to stay close to the tour guide, since there's a lot of peering into crime labs through plate glass windows set at adult height.

Overall Appeal by Age Group:

Pre-school	Grade School	Teens	Young Adults	Over 30	Senior Citizens
★★	★★★★★	★★★★½	★★★★	★★★	★★★

Author's Rating: A boring tour, and the firearms demo lasts about a minute. ★½

How Much Time to Allow: One hour

Average Wait in Line per 100 People in Line ahead of You: One hour. Tours of 30 people depart every 15 minutes during non-peak season; expect delays during peak season.

Description and Comments After a brief introductory video, the tour guide leads your group through a series of displays highlighting the Bureau's fabled history, with heavy emphasis on gangsters (look for John Dillinger's death mask), spies, and drug smugglers. Then a walk past FBI crime labs, with views through windows of technicians at work in DNA-, document-, and material-identification labs. There's also a collection of valuables confiscated in drug raids that includes expensive jewelry and a ten-and-a-half-foot-tall stuffed brown bear. Next is a short Q & A session with a real Special Agent, who then rips off a few live rounds at paper targets. As the lines attest, this is one of the most popular tours in Washington. Families with school-age children should try to work it into a visit—kids love it.

Touring Tips Call first to make sure staff cutbacks haven't eliminated morning tours. If morning tours are scheduled, get in line well before the first tour starts at 8:45. A better alternative is to write your congressperson for a reserved VIP tour that eliminates the uncertainty and long waits in line. Once you're inside, rest rooms are available before the tour begins.

Other Things to Do Nearby If the line at the National Archives is short, scoot inside for a peek at the Declaration of Independence. Or go to the Old Post Office Pavilion for lunch in the food court and a trip to the clock tower for the second-best view in Washington.

Ford's Theatre/Petersen House

Type of Attraction: The restored theater where Abraham Lincoln was assassinated, and the house across the street, where he died. A self-guided tour.

Location: 511 10th Street, NW.

Nearest Metro Station: Metro Center, 11th Street exit

Admission: Free

Hours: 9 A.M. to 5 P.M., closed Christmas Day.

Phone: (202) 426-6924

When to Go: Anytime

Special Comments: The theater (but not the museum) is closed to visitors on Thursday and Sunday afternoons, when matinees are in progress. It may also be closed on other afternoons when rehearsals are in progress.

Overall Appeal by Age Group:

Pre-school	Grade School	Teens	Young Adults	Over 30	Senior Citizens
★	★½	★★	★★½	★★½	★★★

Author's Rating: An interesting, but small, museum; the theater is a reconstruction of the original interior. ★★½

How Much Time to Allow: One hour

Description and Comments Don't miss the recently updated Lincoln Museum in the basement of the theater, featuring the clothes Lincoln was wearing the night he was shot and the derringer used to kill him. Across the street, Petersen House offers a glimpse of nineteenth-century Washington. Ford's Theatre, both the museum and where Lincoln was shot, is small. Unless you're a history buff, this is mostly a fill-in stop, at least for first-time visitors.

Touring Tips Start with the theater, then view the museum in the basement before crossing the street to Petersen House.

Other Things to Do Nearby The FBI, the National Portrait Gallery, and the National Museum of American Art are all close. For lunch, it's four or five blocks to Chinatown, two blocks to the Old Post Office Pavilion, or just down the street to the Hard Rock Cafe.

National Building Museum

Type of Attraction: A museum dedicated to architecture and the construction arts that's an architectural marvel in its own right. Self-guided and guided tours.

Location: 401 F Street, NW.

Nearest Metro Station: Judiciary Square

Admission: Free; suggested donation of $3 for adults.

Hours: Monday through Saturday, 10 A.M. to 4 P.M.; Sundays, 12 noon to 4 P.M. Closed Thanksgiving, Christmas, and New Year's days.

Phone: (202) 272-2448

When to Go: Anytime

Special Comments: Tours are given at 12:30 P.M. on weekdays and at 12:30 and 1:30 P.M. on weekends.

Overall Appeal by Age Group:

Pre-school	Grade School	Teens	Young Adults	Over 30	Senior Citizens
★★	★★★	★★★	★★★½	★★★½	★★★½

Author's Rating: The Great Hall is eye-popping. ★★★½

How Much Time to Allow: 30 minutes

Description and Comments The ideal way to visit this museum would be to walk in blindfolded, then have the blindfold removed. Rather unimposing on the outside, the Pension Building (as this museum is better known to Washingtonians) offers one of the most imposing interiors in Washington, if not the world. The Great Hall measures 316 feet by 116 feet, and at its highest point the roof is 159 feet above the floor. Eight marbleized Corinthian columns adorn the interior. It's a must-see, even if all you do is poke your head inside the door.

Touring Tips The exhibits in the museum are on the thin side: The main attraction is the building itself. But if you're interested in architecture and building construction, check out the permanent and temporary exhibits on the first and second floors. The new Courtyard Cafe is open weekdays, 11 A.M. to 3 P.M.

Other Things to Do Nearby The three-acre National Law Enforcement Officers Memorial is directly across from the National Building Museum's entrance on F Street. Engraved on blue-gray marble walls are the names of 12,500 law enforcement officers who died in the line of duty throughout U.S. history. Four groups of striking statues adorning the park each show a lion protecting her cubs. The Lillian and Albert Small Jewish Museum at 701 3rd Street, NW, offers a glimpse into Washington's historic Jewish presence. The museum features temporary exhibits about the city's Jewish life, while the Adas Israel Synagogue on the second floor is listed in the National Register of Historic Places. Open Sunday through Thursday, noon to 4 P.M. Closed Saturdays and all major Jewish holidays; phone (202) 789-0900 for more information. Chinatown and a large selection of restaurants is only two blocks away.

National Geographic Society's Explorers Hall

Type of Attraction: A small, high-tech exhibition that delights children. A self-guided tour.

Location: 17th and M Streets, NW, four blocks north of the White House.

Nearest Metro Stations: Farragut North, Farragut West

Admission: Free

Hours: Monday through Saturday, 9 A.M. to 5 P.M.; Sundays and holidays, 10 A.M. to 5 P.M.; closed Christmas Day.

Phone: (202) 857-7588

When to Go: Anytime

Special Comments: The downtown exhibit is handy in an area that's spotty on entertaining things for kids to do.

Overall Appeal by Age Group:

Pre-school	Grade School	Teens	Young Adults	Over 30	Senior Citizens
★★★	★★★★	★★★½	★★★	★★	★★

Author's Rating: Well-done exhibits that aren't overpowering. ★★

How Much Time to Allow: One hour

Description and Comments It's like walking through a couple of National Geographic TV specials. Located on the first floor of the National Geographic Society's headquarters, this small collection of exhibits showcases weather, geography, astronomy, biology, exploration, and space science. It's also a bit heavy on quizzes that could prove embarrassing to adults. For example, Earth Station One is a 72-seat amphitheater that simulates orbital flight 23,000 miles above the earth. The interactive program lets kids punch buttons as they answer geography questions posed by the "captain."

Touring Tips Don't miss the extensive sales shop that offers books, videos, maps, and magazines. The courtyard on M Street is a great spot for a brown-bag lunch. Free films are shown on Tuesdays at noon.

Other Things to Do Nearby The *Washington Post* building is around the corner on 15th Street; advance reservations are required for the free tour. The still-imposing Russian embassy is around the corner on 16th Street; you can't go in, but check out the array of antennas on the roof.

National Museum of American Art
(a Smithsonian museum)

Type of Attraction: Galleries displaying painting, sculpture, graphics, folk art, and photography from the eighteenth century to the present, all by American artists. A self-guided tour.

Location: 8th and G Streets, NW.

Nearest Metro Station: Gallery Place/Chinatown

Admission: Free

Hours: 10 A.M. to 5:30 P.M.; closed on Christmas Day.

Phone: (202) 357-2700 (voice); (202) 357-1729 (TTY)

When to Go: Anytime

Special Comments: The museum is housed in the Old Patent Office Building, sharing quarters with the National Portrait Gallery.

Overall Appeal by Age Group:

Pre-school	Grade School	Teens	Young Adults	Over 30	Senior Citizens
★	★½	★★	★★★	★★★★	★★★★

Author's Rating: An off-the-Mall treasure. ★★★★

How Much Time to Allow: Two hours

Description and Comments The collection of paintings (and a few sculptures) spans American history and includes masterworks from the Colonial era, paintings of Indian life, huge 19th-century landscapes, modern and contemporary art, and an in-depth collection of art by African-Americans. Like its neighbor, the National Portrait Gallery, this museum is more intimate than the museums on the Mall. People who don't like art galleries will probably enjoy this one, since there's a good chance of finding something appealing.

Touring Tips While you're here, visit the National Portrait Gallery, also housed inside the Old Patent Office Building. Before your visit, check out the museum's award-winning World Wide Web site at http://www.nmaa.si.edu.

Other Things to Do Nearby For lunch, Chinatown is around the corner on 7th Street, and the Patent Pending cafe in the museum offers above-average museum fare. For additional sight-seeing, it's only a short walk to the National Building Museum and Ford's Theatre.

National Museum of Women in the Arts

Type of Attraction: The world's single most important collection of art by women. A self-guided tour.

Location: 1250 New York Avenue, NW.

Nearest Metro Station: Metro Center

Admission: A $3 donation is requested; $2 for students and children.

Hours: Monday through Saturday, 10 A.M. to 5 P.M.; Sundays, noon to 5 P.M. Closed Thanksgiving, Christmas, and New Year's days.

Phone: (202) 783-5000

When to Go: Anytime

Special Comments: Unfortunately, this beautiful museum is in an inconvenient location on the edge of downtown.

Overall Appeal by Age Group:

Pre-school	Grade School	Teens	Young Adults	Over 30	Senior Citizens
★	★★	★★½	★★★	★★★½	★★★½

Author's Rating: Both the building and the art are superb. ★★★½

How Much Time to Allow: One to two hours

Description and Comments   This relatively new museum has a permanent collection of paintings and sculpture that includes art by Georgia O'Keeffe, Frida Kahlo, and Helen Frankenthaler, as well as art by women from the 16th century to the present. From the outside, it looks like any other office building along crowded New York Avenue. But inside the former Masonic Grand Lodge are striking architectural features such as a crystal chandelier, a main hall and mezzanine, and the Grand Staircase. The second-floor balcony hosts temporary exhibits; the third floor is where you'll find the permanent collection. Next door, a new annex that opened in the fall of 1997 allowed the museum to expand the amount of artwork on display, including sculpture and contemporary works by lesser-known women artists. While this beautiful museum well off the beaten path deserves to be seen by more people, first-time visitors can wait and enjoy it on a later trip.

Touring Tips   Take the elevator to the fourth (top) floor and work your way down. The mezzanine features an attractive cafe offering "light fare," and there's a gift shop on the ground floor.

Other Things to Do Nearby   A block away is the old Greyhound Bus Station, now fully restored into an Art Deco masterpiece; take a peek inside. The Capitol City Brewing Company brews beer on the premises and serves hearty fare like burgers to go with it.

National Portrait Gallery (a Smithsonian museum)

Type of Attraction: An art museum specializing in portraits of noteworthy Americans. Guided and self-guided tours.

Location: 8th and F Streets, NW.

Nearest Metro Station: Gallery Place/Chinatown

Admission: Free

Hours: Daily, 10 A.M. to 5:30 P.M.; closed Christmas Day.

Phone: (202) 357-2700 (voice); (202) 357-1729 (TTY)

When to Go: Anytime

Special Comments: A great museum for the Mall-weary.

Overall Appeal by Age Group:

Pre-school	Grade School	Teens	Young Adults	Over 30	Senior Citizens
★	★½	★★	★★½	★★★	★★★½

Author's Rating: Combines art and education. ★★★½

How Much Time to Allow: One hour

Description and Comments   The Old Patent Office Building, which houses this art museum, is located on the seedy edge of D.C.'s downtown. But don't let the location put you off: If you're interested in U.S. history, you'll enjoy viewing portraits of a panoply of Americans—presidents, statesmen, Native Americans, industrialists, and artists. Unlike most Smithsonian museums, the Portrait Gallery's rooms are on an intimate scale and let you get close to the art. It's not a museum with much appeal to small children, but older kids will enjoy viewing the portraits of U.S. presidents, as will adults. First-time visitors should make the effort.

Touring Tips   The museum shares quarters with the National Museum of American Art, so plan on hitting them both. Keep these museums in mind when the crowds are heavy on the Mall; they're easy to get to and never crowded. At the information desk, request a docent-led tour. On the rainy day I toured the museum, I received a delightful, one-on-one tour from a volunteer who's the wife of a Navy admiral—and she really knew her history! The free tours are available by request between 10 A.M. and 3 P.M. weekdays and from 11 A.M. to 1:30 P.M. weekends. Scheduled tours are also offered on weekends at 11:15 A.M. and 1 P.M.

Other Things to Do Nearby   For lunch, Chinatown is right around the corner: Walk through the atrium and leave the building through the Museum of American Art and turn right. Turn left at the next corner (7th Street) and go one block. Also, the museum's Patent Pending cafe offers above-average museum fare. Other sights: Ford's Theatre and the National Building Museum are only a couple of blocks away.

Washington Post Building

Type of Attraction: The offices of America's number two and D.C.'s number one daily newspaper. A guided tour.

Location: 15th and L Streets, NW.

Nearest Metro Stations: McPherson Square, Farragut North

Admission: Free; no children under age 11.

Hours: 40- to 50-minute guided tours are offered on Mondays from 10 A.M. to 3 P.M. on the hour. Advance reservations are required.

Phone: (202) 334-7969

Overall Appeal by Age Group:

Pre-school	Grade School	Teens	Young Adults	Over 30	Senior Citizens
—	★	★½	★★½	★★★	★★★

Author's Rating: Great fun for current-events fans. ★★★

How Much Time to Allow: One hour

Description and Comments   Renowned for its president-toppling role 20 years ago in the Watergate scandal, the *Washington Post*'s reputation is second only to that of the *New York Times*. This tour shows how a big newspaper is put together, from the newsroom (where reporters write their stories), to the paste-up department (where articles are laid out on pages), to the press room. The big presses may not be rolling, though: Most of the *Post* is printed at night. While kids will enjoy the presses and a small museum full of old Linotype machines, the rest of the tour is quite wordy. This is a tour for people who love newspapers.

Touring Tips   Advance reservations are required to go on a tour; make reservations several months before coming to Washington. During the school year, morning tours are often filled with children on field trips. During peak tourist season, tours are limited to 40, which is a lot of people. Expect to climb many stairs. In the late morning and early afternoon, the newsroom is usually quiet. But as you walk through, keep your eyes peeled for Mr. Woodward's office: Along with Carl Bernstein, rookie reporter Bob

Woodward helped break the Watergate story in the early 1970s. Today, he's a *Post* editor.

Other Things to Do Nearby   Directly behind the Post building on 16th Street is the embassy of the former Union of Soviet Socialist Republics (USSR). You can't get in but the roof still bristles with antennas. National Geographic's Explorers Hall is two blocks away at 17th and M Streets, NW. Walk a block south to K Street and watch well-dressed lobbyists rushing to meetings.

Zone 4: Foggy Bottom

John F. Kennedy Center for the Performing Arts

Type of Attraction: Both presidential memorial and D.C.'s performing arts headquarters. A guided tour.

Location: New Hampshire Avenue, NW, and Rock Creek Parkway.

Nearest Metro Station: Foggy Bottom/GWU

Admission: Free

Hours: 10 A.M. to 12 midnight; closed Christmas Day.

Phone: (202) 467-4600

When to Go: Free tours begin every 15 minutes from 10 A.M. to 1 P.M. daily.

Special Comments: The leisurely tour lasts about 45 minutes but is easy on the feet: The Kennedy Center is well carpeted.

Overall Appeal by Age Group:

Pre-school	Grade School	Teens	Young Adults	Over 30	Senior Citizens
★	★	★	★★	★★½	★★★

Author's Rating: So-so art, a huge building, and a great view. ★★

How Much Time to Allow: One hour

Description and Comments The white rectilinear Kennedy Center facility boasts four major stages, a film theater, and a sumptuous interior shimmering with crystal, mirrors, and deep-red carpets. The Grand Foyer is longer than two football fields. Nations from around the world contributed art and artifacts on display in halls and foyers, such as African art, Beame porcelain, tapestries, and sculptures. If rehearsals aren't in progress, the tour includes peeks inside the intimate Eisenhower Theater, the Opera House (featuring a spectacular chandelier), and the Concert Hall, which seats 2,750. Admirers of JFK and culture vultures will love the tour, while kids will probably get bored. But you don't have to take the tour to enjoy the view; take the elevators to the roof terrace.

Touring Tips While the guided tour is leisurely and informative, the best way to visit the Kennedy Center is to attend a concert, play, or film. Before or after the event, go up to the seventh floor and stroll the roof terrace—the view at night is terrific.

Other Things to Do Nearby   You can lunch or snack at the Kennedy Center's Encore Cafe without securing a second mortgage on your house, but the Roof Terrace Restaurant is expense-account priced. The infamous Watergate project is across G Street from the Kennedy Center and features expensive shops and restaurants, but you won't find any memorial to a certain burglary that occurred there in 1972. A biking and jogging path along the Potomac River is just below the Kennedy Center; follow it upriver to Thompson's Boat Center, which rents canoes and bikes. A little farther is Washington Harbour, an upscale collection of shops, restaurants, and condominiums, featuring life-size and lifelike sculptures of tourists, joggers, workers, and artists that add a bit of whimsy to scenic *al fresco* dining along the river. Hard-core walkers can continue along the path into Georgetown. Walk up Wisconsin Avenue and you enter a world of trendy shops, restaurants, and crowded sidewalks. Before you walk too far, remember that Georgetown lacks a Metro station to get you back to where you started.

U.S. Department of the Interior

Type of Attraction: A museum located inside a square-mile chunk of government bureaucracy; a National Park Service office and a retail map outlet. A self-guided tour.

Location: 1849 C Street, NW, between 18th and 19th Streets.

Nearest Metro Station: Farragut West

Admission: Free

Hours: Weekdays, 8 A.M. to 5 P.M.; closed weekends and federal holidays.

Phone: (202) 208-4743

When to Go: Anytime

Special Comments: Go on a rainy day. Adults must show a photo ID to enter the building.

Overall Appeal by Age Group:

Pre-school	Grade School	Teens	Young Adults	Over 30	Senior Citizens
★	★★	★	★	★	★

Author's Rating: Boring. ★

How Much Time to Allow: 45 minutes

Description and Comments   This six-wing, seven-story limestone edifice includes 16 acres of floors, two miles of corridors—and an old-fashioned museum. Dioramas of mines and geothermal power plants, Native American artifacts, and a historical exhibit of the National Park Service crowd the rather dark and quiet exhibit hall. This is definitely a rainy-day kind of a museum, unless you have a strong interest in national parks.

Touring Tips   Outdoors-people and map-lovers shouldn't miss the U.S. Geological Survey map store, located off the lobby on the E Street side of the building. You can also load up on brochures on any (or all) U.S. national parks at the National Park Service office here. The Indian Craft Shop, across from the museum entrance, sells turquoise and silver jewelry, baskets, and other handicrafts made by Native Americans. The basement cafeteria can seat 1,500 (open weekdays, 7 A.M. to 2:45 P.M.).

Other Things to Do Nearby   The DAR Museum and the Corcoran Gallery of Art are around the corner on 17th Street; the Mall is about two blocks south. The Octagon, one of Washington's earliest and most elegant homes, is half a block north on 18th Street. For places to eat, head north up any numbered street toward Pennsylvania Avenue.

U.S. Department of State Diplomatic Reception Rooms

Type of Attraction: The rooms where visiting foreign dignitaries are officially entertained. A guided tour.

Location: 21st and C Streets, NW.

Nearest Metro Station: Foggy Bottom/GWU

Admission: Free

Hours: Tours are given Monday through Friday at 9:30 A.M., 10:30 A.M., and 2:45 P.M., by reservation only.

Phone: (202) 647-3241; fax (202) 736-4232; TDD (202) 736-4474

Special Comments: See what $90 million in decorative arts can buy. Children under age 12 are not permitted on the tour. Reservations are accepted up to 90 days in advance of your visit. A short, optional public affairs tour is offered after the main tour.

Overall Appeal by Age Group:

Pre-school	Grade School	Teens	Young Adults	Over 30	Senior Citizens
—	—	★★★½	★★★★	★★★★★	★★★★★

Author's Rating: Although most tourists miss this, you shouldn't.
    ★★★★★

How Much Time to Allow: One hour

Description and Comments   While the State Department goes about its important work in a building with architecture best described as "early airport," the interiors on the eighth floor are something else entirely: A fabulous collection of 18th- and early-19th-century fine and decorative arts fills stunning rooms that are used daily to receive visiting heads of state and foreign dignitaries. This is a tour for almost anyone: antique and fine arts lovers, history buffs, and just casual visitors. It's also a sight that the overwhelming majority of D.C. tourists miss. First-time visitors should make the effort to get reservations well in advance of their trip. Then forget about visiting the White House.

Touring Tips   By guided tour only; reservations are required and should be made at least four weeks in advance of your visit. Rest rooms are located near the waiting room and can be visited before and after the tour.

Other Things to Do Nearby   The Lincoln Memorial and Vietnam Veterans Memorial are a short walk away, down 23rd Street to the Mall. The closest places to eat are a few blocks up 23rd Street, away from the Mall.

Zone 5: Georgetown

Dumbarton Oaks and Gardens

Type of Attraction: A mansion/museum and a beautiful terraced garden. Self-guided tours.

Location: 1703 32nd Street, between R and S Streets, NW, in Georgetown.

Admission: Free for the museum, $3 for adults, $2 for seniors and children for the garden (April through October only, free the rest of the year).

Hours: Museum: Tuesday through Sunday, 2 P.M. to 5 P.M.; Garden (weather permitting): November through March, 2 P.M. to 5 P.M., and till 6 P.M. the rest of the year. Closed on national holidays.

Phone: (202) 339-6400

When to Go: Anytime

Special Comments: Don't be put off by the hushed surroundings—this is one of the best museums in Washington.

Overall Appeal by Age Group:

Pre-school	Grade School	Teens	Young Adults	Over 30	Senior Citizens
—	★	★★½	★★★½	★★★★	★★★★

Author's Rating: Intimate and gorgeous. ★★★★

How Much Time to Allow: Two hours

Description and Comments   Most people associate Dumbarton Oaks with the conference held here in 1944 that led to the formation of the United Nations. Today, however, it's a research center for Byzantine and pre-Columbian studies owned by Harvard University. The Byzantine collection is one of the world's finest, featuring bronzes, ivories, and jewelry. The exquisite pre-Columbian art collection is housed in eight interconnected, circular glass pavilions lit by natural light. It's a knockout of a museum. Dumbarton Oaks Gardens is located around the corner on R Street. The terraced ten-acre garden is rated one of the top gardens in the United States, featuring an orangery, a rose garden, wisteria-covered arbors and, in the fall, a blazing backdrop of trees turning orange, yellow, and red. Dumbarton

Oaks isn't the kind of museum with much appeal to small children, and some adults may not find much of interest in the collection due to its narrow focus. But combined with the adjacent gardens, it's a worthwhile place to visit when in Georgetown.

Touring Tips   Because Dumbarton Oaks doesn't open its massive doors until 2 P.M., combine your visit with a morning trip to Georgetown. If it's raining the day you plan to visit, try to rearrange your schedule so you can come on a nice day; the gardens are terrific.

Other Things to Do Nearby   Take a walking tour of Georgetown and see how lobbyists, politicians, media gurus, and other well-connected and monied denizens of Washington live. If you made advance reservations to see Tudor House, Dumbarton Oaks makes a great side trip. When you get hungry, turn left or right on Wisconsin Avenue and you won't have to go far to find an interesting restaurant or cafe. The Chesapeake and Ohio Canal, which starts in Georgetown, can offer near wilderness solace to weary tourists. You may also want to take a stroll through the nearby Montrose and Rock Creek Cemeteries, where Clover and Henry Adams are buried beneath the hooded Saint-Gaudens memorial that Mark Twain called "Grief" but Henry Adams referred to as "The Peace of God."

Zone 6: Dupont Circle/ Adams-Morgan

The Christian Heurich Mansion

Type of Attraction: The lavish home of a wealthy turn-of-the-century Washington businessman. A self-guided tour.

Location: 1307 New Hampshire Avenue, NW (two blocks south of Dupont Circle).

Nearest Metro Station: Dupont Circle

Admission: $3 for adults; $1.50 for students, seniors, and children.

Hours: Wednesday through Saturday, 10 A.M. to 4 P.M. Closed on federal holidays.

Phone: (202) 785-2068

Special Comments: Don't be put off by the grimy exterior.

Overall Appeal by Age Group:

Pre-school	Grade School	Teens	Young Adults	Over 30	Senior Citizens
—	★	★½	★★½	★★★	★★★

Author's Rating: An outrageous Gilded Age interior. ★★★

How Much Time to Allow: One hour

Description and Comments It's doubtful that any amount of money could re-create what wealthy brewer Christian Heurich built in the early 1890s: a regal, 31-room mansion full of richly detailed mahogany and oak woodwork, elaborate plaster moldings, and a musician's balcony that lets live music be heard throughout the first floor. It may be the most opulent home open to the public in Washington. The building also serves as headquarters for the Historical Society of Washington and houses its library. While most first-time visitors to Washington shouldn't feel obliged to spend time here, it's worth a look on a later trip. People who love decorative arts should put it on their "A" list.

Touring Tips The small garden behind the museum is a popular spot for a brown-bag lunch.

Other Things to Do Nearby   Walk to Dupont Circle for a whiff of Washington's bohemian side: Trendy cafes, shops, bookstores, and restaurants crowd Connecticut Avenue. Expect to be panhandled about every 50 feet in fair weather; the street merchants crowding around the Metro entrances suggest a Middle East bazaar. *Note:* Good deals can be had.

House of the Temple

Type of Attraction: A Masonic temple modeled after one of the Seven Wonders of the World. A guided tour.

Location: 1733 16th Street, NW.

Nearest Metro Station: Dupont Circle

Admission: Free

Hours: Guided tours Monday through Friday, 8 A.M. to 2 P.M.

Phone: (202) 232-3579

When to Go: Anytime

Special Comments: Unless you have an abiding interest in Freemasonry, the tour is way too long.

Overall Appeal by Age Group:

Pre-school	Grade School	Teens	Young Adults	Over 30	Senior Citizens
—	★	★	★	★	★

Author's Rating: Spectacular but cold. ★

How Much Time to Allow: Two hours (less if you're willing to fib to the tour guide; see below).

Description and Comments   The walls are 8 feet thick, the exterior is surrounded by 33 massive columns that support a magnificent pyramidal roof and, inside, the Temple Room features a soaring 100-foot ceiling and 1,000-pipe organ. Unfortunately, with the exception of the exterior, you have to take an excruciatingly boring guided tour to see these goodies. You're guaranteed to be bored silly by displays of bric-a-brac and memorabilia belonging to long-dead Masonic leaders. There is one slightly bizarre treat: The J. Edgar Hoover Law Enforcement Room, a shrine to the Mason and lifelong FBI chief. But unless you're a rabid fan of J. Edgar, after about two minutes you'll be . . . bored.

Touring Tips   Arrive around 1 P.M. on a quiet afternoon and tell the tour guide you've got to catch a train at 2:30. Then plead for an abbreviated tour, which he may grudgingly provide if there aren't any other tourists on hand for a tour. But even reduced to an hour, the tour is too long.

Other Things to Do Nearby   The House of the Temple is on the edge of a marginally safe neighborhood, so make a beeline toward Dupont Circle, where you'll find plenty to do. Six blocks west on S Street are the Textile Museum and the Woodrow Wilson House.

Islamic Center

Type of Attraction: A mosque. A self-guided tour.

Location: 2551 Massachusetts Avenue, NW.

Nearest Metro Station: Dupont Circle

Admission: Free

Hours: Daily, 10 A.M. to 5 P.M.; closed Fridays to non-Muslims between 1 P.M. and 2:30 P.M.

Phone: (202) 332-8343

When to Go: Anytime

Special Comments: The mosque enforces a strict dress code: Visitors must remove their shoes to go inside, and no shorts or short dresses are allowed; women must cover their heads and wear long-sleeved clothing.

Overall Appeal by Age Group:

Pre-school	Grade School	Teens	Young Adults	Over 30	Senior Citizens
★	★½	★½	★★★	★★	★★

Author's Rating: Exotic and surprisingly small. ★½

How Much Time to Allow: 15 minutes

Description and Comments   A brilliant white building and slender minaret mark this unusual sight on Embassy Row. Visitors must remove their shoes before stepping inside to see the Persian carpets, elegantly embellished columns, decorated arches, and huge chandelier. Alas, with America's focus on the Middle East and things Islamic, I was disappointed on my visit to the Islamic Center: It fell a little short on giving any useful insight into that troubled part of the world. The small bookstore next to the mosque was filled with Arabic texts and translations of the Koran, but no one was behind the counter to answer my questions. Though close to other tourist sights, the mosque seems to have missed an opportunity to educate D.C. visitors about Islam. Those with a strong interest in the Middle East should call a week in advance for the one-hour guided tour.

Touring Tips Make this small, exotic building a part of a walk down Embassy Row. But unless you have an interest in Islam, it's not worth going out of the way to see.

Other Things to Do Nearby Take a short walk and tour the Textile Museum and the Woodrow Wilson House. On Tuesday through Saturday afternoons, the opulent Anderson House is open. The Phillips Collection is an intimate modern art museum that's a refreshing change of pace from huge Mall museums.

Meridian International Center

Type of Attraction: Two mansions designed by John Russell Pope; art exhibitions displayed in beautiful galleries; handsome gardens and a grove of linden trees. Guided and self-guided tours.

Location: 1624 and 1630 Crescent Place, NW.

Admission: Free

Hours: Wednesday through Sunday, 2 P.M. to 5 P.M. Closed Mondays, Tuesdays, and federal holidays. The cafe is open Monday through Friday from noon to 2 P.M.

Phone: (202) 939-5568

When to Go: Anytime

Special Comments: Call ahead of time or check Friday's "Weekend" section of the *Washington Post* to make sure the center isn't closed (due to a conference) and to find out what's on display in the galleries.

Overall Appeal by Age Group:

Pre-school	Grade School	Teens	Young Adults	Over 30	Senior Citizens
★	★½	★½	★★	★★	★★½

Author's Rating: Architectural grandeur and a glimpse into the world of diplomacy. ★★½

How Much Time to Allow: One hour

Description and Comments Two side-by-side mansions designed by John Russell Pope (architect of the Jefferson Memorial, the National Gallery of Art building, and other Washington treasures) make up the Meridian International Center, a nonprofit organization that promotes conferences, symposiums, lectures, and seminars and provides services to international visitors, diplomats, scholars, politicians, and others.

The 45-room Meridian House (1921) reflects an 18th-century French

Louis XVI style of architecture, while the White-Meyer House (1911) is a salmon-color brick, Georgian-style mansion. Visitors are welcome to tour the ground floors of the gorgeous—though lightly furnished—buildings and the surrounding gardens. About five art exhibits a year rotate through the galleries of the White-Meyer House. The three-acre site, set off from the city by high, elegant walls, takes up an entire city block.

Touring Tips   While folks who enjoy grand architecture won't need additional encouragement to visit these two distinguished buildings, others should plan on coming in the spring when the gardens are in bloom and an art exhibition is on display in the elegant galleries. A small cafe in the basement of the Meridian House (which recently underwent a two-year, $1.8 million restoration) offers coffee, tea, and lunch. For a guided tour of the property, just ask at the front desk in either building.

Other Things to Do Nearby   Adams-Morgan, an eclectic multicultural neighborhood renowned for its ethnic eateries, is only two blocks away on 18th Street, NW.

Phillips Collection

Type of Attraction: The first museum dedicated to modern art in the United States. A self-guided tour.

Location: 1600 21st Street, NW.

Nearest Metro Station: Dupont Circle

Admission: Weekends: $6.50 for adults, $3.25 for seniors over age 62 and full-time students. No charge for visitors under age 18. During the week, the museum suggests contributions at the same level.

Hours: Tuesday through Saturday, 10 A.M. to 5 P.M.; Sundays, noon to 7 P.M. (until 5 P.M. June through August). Open until 8:30 P.M. on Thursdays. Closed New Year's Day, Fourth of July, Thanksgiving, and Christmas.

Phone: (202) 387-2151

When to Go: Anytime

Special Comments: With lots of carpeting and places to sit, the Phillips Collection is a very comfortable museum to tour.

Overall Appeal by Age Group:

Pre-school	Grade School	Teens	Young Adults	Over 30	Senior Citizens
—	★	★★	★★★½	★★★★	★★★★

Author's Rating: One of the best art museums in Washington. ★★★★

How Much Time to Allow: Two hours

Description and Comments Founded by Duncan Phillips, grandson of the founder of the Jones and Laughlin Steel Company, the Phillips Collection is set in the family's former mansion, which helps explain its intimate and comfortable feeling. The collection is too large for everything to be on display at once, so the art is constantly rotated. Expect to see works by Monet, Picasso, Miró, Renoir, and Van Gogh, among other modern masters. The large and ornate Music Room is as spectacular as the art hanging on its walls. If you've seen the Hirshhorn and the National Gallery of Art's East Wing, this should be on your agenda. It's a classy museum on a human scale.

Touring Tips The kids would probably prefer a trip to the zoo. Take advantage of the free, 45-minute guided tours given at 2 P.M. Wednesdays and Saturdays. The well-informed guides do a good job of giving a context for the paintings and sculptures, the building, and its founder's taste in modern art.

Other Things to Do Nearby Cross Massachusetts Avenue and see another eye-popping mansion, the Anderson House (open Tuesday through Saturday from 1 P.M. to 4 P.M.). Dupont Circle hosts a myriad of cafes, restaurants, and fast-food joints to satisfy hunger pangs.

Society of the Cincinnati Museum at Anderson House

Type of Attraction: A combination mansion and Revolutionary War museum. A self-guided tour.

Location: 2118 Massachusetts Avenue, NW.

Nearest Metro Station: Dupont Circle

Admission: Free

Hours: Tuesday through Saturday, 1 P.M. to 4 P.M.; closed national holidays.

Phone: (202) 785-2040

When to Go: Anytime

Special Comments: Children will love the Revolutionary War figurines fighting battles; older folks will marvel at the opulence.

Overall Appeal by Age Group:

Pre-school	Grade School	Teens	Young Adults	Over 30	Senior Citizens
★	★★	★★	★★★	★★★★	★★★★

Author's Rating: Robber-baron decadence. ★★★★

How Much Time to Allow: One hour

Description and Comments   This mansion along Embassy Row is a real sleeper that few visitors ever see. Built in 1906 by Larz Anderson, a diplomat, it's a reflection of fabulous turn-of-the-century taste and wealth. The two-story ballroom is a stunner, tapestries line the crystal chandeliered dining room, and paintings by Gilbert Stuart and John Trumbull hang in the billiard room. Anderson was a member of the Society of the Cincinnati, whose members are descendants of French and American officers who served in the Revolutionary Army. After his death, his widow donated the mansion to the society. Today the building serves the society as both headquarters and museum. Even first-time visitors to D.C. should make the effort to see this spectacular mansion, which is located a block or so from Dupont Circle.

Touring Tips   The first floor contains displays of Revolutionary War artifacts. On the second floor, the mansion remains as it was originally furnished, with 18th-century paintings, 17th-century tapestries from Brussels, and huge chandeliers.

Other Things to Do Nearby   Take a walk along Embassy Row or browse the shops around Dupont Circle. Other sights within walking distance include the Phillips Collection (modern art), the Christian Heurich Mansion, the Textile Museum, and the Woodrow Wilson House.

Textile Museum

Type of Attraction: A museum dedicated to textile arts. A self-guided tour.

Location: 2320 S Street, NW.

Nearest Metro Station: Dupont Circle

Admission: Free; $5 donation suggested.

Hours: Monday through Saturday, 10 A.M. to 5 P.M.; Sundays, 1 P.M. to 5 P.M. Closed federal holidays and December 24.

Phone: (202) 667-0441

When to Go: Anytime

Special Comments: The museum is wheelchair-accessible but not barrier-free. Call ahead if you have special needs.

Overall Appeal by Age Group:

Pre-school	Grade School	Teens	Young Adults	Over 30	Senior Citizens
—	★	★★	★★½	★★½	★★★

Author's Rating: Interesting, but small and esoteric. ★★

How Much Time to Allow: One hour

Description and Comments Cloth, a mass-produced commodity in the West, no longer enjoys much prestige as an art form. But it's a different story in the rest of the world. The museum's collection ranges from countries as diverse as India, Indonesia, and China to Mexico, Guatemala, and Peru. Intricate designs and rich colors grace more than 14,000 textiles and 1,400 carpets dating from ancient times to the present day. Because the items can't be exposed to light for long periods of time, the exhibits are constantly rotated. This museum is much more interesting than it sounds—the rich colors derived from natural dye processes and elaborate details in the fabrics are subtly beautiful. Definitely for distinct tastes, but not to be missed if it appeals to you.

Touring Tips In the new second-floor Textile Learning Center, visitors can touch, feel, and examine textiles close up. It's an opportunity to get a better grip on how and why textiles are cultural carriers that reveal a lot about how people live. Don't miss the pleasant garden behind the museum. The gift shop is chock-full of books and items related to textiles and rugs.

Other Things to Do Nearby The Woodrow Wilson House is next door, and the Islamic Center is around the corner on Massachusetts Avenue. In the other direction, S Street crosses Connecticut Avenue, where you can shop and dine to your heart's content.

Woodrow Wilson House

Type of Attraction: The final home of the 28th U.S. president. A guided tour.

Location: 2340 S Street, NW.

Nearest Metro Station: Dupont Circle

Admission: $5; $2.50 for students and $4 for seniors over age 62

Hours: Tuesday through Sunday, 10 A.M. to 4 P.M. Closed Thanksgiving, Christmas, and New Year's days.

Phone: (202) 387-4062

When to Go: To avoid a crowded tour during spring and summer, arrive before noon.

Special Comments: Lots of stairs, including a steep, narrow descent down a back staircase.

Overall Appeal by Age Group:

Pre-school	Grade School	Teens	Young Adults	Over 30	Senior Citizens
★	★★	★★★	★★★	★★★½	★★★½

Author's Rating: Interesting and informative. ★★★½

How Much Time to Allow: 90 minutes

Description and Comments   After Woodrow Wilson left office in 1921, he became the only former president to retire in Washington, D.C.—and he did so in this house. The tour starts with a 25-minute video narrated by Walter Cronkite that puts this underrated president in perspective and fires you up for the tour. Ninety-six percent of the items in this handsome Georgian Revival townhouse are original, so visitors get an accurate picture of aristocratic life in the 1920s. On the tour you'll see Wilson's library (his books, however, went to the Library of Congress after his death), his bedroom, his old movie projector, and beautiful furnishings.

Touring Tips   The basement kitchen is virtually unchanged from Wilson's day, with original items such as an ornate wooden icebox and a coal- and gas-fired stove. Peek inside the pantry, still stocked with items from the '20s such as Kellogg's Corn Flakes ("wonderfully flavored with malt, sugar and salt"). This is another tour that gives visitors the feeling they've been somewhere special and off the beaten tourist track.

Other Things to Do Nearby   The Textile Museum is next door. Embassy Row is around the corner on Massachusetts Avenue, and in the other direction, Connecticut Avenue bustles with shops and restaurants.

Zone 7: Upper Northwest

Hillwood Museum (closed for renovations from December 1997 until late 1999)

Type of Attraction: A mansion housing fabulous art treasures (a guided tour) and formal gardens on a 25-acre estate (guided and self-guided tours).

Location: 4155 Linnean Avenue, NW.

Nearest Metro Station: Van Ness/UDC. For a pleasant 20-minute walk, go south on Connecticut Avenue past the Star Trek-y Intelsat complex on the right, then turn left on Upton Street. Follow Upton to Linnean, turn right, and walk about a block to the estate entrance. Or grab a cab.

Admission: $10 for the house tour ($5 for full-time students); the garden tour is $5 and $2.50 for students; a combined house and garden tour is $12 ($7.50 for students); $2 to visit the formal gardens and auxiliary buildings only. Guided garden tours are $5 (offered April through June and September through mid-November on Wednesdays, Fridays, and Saturdays only).

Hours: Tuesday through Saturday, house tours begin at 9:30 A.M., 10:45 A.M., 12:30 P.M., 1:45 P.M., and 3 P.M.; the gardens are open 9 A.M. to 5 P.M. Hillwood is closed for renovations from December 1997 until late 1999.

Phone: (202) 686-8500; (202) 686-5807 for reservations

When to Go: Spring is the most beautiful season to tour the house and gardens. But these are popular destinations for garden clubs, so you must secure reservations well in advance. Because of Hillwood's wooded location in Rock Creek Park, it's always five degrees cooler here in D.C.'s hot and humid summers.

Special Comments: The tour involves a lot of walking and standing. No children under age 12 are allowed on the mansion tour.

Overall Appeal by Age Group:

Pre-school	Grade School	Teens	Young Adults	Over 30	Senior Citizens
—	—	★★	★★★	★★★★½	★★★★½

Author's Rating: Stunning. ★★★★½

How Much Time to Allow: Three hours. The tour itself is almost two hours but doesn't include the formal gardens and auxiliary buildings.

Description and Comments She was a girl from Michigan who inherited two things from her father: good taste and General Foods. That, in a nutshell, is the story of Marjorie Merriweather Post, who bought this Rock Creek Park estate in 1955, remodeled the mansion, and filled it with exquisite 18th- and 19th-century French and Russian decorative art. "Fabulous" is not too strong a word to use in describing the collection of Imperial Russian objects on display. Mrs. Post was married to the U.S. ambassador to Russia in the 1930s—a time when the communists were unloading "decadent," pre-Revolution art at bargain prices. Mrs. Post literally bought warehouse-loads of stuff: jewels, dinner plates commissioned by Catherine the Great, Easter eggs by Carl Fabergé, and chalices and icons. She then had the loot loaded onto her yacht, *Sea Cloud* (the largest private ship in the world), for shipment home. The very best of the booty is on display here. The tour provides a glimpse into Mrs. Post's lavish lifestyle.

Touring Tips Advance reservations are required to tour the mansion. Call at least two months in advance for a spring tour, although you may luck into a cancellation by calling a day or two before your planned visit. Children under age 12 are not admitted on the tour. Plan your visit so that you have enough time to stroll the gardens. The estate also has a cafe that serves lunch and tea, a gift shop, and a greenhouse you can tour. A "Behind the Scenes" tour is offered at 3 P.M. on Wednesdays, June through March (except the first Wednesday of the month; $10 per person). Visitors get a glimpse of Hillwood as it was run when Mrs. Post lived here by touring the fallout shelter, the massage room, the silver-polishing room, and other places not seen on the regular house tour. Reservations are suggested for the small cafe.

Other Things to Do Nearby Intelsat, near the Van Ness/UDC Metro station, looks like a building out of the 21st century. That's no surprise, since the firm is an international conglomeration that produces satellites. The lobby features models and prototypes of its products hanging from the ceiling. For lunch, there are plenty of restaurants to choose from near the Metro station on Connecticut Avenue.

National Museum of Health and Medicine

Type of Attraction: A medical museum. A self-guided tour.

Location: On the grounds of Walter Reed Army Medical Center, located between 16th Street and Georgia Avenue, NW, near Takoma Park, Maryland.

Nearest Metro Station: Takoma Park. If you have a car, drive.

Admission: Free

Hours: Daily, 10 A.M. to 5:30 P.M. Closed Christmas Day.

Phone: (202) 782-2200

When to Go: Anytime

Special Comments: Unless you're a health professional or harbor an intense interest in the history of medicine, this small but fascinating museum is simply too difficult to get to. Wait a few years until it relocates to the Mall.

Overall Appeal by Age Group:

Pre-school	Grade School	Teens	Young Adults	Over 30	Senior Citizens
—	★★	★★½	★★½	★★½	★★½

Author's Rating: Some excellent exhibits . . . and a bit unsettling. Though not as gruesome as it used to be, it's still not a place for the squeamish. ★★

How Much Time to Allow: One hour

Description and Comments Excellent exhibits on the human body and the AIDS epidemic make this museum a worthwhile destination. Although there are still plenty of bottled human organs, skeletons, and graphic illustrations of the effects of disfiguring diseases, the emphasis has shifted from the bizarre to education. Exhibits on medicine in the Civil War and an extensive microscope collection (including huge electron microscopes) will probably have more appeal to physicians, scientists, and other health professionals. We're glad to report that the museum has improved the quality of its exhibits and its overall appearance since our first visit.

Touring Tips Finding this place can be tough. By subway, it's a brisk, 15-minute walk to the museum from the Takoma Park Metro station. As you exit the station, turn right and walk under the railroad tracks, then turn right at Blair Road. Walk one block to Dahlia Street and turn left. Walter Reed is about six blocks straight ahead. The museum is directly behind the large white hospital building; you can walk around it on the left. If you're driving, enter the Walter Reed complex through the Dahlia Street gate on Georgia Avenue. The museum is located in the south end of Building 54 (behind the large white hospital building). There's a small parking lot next to the museum.

Other Things to Do Nearby Nothing recommended.

National Zoological Park
(part of the Smithsonian Institution)

Type of Attraction: The Smithsonian's world-class zoo. A self-guided tour.

Location: 3001 Connecticut Avenue, NW.

Nearest Metro Stations: Woodley Park/National Zoo, Cleveland Park

Admission: Free

Hours: Grounds are open from 6 A.M. to 8 P.M. May through October 15, and buildings are open 10 A.M. to 6 P.M.; September 16 through April, grounds are open from 6 A.M. to 6 P.M., and buildings are open from 10 A.M. to 4:30 P.M. The Pollinarium and the invertebrate exhibits are closed Mondays and Tuesdays.

Phone: (202) 673-4800 (recording); or (202) 673-4717 (during business hours)

When to Go: Anytime. In the summer, avoid going during Washington's sweltering afternoons.

Special Comments: Many sections of the paths winding through the Zoo's 163 acres are steep.

Overall Appeal by Age Group:

Pre-school	Grade School	Teens	Young Adults	Over 30	Senior Citizens
★★★★★	★★★★★	★★★★	★★★½	★★★½	★★★½

Author's Rating: A first-rate operation in a beautiful setting. ★★★★½

How Much Time to Allow: Two hours just to see the most popular attractions; a whole day to see it all. Better yet, see the Zoo over several visits.

Description and Comments The National Zoo emphasizes natural environment, with many animals roaming large enclosures instead of pacing in cages. And it's all found in a lush woodland setting in a section of Rock Creek Park. Two main paths link the many buildings and exhibits: Olmstead Walk, which passes all the animal houses, and the steeper Valley Trail, which includes all the aquatic exhibits. They add up to about two miles of trail. The Zoo's nonlinear layout and lack of sight lines make a map invaluable; pick one up at the Education Building near the entrance. The most popular exhibits include Hsing-Hsing, the famous giant panda (formerly a pair, now down to one), the great apes, the white tiger, and the cheetahs.

But for diversity and a good chance of seeing some animal activity, check out the Small Mammal House, the invertebrate exhibit (kids can look through microscopes), and the huge outside bird cages (the condors look the size of Volkswagens). If your visit to Washington is long enough to include forays away from the Mall, make this beautiful park part of your itinerary. Aside from a wide variety of wildlife on view, the wooded setting is a welcome relief from viewing too much marble downtown.

Touring Tips   Plan to visit either early or late in the day. Animals are more active, temperatures are cooler—and crowds are thinner. During busy periods, some exhibits are subject to "controlled access" to prevent crowding; in other words, you may have to wait in line. Panda feeding is at 11 A.M. and 3 P.M. (while it's usually a mob scene, it's also the only time to glimpse some activity from this docile creature). Other feedings and demonstrations occur throughout the day at the cheetah, elephant, seal, and sea lion exhibits; check at the Education Building for times.

Don't miss three new permanent exhibits: Pollinarium, Think Tank, and the Amazonia Science Gallery. Pollinarium, a lush garden housed in a 1,250-square-foot greenhouse, features hundreds of zebra long-wing butterflies that flutter around as visitors get a firsthand look at animal pollinators, plants, and the process of pollination. A glass-enclosed beehive gives an up-close glimpse of the activities of thousands of honeybees.

Think Tank, a 15,000-square-foot exhibit that opened in late 1995, attempts to answer the question, Can animals think? Scientists conduct demonstrations daily on language, tool use, and social organization. Displays, artifacts, graphics, and videos cover topics such as brain size, problem-solving ability, and language. Four animal species are featured in the exhibit: orangutans, Sulawesi macaque monkeys, hermit crabs, and leaf-cutter ants.

The new Amazonia Science Gallery explores the biological diversity of the Amazon rain forest; a biodiversity demonstration lab is equipped with a working electron microscope and with displays of living beetles, frog eggs, tadpoles, and boas. The two-meter-diameter "Geosphere" globe uses projectors, satellite imagery, and computer data to show seasonal changes, weather and land cultivation patterns, population distribution, and other factors that affect life on earth.

Other Things to Do Nearby   If you've done the Zoo justice, your feet will hurt and your energy level will be too depleted for much else: Go back to your room. Lunch spots abound three blocks north on Connecticut Avenue; from there it's a short walk to the Cleveland Park Metro. But if you've got feet of steel, take the half-hour hike to the National Cathedral.

Washington National Cathedral

Type of Attraction: The sixth-largest cathedral in the world. Guided and self-guided tours.

Location: Massachusetts and Wisconsin Avenues, NW.

Nearest Metro Station: The Woodley Park/National Zoo station is about a half-hour walk; drive or take a cab.

Admission: Free; suggested donations are $2 for adults and $1 for children.

Hours: September through April, daily, 10 A.M. to 4:30 P.M.; May through August, weeknights only, till 9 P.M.

Phone: (202) 537-6200 and (202) 537-6207 for guided tour information.

When to Go: Anytime

Special Comments: Take the optional 30- to 45-minute, docent-led tour.

Overall Appeal by Age Group:

Pre-school	Grade School	Teens	Young Adults	Over 30	Senior Citizens
★	★★	★★★½	★★★★★	★★★★★	★★★★★

Author's Rating: A Gothic masterpiece. ★★★★★

How Much Time to Allow: One hour

Description and Comments   If you've been to Europe, you'll experience déjà vu when you visit this massive Gothic cathedral. It's a tenth of a mile from the nave to the high altar; the ceiling is 100 feet high. Don't miss the Bishop's Garden, modeled on a medieval walled garden, or the Pilgrim Observation Gallery and a view of Washington from the highest vantage point in the city. Small children may not enjoy being dragged around this huge cathedral, but just about anyone else will enjoy its magnificent architecture and stone carvings.

Touring Tips   Docent-led tours are offered from 10 A.M. to 3:15 P.M. Monday through Saturday and from 12:30 P.M. to 2:45 P.M. Sundays. While the tours are free, suggested donations are $2 for adults and $1 for children. Try to catch the free organ demonstration given Wednesdays at 12:30 P.M.; carillon recitals are on Saturdays at 12:30 P.M. You can also visit the grave of Woodrow Wilson, the only president buried in Washington. The Cathedral isn't well served by public transportation, but walking there takes you through safe, pleasant neighborhoods that are home to Washington's elite: It's about a half-hour stroll up Cathedral Avenue from the Woodley Park/National Zoo Metro.

Other Things to Do Nearby The National Zoo is about a half-hour walk from the National Cathedral, or take a cab. For lunch, walk two blocks north on Wisconsin Avenue to Cleveland Park and choose between Thai, Chinese, Mexican, and pizza restaurants. The best deals are at G.C. Murphy's, which features gyros, pita sandwiches, minipizzas, subs, pastry, and Italian coffee. Most items on the menu are under $5.

Zone 8: Northeast

Basilica of the National Shrine of the Immaculate Conception

Type of Attraction: The largest Catholic church in the U.S. and the seventh-largest religious structure in the world. Guided and self-guided tours.

Location: 4th Street and Michigan Avenue, NE, on the campus of the Catholic University of America.

Nearest Metro Station: Brookland/Catholic University

Admission: Free

Hours: November 1 through March 31, daily, 7 A.M. to 6 P.M.; till 7 P.M. the rest of the year. Guided tours are conducted Monday through Saturday from 9 A.M. to 11 A.M. and from 1 P.M. to 3 P.M., and on Sundays from 1:30 P.M. to 4 P.M.

Phone: (202) 526-8300

When to Go: Anytime

Special Comments: It's a huge cathedral and it requires a lot of walking.

Overall Appeal by Age Group:

Pre-school	Grade School	Teens	Young Adults	Over 30	Senior Citizens
★	★	★	★	★	★½

Author's Rating: Sterile and cold. ★

How Much Time to Allow: One hour

Description and Comments A huge, blue-and-gold onion dome lends Byzantine overtones to this massive cathedral, as does the wealth of colorful mosaics throughout its interior. Yet the architecture is lean and stark, and many of the figures in the mosaics and stained-glass windows look cartoonish. It's not in the same league with the awe-inspiring National Cathedral across town. Sure is big, though.

Touring Tips Skip the guided tour, which stops in every one of the dozens of chapels. Instead, grab a map at the information desk on the ground (crypt) level and enter Memorial Hall, which is lined with chapels. Then go up the stairs (or elevator) to the Upper Church.

Other Things to Do Nearby   The Franciscan Monastery is a brisk, 20-minute walk away: Continue past the Metro station on Michigan Avenue to Quincy Street, turn right, and walk about four blocks. The Basilica has a small cafeteria on the ground level; a better bet is the Pizza Hut on Michigan Avenue.

Franciscan Monastery and Gardens

Type of Attraction: A working monastery. A guided tour.

Location: 1400 Quincy Street, NE.

Nearest Metro Station: Brookland/Catholic University. From the station exit, turn left, walk up to Michigan Avenue, turn left, and walk over the bridge. Continue on Michigan Avenue to Quincy Street, turn right, and walk four blocks.

Admission: Free

Hours: Guided tours on the hour, Monday through Saturday from 9 A.M. to 4 P.M. (except at noon); Sundays, 1 P.M. through 4 P.M.

When to Go: Anytime

Phone: (202) 526-6800

Special Comments: The tour involves negotiating many narrow, steep stairs and low, dark passageways. A limited number of wheelchairs are available for touring the church and upper grounds.

Overall Appeal by Age Group:

Pre-school	Grade School	Teens	Young Adults	Over 30	Senior Citizens
—	★★½	★★	★★	★★	★★

Author's Rating: Beautiful architecture, peaceful grounds—and kind of spooky. ★★

How Much Time to Allow: One hour

Description and Comments   Built around 1900 and recently restored, this monastery has everything you'd expect: quiet, contemplative formal gardens; a beautiful church modeled after the Hagia Sophia in Istanbul; and grounds dotted with replicas of shrines and chapels found in the Holy Land. What's really unusual is the sanitized crypt beneath the church, which is more Hollywood than Holy Land. (You almost expect to run into Victor Mature wearing a toga.) It's a replica of the catacombs under Rome and is positively—if inauthentically—ghoulish. As you pass open (but phony) grave sites in the walls, the guide narrates hair-raising stories of Christian martyrs eaten by lions, speared, stoned to death, beheaded, and burned at the stake. Shudder.

Touring Tips   If you're driving, parking is easy. Two parking lots are located across from the monastery on 14th Street. If you're visiting Washington in the spring, the beautiful gardens alone are worth the trip.

Other Things to Do Nearby   The Basilica of the National Shrine of the Immaculate Conception—let me catch my breath—is just past the Metro station on Michigan Avenue. For lunch, a Pizza Hut is conveniently located near the Metro.

U.S. National Arboretum

Type of Attraction: A 444-acre collection of trees, flowers, and herbs. A self-guided tour.

Location: Off New York Avenue in Northeast Washington.

How to Get There: Drive. Take New York Avenue from downtown and enter on the service road on the right just past Bladensburg Road.

Admission: Free

Hours: Daily, 8 A.M. to 5 P.M. The information center is open weekdays, 8 A.M. to 4:30 P.M.; the gift shop is open weekdays, 10 A.M. to 3 P.M. The recently expanded National Bonsai and Penjing Museum is open daily from 10 A.M. to 3:30 P.M. Closed on Christmas Day.

Phone: (202) 245-2726

When to Go: In the spring, fields of azaleas are in bloom. The world-class bonsai collection is a treat all year.

Special Comments: The arboretum is mobbed in the spring; the rest of the year is usually tranquil.

Overall Appeal by Age Group:

Pre-school	Grade School	Teens	Young Adults	Over 30	Senior Citizens
★	★½	★½	★★	★★½	★★★

Author's Rating: Interesting and beautiful; hard to get to. ★★½

How Much Time to Allow: One hour to half a day.

Description and Comments   With nine miles of roads and more than three miles of walking paths, the U.S. National Arboretum offers visitors an oasis of quiet and beauty for a drive or a stroll. Even people without green thumbs will marvel at the bonsai collection, whose dwarf trees are more like sculptures than plants. One specimen, a Japanese white pine, is 350 years old. Folks with limited time who aren't gardening enthusiasts, however, shouldn't spend their valuable touring hours on a visit.

Touring Tips Flowering dogwood and mountain laurel bloom well into May. The rest of the year, it's a fine place to go for a long walk. The surrounding neighborhoods aren't safe, so either drive or take a cab.

Other Things to Do Nearby The Kenilworth Aquatic Gardens are only a few minutes away by car.

Zone 9: Southeast

Anacostia Museum (a Smithsonian museum)

Type of Attraction: A museum focusing on African-American history and culture. A self-guided tour.

Location: 1901 Fort Place, SE, in Anacostia.

How to Get There: Budgets permitting, the Smithsonian operates free shuttle buses from the Mall to the Anacostia Museum (and back) during the spring and summer. The shuttles run on the hour, Monday through Friday. For specific information on where to board the buses and the schedule, stop at any museum information desk on the Mall or call (202) 287-3382.

To Drive: From the Mall, take Independence Avenue east past the Capitol to 2nd Street, SE, where it is intersected by Pennsylvania Avenue. Bear right onto Pennsylvania Avenue and go to 11th Street, SE, and turn right. Cross the 11th Street Bridge and follow signs to Martin Luther King, Jr., Avenue (left lanes). Follow MLK Avenue to Morris Road (third traffic signal) and turn left. Go up the hill to 17th Street, SE, where Morris Road becomes Erie Street. In about five blocks, Erie Street becomes Fort Place; the museum is on the right. Because this part of Southeast Washington is unsafe for pedestrians, we don't recommend taking public transportation.

Admission: Free

Hours: Daily, 10 A.M. to 5 P.M.; closed Christmas Day.

Phone: (202) 357-2700 (voice); (202) 357-1729 (TTY)

When to Go: Anytime. But either call first or pick up a brochure at the Castle on the Mall to find out what's on view before making the trip.

Special Comments: This "neighborhood" museum features temporary, special exhibits; between shows, there is often very little to see, so call first. The museum was renovated and reopened in the fall of 1997.

Overall Appeal by Age Group: Since the museum features special exhibitions that change throughout the year, it's not really possible to rate this Smithsonian facility's appeal by age group.

Author's Rating: Again, the temporary exhibitions make it impossible to rate this museum.

How Much Time to Allow: One hour

Description and Comments Located on the high ground of old Fort Stanton, the Anacostia Museum features changing exhibits on black culture and history and the achievements of African-Americans. Unfortunately for out-of-town visitors, it's in a location that's difficult to reach.

Touring Tips To save yourself the frustration of arriving between major shows, either call the museum first or pick up a flyer at the Castle on the Mall.

Other Things to Do Nearby Frederick Douglass National Historic Site is a short drive, but you need to call in advance to make reservations for the house tour. Anacostia is a high-crime area. It's okay to drive through during daylight, but it's not an area we advise visitors to visit on foot or at night.

Frederick Douglass National Historic Site

Type of Attraction: Cedar Hill, the preserved Victorian home of abolitionist, statesman, and orator Frederick Douglass. A guided tour by reservation only.

Location: 1411 W Street, SE, in Anacostia.

How to Get There: Drive; Anacostia is unsafe for pedestrians day or night. From the Mall, take Independence Avenue east past the U.S. Capitol to 2nd Street, SE, where it is intersected by Pennsylvania Avenue. Bear right onto Pennsylvania Avenue and go to 11th Street, SE, and turn right. Cross the 11th Street Bridge and go south on Martin Luther King, Jr., Avenue to W Street, SE. Turn left and go four blocks to the visitor center parking lot on the right.

Another option during the summer and in February (Black History Month) is Tourmobile, which offers a two-and-a-half-hour guided tour to Cedar Hill. Call (202) 554-5100 or stop at a Tourmobile ticket booth at Arlington Cemetery, the Lincoln Memorial, or the Washington Monument to make reservations in person. Rates are $6 for adults and $3 for children.

Admission: $3 per person, $1.50 for seniors 62 and older, free for children 6 and under.

Hours: October through April, daily, 9 A.M. to 4 P.M.; May through September, 9 A.M. to 5 P.M. Closed New Year's, Thanksgiving, and Christmas days.

Phone: (202) 426-5960 and (800) 365-2267 for reservations

When to Go: Call for reservations for a house tour.

Special Comments: Do not take the Metro to Anacostia. The entire area is unsafe; Cedar Hill, administered by the National Park Service, is safe. Due to staff cutbacks, you must call to reserve a spot on a house tour, although you can take a chance by showing up and joining another reserved tour (if there's space). A better bet is Tourmobile (February and summer only).

Overall Appeal by Age Group:

Pre-school	Grade School	Teens	Young Adults	Over 30	Senior Citizens
★	★★	★★★	★★★	★★★½	★★★½

Author's Rating: Informative and interesting. ★★★½

How Much Time to Allow: 60 minutes

Description and Comments This lovely Victorian home on a hill overlooking Washington remains much as it was in Douglass's time. The former slave, who among other achievements became U.S. ambassador to Haiti, spent the final 18 years of his life in this house. Douglass lived here when he wrote the third volume of his autobiography, *Life and Times of Frederick Douglass*. For people interested in the history of the civil rights movement and genteel life in the late 1800s, Cedar Hill is a find. Our well-informed guide provided a detailed commentary on Douglass's life and times. Look for Douglass's barbells on the floor next to his bed. Most children, however, may find it dull.

Touring Tips A late afternoon visit is almost like stepping back into the 19th century, because the house is preserved as it was when Douglass died in 1895: There's no electricity, and the gathering shadows in the house evoke the past. Be sure to see "The Growlery," a small, one-room structure behind the main house Douglass declared off-limits to the household so that he could work alone.

Other Things to Do Nearby The Anacostia Museum is a short drive. However, Anacostia, Washington's first suburb and an area rich in black history, is an area that's economically distressed and crime-ridden. It's okay to drive during daylight, but it's not a part of town to visit on foot or at night.

Kenilworth Aquatic Gardens

Type of Attraction: A national park devoted to water plants. A self-guided tour.

Location: 1900 Anacostia Drive, SE, across the Anacostia River from the National Arboretum.

How to Get There: Drive. Go south on Kenilworth Avenue from its intersection with New York Avenue. Exit at Eastern Avenue and follow signs to the parking lot off Anacostia Avenue.

Admission: Free

Hours: Daily, 7 A.M. to 4 P.M.

Phone: (202) 426-6905

When to Go: June and July to see hardy water plants; July and August to see tropical plants and lotus. On the third Saturday in July the gardens hold a water-lily festival. Year-round it's a great place for bird-watching.

Special Comments: The gardens are located in a dangerous neighborhood. Don't take public transportation.

Overall Appeal by Age Group:

Pre-school	Grade School	Teens	Young Adults	Over 30	Senior Citizens
★	★★	★★	★★★	★★★	★★★

Author's Rating: Unique. ★★★

How Much Time to Allow: One hour

Description and Comments In addition to pools filled with water lilies, water hyacinth, lotus, and bamboo, the gardens teem with wildlife such as opossum, raccoon, waterfowl, and muskrats. It's an amazing place to visit on a clear summer morning.

Touring Tips Come in the morning, before the heat closes up the flowers. Don't take public transportation; the surrounding neighborhood is unsafe. Drive or go by cab.

Other Things to Do Nearby The National Arboretum is only a few minutes away by car.

Washington Navy Yard

Type of Attraction: Three military museums and a U.S. Navy destroyer. Self-guided tours.

Location: 9th and M Streets, SE, on the waterfront.

Nearest Metro Station: Eastern Market. Because this is an unsafe neighborhood any time of day, we recommend that visitors either drive (parking is available inside the gate) or take a cab.

Admission: Free

Hours: Monday through Friday, 9 A.M. to 4 P.M.; Memorial Day through Labor Day, weekends, and holidays, 10 A.M. to 5 P.M. The USS *Barry* opens at 10 A.M.

Phone: Navy Museum: (202) 433-4882; Marine Corps Historical Museum: (202) 433-3534 (closed Tuesdays); Navy Art Gallery: (202) 433-3815; USS *Barry*: (202) 433-3377 (open until 5 P.M. in the summer and until 4 P.M. in the winter; closed Mondays).

When to Go: Anytime

Special Comments: A nice contrast to the look-but-don't-touch Mall museums.

Overall Appeal by Age Group:

Pre-school	Grade School	Teens	Young Adults	Over 30	Senior Citizens
★	★★★½	★★★	★★	★★	★★★

Author's Rating: Hands-on fun for kids; informative for adults. ★★½

How Much Time to Allow: Two hours

Description and Comments   Exhibits in the Navy Museum include 14-foot-long model ships, undersea vehicles *Alvin* and *Trieste*, working sub periscopes, a space capsule that kids (and wiry adults) can climb in and, tied up at the dock, a decommissioned destroyer to tour. The Marine Corps Historical Museum is less hands-on, featuring exhibit cases and Marine Corps mementos. The Navy Art Gallery is a small museum with paintings of naval actions painted by combat artists. A strong interest in the military is a prerequisite for making the trek to the Washington Navy Yard, and it's not a side trip that many first-time visitors make. But kids will love it.

Touring Tips   Don't make my mistake—jumping off at the Metro's Navy Yard station and walking 10 scary blocks to the Navy Yard entrance; drive or take a cab. It's too bad these museums are so far off the beaten path, because there's a lot here to see and do.

Other Things to Do Nearby   Nothing recommended.

Zone 10: Maryland Suburbs

NASA/Goddard Space Flight Visitor Center (Zone 10D)

Type of Attraction: NASA's 1,100-acre, campuslike facility in suburban Maryland, including a small museum and other buildings. Self-guided and guided tours.

Location: Greenbelt, Maryland.

How to Get There: Drive. From downtown Washington, drive out New York Avenue, which becomes the Baltimore-Washington Parkway (I-295). Take the MD 193 East exit, just past the Capital Beltway. Drive about two miles past the Goddard Space Flight Center's main entrance to Soil Conservation Road and turn left. Follow signs to the visitor center.

Admission: Free

Hours: Daily, 9 A.M. to 4 P.M.; closed Thanksgiving, Christmas, and New Year's days.

Phone: (301) 286-8981

When to Go: Anytime

Overall Appeal by Age Group:

Pre-school	Grade School	Teens	Young Adults	Over 30	Senior Citizens
★	★★★	★★★	★★★	★★★	★★★

Author's Rating: Informative but not convenient for most visitors. ★★½

How Much Time to Allow: One hour for the tours; two hours for the Sunday bus tours.

Description and Comments   The small museum inside the visitor center is loaded with space hardware, including a space capsule kids can play in, space suits and real satellites; think of it as a mini–National Air and Space Museum. Outside, some real rockets used to put the hardware into outer space are on display. While most folks will get their fill and then some of spacecraft at the museum on the Mall, a visit to NASA's Greenbelt facility is the icing on the cake for hard-core space cadets.

Touring Tips   The small gift shop offers interesting NASA-related items such as postcards, 35-mm color slides, posters, and publications. One-hour tours are given at 11:30 A.M. and 2:30 P.M. Monday through Saturday, and on the first and third Sundays of the month at 11 A.M.; two-hour bus tours are scheduled on second and fourth Sundays of the month at 11 A.M. and 2 P.M. The Sunday tours of the center are offered on a first-come, first-served basis and take visitors to special working areas that show satellite control and tracking operations, test and evaluation facilities, and communication operations. On the first and third Sundays of the month, model rocket launches are held on the center grounds; bring your own or watch model rocket enthusiasts do their thing. Launches are monitored for safety. In the spring and fall, an all-day Open House features an even wider array of tours, plus entertainment. Call the center for a schedule.

Other Things to Do Nearby   Drive through the adjacent Agricultural Research Center, a collection of farms where the U.S. Department of Agriculture studies farm animals and plants. The roads are narrow and quiet— it's a rural oasis in the heart of Maryland's suburban sprawl. The National Wildlife Visitor Center off nearby Powder Mill Road features nature displays and hiking paths.

National Cryptologic Museum (north of Zone 10D)

Type of Attraction: A small museum offering a glimpse into the secret world of spies, national defense, and ciphers. A self-guided tour.

Location: The National Security Agency, on the grounds of Fort George G. Meade, about 30 minutes north of Washington and east of Laurel, Maryland (Route 32 and the Baltimore-Washington Parkway).

Admission: Free

Hours: Weekdays, 9 A.M. to 3 P.M., and Saturdays, 10 A.M. to 2 P.M. Closed Sundays and holidays.

Phone: (301) 688-5849

When to Go: Anytime

Special Comments: A very small museum that will only appeal to a narrow slice of Washington visitors.

Overall Appeal by Age Group:

Pre-school	Grade School	Teens	Young Adults	Over 30	Senior Citizens
—	★	★½	★½	★½	★★

Author's Rating: Gee, a real World War II vintage German Enigma ciphering machine. Yet this tiny museum's greatest appeal may be its very existence: The National Security Agency (NSA) is the nation's largest spy organization—and its most secretive. ★

How Much Time to Allow: One hour

Description and Comments Tourists are barred from Central Intelligence Agency headquarters in Langley, across the river from Washington in suburban Virginia. Yet all is not lost for visitors lusting for a peek into the world of cloaks and daggers. The ultra hush-hush National Security Agency operates this tiny museum dedicated to codes, ciphers, and spies in a former motel overlooking the busy Baltimore-Washington Parkway.

All the displays are static; they include items such as rare books dating from 1526, Civil War signal flags, KGB spy paraphernalia, and the notorious Enigma, a German cipher machine (it looks like an ancient Underwood on steroids) "broken" by the Poles and British during World War II. (*Spies,* a film on code breaking during World War II, tells the story continuously on a TV in a small theater in the museum.)

Touring Tips Don't miss the "bugged" Great Seal of the U.S. that hung in Spaso House, the U.S. ambassador's residence in Moscow. (The microphone-equipped seal was uncovered in 1952.) The new high-tech room features spy devices used to guard against computer hackers. Outside, you get a glimpse of the huge NSA headquarters complex from Route 32. NSA is called "The Puzzle Palace" for its secretiveness and worldwide electronic eavesdropping capability. The agency's budget, by the way, is a secret.

Other Things to Do Nearby South on the Baltimore-Washington Parkway are the National Wildlife Visitor Center and the NASA/Goddard Space Flight Center (Powder Mill Road exit).

Almost as big a landmark as the spook complex is Henkel's Restaurant, located in nearby Annapolis Junction. It's essentially a roadhouse famous for gargantuan sandwiches "through the garden," meaning heaped with shaved lettuce and tomatoes. Folks with average appetites can split one; a side of cholesterol-laden french fries with gravy is a must. Alas, finding the place is a challenge thanks to a spaghetti bowl of exit and entrance ramps on nearby converging highways. Ask for directions or call Henkel's at (301) 725-4239.

National Wildlife Visitor Center (Zone 10D)

Type of Attraction: A museum featuring wildlife research exhibits located in a 13,000-acre national wildlife refuge about 30 minutes north of Washington. A self-guided tour.

Location: Off Powder Mill Road, two miles east of the Baltimore-Washington Parkway, south of Laurel, Maryland.

Admission: Free

Hours: Daily, 10 A.M. to 5:30 P.M. Closed Christmas Day.

Phone: (301) 497-5760

When to Go: Anytime. Weekends are busier than weekdays.

Special Comments: You'll need a car to get here. Call ahead if you'd rather avoid large groups of schoolchildren on field trips. And there's no restaurant or snack bar on the premises.

Overall Appeal by Age Group:

Pre-school	Grade School	Teens	Young Adults	Over 30	Senior Citizens
★★★★	★★★★	★★★	★★½	★★½	★★½

Author's Rating: Static exhibits and stuffed animals, but a tranquil setting in the heart of the hectic Washington-Baltimore corridor. ★★½

How Much Time to Allow: One to two hours

Description and Comments This large, airy, new musuem operated by the U.S. Department of the Interior is filled with attractive exhibits—dioramas, mostly—focusing on a wide range of wildlife and environmental topics. While the static displays won't accelerate the pulse rates of adults weary from traipsing through Smithsonian edifices on the Mall, children are fascinated by this place. Large dioramas on pollution, overpopulation, forest and ocean degradation, wildlife habitats, wolves, whooping cranes, and other endangered species demonstrate the value of wildlife research.

Touring Tips A "viewing pod" equipped with spotting scopes and binoculars lets youngsters (and adults) observe wildlife through a picture window overlooking acres of pond and natural wildlife habitat. If it's a nice day, enjoy the sights and sounds of real wildlife by taking a stroll on paved trails through woods and around ponds populated by geese, ducks, and other animals that find refuge on the refuge. Thirty-minute narrated tram rides with a wildlife interpreter are offered on weekends in the spring and fall and daily from the end of June through August. Cost is $2 for adults, $1.50 for seniors, and $1 for children. On weekends documentary wildlife films are shown in the center's movie theater.

Other Things to Do Nearby The NASA/Goddard Space Flight Center in Greenbelt, Maryland, is only a few miles away; follow signs posted on Powder Mill Road near the Baltimore-Washington Parkway.

Folks looking for additional outdoor enjoyment and the opportunity to see more wildlife can drive a few miles north to the North Tract of the Patuxent Research Refuge; take the Baltimore-Washington Parkway north two exits to Route 198 east, drive one mile, and turn right onto Bald Eagle Drive to the Visitor Contact Station. The 8,100-acre tract features forest, wetlands, a wildlife viewing area (with an observation tower), and eight miles of paved roads for car touring and bicycling. There's another ten miles of graded gravel roads for hiking, mountain biking, and horseback riding. For more information, call (410) 674-3304.

The National Cryptologic Museum is located next to the huge National Security Agency complex near the intersection of the Baltimore-Washington Parkway and Route 32; drive north on the parkway a few miles and follow the signs. For a large selection of fast-food options, take the parkway north a few miles to Route 197.

Zone 11: Virginia Suburbs

Mount Vernon (south of Zone 11C)

Type of Attraction: George Washington's 18th-century Virginia plantation on the Potomac River. A self-guided tour.

Location: 16 miles south of Washington.

How to Get There: To drive from Washington, cross the 14th Street Bridge into Virginia, bear right, and get on the George Washington Memorial Parkway south. Continue past National Airport into Alexandria, where the Parkway becomes Washington Street. Continue straight; Washington Street becomes the Mount Vernon Memorial Parkway, which ends at Mount Vernon.

Tourmobile offers four-hour, narrated bus tours to Mount Vernon daily, April through October. Departures are at 10 A.M., 12 P.M., and 2 P.M. Tickets are $20 for adults and $10 for children ages 3 to 11. The price includes admission to Mount Vernon. Call Tourmobile at (202) 554-5700 for more information. Gray Line offers four-hour coach trips to Mount Vernon and Old Town Alexandria that depart at 8:30 A.M. daily from Union Station. No tours are scheduled on New Year's, Thanksgiving, and Christmas days. Fares are $22 for adults and $11 for children. For more information call Gray Line at (202) 289-1995.

Admission: $8 for adults, $7.50 for senior citizens age 62 and over, and $4 for children ages 6 through 11.

Hours: April through August, 8 A.M. to 5 P.M.; November through February, 9 A.M. to 4 P.M.; March, September, and October, 9 A.M. to 5 P.M. Open every day, including Christmas.

Phone: (703) 780-2000

When to Go: Generally, before 10 A.M., especially in hot weather. But sometimes tour and school buses arrive before the gates open, creating a line to buy tickets and tour the mansion. Come around 3 P.M. and you're sure to avoid the buses—and the lines. When longer hours are in effect, you must clear the grounds by 5:30.

Special Comments: Mount Vernon is probably the only major D.C. attraction that opens at 8 A.M., making it a prime place to hit early in hot weather—if you have a car to get you there. During Christmas, the decorated mansion's seldom-seen third floor is open to the public.

Overall Appeal by Age Group:

Pre-school	Grade School	Teens	Young Adults	Over 30	Senior Citizens
★★	★★★★	★★★	★★★★½	★★★★★	★★★★★

Author's Rating: Not to be missed. ★★★★★
How Much Time to Allow: Two hours

Description and Comments Folks on a quick trip to Washington won't have time to visit Mount Vernon, but everyone else should. The stunning view from the mansion across the Potomac River is pretty much the same as it was in Washington's day. Unlike most historic sites in D.C., Mount Vernon gives visitors a real sense of how 18th-century rural life worked, from the first president's foot-operated fan chair (for keeping flies at bay while he read) to the rustic kitchen and outbuildings. Historic interpreters are stationed throughout the estate and mansion to answer questions and give visitors an overview of the property and Washington's life.

Mount Vernon is more than just a big house. Special 30-minute landscape and garden tours leave at 11 A.M., 1 P.M., and 3 P.M. April through October. "Slave Life at Mount Vernon" is a 30-minute walking tour to slave quarters and workplaces that starts at 10 A.M., noon, 2 P.M., and 4 P.M., daily, April through October. There's no additional charge for either tour.

Mount Vernon has opened several new attractions on the 30-acre plantation to help diffuse huge crowds that throng the mansion. The newest is a four-acre colonial farm site where visitors can view costumed interpreters using 18th-century farm methods and tools. Hands-on activities are available March through November, and wagon rides are offered on Fridays, Saturdays, and Sundays.

During the summer months, a "Hands-On History" area lets children handle 18th-century objects, play games such as rolling hoops, and learn about early American life; hours are 10 A.M. to 1 P.M. daily from Memorial Day through Labor Day.

Touring Tips Mount Vernon is *very* popular, and tourists pull up by the busload in the spring and summer months—sometimes before the grounds open. During the high tourist season, Monday, Friday, and Sunday mornings before 11 A.M. are the least busy periods. If you want to avoid big crowds, go around 3 P.M., but you must leave the grounds by 5:30 P.M. When crowds are small in the winter, visitors are frequently given guided tours of the mansion in groups of 20 to 30 people.

Other Things to Do Nearby Mount Vernon offers a snack bar, two gift shops, a post office, and a sit-down restaurant. Rest rooms can be found near the museum on the grounds or between the gift shop and snack bar near the entrance. Visit Old Town Alexandria on your way to or from Mount Vernon. A stop at Gadsby's Tavern is appropriate, because that's what George Washington used to do.

Newseum (Zone 11B)

Type of Attraction: A journalism museum and "interactive" gallery. A self-guided tour.

Location: 1101 Wilson Boulevard, in Rosslyn, across the Potomac River from Georgetown and near Arlington National Cemetery.

Nearest Metro Station: Rosslyn. The Newseum is two blocks down Wilson Boulevard, opposite the silvery twin towers of *USA Today* and the Gannett Company.

Admission: Free

Hours: Wednesday through Sunday, 10 A.M. to 5 P.M. Closed Mondays, Tuesdays, and Thanksgiving, Christmas, and New Year's days.

Phone: (703) 284-3722 or toll-free (888) NEWSEUM

When to Go: Anytime

Special Comments: The museum is fully accessible to folks with physical handicaps. On crowded days, timed-entry passes for same-day admission may be distributed beginning at 9:45 A.M. A small cafe on the first floor sells snacks and cold drinks.

Overall Appeal by Age Group:

Pre-school	Grade School	Teens	Young Adults	Over 30	Senior Citizens
★★	★★★	★★★	★★★	★★½	★★½

Authors' Rating: Sleek, nifty, and new. But it's small—and while Metro makes it easy to get to, it's well off the main tourist path. ★★½

How Much Time to Allow: Two hours

Description and Comments First, some background: This new, $50 million museum is owned and operated by the Freedom Forum, a pro-journalism foundation established in 1935 with $100,000 in stock donated by Frank E. Gannett and with assets currently valued at $850 million. Today the Gannett Company is publisher of *USA Today*, which is located in one of the mid-rise office towers nearby. So it shouldn't come as a surprise that the Newseum is a lavish homage to journalism that purports to take visitors behind the scenes to experience how news is reported and presented.

The third-floor history museum is jam-packed with exhibits that show how news evolved from shared stories to today's information overload. Artifacts on display include Middle Eastern cuneiform tablets dating from 2176 B.C.; Asian and African drums, bells, and other sounding devices used to transmit messages; a first edition of Thomas Paine's *Common Sense* (1776); ancient printing presses and a not-so-ancient Linotype printing machine; Paul Revere's glasses; a Civil War–era camera used by Mathew Brady; Mark Twain's pipe; the microphone used by Edward R. Murrow to report the bombing of London; Bob Woodward's handwritten Watergate notes . . . and lots more. Overhead, video screens scroll famous photographs by renowned photojournalists and play clips of famous and not-so-famous events, ranging from dancing Jazz Age flappers (1925) to Walter Cronkite announcing the death of John F. Kennedy on network TV (1963). There's so much crammed into the exhibition hall that you may not notice how small it is.

The second-floor interactive gallery features a wide array of touch-screen video monitors that let visitors play reporter or editor, mini–video studios where visitors can act out fantasies as TV news anchors or sportscasters (and later purchase tapes of their performances), and a real broadcast studio where actual news programs are produced. A 126-foot-long "video news wall" features breaking news and broadcasts from around the world; news photos from wire services; a news "zipper" displaying the day's headlines, sports scores, and stock quotes; and the current day's front pages of newspapers from all 50 states. Throw in a large crowd on a busy day, and the place can be quite overwhelming.

What you won't find in this dazzling, but somewhat confusing, hodge-podge of late-20th-century electronic glitz and slick museum packaging is any analysis of current dilemmas in modern journalism: the blurring of news and entertainment, the spreading blandness of news coverage, the impossibility of explaining increasingly complex problems in ever-shrinking sound bites, and the growing trend of corporate ownership of media. For that, you'll have to wait for a journalism museum not sponsored by *USA Today*.

Touring Tips After entering the Newseum on the first floor, take the escalator to the next level. Then enter the domed, 220-seat high-definition TV theater to watch a slick, 13-minute film that explains the Newseum's mission. After the movie, you'll exit to the third-floor museum exhibition; if the theater was anywhere near full, it will be elbow to elbow as you view the exhibits in the long, narrow room. Our advice: Take the stairs down a level and kill a few minutes browsing in the museum shop until the crowd thins.

Then go back to the third floor and the 50-seat Bijou Theater to see the 10-minute film *Fact or Fiction: Hollywood Looks at the News*, a terrific montage of clips from Tinseltown classics ranging from *The Front Page* (1931) to *Network* (1976). It's a hoot.

Other Things to Do Nearby   Just outside is Freedom Park, featuring the Freedom Forum Journalists Memorial to nearly 1,000 journalists from around the world killed in the line of duty; other outdoor displays include segments of the Berlin wall, a headless statue of Vladimir Ilyich Lenin, a Cuban refugee kayak, and replicas of woman suffrage banners. This unusual park is perched high atop Rosslyn on a never-used elevated highway that was so badly constructed it couldn't be used for its intended purpose. Now the former eyesore is an unusual—to say the least—urban oasis. And the view of downtown D.C. across the river ain't bad, either. Rosslyn abounds in places to grab lunch or dinner.

Old Town Alexandria (Zone 11C)

Type of Attraction: A restored colonial port town on the Potomac River, featuring 18th-century buildings on cobblestone streets, trendy shops, bars and restaurants, parks, and a huge art center. Guided and self-guided tours.

Location: In suburban Virginia, eight miles south of Washington.

Nearest Metro Station: King Street

Admission: Some historic houses charge $3 for admission. Admission to the Torpedo Factory Art Center, the Lyceum, the Lloyd House, and the George Washington Masonic National Memorial is free. Tickets that get you into five historic sites for $12 ($5 for children ages 11 to 17 years) are sold at Ramsay House, the main visitor center on King Street.

Hours: Historic houses, shops, and the Torpedo Factory Art Center open by 10 A.M. and remain open through the afternoon.

Phone: For more information on Old Town, call the Alexandria Convention & Visitors Association at (703) 838-4200. Press 4 for a recording of special events that's updated regularly.

When to Go: Anytime

Special Comments: The most scenic spot for a brown-bag lunch is the picnic tables located at the foot of 1st Street, on the Potomac River.

FIRST NATIONAL
Alexandra
Anne Kinnaird Real Estate Ltd
MREINZ

With Compliments
ANNE KINNAIRD
MARKETING CONSULTANT

Bus: 03-440 2088
A/Hrs: 03-449 2428
Mobile: 025-221 9813
Fax: 03-448 8196
Email: alexfirstnat@xtra.co.nz

Overall Appeal by Age Group:

Pre-school	Grade School	Teens	Young Adults	Over 30	Senior Citizens
★★	★★★	★★★	★★★★½	★★★★½	★★★★½

Author's Rating: A satisfying contrast to awesome D.C. ★★★★

How Much Time to Allow: Half a day. If it's the second half, stay for dinner; Old Town Alexandria has a great selection of restaurants.

Description and Comments Alexandria claims both George Washington and Robert E. Lee as native sons, so history buffs have a lot to see. Topping the list are period revival houses that rival those in Georgetown, another old port up the river; Gadsby's Tavern (open Tuesday through Saturday, 10 A.M. to 5 P.M., April through September, and 1 P.M. to 5 P.M. Sundays; guided tours at quarter of and quarter past the hour); Christ Church; and the Lee-Fendall House. This hip, revitalized city on the Potomac is crammed with exotic restaurants (Thai, Indian, Lebanese, Greek) and shops (art, jewelry, children's books, antiques, Persian carpets). And, unlike those in Georgetown, the eating and drinking establishments in Old Town aren't overrun by suburban teenagers on weekends.

Touring Tips As you exit the King Street Metro station, either board a DASH bus for a quick trip down King Street to Old Town (75 cents), or walk to your left and turn right onto King Street for a pleasant 15-minute stroll toward the river. The closest visitor center is at the Lyceum, where two exhibition galleries and a museum of the area's history are featured; from King Street, turn right onto Washington Street and walk a block. There's also a small museum featuring prints, documents, photographs, silver, furniture, and Civil War memorabilia. Farther down King Street on the left is *Ramsay House*, built in 1724 and now Alexandria's official visitor center, open daily from 9 A.M. to 5 P.M., except Thanksgiving, Christmas, and New Year's days. Ramsay House makes a good starting point for a walking tour of Old Town Alexandria. The *Torpedo Factory Arts Center* at the foot of King Street features more than 150 painters, printmakers, sculptors, and other artists and craftspeople. Visitors can watch artists at work in their studios housed in the former munitions factory. If you drive to Alexandria, park your car in a two-hour metered space, feed it a nickel or a dime, and go to a visitor center to pick up a pass that lets you park free for 24 hours in any two-hour metered zone inside Alexandria city limits (renewable once); you'll need your vehicle's license plate number. But parking is scarce and the King Street Metro is conveniently located.

Other Things to Do Nearby About a mile west of the center of Alexandria is the George Washington National Masonic Memorial. A free tour features a view from the 333-foot tower, Washington memorabilia, a 370-year-old Persian rug valued at $1 million, and more information about Masonry than you probably want. The tours are given Monday through Saturday on the half-hour in the mornings and on the hour in the afternoons; the Memorial is open daily, 9 A.M. to 5 P.M. Mount Vernon, George Washington's plantation on the Potomac, is eight miles downriver.

PART ELEVEN

Dining and Restaurants

Experiencing Washington Cuisine

■ **The New Washington Cookery** ■

The great calorie inflation is over in Washington. Dollar for dollar (and pound for pound), dining in Washington has never been better: more varied, healthier, more affordable—and, when it is pricey, it's more apt to be worth the expense. And in addition, Washington restaurant patrons benefit from both "insider" trends and outside influences—from general trends in the restaurant business and from D.C.'s unique demographics.

Ethnic Influence

This onetime cholesterol capital of the world has discovered not only its natural resources—its regional specialties and farm produce—but also its imported ones, the rainbow of immigrant chefs and cuisines and the even more intriguing pidgin cuisines that are constantly being created here. Consider the possibilities in a restaurant called "Cajun Bangkok" or "Thai Roma," or one that advertises Chinese-Mexican or Italian-Creole.

One of the most enjoyable aspects of dining out in Washington is exploring more exotic cuisines and new trends—even, for the newly watchful, haute health restaurants, where additives and chemicals are banned or heart-healthy cuisine is custom-tailored. What follows is not a list of the 85 "best" kitchens in the Washington area; it's a compendium of the best and the broadest, with an eye toward the unusual and even the mercurial.

New Restaurant Districts

Along with the awakening of the Washington palate has come a rearrangement of the dining map. While Georgetown remains a busy shopping and nightlife area, it is no longer the dominant restaurant strip. The revitalized downtown arts district, particularly the hip/conspicuous strip of Seventh Street, NW, between E and I Streets; the ethnically mixed Adams-Morgan neighborhood; and the northwest suburbs—particularly the Asian polyglot neighborhoods of Wheaton and Bethesda with their "golden triangles" of restaurants—have all emerged as livelier locations, with Gaithersburg and Germantown hot on their heels. At the same time, restaurant dining has become so diversified that one no longer needs to go to the "Little Saigon" neighborhood around Clarendon for good Vietnamese cooking (although Adams-Morgan is still home to most of the Ethiopian restaurants); in fact, it's hard to imagine that anyone living in the Washington metropolitan area is more than a mile from three or four different ethnic restaurants.

Scoping Out the Lunch Crowd

In the old days the price of a Washington meal proved its importance—and by implication, the diners'. These days the appeal of a D.C. restaurant rests more on a kitchen's imagination, its beer selection, its service, even its bottled water. Half the fun of lunching out is scoping out the midday clientele: power lunchers (at the old standbys and some well-kept secret spots), hour lunchers (very often at ethnic restaurants, which are rather quicker on the uptake than traditional white-linen establishments), flower lunchers (the remnants of the leisure class), and shower lunchers (those roving bands of office workers who seem always to be celebrating someone's great occasion but who want individual checks).

If you're not sure which kind of restaurant you've just walked into, glance around at the beverage glasses. Power lunchers are more likely to order a cocktail, hour lunchers a beer, flower lunchers wine, and shower lunchers soft drinks or pitchers with paper fans.

Incidentally, there's a new "power meal" in Washington: afternoon tea. Over finger sandwiches and scones at the Four Seasons, Hay-Adams, and Jefferson hotels, you will see just as many pin-striped suits as flowered skirts—and a lot more briefcases than either. Lower-pressure than traditional conferences but still face-to-face, tea has become a very popular way for lawyers and lobbyists to take meetings. And it also fits the two-career-family lifestyle better than long, expensive dinners.

Industry Trends

The end of price-padding inflation has had a rather more serious impact on the restaurant industry in Washington. Several of the finer establishments, caught between the pincers of exorbitant rent and declining expense-account business, have closed. A few have downscaled, and some of the most influential chefs in the area are opening what might be called "off-the-rack" restaurants (cafes and pizzerias) in addition to their designer rooms. More intriguing, some mixed-metaphor chefs are becoming partners: Galileo godfather Roberto Donna, who started the off-price trend with his Adams-Morgan kitchen I Matti, and Jean-Louis Palladin of the Watergate, arguably the two finest chefs in the city, created Pesce. Yannick Cam of Provence and Savio Racino of Primi Piatti founded Provencal, Coco Loco, and are about to open El Catalan, too. Donna also owns the retro-trendy spaghetti gardens Il Radicchio, Dolcetto, and Arucola and, with i Ricchi founder Francesco Ricchi, Cesco in Bethesda.

The 85 restaurant profiles that follow (we say 85, although it's closer to 100, since several profiles cover more than one location) are intended to give you a sense of the atmosphere and advantages of a particular establishment as well as its particular cuisine. None should be taken as gospel, because one drawback of Washington's new appetite for adventure is that restaurants open and close—and promising chefs play musical kitchens—with breathtaking speed. This also means that we have for the most part profiled only restaurants that have been in operation for at least a year, or that have chefs with such strong track records that they are of special interest.

And, blame it on yuppie consciousness, gourmet magazine proliferation, or real curiosity, the increased interest in the techniques of cooking has also produced a demand for variety, for constantly challenging presentations and guaranteed freshness. Consequently, many of the fancier restaurants change their menus or a portion thereof every day, and more change seasonally, so the specific dishes recommended at particular places may not be available on a given night. Use these critiques as a guide, an indication of the chef's interests and strengths—and weaknesses, too. We'll tell you what's not worth trying.

The New Hotel Dining

When it comes to hotel dining rooms, Washington contradicts the conventional wisdom that hotel restaurants are not worth seeking out. In D.C., many of the better chefs (including a dozen or so profiled in depth here) are working in hotels. This is a mutually beneficial arrangement, allowing the chefs to concentrate on managing a kitchen, not a business, and providing an extra attraction to potential clients. Since Washington's hotels count on a great deal of expense-account business, they generally offer menus on the expensive side. In addition to the restaurants listed, we recommend those at the George Washington Inn (**Zuki Moon**), Henley Park (**Coeur de Lion**), the Lansdowne Resort in Leesburgh (**Potomac Grille**), the Ritz-Carlton downtown (**Jockey Club**), The Stratford Motor Inn in Falls Church (**Cafe Rose**), the Westin (**Cafe on M**), and the Mayflower (**Cafe Promenade**), to name a few.

The Inns and Outs

The Washington area is also blessed with some very fine country inns within a couple of hours' drive. We have actually profiled only the **Inn at Little Washington** and **L'Auberge Chez François** in this edition, but in addition, we would recommend looking into such restaurants as **Antrim 1844** in Taneytown, **Willow Grove** in Orange, **Stone Manor** in Middleton, **the Turning Point Inn** in Urbana, **Four and Twenty Blackbirds** in Flint Hill, and the **Ashby Inn** in Paris.

Diners' Special Needs

The following profiles attempt to address the special requirements of diners who use wheelchairs or leg braces. Because so many of Washington's restaurants occupy older buildings and row houses, options for wheelchair users are unfortunately limited. In most cases, wheelchair access is prevented right at the street, but many restaurants offering easy entrance to the dining room keep their rest rooms up or down a flight of stairs. In either case, we list them as having "no" disabled access. "Fair" access suggests that there is an initial step or small barrier to broach, or that passage may be a bit tight, but that once inside the establishment, dining is comfortable for the wheelchair user. Again, hotel dining rooms are good bets—the same wide halls and ramps used for baggage carts and deliveries serve wheelchair users as well. Newer office buildings and mixed shopping and entertainment complexes have ramps and elevators that make them wheelchair-accessible; the ones above subway stations even have their own elevators.

We have not specially categorized restaurants as offering vegetarian or other restricted diets, because almost all Washington restaurants now offer either vegetarian entrees on the menu or will make low-salt or low-fat dishes on request, although some are particularly amenable to doing this, and we have said so. Use common sense: A big-ticket steakhouse is unlikely to have many nonmeat options (though even Morton's of Chicago has become accustomed to making veggie plates), but since few countries in the world eat as much meat as Americans, most ethnic cuisines are good bets for vegetarians.

■ Places to See Faces ■

Washington may not really be Hollywood on the Potomac, but there are celebrity faces aplenty (so many movie stars come to town to lobby for their pet causes, it's getting close).

Consequently, out-of-towners often list "famous people" right after the Air & Space Museum on the required-viewing list. And since being seen is part of the scene—and getting star treatment is one of the perks of being famous—celebrities tend to be visible in dependable places, particularly at lunch.

The venerable steak-and-lobster **Palm** (1225 19th Street, NW; (202) 293-9091), with its wall-to-wall caricatures of famous customers and its bullying waiters, is still a popular media and legal-eagle hangout. Among its regulars: strange political bedfellows James Carville and Mary Matalin, who sometimes eat in and carry out simultaneously.

The **Capital Grille** is particularly well located in this expansive economy; only a short stroll from the Capitol grounds, it serves as both boardroom and back room for the GOP. After the party's gala in January 1995, a couple hundred of the black-tie guests dropped by the Grille for drinks and cigars; but only a few nights before, when a clutch of budget-crunching Republican senators had peeked in after last call, the general manager had rolled up his sleeves and grilled a dozen strategic burgers. Among those with preferred tables are House Speaker Newt Gingrich and lawyer-turned-lobbyist-turned-actor-turned-populist Sen. Fred Thompson. But the Capital Grille gets its share of odd couples, too: Right-Republican Sen. Lauch Faircloth and liberal intellectual Sen. Pat Moynihan once arrived for dinner, Faircloth announcing the pair to staff as "the redneck and the aristocrat."

Galileo, the flagship restaurant of Washington's *capo di tutti capi* chef Roberto Donna, is a favorite of both Ted Kennedy and Bob Dole, as well as Treasury Secretary Robert Rubin. **Restaurant Nora** was an early favorite of the Clintons and Gores; its sibling **Asia Nora** draws Attorney General Janet Reno and other Cabinet shakers; and Energy Secretary Hazel O'Leary, Bosnian peacemeister Richard C. Holbrooke, and Clinton insider Vernon Jordan like **Melrose**. The old-clubby **Monocle** (107 D Street, NE; (202) 546-4488), the unofficial transfer point between the Senate and its office buildings, draws the Republican money men—Alfonse D'Amato and Pete Domenici, chairmen of the Senate banking and finance committees, respectively, and John Kasich, chairman of the House budget committee.

The elegant Raj-redux **Bombay Club** across the street from the White House attracts presidential-advisor-cum-commentator George Stephanopoulos, Reno, and John Glenn. Sen. Frank Lautenberg of New Jersey (who wrote the bill banning smoking on airlines), Stephanopolous, D'Amato, and Bob Kerrey have taken the steak-and-stogie course at **Les Halles**.

Pol-watchers should also check out **Two Quail** (320 Massachusetts Avenue, NE; (202) 543-8030) for congresswomen or **La Colline** for committee staffers. **Bullfeathers** is full of national committee staffers from both parties (410 1st Street, NW; (202) 543-5005). **The Hay-Adams** is where the power breakfast was born, starring White House staff and federal bureaucrats, and the **Powerscourt** (under renovation at press time) is the branch office of Bostonian politicians. Behind-the-scenes power-wielders, "spouses of," and social arbiters congregate at the Ritz-Carlton's **Jockey Club** (2100 Massachusetts Avenue, NW; (202) 659-8000) and **Maison Blanche** (1725 F Street, NW; (202) 842-0070).

Treasury and White House staff crowd the neighboring **Old Ebbitt Grill**, the **Occidental Grill** (1475 Pennsylvania Avenue, NW; (202) 783-1475), and **Georgia Brown's**. And, among the low-profile politicians and working press who frequent the **Market Inn**, especially in shad roe season, are rumored to be CIA and other professionals incognito (200 E Street, SW; (202) 554-2100).

World Bank and OAS suits lunch at **Taberna del Alabardero**; corporate write-offs go to the **Prime Rib** (2020 K Street, NW; (202) 466-8811) and the new midtown **Morton's**, which is also where Art Buchwald, who lost his longtime favorite table when Tiberio's closed, is imperially re-ensconced.

The Restaurants

Our Favorite Washington Restaurants

We have developed detailed profiles for the best and most interesting restaurants (in our opinion) in town. Each profile features an easily scanned heading that allows you, in just a second, to check out the restaurant's name, cuisine, star rating, cost, quality rating, and value rating.

Cuisine This is actually less straightforward than it sounds. A couple of years ago, for example, "pan-Asian" restaurants were generally serving what was then generally described as "fusion" food—Asian ingredients with European techniques, or vice versa. Since then, there has been a pan-Asian explosion in the area, but nearly all specialize in what would be street food back home: noodles, skewers, dumplings, and soups. Once-general categories have become subdivided—French into bistro fare and even Provençal; "new continental" into regional American and "eclectic"—while others have broadened and fused: Middle Eastern and Provençal into Mediterranean, Spanish and South American into nuevo Latino, and so on. In these cases, we have generally used the broader terms (i.e., "French") but sometimes added a parenthetical phrase to give a clearer idea of the fare. Again, though, experimentation and "fusion" is ever more common, so don't hold us, or the chefs, to too strict a style.

Star Rating The star rating is an overall rating that encompasses the entire dining experience, including style, service, and ambience in addition to the taste, presentation, and quality of the food. Five stars is the highest rating possible and connotes the best of everything. Four-star restaurants are exceptional, and three-star restaurants are well above average. Two-star restaurants are good. One star is used to indicate an average restaurant that demonstrates an unusual capability in some area of specialization—for example, an otherwise unmemorable place that has great barbecued chicken.

Cost To the right of the star rating is an expense description that provides a comparative sense of how much a complete meal will cost. A complete meal for our purposes consists of an entree with vegetable or side dish and choice of soup or salad. Appetizers, desserts, drinks, and tips are excluded.

Inexpensive	$14 and less per person
Moderate	$15–30 per person
Expensive	Over $30 per person

Quality Rating   On the far right of each heading appears a number and a letter. The number rates the food quality on a scale of 0–100, with 100 being the best rating attainable. It is based expressly on the taste, freshness of ingredients, preparation, presentation, and creativity of food served. There is no consideration of price. If you are a person who wants the best food available, and cost is not an issue, you need look no further than the quality ratings.

Value Rating   If, on the other hand, you are looking for both quality and value, then you should check the value rating, expressed in letters. The value ratings are defined as follows:

A	Exceptional value, a real bargain
B	Good value
C	Fair value, you get exactly what you pay for
D	Somewhat overpriced
F	Significantly overpriced

Locating the Restaurant   Just below the heading is a designation for geographic zone. This zone description will give you a general idea of where the restaurant described is located. We've divided Washington, D.C., into the following 11 geographic zones:

Zone 1.	The Mall
Zone 2.	Capitol Hill
Zone 3.	Downtown
Zone 4.	Foggy Bottom
Zone 5.	Georgetown
Zone 6.	Dupont Circle/Adams-Morgan
Zone 7.	Upper Northwest
Zone 8.	Northeast
Zone 9.	Southeast
Zone 10.	Maryland Suburbs
Zone 11.	Virginia Suburbs

The Maryland suburbs are divided into four smaller areas: Zones 10A (Bethesda) and 10B (Rockville-Gaithersburg) are bounded by the Potomac and Georgia Avenue and divided by the Beltway; Zone 10C is defined by 16th Street/Georgia Avenue, the District Line, New Hampshire Avenue, and I-95 as a wedge that runs north from Silver Spring and that necessarily splits Wheaton down the middle; and Zone 10D reaches from the District Line up New Hampshire and I-95 around to the Virginia line.

The Virginia suburbs are marked off more cleanly along I-66 and I-95/395 into three slices: Zone 11A covers Tysons Corner, McLean, Vienna, and Reston; Zone 11B includes Arlington, Annandale, and Fairfax; and Zone 11C is Alexandria, Old and otherwise. See pages 9–19 for detailed zone maps.

Payment We've listed the type of payment accepted at each restaurant using the following code: AMEX equals American Express (Optima), CB equals Carte Blanche, D equals Discover, DC equals Diners Club, MC equals MasterCard, and VISA is self-explanatory.

Who's Included Because restaurants are opening and closing all the time in Washington, we have tried to confine our list to establishments with a proven track record over a fairly long period of time. Franchises and national chains are not included, although local "chains," restaurant groups of three or four, may be. Newer or changed establishments that demonstrate staying power and consistency will be profiled in subsequent editions. Also, the list is highly selective. Noninclusion of a particular place does not necessarily indicate that the restaurant is not good, but only that it was not ranked among the best in its genre. Detailed profiles of individual restaurants follow in alphabetical order at the end of this chapter.

Restaurants by Cuisine

Name	Star Rating	Price Rating	Quality Rating	Value Rating	Zone
American (See also Modern American)					
Clyde's	★★★	Mod	81	B	5, 10A, 11A, 11B
Old Ebbitt Grill	★★★	Mod	80	C	3
Barbecue					
Rocklands	★★★	Inexp	80	C	5, 11B
Old Glory	★★½	Mod	78	B	5

Restaurants by Cuisine (continued)

Name	Star Rating	Price Rating	Quality Rating	Value Rating	Zone
Chinese					
Seven Seas	★★★½	Mod	85	B	10B
China Inn	★★★	Inexp	83	B	3
City Lights of China	★★★½	Mod	81	B	6
Vegetable Garden	★★★	Mod	80	B	10B
Tony Cheng's Mongolian Restaurant	★★½	Inexp	75	A	3
Ethiopian					
Meskerem	★★★½	Inexp	86	A	6
French					
L'Auberge Chez François	★★★★	Mod	92	A	11A
Gerard's Place	★★★★	Exp	90	C	3
Le Lion d'Or	★★★½	Exp	86	C	6
La Colline	★★★	Mod	84	A	2
La Chaumière	★★★	Mod	81	C	5
Bistro Français	★★½	Inexp	79	B	5
Le Refuge	★★	Mod	73	B	11C
French (Provençal)					
Provence	★★★½	Mod	87	C	6
La Provence	★★★½	Inexp	85	B	11A
La Côte d'Or Cafe	★★½	Exp	78	C	11B
Greek					
Athenian Plaka	★★½	Mod	75	B	10A
Indian					
Bombay Club	★★★½	Exp	89	C	3
Bombay Bistro	★★★	Inexp	83	A	10B, 11B
Italian					
Galileo	★★★★★	Exp	98	C	6
Obelisk	★★★½	Exp	89	B	6
Goldoni	★★★½	Inexp	85	C	6
i Ricchi	★★★	Exp	84	B	6
Vincenzo al Sole	★★★	Exp	82	C	6
Jamaican					
Hibiscus Cafe	★★★½	Inexp	85	B	5

Restaurants by Cuisine (continued)

Name	Star Rating	Price Rating	Quality Rating	Value Rating	Zone
Japanese					
Sushi-Ko	★★★★	Mod	92	B	5
Tako Grill	★★★★	Mod	92	B	10A
Tachibana	★★★½	Mod	88	B	11A
Matuba	★★★½	Inexp	85	B	10A, 11B
Korean					
Woo Lae Oak	★★★	Mod	82	A	11B
Jin-Ga	★★½	Mod	79	B	5
Korean/Japanese					
Ichiban	★★★	Mod	83	B	10B
Lebanese					
Bacchus	★★★	Mod	73	B	6, 10A
Mediterranean					
George	★★★½	Mod	85	B	3
Isabella	★★★	Mod	83	B	3
Il Ritrovo	★★★	Mod	80	B	10A
Modern American					
The Inn at Little Washington	★★★★★	Exp	98	B	11B
Seasons	★★★★	Exp	93	B	5
Vidalia	★★★★	Exp	93	B	6
Kinkead's	★★★★	Mod	91	C	4
Old Angler's Inn	★★★½	Exp	89	C	10B
New Heights	★★★½	Mod	88	C	6
Elysium	★★★½	Exp	88	B	11C
Melrose	★★★½	Mod	87	C	5
Lafayette	★★★½	Mod	85	B	3
Greenwood	★★★	Mod	84	B	7
Morrison-Clark Inn	★★★	Mod	83	B	3
1789	★★★	Exp	83	C	5
Cashion's Eat Place	★★★	Mod	83	B	6
Carlyle Grand Café	★★★	Mod	81	C	11B
Citronelle	★★★	Exp	81	C	5
Nora	★★★	Mod	80	C	6
Market Street Bar & Grill	★★½	Mod	79	C	11A

Restaurants by Cuisine (continued)

Name	Star Rating	Price Rating	Quality Rating	Value Rating	Zone
Modern Continental					
Lespinasse	★★★★	Exp	92	B	3
Moroccan					
Dar es Salaam	★★½	Mod	79	B	5
New Southwestern					
Red Sage	★★★★	Exp	94	B	3
Cottonwood Cafe	★★★	Mod	80	B	10A
Nuevo Latino					
Cafe Atlantico	★★★½	Mod	85	B	3
Coco Loco	★★★	Mod	84	A	3
Gabriel	★★★	Mod	84	A	6
Jaleo	★★★	Mod	77	B	3
Pan Asian					
Asia Nora	★★★½	Mod	86	B	6
Raku: An Asian Grill	★★★	Inexp	82	A	6, 10A
Germaine's	★★★	Mod	81	B	5
Pizza					
Pizzeria Paradiso	★★★	Inexp	83	A	6
Seafood					
Sea Catch	★★★	Mod	83	B	5
Legal Sea Foods	★★½	Mod	78	B	4, 11A
Southern					
Georgia Brown's	★★★	Mod	80	B	3
Spanish					
Taberna del Alabardero	★★★½	Exp	88	C	3
Steak					
Morton's of Chicago	★★★½	Exp	89	B	3, 5, 11A
Les Halles	★★★	Mod	84	B	3
Sam & Harry's	★★★	Exp	84	C	6
The Capital Grille	★★½	Exp	78	C	3
Tex-Mex					
Austin Grill	★★★	Inexp	83	A	5, 10A, 11B, 11C
Rio Grande Cafe	★★½	Mod	78	C	10A, 11B
Thai					
Benjarong	★★★½	Inexp	87	B	10B
Busara	★★★½	Mod	87	B	5, 11A
Tara Thai	★★★½	Mod	85	A	10A, 11A

Restaurants by Cuisine (continued)

Name	Star Rating	Price Rating	Quality Rating	Value Rating	Zone
Vietnamese					
Taste of Saigon	★★★½	Mod	86	A	10B, 11A
Miss Saigon	★★½	Inexp	79	B	5, 6

■ More Recommendations ■

The Best Afternoon Teas

Four Seasons Hotel   2800 Pennsylvania Avenue, NW (202) 342-0444

The Hay-Adams Hotel   16th and H Streets, NW (202) 638-6600

Henley Park Hotel   926 Massachusetts Avenue, NW (202) 638-5200

Jefferson Hotel   1200 16th Street, NW (202) 347-2200

Park Hyatt Hotel   24th and M Streets, NW (202) 955-3899

The Tea Cozy   119 South Royal Street, Alexandria (703) 836-8181

Teaism   2009 R Street, NW (202) 667-3827

The Best Bagels

Bagel City   12119 Rockville Pike, Rockville (301) 231-8080

Bethesda Bagel   4819 Bethesda Avenue, Bethesda (301) 652-8990

Bruegger's Bagels   Many area locations

Chesapeake Bagel Bakery   Many area locations

The Best Bar Food or Appetizers

Citronelle Latham Hotel   3000 M Street, NW (202) 625-2150

Cottonwood Cafe   4844 Cordell Avenue, Bethesda (301) 656-4844

Red Sage   605 14th Street, NW (202) 638-4444

The Freshest Beers (Brewed on Site)

Bardo Rodeo   2000 Wilson Boulevard, Arlington (703) 527-9399

Blue-N-Gold Brewing Company   Corner of Washington Boulevard and Highland Street, Arlington (703) 908-4995

Brewer's Alley   124 N. Market Street, Frederick (301) 631-0089

Capitol City Brewing Co.   1100 New York Avenue, NW
(202) 628-2222
   2700 South Quincy Street, Arlington (703) 578-3888
   7735 Old Georgetown Road, Bethesda (301) 652-2282

DuClaw Brewing Co.   16-A Bel-Air South Station Parkway, Bel Air
(410) 515-3222

John Harvard's Brewhouse   1299 Pennsylvania Avenue, NW (202)
783-2739

Mount Airy Brewing Co.   223 South Main Street, Mount Airy (410)
795-5557

Old Dominion Brewing Co.   44633 Guilford Drive, Ashburn (703)
689-1225

Olde Towne Taverne & Brewing Co.   Summit and Diamond Avenues,
Gaithersburg (301) 948-4200

Potomac River Brewing Co.   14141-A Parke Long Court, Chantilly
(703) 631-5430

Rock Bottom Restaurant & Brewery   7900 Norfolk Avenue, Bethesda
(301) 652-1311

Sweetwater Tavern   14250 Sweetwater Lane, Centreville (703) 449-1100

Virginia Beverage Co.   607 King Street, Alexandria (703) 684-5397

The Best Burgers

Brewbaker's   6931 Arlington Road, Bethesda (301) 907-2600

The Brickskeller   1523 22nd Street, NW (202) 293-1885

Clyde's   3236 M Street, NW (202) 333-9180
   8332 Leesburg Pike, Tysons Corner (703) 734-1901
   Reston Town Center, Reston (703) 787-6601

Old Ebbitt Grill   675 15th Street, NW (202) 347-4801

Union Street Public House   121 South Union Street, Alexandria
(703) 548-1785

The Best Coffee

Dean & DeLuca   3276 M Street, NW (202) 342-2500
   1299 Pennsylvania Avenue, NW (202) 628-8155
   1919 Pennsylvania Avenue, NW (202) 296-4327

Pop Shop   1513 17th Street, NW (202) 328-0880

Puccini's 1620 L Street, NW (202) 223-1975

Starbuck's Many area locations

The Best Desserts

Citronelle 3000 M Street, NW (Latham Hotel) (202) 625-2150

Dean & DeLuca 3276 M Street, NW (202) 342-2500

Dolci Finale 2653 Connecticut Avenue, NW (Pettito's) (202) 667-5350

Patisserie Cafe Didier 3206 Grace Street, NW (202) 342-9083

Lespinasse 16th and K Streets, NW (Carlton Hotel) (202) 879-6900

The Kennedy Center Roof Terrace Virginia and New Hampshire Avenues, NW (202) 416-8555

The Best Pizza

Faccia Luna 2400 Wisconsin Avenue, NW (202) 337-3132
   23 Washington Boulevard, Alexandria (703) 838-5998
   2909 Wilson Boulevard, Arlington (703) 276-3099

Pizza de Resistance 2300 Clarendon Boulevard, Arlington (703) 351-5680

Pizzeria Paradiso 2029 P Street, NW (202) 223-1245

Primi Piatti 2013 I Street, NW (202) 223-3600
   8045 Leesburg Pike, Tysons Corner (703) 893-0300

Zio's 9083 Gaither Road, Gaithersburg (301) 977-6300

The Best Raw Bars

Blue Point Grill 600 Franklin Street, Alexandria (703) 739-0404

Georgetown Seafood Grill 3063 M Street, NW (202) 333-7038
   1200 19th Street, NW (202) 530-4430

Old Ebbitt Grill 675 15th Street, NW (202) 347-4801

Kinkead's 2000 Pennsylvania Avenue, NW (202) 296-7700

The Sea Catch 1054 31st Street, NW, rear (202) 337-8855

The Most Entertaining Decor

Bangkok St. Grill and Noodles 5872 Leesburg Pike, Falls Church (703) 379-6707

Busara   2340 Wisconsin Avenue, NW (202) 337-2340
  8142 Watson Street, McLean (703) 356-2288

Clyde's of Chevy Chase   70 Wisconsin Circle, Chevy Chase
(301) 951-9600

Filomena's   1063 Wisconsin Avenue, NW (202) 337-2782

Hibiscus Cafe   3401 K Street, NW (202) 965-7170

Pizzeria Paradiso   2029 P Street, NW (202) 223-1245

Planet Hollywood   101 Pennsylvania Avenue, NW (202) 783-7827

Provence   2401 Pennsylvania Avenue, NW (202) 296-1166

Rain Forest Cafe   Routes 7 and 123 (Tysons Corner Center), Tysons
Corner (703) 821-1900

Raku: An Asian Diner   19th and Q Streets, NW (202) 265-7258
  7240 Woodmont Avenue, Bethesda (301) 718-8681

Red Sage   605 14th Street, NW (202) 638-4444

Tara Thai   226 Maple Avenue West, Vienna (703) 255-2467
  4828 Bethesda Avenue, Bethesda (301) 657-0488

The Best Family Dining

Generous George's   7031 Little River Turnpike, Annandale
(703) 941-9600
  6131 Backlick Road, Springfield (703) 451-7111
  3006 Duke Street, Alexandria (703) 370-4303

Guapo's   4515 Wisconsin Avenue, NW (202) 686-3588
  9811 Washingtonian Boulevard (Rio Centre), Gaithersburg
(301) 977-5655

Hard Rock Cafe   999 E Street, NW (202) 737-ROCK

Olney Ale House   2000 Sandy Spring Road (Route 108), Olney
(301) 774-6708

Oodles Noodles   1120 19th Street, NW (202) 293-3138
  4907 Cordell Avenue, Bethesda (301) 986-8833

Radio Free Italy   5 Cameron Street (Torpedo Factory) (703) 683-0361

Rain Forest Cafe   Routes 7 and 123 (Tysons Corner Center), Tysons
Corner (703) 821-1900

The Best Sunday Brunches

Clyde's   3236 M Street, NW (202) 333-9180
8332 Leesburg Pike, Tysons Corner (703) 734-1901

The Four Seasons Hotel Garden Terrace   2800 Pennsylvania Avenue, NW (202) 342-0444

Gabriel   2121 P Street, NW, in Radisson Barceló Hotel
(202) 956-6690

The Inn at Glen Echo   MacArthur Boulevard and Clara Barton Parkway, Glen Echo (301) 229-2280

The Kennedy Center Roof Terrace   Virginia and New Hampshire Avenues, NW (202) 416-8555

Old Ebbitt Grill   675 15th Street, NW (202) 347-4801

The Best Sushi Bars

Atami   3155 Wilson Boulevard, Arlington (703) 522-4787

Blue Ocean   9440 Main Street, Fairfax (703) 425-7555

Ginza   1009 21st Street, NW (202) 833-1244

Matuba   2915 Columbia Pike, Arlington (703) 521-2811
4918 Cordell Avenue, Bethesda (301) 652-7449

Miyagi   6918 Curran Street, McLean (703) 893-0116

Niwano Hana   887 Rockville Pike (Wintergreen Plaza)
(301) 294-0553

Sakana   2026 P Street, NW (202) 887-0900

Shiro-Ya   2512 L Street, NW (202) 659-9449

Sushi Kappo Kawasaki   1140 19th Street, NW (202) 466-3798

Sushi-Ko   2309 Wisconsin Avenue, NW (202) 333-4187

Tachibana   6715 Lowell Avenue, McLean (703) 847-7771

Tako Grill   7756 Wisconsin Avenue, Bethesda (301) 652-7030

Yosaku   4712 Wisconsin Avenue, NW (202) 363-4453

The Best Views

America   50 Massachusetts Avenue, NE (Union Station)
(202) 682-9555

Hotel Washington Roof 515 15th Street, NW (202) 638-5900

Lafayette 16th and I Streets, NW (Hay-Adams Hotel) (202) 638-2570

New Heights 2317 Calvert Street, NW (202) 234-4110

Sequoia 3000 K Street, NW (202) 944-4200

Tony & Joe's 3000 K Street, NW (202) 944-4545

J.W.'s View 1401 Lee Highway (Key Bridge Marriott), Arlington (703) 243-1745

Perry's 1811 Columbia Road, NW (202) 234-6218

Potowmack Landing Washington Marina, George Washington Parkway, Alexandria (703) 548-0001

The Best Wee-Hours Service

Afterwords Cafe 1517 Connecticut Avenue, NW (202) 387-1462

American City Diner 5532 Connecticut Avenue, NW (202) 244-1949
  Wisconsin Avenue at East-West Highway, Bethesda (301) 654-3287

Amphora 377 Maple Avenue West, Vienna (703) 938-7877

Bistro Français 3128 M Street, NW (202) 338-3830

Full Kee 509 H Street, NW (202) 371-2233

Hunan Number One 3033 Wilson Avenue, Arlington (703) 528-1177

Il Ritrovo 4838 Rugby Avenue, Bethesda (301) 986-1447

Polly's Cafe 1342 U Street, NW (202) 265-8385

Tastee Diner 7731 Woodmont Avenue, Bethesda (301) 652-3970
  8516 Georgia Avenue, Silver Spring (301) 589-8171
  10536 Lee Highway, Fairfax (703) 591-6720

Thai Flavor 2605 Connecticut Avenue, NW (202) 745-2000

Tables in the Kitchen

Aquarelle 2650 Virginia Avenue, NW (Watergate Hotel) (202) 298-4455

Bice 601 Pennsylvania Avenue, NW (202) 638-2423

Citronelle 3000 M Street, NW (Latham Hotel) (202) 625-2150

Galileo 1110 21st Street, NW (202) 293-7191

Hibiscus Cafe 3401 K Street, NW (202) 965-7170

Melrose 24th and M Streets, NW (Park Hyatt Hotel) (202) 955-3899

Restaurant Nora   R Street and Florida Avenue, NW (202) 462-5143

The Kennedy Center Roof Terrace   Virginia and New Hampshire Avenues, NW (202) 416-8555

ASIA NORA			
Pan Asian	★★★½	Moderate	**QUALITY** 86
2213 M Street, NW			**VALUE** B
(202) 797-4860 Zone 6, Dupont Circle/Adams-Morgan			

Reservations: Recommended	Parking: Pay lots, meters
When to go: Anytime	Bar: Full service
Entree range: $18–23.50	Wine selection: Limited
Payment: VISA, MC	Dress: Business, informal
Service rating: ★★★	Disabled access: No
Friendliness rating: ★★★½	Customers: Local, tourist, business

Dinner: Monday–Thursday, 6–10 P.M.; Friday and Saturday, 6–10:30 P.M.; Sunday, closed.

Atmosphere/Setting: A small but very romantic two-story Indonesian jewel box (or fantasy boudoir) of a room, with carved wood, mirrors, and intriguing booths and balcony niches.

House Specialties: Rockfish with lemongrass and chiles; lacquered spit-roasted duck with a crêpe-light mushroom pancake and chile-hoisin sauce; salmon glazed with Japanese miso and served with ginger-flavored soba noodles.

Other Recommendations: Grilled "satays" of shiitake mushrooms and tofu; Asian veal-rice sausage; vegetable or seafood tempura; Vietnamese-style garden rolls with crabmeat, cilantro, mint, and peanut sauce; hot-and-sour coconut soup. At lunch, the "grill of the day" or Japanese-style bento box lunches. A selection of quality sakés and green teas.

Summary & Comments: This is a restaurant designed for dawdling. The menu, which is seasonally adjusted, is divided into "small dishes" of three or four bites each and larger dishes of six to eight bites, so that a series of different tastes can be shared. (Of course, this means that you can spend rather more money here if you want.) The dishes are more traditional in attitude than in strict recipes: Japanese udon noodles are topped with portobello mushrooms; salmon "tartare" is lightly pickled, like seviche; and the tuna "sashimi" is seared, just as the flounder "sashimi" is dressed with sizzling-hot oil—a trick made famous by bicoastal star Nobu.

ATHENIAN PLAKA

			QUALITY
Greek	★★½	Moderate	75

	VALUE
	B

7833 Woodmont Avenue, Bethesda
  (301) 986-1337   Zone 10A, Maryland suburbs

Reservations: Accepted
When to go: Anytime
Entree range: $8.95–14.95
Payment: VISA, MC, AMEX, CB,
  DC, D
Service rating: ★★★
Friendliness rating: ★★★

Parking: Validated, free valet
  (weekends)
Bar: Full service
Wine selection: Limited
Dress: Informal, casual
Disabled access: Good
Customers: Locals

Open: Monday–Thursday, 11 A.M.–10 P.M.; Friday and Saturday, noon–11 P.M.; Sunday, noon–10 P.M.

Atmosphere/Setting: A quietly proud little dining room, with fresh linen and greenery, plaster arches, and vivid travel-mag murals of the home country. (In fact, it shares ownership with the nearby La Panetteria Italian restaurant.) In good weather, tables are set up on the sidewalk.

House Specialties: Among entrees, veal baked with eggplant, wine, and two cheeses; exohikon, lamb sautéed with artichokes, calamata olives, and cheese and then baked in phyllo; pan-fried baby squid. Among appetizers, a combination platter of calf's liver, sweetbreads, meatballs, sausage, and lamb (for two); eggplant stuffed with pine nuts, raisins, and tomato; pan-fried smelt.

Other Recommendations: Broiled red snapper; shrimp baked with tomatoes and feta; swordfish.

Summary & Comments: Don't let the suburban storefront location fool you; this is not your father's greasy Greek joint. The kitchen says it takes time to prepare dishes to order, and they mean it—it's a little slow, but it's right. A surprising number of these dishes are also available at lunch for a couple of dollars less.

AUSTIN GRILL

			QUALITY
Tex-Mex	★★★	Inexpensive	**83**
			VALUE
			A

2404 Wisconsin Avenue, NW
  (202) 337-8080   Zone 5, Georgetown

801 King Street, Alexandria
  (703) 684-8969   Zone 11C, Virginia suburbs

8430-A Old Keene Mill Road (Old Keene Mill Center), West
  Springfield   (703) 644-3111   Zone 11B, Virginia suburbs

7278 Woodmont Avenue, Bethesda
  (301) 656-1366   Zone 10A, Maryland suburbs

Reservations: Not accepted	Parking: Street
When to go: Late afternoon, late	Bar: Full service
night	Wine selection: Fair
Entree range: $5.75–13.95	Dress: Casual
Payment: VISA, MC, AMEX, D, DC	Disabled access: Good, except for
Service rating: ★★★	Georgetown
Friendliness rating: ★★★	Customers: Local, student

Breakfast: West Springfield: Saturday and Sunday, 9 A.M.–3 P.M.
Brunch: Saturday and Sunday, 11 A.M.–3 P.M.
Lunch/Dinner: Tuesday–Thursday, 11:30 A.M.–11 P.M.; Friday and
  Saturday, 11 A.M.–midnight; Sunday, 11 A.M.–10 P.M.; Monday,
  11:30 A.M.–10 P.M.

Atmosphere/Setting: Hot adobe pastels, Crayola-colored tile, buffalo and
lizard stenciling, angular art-joke graphics, and Tex-Mex pun art and T-
shirts in a funky vinyl-booth roadhouse setting. Great Texas music on the
PA. If not a mom-and-pop joint, it's a friends franchise: One of the original prep cooks who started at age 19 in Georgetown became the head chef
in Bethesda.

House Specialties: Potent quesadillas with chorizo or delicate ones with
crabmeat; grilled fish of the day; real all-beef chunky chili; "Austin special
enchilada" with three sauces; green chicken chili; grilled chile-rubbed
shrimp and scallops; grilled fish; pork loin enchilada with mole sauce.

Other Recommendations: Margaritas; chili-flavored rib eye; pork chops
adobado; eggs Benedict with jalapeño hollandaise (brunch); barbecued
brisket.

Summary & Comments: The perfect antidote for designer chili cuisine
(not that these are plain-Jane spots; in fact, they're corporate cousins of the
slick-chic Jaleo). The original Georgetown branch made its first friends just
from the smell of the smoker out back. The hot-hot sauces—a choice of

four—were the local endorphin addict's drugs before chiles were cool, so to speak. Incidentally, the Springfield location has been experimenting with serving breakfast, but a fairly straight version.

BACCHUS			
			QUALITY
Lebanese	★★★	Moderate	73
			VALUE
			B

1827 Jefferson Place, NW
  (202) 785-0734   Zone 6, Dupont Circle/Adams-Morgan
7945 Norfolk Avenue, Bethesda
  (301) 657-1722   Zone 10A, Maryland suburbs

Reservations: Suggested
When to go: Anytime
Entree range: $14.25–16.25
Payment: VISA, MC, AMEX
Service rating: ★★½
Friendliness rating: ★★
Parking: Street; valet (dinner only)

Bar: Full service
Wine selection: Brief
Dress: Informal, casual
Disabled access: Jefferson Street, no;
  Norfolk Avenue, good
Customers: Local, business

Lunch: Monday–Friday, noon–2:30 P.M.
Dinner: Monday–Thursday, 6–10 P.M.; Friday and Saturday,
  6–10:30 P.M.; Sunday, 6–10 P.M. (Bethesda only; downtown closed)

Atmosphere/Setting: The D.C. location is a simple, pleasantly crowded English basement downtown; in Bethesda, it's a villa with carved screens, whitewashed walls, a balcony, and a more leisurely atmosphere.
House Specialties: Meze (or "maza" here), a platter of two-bite appetizers served simultaneously, including stuffed phyllo turnovers of spinach or cheese; kibbeh, a steak tartare with cracked wheat; zucchini pancakes; grilled sausages; stuffed baby eggplant; spicy sausages; stuffed grape leaves.
Other Recommendations: Lamb almost any fashion, including layered over a fried pita and yogurt or with eggplant; fried smelts; fatayer bel sbanegh, a spinach and coriander pastry; stuffed cabbage with pomegranate sauce; kebabs.
Summary & Comments: For whatever reason, the Bethesda location is more consistent, the specials are more interesting, and the food is just a little sprightlier (perhaps because the pace is less frantic), but appetizers in particular are always good at both sites. The Washington location has no separate nonsmoking section.

BANGKOK GARDEN

Thai	★★½	Inexpensive	QUALITY 79
			VALUE B

4906 St. Elmo Avenue, Bethesda
  (301) 951-0670   Zone 10A, Maryland suburbs

Reservations: Accepted on weekends
When to go: Anytime
Entree range: $6.25–17.25
Payment: VISA, MC, AMEX
Service rating: ★★★½
Friendliness rating: ★★★★

Parking: Street, free lot after 6 P.M.
Bar: Full service
Wine selection: House
Dress: Casual
Disabled access: Fair
Customers: Local, ethnic

Open: Monday–Thursday, 11 A.M.–10:30 P.M.; Friday and Saturday, 11 A.M.–11 P.M.; Sunday, 4–10 P.M.

Atmosphere/Setting: Small, cheery, and so crowded with brass and plaster animals—giraffes, elephants, temple foo dogs, peafowl, deer—that the enshrined young Buddha resembles a Thai Francis of Assisi. Enlarged and framed colorful Thai currency and portraits of the ruling family are also prominent.

House Specialties: A rich, skin-and-fat duck in five-flavor sauce; fat "drunken" noodles with beef; hoy jawh, a crispy pork and crab appetizer cake; squid with basil and chili (unusually, almost purely squid and scarce vegetable filler); the tangy rather than searing seafood combination.

Other Recommendations: Soft-shell crabs in a choice of five sauces, four spicy and one very light version with asparagus and oyster sauce; steamed crab dumplings; shrimp in chili oil.

Summary & Comments: Though relatively low-profile amidst the Thai boom, this family-run restaurant rewards regular attendance and obvious interest because some of the best dishes aren't on the English menu, but are available to anyone who knows to ask. A particularly delicious example is the "Thai steak tartare," a beef version of a Thai pork classic that is rich with garlic, cilantro, and basil and served with a steaming basket of "sticky rice" intended to be used as the utensil: Take a pinch of rice—about a tablespoon—slightly flatten it and grasp a bite of meat with it and pop the whole morsel into your mouth. At $7.95, it's a steal of a meal.

BENJARONG

			QUALITY
Thai	★★★½	Inexpensive	**87**

	VALUE
	B

855-C Rockville Pike (Wintergreen Plaza), Rockville
  (301) 424-5533   Zone 10B, Maryland suburbs

Reservations: Suggested	Parking: Free lot
When to go: Anytime	Bar: Full service
Entree range: $7.95–11.95	Wine selection: House
Payment: VISA, MC, AMEX, DC, D	Dress: Informal
Service rating: ★★★	Disabled access: Good
Friendliness rating: ★★★★	Customers: Local, ethnic

Open: Monday–Thursday, 11:30 A.M.–9:30 P.M.; Friday and Saturday, 11:30 A.M.–10:30 P.M.; Sunday, 5–9:30 P.M.

Atmosphere/Setting: A simple but soothing room decorated with off-white grass wallpaper, pink linens, black lacquer chairs, and a few Thai carvings and figurines.

House Specialties: Duck with asparagus (in season); spicy duck and coriander salad; mussels steamed in lemongrass and spices; sliced beef filet in red wine sauce; fresh squid sautéed with chiles and basil; and the best pra pla mug—a sort of squid seviche with lime juice and chiles—even in this Thai-smart town.

Other Recommendations: Steamed whole snapper with delicate scallions and ginger sauce or crispy fried flounder; spicy shrimp in red curry sauce; red curry duck; seafood combination chow foon noodles; a rattle-shaped chicken drummette appetizer stuffed with ground chicken and pork; soft-shell crabs in a choice of sauces; and a sort of barbecue beef in chili paste with scallions.

Summary & Comments: Benjarong (the name refers to a type of multi-colored Thai porcelain) used to be part of a local chain called Thai Taste, but like its next-door neighbor, the Kashmir Palace, it seems to have become much stronger since going independent. Many of the dishes here are Southern Thai, meaning the curries are creamier and there's a good pork satay on the menu. There are also several good vegetarian choices, including a delicately peppery sautéed watercress.

BISTRO FRANÇAIS

			QUALITY
French	★★½	Inexpensive	**79**

	VALUE
	B

3128 M Street, NW
   (202) 338-3830   Zone 5, Georgetown

Reservations: Recommended	Parking: Street (valet on weekends)
When to go: Anytime	Bar: Full service
Entree range: $12.95–19.95	Wine selection: House
Payment: VISA, MC, AMEX, DC	Dress: Casual
Service rating: ★★★	Disabled access: Good
Friendliness rating: ★★★	Customers: Local, ethnic

Open: Sunday–Thursday, 11 A.M.–3 A.M.; Friday and Saturday, 11 A.M.–4 A.M.

Atmosphere/Setting: This hasn't changed much since the word "bistro" was new to Washington—hanging pots, rotisserie spits, and clanking trays. In other words, just right.

House Specialties: This is the sort of place where as nice as the menu is—especially Dover sole, coq au vin, quennelles of pike, its signature spit-roasted chicken—the daily specials are even better: for instance, duck confit, roast game birds, or lamb with artichokes.

Other Recommendations: The steak-and-fries here is probably the standard against which all others should be measured. And there are fixed-price lunch and pretheater menus for $18, including wine.

Summary & Comments: For all its many pleasures—its famous late-night service and the especially telling fact that many local chefs eat here after-hours—it sometimes seems as if this old favorite gets the Rodney Dangerfield treatment from the fashionable crowds.

BOMBAY BISTRO

			QUALITY
Indian	★★★	Inexpensive	**83**

	VALUE
	A

98 West Montgomery Avenue, Rockville
   (301) 762-8798   Zone 10B, Maryland suburbs
3570 Chain Bridge Road, Fairfax
   (703) 359-5810   Zone 11B, Virginia suburbs

Reservations: Not accepted	Entree range: $6.95–15.95
When to go: Early evening; lunch buffet	Payment: VISA, MC, AMEX, DC, D
	Service rating: ★★★

(Bombay Bistro)

Friendliness rating: ★★★
Parking: Free lot
Bar: Beer and wine
Wine selection: House

Dress: Casual
Disabled access: Yes
Customers: Local, ethnic, business

Lunch: Rockville: Monday–Friday, 11 A.M.–2:30 P.M.; Saturday and Sunday, noon–3 P.M.; Fairfax: Monday–Friday, 11:30 A.M.–2:30 P.M.

Dinner: Rockville: Sunday–Thursday, 5–9:30 P.M.; Friday and Saturday, 5–10 P.M.; Fairfax: Sunday–Thursday, 5–10 P.M.; Friday and Saturday, 5–10:30 P.M.

Atmosphere/Setting: This storefront family-style diner is made cheery in an almost Christmasy way, with red and green native costumes and gilded slippers hung on the wall along with strings of stuffed birds above wooden booths. Its new offshoot is equally simple and comfy.

House Specialties: Tandoori chicken or, even better, tandoori salmon; lamb vindaloo, the hottest item on the menu; el maru, a bowlful of rice and crispy noodles with a texture between granola and trail mix; Goan fish curry with a golden sauce; many fine vegetarian choices, notably an aromatic clove-and-cinnamon-flavored okra curry and baingan bhartha (tandoori eggplant); roasted vegetables; mild chicken tikka or spicy chicken madras; oothapam, a South India "crêpe" of lentil and rice dough, stuffed with onions, tomatoes, and green peppers.

Other Recommendations: Lamb rogan josh or shish kebab; chicken or vegetable biryani; beef badam pasandra, an almond-spiked stew; a sampler platter with chicken tikka, rogan josh, cucumber raita, puri, lentils, and spinach or eggplant.

Summary & Comments: Located among the lawyers' warrens of historic Rockville, this squeeze-'em-in eatery started out as an Indians' Indian lunch spot, but the word leaked out. Now, even with three or four cooks working, you may have to wait at dinner for a table at the original location, which is the second good reason to go for the all-you-can-eat lunchtime buffet (at both branches). The first good reason is the price: $6.95 on weekdays and $8.95 on weekends. Meanwhile, the cooking keeps getting better.

BUSARA

			QUALITY
Thai	★★★½	Moderate	87
			VALUE
			B

2340 Wisconsin Avenue, NW
  (202) 337-2340   Zone 5, Georgetown
8142 Watson Street, McLean
  (703) 356-2288   Zone 11A, Virginia suburbs

Reservations: Recommended	Parking: Street, lot, valet after 6 p.m.
When to go: Before 7:30 or after 9:30	Bar: Full service
Entree range: $7.50–22.95	Wine selection: Fair
Payment: VISA, MC, AMEX, DC, D	Dress: Informal
Service rating: ★★★½	Disabled access: No
Friendliness rating: ★★★	Customers: Local, ethnic

Lunch: Monday–Friday, 11:30 A.M.–3 P.M.; Saturday and Sunday, 11:30 A.M.–4 P.M.

Dinner: Sunday–Thursday, 5–11 P.M.; Friday and Saturday, 5 P.M.–midnight

Atmosphere/Setting: These Thai siblings are aggressively and cheekily modern. The decor of molded hard black rubber, brushed steel, slate, and heavily lacquered flame-streaked tabletops looks as if it were created by a former hot rod customizer—not to mention the ice-blue neon overhead ("busara" means "blue topaz") and post-Pop art. Outside, a partially covered patio curves around a miniature, but elegant, Japanese garden with a fountain. The Tysons Corner branch is even brighter, and although it doesn't yet have a garden, it may in the future.

House Specialties: Rice-fattened eesan sausage with pork and cabbage; roasted quail with asparagus and oyster sauce; cellophane noodles with three kinds of mushrooms; fillet of sea trout with salmon mousse served on a banana leaf; marinated pork satay with both a tomato-peanut sauce and a chile-spiked vinegar dip; duck in red curry; Thai bouillabaisse in coconut milk; country-style lamb curry.

Other Recommendations: Tiger shrimp grilled over watercress; vegetarian pad thai; soft-shell crabs and whole flounder; lobster tail in white pepper. The Tysons branch has a grill that turns out chicken, lean pork, and assorted fresh fish and shellfish as well.

Entertainment & Amenities: Live jazz in the upstairs bar suite in town, Wednesday through Saturday.

Summary & Comments: These are Siamese grins with the emphasis on presentation as much as preparation and a lightened-up attitude toward greens and veggies that makes them crisp and filling. A wide variety of spicing is represented (the chile-pod symbols next to menu items are fairly reliable for gauging heat; the Tysons branch sticks to the more familiar stars), and extra sauces or peppers are easy to obtain. Even nicer, there is no MSG in anything.

CAFE ATLANTICO			
Nuevo Latino	★★★½	Moderate	**QUALITY** 85
			VALUE B

405 8th Street, NW
  (202) 393-0812   Zone 3, Downtown

Reservations: Recommended	Parking: Street, valet (dinner only)
When to go: Anytime	Bar: Full service
Entree range: $12.95–16.95	Wine selection: Good
Payment: VISA, MC, AMEX, DC	Dress: Casual
Service rating: ★★★	Disabled access: Good
Friendliness rating: ★★★	Customers: Local, ethnic

Open: Monday, 11:30 A.M.–10 P.M.; Tuesday–Thursday, 11:30 A.M.–11 P.M.; Friday, 11:30 A.M.–midnight; Saturday, 5:30 P.M.–midnight; Sunday, 5:30–10 P.M.

Atmosphere/Setting: A very stylish salon, like the living room of an art collector: brilliant fabrics, large and vibrant paintings, loft-like balconies and windows, mosaics, and richly oiled wood. The clientele tends to match the decor—very vibrant, very "on," and frequently very loud.

House Specialties: Baby fowl with Mexican mole (cocoa-cinnamon) sauce; a miniature (traditionally speaking) Argentine mixed grill with steak, two kinds of sausage, and the teaspoon-sized sweetbread; mushroom-stuffed boned quail; and a nueva feijoada, the Brazilian national stew that vaguely resembles cassoulet.

Other Recommendations: Guacamole prepared tableside; chicken pieces skewered on sugar cane; the Portuguese-imported brandade of salt cod appetizer; fresh fish Veracruzano.

Summary & Comments: Cafe Atlantico is riding two waves at once: location and cuisine. It has moved into the heart of the new arts-intelligentsia neighborhood around the Shakespeare Theatre and Lansburg Building, and it's the first major restaurant in this area to specialize in cocina nueva, the Latin version of New Continental. That means that although dishes salute various Central and South American traditions, they are apt to be lighter, more fashionably presented and, depending on your perspective, less homey and more expensive than the originals.

THE CAPITAL GRILLE

			QUALITY
Steak	★★½	Expensive	**78**

	VALUE
	C

601 Pennsylvania Avenue, NW
  (202) 737-6200   Zone 3, Downtown

Reservations: Recommended	Bar: Full service
When to go: Anytime	Wine selection: Good
Entree range: $15.95–27.95	Dress: Business, informal
Payment: VISA, MC, AMEX, DC, D	Disabled access: Good
Service rating: ★★★	Customers: Politicos, lawyers, lobby-
Friendliness rating: ★★★	ists, and tourists looking for them
Parking: Valet after 5 P.M.; paid lots	

Lunch: Monday–Friday, 11:30 A.M.–2:30 P.M.
Dinner: Sunday–Thursday, 5–10 P.M.; Friday and Saturday, 5–11 P.M.

Atmosphere/Setting: Very gentlemen's clubbish, with dark wood, white linen, and polished brass. The streetside bar is quite atmospheric, combining as it does the old-boys' look and the Fed City vista. (The gas lanterns at the doorway, à la carriage house chic, are almost always lit: Bring me your prosperous, your power-tied, your huddled lobbyists yearning to eat free.) However, some may find the display of darkening and apparently somewhat dessicated dry-aged slabs of meat stacked like firewood in the vestibule window a little stark.

House Specialties: Pan-fried, chile-spiked calamari; cold baby lobster; and lobster-crab cakes (appetizers); porterhouse; the house special Delmonico, a classic but nowadays less popular cut; and a signature veal steak.

Other Recommendations: Fresh grilled swordfish or salmon; double-cut lamb chops; a near-pound of filet mignon; lobsters by the pound.

Summary & Comments: Capital Grille steaks come in either merely greedy portions (10 or 14 ounces) or true pig-out sizes (in the 20- to 24-ounce range). "Dry-aging" means that instead of being kept in vacuum bags, which keeps the blood in and the weight higher, the meat is allowed to drain, making for a heartier texture that either does or doesn't attract you. Otherwise, its menu and its side orders of asparagus hollandaise, creamed spinach, and potatoes don't differ much from the other red-blooded steakhouses in town such as Morton's and Ruth's Chris, except perhaps that its propinquity to Congress makes it a political hot spot.

CARLYLE GRAND CAFÉ

			QUALITY
			81

Modern American ★★★ Moderate

VALUE
C

4000 South 28th Street, Arlington
  (703) 931-0777   Zone 11B, Virginia suburbs

Reservations: Recommended for 6
  or more
When to go: Late night, afternoon
Entree range: $10.95–15.95
Payment: VISA, MC, AMEX
Service rating: ★★½
Friendliness rating: ★★★

Parking: Free lot, street
Bar: Full service
Wine selection: Good
Dress: Casual
Disabled access: Good
Customers: Locals

Open: Monday–Wednesday, 11:30 A.M.–11 P.M.; Thursday,
  11:30 A.M.–midnight; Friday and Saturday, 11:30 A.M.–1 A.M.;
  Sunday, 10:30 A.M.–11 P.M.

Atmosphere/Setting: Simple and attractive, though often over-bustly, a
mix of black-and-white and pink paint upstairs, but bistro style rather than
Deco.

House Specialties: Lobster pot stickers with a spicy ginger sauce; porter-
house-cut lamb chops with minted papaya chutney; roast duck with
mango sauce and curried greens; barbecue-spiced oysters; sautéed scallops
on lemon fettuccine with a hint of bacon and ginger.

Other Recommendations: A smoked chicken and wild mushroom tamale
with roasted chili sauce; rock shrimp and sea scallop risotto (an appetizer);
a big salad with seared rare tuna or grilled tuna steak with mango relish.

Summary & Comments: Chef Bill Jackson, who's popular with his peers
as well as his patrons, is interested in providing varied and unobtrusively
healthful food and air: It's a smoke-free zone, and there are plenty of heart-
healthy options as well as hearty ones. He likes to mix and match styles,
although it isn't fusion food, just fun. He believes in light spirits as well as
light food: consider his own description, "chef and fearless sailboarder," on
the menu, and the name of his adjoining bread bakery, Best Buns. Note
that while the downstairs area is open all afternoon and into the late hours,
the more formal upstairs dining room closes between lunch and dinner and
also shuts down earlier in the evening.

CASHION'S EAT PLACE

			QUALITY
Modern American	★★★	Moderate	**83**
			VALUE
			B

1819 Columbia Road, NW
   (202) 797-1819   Zone 6, Dupont Circle/Adams-Morgan

Reservations: Recommended
When to go: Anytime
Entree range: $12.95–17.95
Payment: VISA, MC
Service rating: ★★★
Friendliness rating: ★★★★

Parking: Street, valet (evenings)
Bar: Full service
Wine selection: Good
Dress: Business/casual
Disabled access: Fair
Customers: Locals

Brunch: Sunday, 11:30 A.M.–2:30 P.M.
Dinner: Tuesday, 5:30–10 P.M.; Wednesday–Saturday, 5:30–11 P.M.;
   Sunday, 5:30–10 P.M.

Atmosphere/Setting: Crammed into the hodgepodge wedge of Columbia Road, this tongue-in-cheekily modest bistro ("Eat Place," indeed) manages to seem bustling, lively, streetwise, and sleek all at the same time, thanks to a smart mix of old photos, exposed wine bins, and architectural detailing.

House Specialties: "Old-fashioned rabbit and dumplings"; sautéed scallops with a gingery "bordelaise" over tender savoy cabbage; osso bucco; hearty but moist pork chops; big-flavor-for-the-bite buffalo hanger steak.

Other Recommendations: Roast chicken or Cornish hen is a frequent theme, and any version of it is welcome. Ditto with grilled seafood or mussels.

Summary & Comments: Ann Cashion's Southwest-flavored cooking helped launch the Austin Grills and Jaleo; however, her style here is what you might think of as boomer comfort food. It's a little bit mid-America, a little bit Euro-peasant, a bit o' bistro, a fillip of fusion . . . and all with a solid comprehension of the pleasures of texture. You can have light or filling, rich or delicate, and side dishes are sauced as complementary, not "creative." It may be the kind of stuff some people would make at home, but they'd have to have subscriptions to gourmet mags and time to cruise the markets for inspiration. And with "homestyle" places like this, who needs a kitchen, anyway?

CHINA INN

			QUALITY
			83

Chinese   ★★★   Inexpensive

	VALUE
	B

631 H Street, NW
(202) 842-0909   Zone 3, Downtown

Reservations: Helpful
When to go: Lunch for dim sum,
  late night
Entree range: $9.95–24.95
Payment: VISA, MC, AMEX, DC
Service rating: ★★½
Friendliness rating: ★★½

Parking: Street
Bar: Full service
Wine selection: House
Dress: Casual, informal
Disabled access: No
Customers: Ethnic, local, tourist

Open: Sunday–Thursday, 11 A.M.–1 A.M.; Friday and Saturday,
11 A.M.–2 A.M.

Atmosphere/Setting: This isn't a place that feels the need to look "authentic" (meaning touristy) or dangle roasted ducks in the window. It's just a hodgepodge of small dining rooms on various levels, simply painted teal and pink, but what you do see—the large number of Chinese diners—is more telling.

House Specialties: Crabs "smoked" in ginger and scallions; boneless duck in watercress (not on the menu, but ask); "fish dipping in boiling water with spices" (a fantastic poached sea bass); hearty chow foon noodle dishes; seafood dumplings.

Other Recommendations: One of the most fun lunches in any Chinatown is dim sum, the little wheelabout trays of hot dumplings, stuffed bean curd, spare ribs, and so on that you order by the dish (usually three pieces or servings). It goes like this: The cook sends out something hot; the waiter wheels it by; you point; they put a check on your bill and the plate on your table. Most restaurants make dim sum only on the weekends, but China Inn offers this traditional teahouse fare every day between 11 A.M. and 3 P.M.

Summary & Comments: China Inn has a very strong and loyal following in the Chinese community, and like many such places, it has more than one menu—the "authentic" version and the tourist guide (although here, even some of the more revisionist dishes are very good). Peruse the "chef's specials," and if you see something on someone else's table that attracts you, be brave and order it. And since it's only a block from the subway and near the great Chinese arch, it's a great place for tourists.

CITRONELLE

			QUALITY
Modern American	★★★	Expensive	**81**
			VALUE
			C

Latham Hotek, 3000 M Street, NW
  (202) 625-2150   Zone 5, Georgetown

Reservations: Recommended
When to go: Lunch; before 9
Entree range: $24–28
Payment: VISA, MC, AMEX, DC, D
Service rating: ★★½
Friendliness rating: ★★★

Parking: Valet
Bar: Full service
Wine selection: Good
Dress: Business, dressy
Disabled access: Excellent
Customers: Local, tourist, business

Brunch: Sunday, 10:30 A.M.–3:30 P.M.
Lunch: Every day, 11:30 A.M.–2 P.M.
Dinner: Sunday–Thursday, 6–10 P.M.; Friday and Saturday,
  5:30–10 P.M.

Atmosphere/Setting: Using a series of small level shifts and cutaway ceilings, the designers of this pretty but not showy establishment have made the space seem both intimate and expansive. The upstairs lounge is classic flannel grey and green; the downstairs rooms have a conservatory touch, with dark green wicker armchairs, glass accent doors, and blessedly simple greenery. The star attractions are the exposed kitchen and its six chefs, two preppers, and salad chef.

House Specialties: Appetizers: white tuna carpaccio (actually yellowtail) with ginger vinaigrette; luxuriant sautéed foie gras with chanterelles; creamy crab coleslaw wrapped in savoy cabbage; crab cannelloni; wild mushroom napoleon. Entrees: roasted lobster; veal chop with mini–goat cheese ravioli; penne with shiitakes and veal glacé; grilled swordfish; rib eye; rare tuna Châteaubriand; rack of lamb.

Summary & Comments: It's tempting to pass up the entrees and load up on appetizers which, at between $8 and $14, make more of a meal for the money and are more reliably handled. This is food art: Simple grilled swordfish is made memorable by a wreath of angelhair-fine potato crisps and a bed of lentils; the peony of transparently sliced yellowtail lies on a painted bed of sauce and under a garnish of seaweed and baby endive. Monkfish is bacon-wrapped à la tournedo and accompanied by a standing pastry "vase" filled with wild mushrooms; a crabmeat "cannelloni" is actually a seafood terrine rolled in a broad noodle canopy and striped with saffron and squid ink.

CITY LIGHTS OF CHINA

			QUALITY
Chinese	★★★	Moderate	81

VALUE
B

1731 Connecticut Avenue, NW
(202) 265-6688   Zone 6, Dupont Circle/Adams-Morgan

Reservations: Helpful	Parking: Validated after 6 P.M.
When to go: Anytime	Bar: Full service
Entree range: $6.95–21.95	Wine selection: House
Payment: VISA, MC, AMEX, DC, D	Dress: Informal or casual
Service rating: ★★½	Disabled access: Yes
Friendliness rating: ★★½	Customers: Local

Open: Monday–Thursday, 11:30 A.M.–10:30 P.M.; Friday, 11:30 A.M.–11 P.M.; Saturday, noon–11 P.M.; Sunday, 11:30 A.M.–11 P.M.

Atmosphere/Setting: A surprisingly cheery underground warren with a reasonable volume setting. It has expanded a couple of times, which may explain the minimal decor of celadon paint; it's sort of like those portable walls in office buildings that are made to be reconfigured at any time.

House Specialties: Tinkling bells pork, named for the spitting noises produced when the fried wontons and pork tidbits hit the hot metal platter; a peppery version of caramelized shredded beef; a strongly flavored Szechuan lamb; twice-cooked duck; pan-fried dumplings; lobster so fresh you're introduced to it first.

Other Recommendations: Shredded pork with chiles; Peking duck; sea cucumber with scallions; bean curd with crabmeat.

Summary & Comments: One of the great attractions of this young-professional-neighborhood restaurant is the breadth of its menu, from the authentic and authentically filling entree soups (combination chicken, pork, and shrimp; pork and pickle mustard with noodles; etc.), through a sort of middle-class range of seafood and meat dishes, up to perfectly executed steamed whole sea bass and shrimp on coarse salt. One of its drawbacks is the lack of "serious" dishes—no organ meats or more exotic sea creatures—but then the really ethnic eaters aren't the target audience here. The nouvelle attitude toward traditional sauces is something of a toss-up; when they're good, they're very, very good, but when they're bland, they're boring.

CLYDE'S

			QUALITY
American	★★★	Moderate	81
			VALUE
			B

3236 M Street, NW
   (202) 333-9180   Zone 5, Georgetown

70 Wisconsin Circle (Chevy Chase Center), Chevy Chase
   (301) 951-9600   Zone 10A, Maryland suburbs

8332 Leesburg Pike, Tysons Corner
   (703) 734-1901   Zone 11A, Virginia suburbs

Market Street, Reston Town Center, Reston
   (703) 787-6601   Zone 11B, Virginia suburbs

Reservations: Recommended
When to go: Anytime
Entree range: $6.95–14.95
Payment: VISA, MC, AMEX, DC, D
Service rating: ★★★½
Friendliness rating: ★★★½
Parking: Free lots; pay lots in George-
   town

Bar: Full service
Wine selection: Limited
Dress: Business, casual
Disabled access: Good
Customers: Local, business

Brunch: Georgetown: Saturday and Sunday, 9 A.M.–4 P.M.;
Reston: Sunday, 10 A.M.–4 P.M.

Lunch/Dinner: Georgetown: Monday–Thursday, noon–10 P.M.; Friday,
noon–11 P.M.; Saturday, 4:30–11 P.M.; Sunday, 4:30–10 P.M.; Reston:
Monday–Saturday, 11 A.M.–midnight; Sunday, 4–10 P.M.; Chevy Chase
and Tysons: Monday–Saturday, 11 A.M.–2 A.M.; Sunday, 10 A.M.–2 A.M.

Atmosphere/Setting: Although all the Clyde's branches resemble the original M Street gaslight-era chophouse in atmosphere, they each have a
theme: Reston's is a sporting club, with paraphernalia from sculls to sail-
boat models; Tysons Corner has a pseudo-European style, with murals of
nude bathers and lots of neo-nouveau glass and sculpture; and the branch
in Columbia Mall is that sort of helter-skelter fake Tiffany and patent
medicine sort of saloon. The Clyde's of Chevy Chase is a showplace of
etched "Orient Express" glass, model cars—we mean production models
—and real race cars, plus a huge downstairs bar larger than many nightclubs.

House Specialties: The foods vary somewhat, too, with some similarities
(and slight variations in price range). In general, look for smoked salmon,
one of the company's signatures; lamb stew; beer-batter shrimp with an
orange marmalade/mustard sauce; crab cakes; real old-fashioned burgers.
(Which is to say, these kitchens are still American at heart.) However, a

new, more serious attitude toward cooking is beginning to manifest itself; watch these spaces.

Other Recommendations: Steaks; scallop and shrimp sautées; a chili that many people swear by (it's the company's other signature dish, canned and sold by neo-prep catalogs); seafood specials (including the annual halibut feasts, lobster specials, and in Reston, huge clambakes and Oktoberfest feeds). The menus and prices vary a bit from site to site but have obvious family relationships.

Entertainment & Amenities: Bar nibbles at happy hour, most notably an old-fashioned club cheese or smoked salmon tray at M Street and hot, fresh, butter-dipped soft pretzels in Reston—worth the trip alone. So are the sweet rolls served at Sunday brunch in Tysons.

Summary & Comments: Clyde's was Georgetown's first "scene" bar, a sort of party and political hangout for post-grads who couldn't let go. Now it's almost an institution, but always dependable and welcoming. The Tysons Corner branch is a major singles center; Reston and Columbia are more family-oriented. Chevy Chase is a more serious restaurant, with sweetbreads, smoked duck, and other slightly more Bethesda-neighborhood entrees. All are heavy on the ice cream and spiked coffee drinks, and on cholesterol-spiking desserts.

COCO LOCO

			QUALITY
Nuevo Latino	★★★	Moderate	**84**
			VALUE
810 Seventh Street, NW			**A**
(202) 289-2626 Zone 3, Downtown			

Reservations: Strongly recommended on weekends

When to go: Early or late; lunch for lower prices

Entree range: $29.95 fixed price

Payment: VISA, MC, AMEX

Service rating: ★★★

Friendliness rating: ★★★½

Parking: Street, garage, valet (dinner only)

Bar: Full service

Wine selection: Good

Dress: Business, informal

Disabled access: Fair

Customers: Local, international

Lunch: Monday–Friday, 11:30 A.M.–2:30 P.M.
Dinner: Monday–Thursday, 6–10:30 P.M.; Friday and Saturday, 6–11 P.M.

(Coco Loco)

Atmosphere/Setting: Splashily modern tropical decor includes tile floors, bright primary colors and parrot-print uniforms, suspended canoes, and geometrically shaped columns. The cafe in front and big horseshoe bar serve tapas; the main dining room features an all-you-can-eat Brazilian-style mixed grill.

House Specialties: The all-you-can-eat churrascaria grill includes skewered meats—lamb, beef flank and tenderloin, pork spareribs, chicken, and chorizo—carved directly onto your plate, plus a huge salad bar with fruit, asparagus, marinated mushrooms, couscous, etc. From the tapas menu: beef brochette with chili sauce; crab cakes; mini-paella; duck enchiladas with mole sauce.

Other Recommendations: Bacon-wrapped shrimp; chicken-stuffed ravioli with poblanos; steamed salmon; side dishes of coconut rice.

Entertainment & Amenities: Good-weather dining in a walled courtyard; hot Latin dancing after 11 P.M. Wednesday through Saturday, with Rio-style "pros" atop the bar on Saturdays.

Summary & Comments: This is a very high-energy joint, a crowd- and trend-watcher's paradise; even with reservations you may have to wait a while. The mixed grill is more food than anyone but a pro football player could eat. The wine list includes several lesser-known but good and bargain-priced Chilean and Argentine wines. If you can afford to go straight to bed at 4 in the afternoon, go for the all-you-can-eat churrascaria at lunch, when it's only $20.95.

COTTONWOOD CAFE

New Southwestern	★★★	Moderate	QUALITY
			80
4844 Cordell Avenue, Bethesda			VALUE
(301) 656-4844 Zone 10A, Maryland suburbs			**B**

Reservations: Recommended	Parking: Lot, valet (dinner only)
When to go: Anytime	Bar: Full service
Entree range: $9.95–20.95	Wine selection: Fair
Payment: VISA, MC, AMEX	Dress: Informal, business, casual
Service rating: ★★★	Disabled access: Good
Friendliness rating: ★★★	Customers: Local, business

Open: Monday–Thursday, 11:30 A.M.–10 P.M.; Friday and Saturday, 11:30 A.M.–11 P.M.; Sunday, 5:30–10 P.M.

(Cottonwood Cafe)

Atmosphere/Setting: A very pretty, jewel-toned bow to the American Southwest, with terra-cotta walls, murals of pueblos, wall sconces like mood rings, a few artifacts, and wrought-iron salamander door pulls—and a staff uniformed in turquoise and amethyst shirts with bolos and boots.

House Specialties: Real "rattlesnake bites" (jalapeños stuffed with rattlesnake meat and cheese); blue cornmeal–crusted calamari with tomato chili glaze; a Southwest-style paella with sun-dried Indian corn and black beans amongst the shellfish; roast duck glazed with habanero-flavored molasses.

Other Recommendations: Chile sausage and smoked shrimp tossed with black pepper pasta, sun-dried tomatoes, and shiitakes; Navajo fry bread topped with smoked salmon.

Summary & Comments: Cottonwood continues to experiment with chile peppers, varying its flavors as well as heat levels. Sauces are cleaner and lighter than before, the quality is consistent, and the experimentation informed, not frantic. Lunch is a real bargain. The wine list is all-American, and the beer list is fair.

DAR ES SALAAM

Moroccan	★★½	Moderate	**QUALITY**	**79**
			VALUE	**B**

3056 M Street, NW
   (202) 337-6680   Zone 5, Georgetown

Reservations: Helpful	Parking: Street
When to go: Anytime	Bar: Full service
Entree range: $11.95–14.95	Wine selection: House
Payment: VISA, MC, AMEX	Dress: Casual
Service rating: ★★★	Disabled access: Limited
Friendliness rating: ★★★	Customers: Local, ethnic

Dinner: Every day, 5–11 p.m.

Atmosphere/Setting: Even after being closed for several years, the authentic tilework and plaster of this escapist fantasy is in beautiful condition; add the flowery pillowcases, brass jugs, and background music, and you have a romantic date to reckon with.

House Specialties: Mechoui, roast whole lamb (requires 24 hours' notice); an unusual tajine of red snapper and more common lamb and chicken versions of this classic preserved-citrus and olive stew.

Other Recommendations: Bisteeya, the sugar-dusted pastry filled with chicken and used not as dessert but as first course; harrira, a pepper-potent stew-thick soup with lamb and lentils.

Summary & Comments: It's a little sad that, while so many other ethnic restaurants in Washington feel increasingly emboldened to ask diners to eat traditional style, Dar es Salaam has gone the other way: The handwashing ceremony which formerly preceded eating with fingers has given way to forks and knives, and the low banquette seating has been topped with another layer of cushions. But the food is as good as ever. (Some people complain that the couscous seems skimpy, compared to the typically exaggerated versions served around town, but it's plenty filling and more traditional.)

ELYSIUM

Modern American	★★★½	Expensive	QUALITY
			88
			VALUE
			B

116 South Alfred Street, Old Town Alexandria
   (703) 838-8000   Zone 11C, Virginia suburbs

Reservations: Recommended	Parking: Valet, street
When to go: Anytime	Bar: Full service
Entree range: Fixed price: $35, $45, and $55	Wine selection: Very good
Payment: VISA, MC, AMEX, DC	Dress: Jacket and tie (dining room); informal (grill)
Service rating: ★★★★	Disabled access: No
Friendliness rating: ★★★½	Customers: Local, tourist

Dinner: Dining room: Tuesday–Saturday, 6–10 P.M.; Grill: Every day, 6–10 P.M.

Atmosphere/Setting: A lovely newer but Old Town–style inn, with a curving white marble stairway and various small, pretty dining rooms; some more formal with classic white linen, oil paintings, and definitely modern but stylish china; some more like libraries and old smoking rooms.

House Specialties: For such a shifting menu, it's hard to specify, but game dishes, including ostrich in a rich wine reduction and wild boar with a mole sauce and Cervena venison, are beautifully handled; a mini-bouillabaisse, though not the richest, was light and succulent; and a cannelloni of pheasant and duck was rich without being cloying. Grilled marinated quail with red cabbage choucroute is a good example of traditional recipes made fresh.

(Elysium)

Summary & Comments: Under different chefs, different names, and different cuisines, this restaurant has wandered from fine to frustrating, but it's been riding high lately as a showcase for chef Jim Garrison's fancies. The menu changes almost nightly, which is good for those intrigued by market-fresh ingredients, but not all Washingtonians are so off-the-cuff, and some may find this a little overwhelming. In addition, some dishes seem more carefully considered and original than others. But there is no doubt that if you're at all food-savvy, his chef's menus—$35 for three courses, $45 for four, and $55 for five, each including dessert and quite likely a little lagniappe from the kitchen—are as intriguing as any. And you can opt for a glass of wine or even a tasting flight recommended for each course as well.

GABRIEL

			QUALITY
Nuevo Latino	★★★	Moderate	**84**
			VALUE
2121 P Street, NW (Radisson Barceló Hotel)			**A**

(202) 956-6690   Zone 6, Dupont Circle/Adams-Morgan

Reservations: Recommended	Parking: Street, hotel valet
When to go: Lunch, brunch, happy hour	Bar: Full service
	Wine selection: Good and affordable
Entree range: $15.50–22	Dress: Business, casual
Payment: AMEX, VISA, MC, DC, D	Disabled access: Good
Service rating: ★★½	Customers: Business, local
Friendliness rating: ★★★	

Breakfast: Monday–Friday, 6:30–11 A.M.; Saturday and Sunday, 7–10:30 A.M.

Brunch: Sunday, 11 A.M.–3 P.M.

Lunch: Monday–Friday, 11:30 A.M.–2:30 P.M.

Dinner: Monday–Thursday, 6–10 P.M.; Friday and Saturday, 6–10:30 P.M.; Sunday, 6–9:30 P.M.

Atmosphere/Setting: Sunny yellow paint, ocre and red art, and lots of wood and windows makes this English basement seem like an enclosed courtyard.

House Specialties: Tapas: grilled quail stuffed with sausage; neo-Salvadoran pupusas with a crunchy cornmeal batter; scallops and spicy chorizo with cilantro and lime; figs stuffed with chorizo. Entrees: vegetable stew with rice croquettes; roast monkfish with caramelized oranges and corn fungus sauce; seared salmon with serrano ham and saffron-tomato broth.

(Gabriel)

Summary & Comments: At $9.50, the lunch buffet might seem to be the best bargain, usually including paella, quesadillas, rice and vegetable salads, and sliced cured meats and cheeses. And the $7.95 happy-hour spread, 5–8:30 P.M. Wednesday through Friday, could easily pass for dinner. The real pig-out, so to speak, is Sunday brunch, complete with suckling pigs carved from the spit; paella; cassoulet; rolls, danishes, and pastries; cheese and fruit; vegetable and couscous salads; sardines and cold cuts; omelets; polenta and potatoes; roast beef, lamb, and ham; plus unlimited champagne and a whole dessert bar, all for $16.75. Holy mole!

GALILEO				
Italian	★★★★★	Expensive	**QUALITY**	98
			VALUE	C

1110 21st Street, NW
(202) 293-7191   Zone 6, Dupont Circle/Adams-Morgan

Reservations: A must
When to go: Anytime
Entree range: $19.95–29.95
Payment: VISA, MC, AMEX, CB, DC, D
Service rating: ★★★★
Friendliness rating: ★★★½
Parking: Lot, valet (dinner, except Sunday)
Bar: Full service

Wine selection: Excellent
Dress: Dressy, business
Disabled access: Good
Customers: Local, tourist, business, gourmet mag groupies

Breakfast: Monday–Friday, 7:30–9 A.M.
Lunch: Monday–Friday, 11:30 A.M.–2 P.M.
Dinner: Monday–Thursday, 5:30–10 P.M.; Friday and Saturday, 5:30–10:30 P.M.; Sunday, 5–10 P.M.

Atmosphere/Setting: A gracious stone and plaster palazzo with vaulted recessed booths and a trompe l'oeil mural leading into a Renaissance eternity.
House Specialties: Five-course menus du gustacione for about $50. Among the frequent offerings are game birds—squab, woodcock, guinea hen—and red game such as venison and wild hare. Sea urchin appears fairly often, usually caressing a delicate pasta, as do wild mushrooms or truffles.
Other Recommendations: Ravioli stuffed with scallops and served with black truffles, or stuffed with veal and topped with roasted foie gras; grilled rack of veal or venison; sweetbreads; grilled or roasted seafood; gnocchi.

(Galileo)

Summary & Comments: Among the city's finest restaurants by any account. Chef Roberto Donna's creations quickly appear on menus elsewhere in town. He also offers the longest, best, and probably priciest Italian wine list in Washington, but with style: Even the bread sticks and loaves, which come in a half-dozen flavors, are to be savored. Sauces and presentations are rarely showy, and purees often stand in for cream. Regular customers get white-glove treatment; tourists (and obvious food-trend victims) may find the staff showily condescending, but spit-and-polish precise nonetheless.

GEORGE

Mediterranean	★★★½	Moderate	QUALITY
			85
			VALUE
			B

2020 K Street, NW
   (202) 452-9898   Zone 3, Downtown

Reservations: Recommended	Parking: Valet at night; street or lot
When to go: Anytime; lunch	Bar: Full service
Entree range: $13.50–20.50	Wine selection: Good
Payment: VISA, MC, AMEX, DC	Dress: Business, informal
Service rating: ★★★	Disabled access: Good
Friendliness rating: ★★★★	Customers: Local

Lunch: Monday–Friday, 11:30 A.M.–2 P.M.
Dinner: Monday–Thursday, 5:30–10 P.M.; Friday and Saturday, 5:30–10:30 P.M.

Atmosphere/Setting: A stately, but not stiff, room with a hint of Riviera-style stucco paint, Italian marble floor, and polished wood.

House Specialties: Scallop-stuffed lasagna with eels and white wine sauce; chunky lobster ravioli with lime, ginger, shiitakes, and roasted fennel; a novel seafood soup with kohlrabi, tomatoes, and crab fritters.

Other Recommendations: A sort of pared-down couscous with honey-ginger-marinated lamb chops, eggplant mousse, and fennel; a rich-spirited agnolotti stuffed with wild mushrooms and topped with a ham-asparagus cream; lemony chicken over caponata; pork chops marinated in buttermilk and honey with horseradish; roasted shiitake and lamb kidney salad.

Summary & Comments: It may seem as odd a name for a restaurant as for a magazine, but it has a better excuse: It's the eponymous kitchen of chef George Vetsch, who not only was one of the first chefs to offer a combination of North African/Middle Eastern/Riviera cooking at the

(George)

Mediterraneo restaurant in Arlington, but who pushed the envelope even more by making the real stuff, like sautéed rabbit giblets and brandied lamb liver. The menu here is only a little more subdued, but the rich flavors—fennel, chicken livers, calamata olives, goat cheese, eggplant, and spicy harissa—are the same. And the majority of these dishes are available at lunch for a few dollars less. Even the supposedly jaded sophisticates of K Street ought to find real pleasure in some of these combinations.

GEORGIA BROWN'S

Southern	★★★	Moderate	QUALITY
			80
			VALUE
			B

950 15th Street, NW
  (202) 393-4499   Zone 3, Downtown

Reservations: Suggested	Parking: Street, valet (after 6 P.M.), $5
When to go: Anytime	
Entree range: $10.95–19.95	Bar: Full service
Payment: VISA, MC, AMEX, DC, CB, D	Wine selection: Very good
Service rating: ★★★½	Dress: Business, informal
Friendliness rating: ★★★½	Disabled access: Good
	Customers: Business, local, tourist

Brunch: Sunday, 11:30 A.M.–3 P.M.
Lunch/Dinner: Monday–Thursday, 11:30 A.M.–11 P.M.; Friday, 11:30 A.M.–midnight; Saturday, 5:30 P.M.–midnight; Sunday, 5:30–11 P.M.

Atmosphere/Setting: An almost too-sophisticated take on Southern garden district graciousness, with vinelike wrought iron overhead, sleek wood curves and conversation nooks; window tables are prime.
House Specialties: A very in-joke take on osso bucco made with ham hock (possibly the smartest pun in Washington cuisine); beautiful white shrimp, heads still on, with spicy sausage over grits; the same extravagant shrimp in an untypical coconut milk–rum–green onion gravy; grilled black grouper with peach chutney; spicy duck sausage gumbo; pan-crisped sweetbreads with Madeira.
Other Recommendations: Braised rabbit with wild mushrooms; crab cakes; medallions of beef with bourbon-pecan sauce; a Caribbean-spiced catfish fried in cornmeal; an appetizer of eggplant rolls stuffed with bleu cheese and fried.
Entertainment & Amenities: Live jazz at Sunday brunch.

(Georgia Brown's)

Summary & Comments: This is not low-country cuisine (except perhaps for the high-octane planter's punch); it's haute country, updated versions of dishes you might have found in Charleston or Savannah. Presentation is distinctive without being showy, and portions are generous. Homesick Southerners can indulge in the fried chicken livers and the farm-biscuit-like scones and still look uptown. The wine list is all-American and fairly priced; barrel-aged bourbons and single-malt Scotches available as well.

GERARD'S PLACE

French	★★★★	Expensive	**QUALITY** 90
			VALUE C

915 15th Street, NW
   (202) 737-4445   Zone 3, Downtown

Reservations: Recommended
When to go: Monday
Entree range: $16.50–29.50
Payment: VISA, MC, AMEX, CB, DC
Service rating: ★★★
Friendliness rating: ★★½
Parking: Street, valet (evenings)

Bar: Full service
Wine selection: Good
Dress: Business, casual
Disabled access: Very good
Customers: Business, local, tourist

Lunch: Monday–Friday, 11:30 A.M.–2:30 P.M.
Dinner: Monday–Thursday, 5:30–10 P.M.; Friday and Saturday, 5:30–10:30 P.M.; Sunday, closed.

Atmosphere/Setting: A quietly powerful room, painted simply in charcoal and terra-cotta and studded with a series of stark pencil lithographs.

House Specialties: The menu changes weekly, but look for any sweetbread or venison dish; perfectly poached lobster topped with a tricolor confetti of mango, avocado, and red bell pepper in lime-sauterne sauce; "foie gras of the sea" (known to sushi connoisseurs as ankimo or monkfish liver), lightly crusted and grilled rare, as rich as real foie gras but with a fraction of the calories and guilt; terrine of quail bound by quail liver; boned rabbit rolled and wrapped in Japanese seaweed; soft-shell crabs not with almonds but sweeter, unexpected hazelnuts.

Other Recommendations: Hearty bistro-max dishes such as pot-au-feu of cured duck and savoy cabbage; cod cheeks; braised oxtail; breast of duck with shepherd's pie of the leg. Or you can try the tasting menu, five courses for $58 or with wine for $85. A vegetarian tasting menu is also offered.

Entertainment & Amenities: On Monday, Gerard's Place waives not only the corkage fee on wines but the markup as well.

Summary & Comments: Gerard Pangaud prepares classic food, often long-cooked and incredibly tender, but unobtrusively lightened to modern nutritional standards and keyed to seasonal specialties. Presentation is discreet but stunning.

Honors & Awards: Pangaud's restaurant in Paris earned two Michelin stars.

GERMAINE'S

Pan Asian	★★★	Moderate	QUALITY
			81
			VALUE
2400 Wisconsin Avenue, NW			B
(202) 965-1185 Zone 5, Georgetown			

Reservations: Recommended	Parking: Valet (dinner), meters
When to go: Anytime	Bar: Full service
Entree range: $14–22	Wine selection: Fair
Payment: VISA, MC, AMEX, DC	Dress: Business, informal
Service rating: ★★★	Disabled access: No
Friendliness rating: ★★★	Customers: Local, media, tourist

Lunch: Monday–Friday, 11:30 A.M.–2:30 P.M.

Dinner: Sunday–Thursday, 5:30–10 P.M.; Friday and Saturday, 5:30–11 P.M.

Atmosphere/Setting: Oriental only in its discretion and elegance, with airy skylights, semiformal banquettes, and large and striking plants for dividers.

House Specialties: Cha gio, the traditional spring rolls (better than most); chicken or pork satay; Thai chicken with basil; tea-leaf seafood in a coconut milk sauce; sautéed calamari with tomato and leeks; grilled fresh fish.

Other Recommendations: Rockfish steamed in foil with shrimp and chopped seafood; shrimp or mixed seafood in fried-noodle baskets; Peking duck.

Summary & Comments: Despite the owner's Vietnamese heritage, Germaine's has turned into what is even more pan-hemispheric than pan-Asian. Elements of Korean, Japanese, Filipino, Indonesian, Thai, Chinese, Burmese, and French cuisines are mixed together in what is really the chef's best interest. She cooks what she likes, which is, after all, the definition of any art. After 15 years, it may not be quite the prime people-watching spot it used to be (image is everything) but it's still intelligently populated, particularly by professionals who haven't rotated with the administrations.

GOLDONI			
			QUALITY
Italian	★★★½	Inexpensive	85
			VALUE
1113 23rd Street, NW			C

(202) 293-1511   Zone 6, Dupont Circle/Adams-Morgan

Reservations: Recommended
When to go: Anytime
Entree range: $9.95–24.95
Payment: VISA, MC, AMEX, D, DC
Service rating: ★★★½
Friendliness rating: ★★★

Parking: Free lot
Bar: Full service
Wine selection: Good
Dress: Business/informal
Disabled access: No
Customers: Local, ethnic

Lunch: Every day, 11:30 A.M.–2 P.M.
Dinner: Monday–Thursday, 5:30–10 P.M.; Friday and Saturday, 5–10:30 P.M.; Sunday 5–9:30 P.M.

Atmosphere/Setting: This has always been a beautiful restaurant, no matter under which regime: The skylights and white marble bar contrast with deep green tones and old-fashioned candelabra.

House Specialties: Pappardelle with duck ragout or fettuccine with lamb ragout and mushrooms; portobello-stuffed tortellini; veal that goes cordon bleu one better, on a roll with asparagus, prosciutto, spinach, and egg frittata; veal-stuffed ravioli; appetizers such as a terrine of rabbit and sweetbreads with black olive sauce or a salad composed of smoked salmon, goat cheese, and asparagus.

Other Recommendations: Dishes wrapped for delicacy, including a scallop wrapped in spinach and a snapper en papillote; break-your-resolution risottos with mascarpone or even sausage; rack of lamb pan-sautéed rather than roasted (and more tender for it) but served, with a wink to Tuscany, with cannellini beans and Swiss chard; and surprisingly light but flavorful mixed grilled seafoods.

Summary & Comments: Chef Fabrizio Aielli is one of Roberto Donna's former sous-chefs, and it shows: The dishes here (and their menu descriptions) are every bit as elaborate as those at Galileo—and, as at Galileo, you're always surprised at just how satisfying such imagination can be. These are richly flavored dishes, particularly the pastas: Notice the number of gamey ragout sauces.

GREENWOOD

Modern American	★★★	Moderate	QUALITY
			84
			VALUE
			B

3311 Connecticut Avenue, NW
   (202) 833-6572   Zone 7, Upper Northwest

Reservations: Accepted	Bar: Full service
When to go: Anytime	Wine selection: Limited
Entree range: $11.50–16.95	Dress: Business, casual
Payment: VISA, MC, AMEX	Disabled access: Yes
Service rating: ★★★	Customers: Youngish, nutrition-
Friendliness rating: ★★★★	conscious locals
Parking: Street	

Lunch: Monday–Friday, noon–3 P.M.
Dinner: Every day, 6–10 P.M.

Atmosphere/Setting: A simple but inviting cafe, pretty in pink but smartly modernized by antique tablecloths, faux marbling, and iron sconces.

House Specialties: "New-wave salmon," served over a red lentil dhal with cucumber salad, is a signature dish; "mile-high" lobster or shrimp pad thai; open-faced buckwheat ravioli with mushrooms, potato, and smoked mozzarella filling; lobster-scallop cakes; open-faced spinach ravioli filled with potatoes, chanterelles, spinach, and smoked mozzarella; a signature appetizer of three dips: Mediterranean carrot-cashew, spicy lentil, and beet with caraway.

Other Recommendations: A vegetable pho, the Vietnamese noodle soup; seared rare tuna; artichoke and mushroom risotto; baklava stuffed with eggplant, potato, roasted onion, and walnuts; a bastila, the North African pastry filled with red snapper, caramelized onions, and spices and served with almond couscous and preserved lemons.

Entertainment & Amenities: Live music on Sunday evenings only, ranging from virtuoso guitar to progressive pop; but several of the staff are or have been musicians, so even the recorded music tends to be interesting.

Summary & Comments: Greenwood, named for owner/chef Carole Wagner Greenwood, is billed as providing "seasonal California cooking," and that pretty much sums it up: light, market-savvy, and not recipe-bound. Meals can be either light or heavy (in fact, the menu is divided into small and large dishes, so you can nibble in the neo-Asian fashion). Her cooking is still worldview, however, working in Asian and Middle Eastern flavors in ways that don't overwhelm the palate. This is home-style fusion, if you can understand that.

HIBISCUS CAFE

			QUALITY
Jamaican	★★★½	Inexpensive	85

VALUE: B

3401 K Street, NW
  (202) 965-7170   Zone 5, Georgetown

Reservations: Accepted; required for
  6 or more
When to go: Anytime
Entree range: $12.50–18.50
Payment: AMEX, VISA
Service rating: ★★★
Friendliness rating: ★★★½

Parking: Street
Bar: Beer and wine
Wine selection: Moderate
Dress: Casual
Disabled access: Fair
Customers: Local, international

Dinner: Tuesday–Thursday, 6–11 P.M.; Friday and Saturday,
  6 P.M.–midnight; Sunday and Monday, closed.

Atmosphere/Setting: A bright and roadhouse-cheery but extremely modern cafe, with oversized art-metal furnishings, multiple seating levels, potted mini-trees (to earn the name), and infectious music.

House Specialties: Jerk quail; smoked rack of lamb with plantain mousse; blackened Creole grouper; lobster and shrimp in spicy coconut butter sauce; "shark and bake" (shark-filled fried appetizers); and a searing habanero-marinated "peppa shrimp," head-on and wildly pungent.

Other Recommendations: A yuppie but addictive smoked salmon and Brie pizza; salmon, shrimp, and mussels Creole; homemade ginger beer. For the less spicy-minded, chicken breasts stuffed with spinach and crabmeat; grilled salmon or veal chops.

Summary & Comments: The menu changes a bit every day, mostly depending on the choices of fish and curry meat available. The newest weekend special is whole-roasted goat, the most aromatic dish on the riverfront. The jerk chicken wings here are legendary (owners Sharon and Jimmie Banks started out at Adams-Morgan's legendary—and never quite replaced—Fish Wings & Tings). There is a mixed-veggie curry as well that is popular among PC neighbors.

I RICCHI

			QUALITY
Italian	★★★	Expensive	**84**
			VALUE
			B

Zone 6, Dupont Circle/Adams-Morgan
  1220 19th Street, NW   (202) 835-0459

Reservations: Suggested
When to go: Lunch (almost the same
  menu but a few dollars less) or
  early dinner
Entree range: $10.50–29.95
Payment: VISA, MC, AMEX
Service rating: ★★★★
Friendliness rating: ★★★★

Parking: Street, garage, valet (dinner
  only)
Bar: Full service
Wine selection: Fine
Dress: Dressy, business
Disabled access: Good
Customers: Business, local, tourist

Lunch: Monday–Friday, 11:30 A.M.–2 P.M.
Dinner: Monday–Saturday, 5:30–10 P.M.; Sunday, closed.

Atmosphere/Setting: This stone and terra-cotta-tile room evokes a villa courtyard with *Better Homes & Gardens* detailing—gilded magnolia branches draped in muslin, floral tiles, and heavy cloth. The wood-burning stove makes the whole restaurant smell like fresh bread.

House Specialties: Brick-pressed grilled half-chicken; rolled florentine of pork and rabbit; pasta with hare; a miraculously light fritto misto; a mixed grill of sausage, quail, and veal; scottiaglia, a mixed platter of braised meats.

Other Recommendations: The risotto of the day; grilled fresh fish; the warm salad of shrimp, cannellini, and green beans; the punning "ricchi e poveni," roasted goat chops; thick winter soups; Tuscan toast slathered with chicken livers.

Summary & Comments: The oak-fired grill is the other fiery attraction, and the fresh breads and grilled meats and seafoods taste, with pure Tuscan assurance, of smoke and rosemary. (Like many of the finer restaurants in town, i Ricchi changes its menu seasonally and has moved beyond strictly regional fare, but the grill is always featured.) Despite its prime law-and-lobby location, i Ricchi is arguably the most affordable fancy Italian restaurant in town, although the competition is quickening. Incidentally, it's a rare tribute to someone's cooking when he can leave and people still take his name with pleasure: Founding chef and former co-owner Francesco Ricchi is now trying to rescue the Bice reputation.

ICHIBAN

			QUALITY
Korean/Japanese	★★★	Moderate	**83**
			VALUE
			B

637 North Frederick Avenue, Gaithersburg
   (301) 670-0560   Zone 10B, Maryland suburbs

Reservations: Recommended
When to go: Anytime
Entree range: $9.95–20.95
Payment: VISA, MC, AMEX, DC, D
Service rating: ★★★
Friendliness rating: ★★★

Parking: Free lot
Bar: Full service
Wine selection: House
Dress: Informal
Disabled access: Good
Customers: Local, ethnic

Open: Every day, 11:30 A.M.–10:30 P.M.

Atmosphere/Setting: A pleasant, simple room with screened-off tatami (or banquet) rooms for special parties, a stone garden lantern at the entrance, a sushi bar with a few stools, and hoods and built-in gas grills in the booths.

House Specialties: Grilled split squid that you barbecue yourself on a portable grill top; tripe casserole (for two); choice yook hwe bibimbap, the Korean steak tartare; negimayaki, marinated beef sliced thin and pin-rolled around scallions; sushi and sashimi; rice vermicelli with chopped beef and vegetables.

Summary & Comments: Although Korean-Japanese restaurants competent at both cuisines aren't so rare anymore, Ichiban was one of the first. It also braved what was then the frontier of mid-county business traffic and managed to make bulgoki a household word in Germantown. Sushi order prices here are a touch higher than some, but the quality is usually very high, and the sushi staff more knowledgeable than at some other non-Japanese bars. And as it has become more of a neighborhood fixture, it has become more self-assured: its spices more assertive and the staff more outgoing.

IL RITROVO

			QUALITY
Mediterranean	★★★	Moderate	**80**
			VALUE
			B

4838 Rugby Avenue, Bethesda
(301) 986-1447   Zone 10A, Maryland suburbs

Reservations: Helpful	Parking: Street, lot (free after 5:30 P.M.)
When to go: Anytime	Bar: Full service
Entree range: $7.95–17.95	Wine selection: Limited
Payment: MC, VISA, AMEX, DC, D	Dress: Business, informal
Service rating: ★★★★	Disabled access: Good
Friendliness rating: ★★★★	Customers: Locals

Lunch: Monday–Friday, 11:30 A.M.–2:30 P.M.
Dinner: Every day, 5:30–11 P.M.

Atmosphere/Setting: Simple but attractive, with whitewashed brick, white linen, and a sort of schoolroom-sized mural map of the Mediterranean.

House Specialties: Moroccan lamb scaloppine marinated with mint; paella and couscous offered with meat or seafood; potato gnocchi with spinach, fresh tomatoes, feta cheese, and black olives; and specials of grilled fresh fish. Daily specials have included duck-stuffed ravioli; Lebanese-style trout with tahini; bouillabaisse and even the classic escargot Escoffier in puff pastry.

Other Recommendations: A heart-stoppingly rich risotto of four cheeses, including Gorgonzola; seafood brochette; vegetarian options including the risottos and pasta and a couscous with seven vegetables.

Summary & Comments: "All menu items are just suggestions," the menu says, and you can certainly have it your own way, but you might never want to. The chef and owners between them have worked at a half-dozen well-liked area restaurants, mostly French and Italian, but this restaurant encompasses Greece, Spain, and North Africa as well. It even offers tasting each course with wines from different countries. And although it hasn't been so highly publicized as some places, it's developed a strong enough following that it's branched out into catering and broadened the menu a little more. In fact, the menu has been broadened almost into confusion: There are four fixed-price menus from $17.50 to $32 and a nightly raft of specials.

THE INN AT LITTLE WASHINGTON

			QUALITY
Modern American	★★★★★	Expensive	98
			VALUE
			B

Middle and Main Streets, Washington, VA
(540) 675-3800   Zone 11B   Virginia suburbs

Reservations: Recommended	Friendliness rating: ★★½
When to go: Anytime	Parking: Free lot
Entree range: Prix fixe: $78 during	Bar: Full service
the week, Friday $98, and Saturday	Wine selection: Very good
$108	Dress: Dressy, informal
Payment: VISA, MC	Disabled access: Fair
Service rating: ★★★½	Customers: Local, tourist

Dinner: Monday, Wednesday–Friday, 6–9:30 P.M.; Saturday, seatings at 5:30, 6, 9, and 9:30 P.M.; Sunday, 4–8:30 P.M.; Tuesday, closed.

Atmosphere/Setting: An elegantly appointed but unfussy frame building with an enclosed garden (with many romantic seatings on the patio) and rich, hand-painted walls, velvet upholstery, and the clean glint of real crystal and silver in all directions.

House Specialties: The menu changes continually, but look for dishes such as seafood and wild mushroom risotto; veal or lamb carpaccio; tenderloin of beef that reminds you why that's such a classic entree; homesmoked trout; sweetbreads with whole baby artichokes; baby lamb morsels with lamb sausage alongside. And although the dinner is purportedly four courses, here, as at several other top-flight restaurants, there are apt to be extras along the way.

Other Recommendations: Soft-shell crabs however offered (usually respectfully simple); a signature appetizer of black-eyed peas and Smithfield ham topped with foie gras; that same ham, sliced thin as prosciutto, wrapped around fresh local figs; portobello mushroom pretending to be a filet mignon.

Summary & Comments: Like Roberto Donna, Yannick Cam, and Jean-Louis Palladin, chef Patrick O'Connell is a name to conjure within gourmet (and gourmand) circles all over the country. O'Connell's strength is a sense of balance: Dishes are never overwhelmed or overfussy; local produce is emphasized (which guarantees freshness); and a lot of fine ingredients are allowed to speak for themselves, which is sadly rare. Everyone remembers his or her first passion here—homemade white chocolate ice cream with bitter chocolate sauce—and for some Washingtonians, driving down to the other Washington becomes an addiction, a compulsion. It's the single biggest reason (besides horses, perhaps) for the boom in yuppie commuting to the hills. Incidentally, for fans of Cam, it was O'Connell who bought up the wine cellar when Le Pavilion went bankrupt; and one can almost not regret it.

ISABELLA

Mediterranean	★★★	Moderate	QUALITY
			83

			VALUE
			B

809 15th Street, NW
  (202) 408-9500   Zone 3, Downtown

Reservations: Recommended	Bar: Full service
When to go: Anytime	Wine selection: Good
Entree range: $13–21	Dress: Business, casual
Payment: VISA, MC, AMEX	Disabled access: Good
Service rating: ★★★	Customers: Local, ethnic
Friendliness rating: ★★★	
Parking: Valet ($3 after 5:30 P.M.),	
street	

Lunch: Monday–Friday, 11:30 A.M.–3 P.M.
Dinner: Monday–Saturday, 5:30–10 P.M.

Atmosphere/Setting: A smart and fresh take on Spanish Mediterranean decor: leopard-like patina'd copper panels, carved wood, bits of iron, touches of deep marine blue (particularly the taverna-like heavy cobalt glassware); a richly appointed galleon of a room that rides the eye line back to the great curving wave of the chef's table. The mood is light, however; check out the funky videos and the world beat music.

House Specialties: Seared lamb carpaccio with roasted eggplant; duck-stuffed rigatoni dressed with calamata olives, artichokes, and oven-dried tomatoes on a pool of broth; lamb tagine, the citrusy North African stew; grilled snapper on wilted Swiss chard.

Other Recommendations: For unrepentant foie gras fanatics, a different tack with artichokes, potato, and tomato jam; tabbouleh-crusted lamb chops with mint and pomegranates; black bass with preserved lemons.

Summary & Comments: This is the new home of prodigal popular chef Will Greenwood, long of the Jefferson Hotel and back near his old digs after a stint in Nashville. It may surprise some people that he's abandoned his old regional American style for this rich Moorish Mediterranean stew, but Greenwood has lightened his hand with sauces (check his personal profile for evidence) and here takes up the romance of 15th-century Spain —well, mood is mood—with a flourish.

JALEO

				QUALITY
Nuevo Latino		★★★	Moderate	**77**
				VALUE
				B

480 7th Street, NW
  (202) 628-7949   Zone 3, Downtown

Reservations: Limited
When to go: Early evening
Entree range: $9.75–14.95
Payment: VISA, MC, AMEX, DC, D
Service rating: ★★★
Friendliness rating: ★★★
Parking: Street, valet, $5 (after
  5:30 P.M.)

Bar: Full service
Wine selection: Good
Dress: Business, casual
Disabled access: Good
Customers: Local, tourist

Brunch: Sunday, 11:30 A.M.–2:30 P.M.
Lunch/Dinner: Sunday and Monday, 11:30 A.M.–10 P.M.;
  Tuesday–Thursday, 11:30 A.M.–11:30 P.M.; Friday and Saturday,
  11:30 A.M.–midnight

Atmosphere/Setting: A combination tapas bar, chic competition, and piazza, with bits of wrought iron, a lush suedelike gray decor, and a partial copy of the John Singer Sargent painting from which it takes its name.

House Specialties: Tapas—bite-sized appetizers (four to a plate) meant to help wash down glasses of sangria and sherry and pass hours of conversation. Among the best: tuna carpaccio; grilled quail; spinach with apples; pine nuts and raisins; salmon with artichokes; eggplant flan with roasted peppers; serrano ham and tomatoes on focaccia. Daily specials, frequently of shrimp or shellfish, are extremely good bets.

Other Recommendations: Sausage with white beans; grilled portobello mushrooms (getting to be a local staple); lightly fried calamari; paella.

Summary & Comments: Jaleo has taken tapas, a late-blooming bar fad, and built an entire menu around them—there are five times as many tapas as whole entrees. And if you're with three or four people, you can just about taste everything in sight. (In fact, the first time, you may want to go extra slow: The plates look so small, and the palo cortada goes down so smoothly, that you can overstuff yourself without realizing it.) The bar does a heavy business, too, especially pre- and post-theater. It's already so trendy that if you really want to celeb-spot, go off rush hour; they're already ducking the crowds.

JIN-GA

| Korean | ★★½ | Moderate | QUALITY 79 |
| | | | VALUE B |

1250 24th Street, NW
(202) 785-0720   Zone 5, Georgetown

Reservations: Helpful
When to go: Anytime
Entree range: $12–20
Payment: MC, VISA, AMEX, DC, D
Service rating: ★★
Friendliness rating: ★★★
Parking: Validated

Bar: Full service
Wine selection: House
Dress: Business, informal
Disabled access: Good
Customers: Primarily Asian; mixed
    business crowd at lunch

Open: Every day, 11:30 A.M.–10:30 P.M.

Atmosphere/Setting: Very sleek—mostly wood-paneled with a small stone garden outside and a few private tatami (straw mat) rooms: You might think of it as the gentlemen's club version of Seoul food.

House Specialties: The marinated, cook-it-yourself (if you like) barbecues prepared on grill-top tables are the most visible options, and there are a dozen choices: short ribs, chicken, pork tenderloin, squid. However, the rice or noodle and broth casseroles, topped with a variety of seafood or meats, are what you see the older Koreans enjoying. Also look at the upscale appetizers for grazing on a fine international scale. And if you like the family of dip-into dishes called "hot pots," this is a great place for the Japanese version called shabu shabu in meat, veggie, or seafood versions (all served for two).

Other Recommendations: Although Korean restaurants back home tend to specialize in one sort of food—barbecue, casseroles, noodles, sushi, even the rarer (in the United States) vegetarian cuisine—here you can wander happily through the whole countryside. If you really want to wow 'em, or have a business dinner with top Asian or gourmet clients, give the restaurant 24 hours' notice and they'll make up one of three elaborate and fascinating multicourse menus at $30, $40, or $60 a head.

Summary & Comments: This is the first downtown Korean restaurant (other than a lunch carryout), and it's a first-class branch of a prosperous Asian chain, but its ambitions haven't been matched by its clientele, so the kitchen has scaled back a little.

KINKEAD'S

			QUALITY
Modern American	★★★★	Moderate	**91**
			VALUE
			C

2000 Pennsylvania Avenue, NW
  (202) 296-7700   Zone 4, Foggy Bottom

Reservations: Recommended;
  required for the dining room
  upstairs
When to go: Anytime
Entree range: $16–24
Payment: VISA, MC, AMEX, DC, D
Service rating: ★★★
Friendliness rating: ★★★

Parking: Valet at dinner; pay lots,
  meters
Bar: Full service
Wine selection: Good
Dress: Business, informal
Disabled access: Good
Customers: Business, local

Brunch: Sunday, 11:30 A.M.–2:30 P.M.
Lunch: Monday–Saturday, 11:30 A.M.–2:30 P.M.
Dinner: Every day, 5:30–10:30 P.M.

Atmosphere/Setting: Pleasantly restrained, ranging over two floors and divided into a series of elevated or glass-enclosed areas. The kitchen staff is visible upstairs, as is commonplace these days; it's a little less common to see chef-owner Robert Kinkead, on the consumer side of the glass wall, barking at his cooks via headset like a football coach talking to the booth.

House Specialties: A melting char-grilled squid over polenta with tomato confit (appetizer); delicate grilled skate with a veal reduction; rockfish with artichokes; seared tuna with portobellos and flageolets; lobster specials; crispy-fried red snapper with Chinese black bean sauce; hearty seafood chowder.

Other Recommendations: Grilled squid, shrimp, and crab pupusa with pickled cabbage; Ipswich-style fried soft-shell clams and crab and lobster cakes (appetizers); lamb shanks with braised leg of lamb and white beans; sautéed cod cheeks; Sicilian swordfish with fennel, olives, currants, and arugula.

Entertainment & Amenities: Live jazz weeknights.

Summary & Comments: Kinkead's style is simple and straightforward but not shrinking; his sauces are balanced but assured, designed to highlight the food, not the frills. Any available seafood can be ordered broiled or grilled, but "simply grilled" here is almost an oxymoron. And Kinkead, whose first fame came from his Nantucket restaurant, has installed a little home-away-from-home downstairs by way of a raw bar. For those who count Mobil stars, Kinkead's has four.

L'AUBERGE CHEZ FRANÇOIS

French	★★★★	Moderate	**QUALITY** **92**

VALUE
A

332 Springvale Road, Great Falls
  (703) 759-3800   Zone 11A, Virginia suburbs

Reservations: Required 4 weeks in
  advance
When to go: Summer evenings in
  good weather for the terrace
Entree range: $30–39
Payment: VISA, MC, AMEX, DC
Service rating: ★★★★
Friendliness rating: ★★★★

Parking: Free lot
Bar: Full service
Wine selection: Very good
Dress: Dressy, business (jacket
  required for men at night)
Disabled access: Very good
Customers: Locals

Dinner: Tuesday–Saturday, 5:30–9:30 P.M.; Sunday, 1:30–8 P.M.

Atmosphere/Setting: One of the most beloved and romantic dining sites in the area, a real country inn with exposed beams, a mix of views of Alsace (home of pater familias/executive chef Jacques Haeringer), only-a-family-could-love drawings, and a travel-brochure veranda. It's so widely known as an engagement and anniversary mecca that *Regrets Only*, Sally Quinn's semi–roman à clef about journalistic and political circles, included a rather improbable but dramatic tryst in the parking lot (in an MG with a stick shift, no less).

House Specialties: Classics such as rack of lamb ($36.50 for one, $72 for two), Châteaubriand for two ($73), and duck foie gras either sautéed with apples or "plain"; the true choucroute royal garni, with Alsatian sauerkraut, sausages, smoked pork, duck, pheasant, and quail; game in season, such as medallions of venison and roast duck; veal kidneys in a rich, mustardy sauce; sweetbreads with wild mushrooms in puff pastry; roasted boneless duck breast paired with the stuffed leg and fruit-dotted rice; seafood fricassee with shrimp, scallops, lobster, rockfish, and salmon in Riesling.

Other Recommendations: Various seafood and game pâtés; red snapper braised in beer; boneless rabbit stuffed with leeks and fennel; soft-shell crabs with extra crabmeat stuffed into the body; big scallops in a bright (but not overwhelming) tomato–bell pepper sauce.

Summary & Comments: Although theoretically L'Auberge falls into the "expensive" range, it ought to be called "moderate" to give a fair comparison. What look like entrees on the menu are really whole dinners, and with salads, fancy appetizers, and dessert—not to mention bread and cheese and a bit of sorbet—this is a lot of food. Although the two-to-four weeks' notice rule still applies, competition has increased, along with cancellations: It may be worth a flyer to call in the late afternoon, especially during the week. You can't make reservations for the outdoor terrace, incidentally; just call to make sure it's open (about May through September) and then show up.

LA CHAUMIÈRE

French	★★★	Moderate	QUALITY
			81

	VALUE
	C

2813 M Street, NW
(202) 338-1784   Zone 5, Georgetown

Reservations: Recommended
When to go: Anytime
Entree range: $13.75–23.95
Payment: VISA, MC, AMEX, CB, DC
Service rating: ★★★
Friendliness rating: ★★★

Parking: Two-hour parking at Four Seasons Hotel (dinner), street
Bar: Full service
Wine selection: Good
Dress: Business, informal
Disabled access: Good
Customers: Local, embassy, business

Lunch: Monday–Friday, 11:30 A.M.–2:30 P.M.
Dinner: Monday–Saturday, 5:30–10:30 P.M.; Sunday, closed.

Atmosphere/Setting: After 20 years in the often tumultuous Georgetown culinary competition, the cooking in this big-beamed, in-town country inn, with its freestanding fireplace in the center and old iron tools on the wall, remains solid. And what goes around comes around: Bistro fare of owner Gerard Pain's sort is suddenly booming around him.

House Specialties: Oysters; seasonal specials of venison (as uptown as medallions with chestnut puree or as down-home as pot pie), rabbit, or choucroute; seafood crêpes; bouillabaisse; traditional tripe à la mode in Calvados. Here, as at the Bistro Français across the street, the daily specials are even more amazing: terrine of duck foie gras or fresh foie gras with cassis; ostrich loin wrapped in bacon; hearty choucroute with Riesling; seared sea bass with portobello-turnip risotto.

Other Recommendations: Calf's liver or brains; quenelles of pike in lobster.

Summary & Comments: Part of La Chaumière's charm is its weekly treats: Wednesday it's couscous, and Thursday, cassoulet. This is family-style food, and most of its regulars are treated like family. Actually, "regulars" is a key word here; La Chaumière hearkens back to the time when Georgetown was more neighborhood than shopping mall, and a lot of its customers feel as if they graduated into adult dinner-dating here. The fireplace is one of the area's hottest (sorry) soulful-gazing areas.

LA COLLINE

			QUALITY
French	★★★	Moderate	**84**
			VALUE
			A

400 North Capitol Street, NW
   (202) 737-0400   Zone 2, Capitol Hill

Reservations: Recommended
When to go: Anytime
Entree range: $14.50–19.75
Payment: VISA, MC, AMEX, CB, DC
Service rating: ★★★★
Friendliness rating: ★★★★
Parking: Garage, validation after 5

Bar: Full service
Wine selection: Good
Dress: Casual, elegant
Disabled access: Good
Customers: Business, local, tourist

Breakfast: Monday–Friday, 7–10 A.M.
Lunch: Monday–Friday, 11:30 A.M.–3 P.M.
Dinner: Monday–Saturday, 6–10 P.M.; Sunday and holidays, closed.

Atmosphere/Setting: An unfussy, conference-style reception room at one side is the only concession to the office-building shoebox exterior; the main dining room is large, two-tiered, and made less "executive" with nostalgic paintings, a mix of booths and tables, and French country-kitchen cupboards.

House Specialties: Foie gras and homemade pâté; lobster and shellfish fricassee; sweetbreads with wild mushrooms; tripe; cool lobster salad; stuffed quail; venison tournedos.

Other Recommendations: Roasted monkfish; crab cakes; appetizers of smoked duck breast, wild mushroom ravioli, or spicy lamb-stuffed pastries.

Summary & Comments: La Colline manages to serve old-homey French food in such quantity (and with such hospitable style) that you'd expect the quality to fall off, but somehow it never does. The quantity of business of this Senate-side favorite also keeps the prices steady. Presentation is simple and untrendy, but exact: salmon or swordfish steaks on beds of vermouth-flavored sauce, sweetbreads bull's-eyed over concentric circles of bordelaise and herb wine deglaze. Game dishes and rowdy, hearty stews, along with the organ meats most Americans are still only discovering, are always good bets.

LA CÔTE D'OR CAFE

French (Provençal) ★★½ Expensive

QUALITY
78

VALUE
C

6876 Lee Highway, Arlington
  (703) 538-3033   Zone 11B, Virginia suburbs

Reservations: Suggested
When to go: Anytime
Entree range: $18.95–24.50
Payment: VISA, MC, AMEX
Service rating: ★★★
Friendliness rating: ★★½

Parking: Street, lot
Bar: Full service
Wine selection: Good
Dress: Business, informal
Disabled access: Good
Customers: Local, business

Lunch: Monday–Saturday, 11:30 A.M.–3 P.M.
Dinner: Monday–Saturday, 5:30–11:30 P.M.; Sunday, 5:30–9 P.M.

Atmosphere/Setting: Although seeming rather out of place at first glance—a stone's throw from I-66 and associated with a motel—this is a very pretty, two-room French townhouse with armchairs, attractive but not overly formal silver and porcelain, and lots of flowers and windows. There's even a small deck for warm-weather dining, although the view is a little . . . urban.

House Specialties: Wild mushrooms with delicate duck "ham" (appetizer); grilled tuna with basil and tomato; rabbit stew with mustard sauce over pasta; entrecôte with bleu cheese sauce; loin of lamb; monkfish with mustard sauce.

Other Recommendations: Bouillabaisse with lobster and powerful aïoli; steamed mussels; scallop and shrimp soup; calamari with salmon mousse.

Summary & Comments: This menu is part traditional country French, part southern French, and occasionally old-fashion "continental," but all hearty and aromatic comfort food. Sometimes the seasoning can seem overpowering (especially if you've been gradually accustomed to "new" Americanized versions of continental food), but many people will find that one of its virtues. The message is sometimes mixed, however: Suburbanizing seems to have increased the staff's desire to seem uptown, so they can be patronizing in the way that used to give continental dining a bad name. A little more consistency from the kitchen, too, would bring in another star.

LA PROVENCE

			QUALITY
French (Provençal)	★★★½	Inexpensive	85

	VALUE
	B

144 West Maple Avenue, Vienna
(703) 242-3777   Zone 11A, Virginia suburbs

Reservations: Recommended	Parking: Free lot
When to go: Anytime	Bar: Full service
Entree range: $15.95–21.95	Wine selection: Good
Payment: VISA, MC, AMEX, D, DC	Dress: Informal
Service rating: ★★★	Disabled access: Good
Friendliness rating: ★★★	Customers: Local, ethnic

Lunch: Monday–Saturday, 11:30 A.M.–2:30 P.M.
Dinner: Monday–Saturday, 5:30–10 P.M.

Atmosphere/Setting: A surprisingly evocative little place, done up in sea-side blues and sunny yellows representing the "sun cuisine" of its Provençal fare. The intriguingly offsetting touches, such as the minimal and vaguely Asian flower arrangements (which are also practical, as they don't interfere with your vision) are a subtle reminder of the chef's Franco-Lao mindset.

House Specialties: Grilled tuna (or other fish of the day) with fresh tomatoes, anchovies, and garlic; breast of duck on a mint-flavored mousse; monkfish in a caramelized apple cider sauce with fennel; saddle of rabbit in anise; bourride, a close cousin to bouillabaisse, as well as the Pernod-flavored real thing; or a homey pot-roasted Cornish hen.

Other Recommendations: A variety of appetizers intriguing enough to make a grazing meal: calamari stuffed with herbs, duck pâté studded with pistachios, codfish mousse; roasted vegetables on semolina (like a mini-couscous) and the roasted eggplant "cake" with Roquefort cheese, pine nuts, capers, and sweet pepper.

Summary & Comments: Keo Koumtakoun, former chef at Lavandou and, until recently, chef-owner of Le Paradis, is entirely at home with the flavors of Provence (as is his French wife): basil, olives, garlic, anchovies, saffron, and fennel. But his Asian background serves even this rich style well by keeping things from being over-rich; the mint mousse, for instance, will make you blink with simple pleasure and surprise. The recipes here seem even more assured, more personalized, than at Le Paradis. This is one of the area's greatest (as yet) undiscovered pleasures.

LAFAYETTE

			QUALITY
Modern American	★★★½	Moderate	85

	VALUE
Hay-Adams Hotel, 16th and H Streets, NW	B
(202) 638-2570 Zone 3, Downtown	

Reservations: Recommended	Bar: Full service
When to go: Pretheater, lunch	Wine selection: Good
Entree range: $14.50–29.75	Dress: Business, informal
Payment: VISA, MC, AMEX, DC, CB, D	Disabled access: No
Service rating: ★★★	Customers: Business, local, tourist
Friendliness rating: ★★½	
Parking: Valet	

Breakfast: Monday–Friday, 6:30–11:30 A.M.
Brunch: Saturday and Sunday, 11:30 A.M.–2 P.M.
Lunch: Monday–Friday, 11:30 A.M.–2 P.M.
Dinner: Every day, 6–10 P.M.

Atmosphere/Setting: A pretty room, almost formal but given a lighter, "parlor-ish" warmth by a mix of armchairs and highbacks, florals, abundant flowers, and light, sunny, yellow walls. The arched windows look across Lafayette Park to the White House (the view Lincoln's secretary John Hay and his good friend Henry Adams had when their houses occupied this spot).

House Specialties: Roasted Moroccan-barbecued salmon or grilled lacquered swordfish; sautéed veal medallions with a Parmesan soufflé and artichoke puree; roasted lobster over polenta; duck terrine paired with smoked duck. There are heart-healthy options to satisfy the most reluctant dieter, such as sesame-and-ginger-crusted tuna; steamed lobster over couscous; or tomato linguine with grilled chicken.

Entertainment & Amenities: Piano music, mostly pops, during dinner.

Summary & Comments: Although chef Martin Saylor had big shoes to fill when Patrick Clark moved to New York's Tavern on the Green, his lightened-up classic cuisine fills the bill: One night's pretheater prix fixe (three courses for $30 or with two glasses of wine for $40) began with a seafood risotto that included four huge shrimp, four scallops, and four mussels, moved on to a hearty strip of salmon over couscous, and ended with a frieze of three sherbets and fresh fruit—about twice the amount of food anyone could eat.

LE LION D'OR

French   ★★★½   Expensive

QUALITY
86

VALUE
C

1150 Connecticut Avenue, NW
   (202) 296-7972   Zone 6, Dupont Circle/Adams-Morgan

Reservations: Required
When to go: Anytime
Entree range: $24–36
Payment: VISA, MC, AMEX, CB, DC
Service rating: ★★★★
Friendliness rating: ★★★
Parking: Validation for lot

Bar: Full service
Wine selection: Very good
Dress: Jacket and tie required
Disabled access: No
Customers: Local, business, tourist

Dinner: Monday–Saturday, 6–10 P.M.; Sunday, closed.

Atmosphere/Setting: Old continental-style room with leather banquettes, tableside service carts, and faience platters around the walls.

House Specialties: Whole lobster presented with pasta; lobster soufflé; rack of lamb; roast game birds. Daily specials are the key here—high interest for both parties.

Other Recommendations: Seasonal game specials, including venison, guinea hen, hare, and so on; rolled crêpes with oysters and caviar; squab; red snapper baked in a papillote of thinly sliced potatoes.

Summary & Comments: Chef/owner Jean-Pierre Goyenvalle is a Washington institution, a purveyor of the best in classic French cuisine who does not believe nouvelle is necessarily better. You might almost call him the last of an endangered species. Whole fresh fish is broiled in salt and skinned at the table; pâté is wrapped in pastry; squab and filet of lamb are pan-sautéed and simply deglazed. But classic need not be hidebound: An almost guilt-free morsel of foie gras is served in ravioli or melted over pasta. Seafood is always a fine bet.

LEGAL SEA FOODS

			QUALITY
Seafood	★★½	Moderate	**78**
			VALUE
			B

2020 K Street, NW
  (202) 496-1111   Zone 4, Foggy Bottom

2001 International Drive (Tysons Galleria), McLean
  (703) 827-8900   Zone 11A, Virginia suburbs

Reservations: Recommended
When to go: Early dinner
Entree range: $12.95–19.95
Payment: VISA, MC, AMEX, DC,
  D, CB
Service rating: ★★★
Friendliness rating: ★★★½

Parking: Valet after 5 P.M. (downtown); valet or self-park (Virginia)
Bar: Full service
Wine selection: Fair
Dress: Business, casual
Disabled access: Good
Customers: Business, local

Open: Foggy Bottom: Monday–Thursday, 11 A.M.–10:30 P.M.; Friday, 11 A.M.–11 P.M.; Saturday, noon–11 P.M.; Sunday, noon–10 P.M.; Tysons: Monday–Thursday, 11 A.M.–10 P.M.; Friday and Saturday, 11 A.M.–10:30 P.M.; Sunday, noon–9 P.M.

Atmosphere/Setting: Both have slightly upscale takes on classic Boston style, with booths, ice-packed raw bar displays, and oversized napkins. In Tysons, two long glass walls, one downstairs overlooking the mall and one upstairs opening to the outside, make it brighter and a little more cheery.

House Specialties: Smoked bluefish pâté; crab cakes; bouillabaisse; salmon in parchment; a clam chowder that was a JFK fave; steamed or crab-stuffed lobsters by weight, brushing the $70 mark; raw oysters and clams; a dozen types of fish and seafood available every day either grilled or Cajun style; crab-stuffed shrimp.

Summary & Comments: Although seafood is, as they say, their middle name (and although their rigorous oyster-testing makes the first name even more appropriate), Legal Sea Foods is also steak- and sandwich-friendly, offering porterhouse and sirloin, pork and veal chops, and surf-and-turf.

LES HALLES

			QUALITY
Steak	★★★	Moderate	**84**

VALUE: B

1201 Pennsylvania Avenue, NW
   (202) 347-6848   Zone 3, Downtown

Reservations: Accepted	Parking: Valet at dinner
When to go: Anytime	(Tuesday–Saturday after
Entree range: $14.50–20	6:30 P.M.); pay lots
Payment: VISA, MC, AMEX, DC, D	Bar: Full service
Service rating: ★★★	Wine selection: Good
Friendliness rating: ★★★½	Dress: Business, informal
Disabled access: Good	Customers: Business, local

Open: Every day, 11:30 A.M.–midnight

Atmosphere/Setting: Considering it's in a downtown office building, Les Halles manages to create quite a bit of French brasserie atmosphere, particularly thanks to the buy-your-own meat market at the lobby entrance, the old tin ceiling, and the occasional burst of song from the maître d'. The staff is very cheery, some rather more authentic than others, but quite entertaining. There are several seating areas over three levels, with the cigar smoking segregated upstairs.

House Specialties: The long, narrow cut of beef called onglet, a Parisian favorite; a classic pork loin; grilled fish of the day; a very hearty cassoulet, the stew of white beans, pork, and duck. This is the only place in town that still has steak tartare on the menu, and it's a fine, spicy version.

Other Recommendations: Romantic traditional dishes such as Caesar salad and lentils with sausage; the bistro classic skillet steak with steak fries; onion soup that reminds you why soup and salad used to be a whole meal.

Entertainment & Amenities: Cigar-smokers have their own room on the third floor. And, if you're lucky, the host may sing a little.

Summary & Comments: Although best known for its steaks ("American beef, French style," meaning less aged and more muscular than the prime beef more familiar at a Morton's), this is really a brasserie, where you can nibble on a light meal of pâté and salad and get the same attentive service you would get if you had ordered the most expensive entree. More people are beginning to prefer the assertive flavor of the beef here.

LESPINASSE

			QUALITY
Modern Continental	★★★★	Expensive	92
			VALUE
			B

Carlton Hotel, 923 16th Street, NW
  (202) 879-6900   Zone 3, Downtown

Reservations: Recommended
When to go: Anytime
Entree range: Fixed price, $65 and
  $110; à la carte, $28–36
Payment: VISA, MC, AMEX, D, DC
Service rating: ★★★★
Friendliness rating: ★★★½
Parking: Valet at dinner

Bar: Full service
Wine selection: Excellent
Dress: Business, dressy; jacket
  required
Disabled access: Good
Customers: Local gourmets and
  food-mag trendies, business

Lunch: Monday–Friday, 11:30 A.M.–2:30 P.M.
Dinner: Monday–Saturday, 6–10 P.M.

Atmosphere/Setting: One of the most beautiful rooms in Washington, rich gold and royal blue with a high, hand-painted ceiling, fleur-de-lis upholstery, broad-shouldered armchairs and plush sofas, fine china, and serious, hefty silver. The adjoining bar has also been restored to old grand-hotel splendor, with the sort of library walls and club chairs that made lobby lounges famous.

House Specialties: The chef's sampler, six nominal courses (tidbits may appear at any time) for $110 or a simpler, seasonal sampling menu for $65. There is an unusually good list of wines by the glass, and if you aren't an expert, ask sommelier Vincent Ferraut, longtime wine steward at Jean-Louis.

Other Recommendations: The à la carte list is fairly short—this is very labor-intensive cooking, after all, with beautiful presentations—but fine.

Summary & Comments: As the closing of Jean-Louis at the Watergate (and Le Pavilion before that) demonstrates, New York–style prices are hard to get in Washington, even for New York–style quality. But if any restaurant can hold to the gold standard, it's this one. The original Lespinasse in the St. Regis in Manhattan, home of cuisine star Gray Kunz, has a Mobil five-star rating (and nobody is arguing), and the Washington chef, Troy Dupuy, has been Kunz's sous-chef for many years and knows Kunz's Asian-tinged style inside and out. If this Lespinasse continues on its current course, it will almost certainly earn five stars here, too. Pastry chef Jill Rose has her own full-sized kitchen; sometimes, even if you claim not to need another bite, a tiny palette of sweet gems will come your way.

MARKET STREET BAR & GRILL

			QUALITY
Modern American	★★½	Moderate	79
			VALUE
			C

Hyatt Regency, 1800 Presidents Street, Reston
  (703) 709-6262   Zone 11A, Virginia suburbs

Reservations: Recommended	Parking: Street, garage
When to go: Anytime	Bar: Full service
Entree range: $10.95–22.75	Wine selection: Good; all domestic
Payment: VISA, MC, AMEX, DC, D	Dress: Business, informal
Service rating: ★★★★	Disabled access: Good
Friendliness rating: ★★★	Customers: Local, tourist, business

Brunch: Sunday, 10:30 A.M.–2:30 P.M.
Lunch: Monday–Friday, 11:30 A.M.–2:30 P.M.
Dinner: Monday–Thursday, 5:30–10 P.M.; Friday and Saturday,
  5:30–10:30 P.M.; Sunday, 5:30–9:30 P.M.

Atmosphere/Setting: Bright and chic, with black-and-white checks the theme (even on the staff's trousers), green marble bars, and brass trim.
House Specialties: Grilled wild boar sausage with fried green tomatoes; sautéed lobster meat with grits, leeks, and mushrooms and a warm lobster salad like an updated Niçoise; saffron and squid-ink ravioli with cheese (all appetizers); a pretty toss of lemon and black-pepper linguine with seared scallops; braised lamb shank with couscous; roast pheasant with white truffle risotto.
Other Recommendations: Grilled fish; squash risotto with rabbit sausage.
Entertainment & Amenities: Live jazz Friday through Sunday.
Summary & Comments: Having careened from too-conservative to overly ambitious and scattered, this kitchen has finally begun to find a compromise rhythm (though still paying attention to prevailing winds). This hotel restaurant provides enough trendy dishes for the pleasure diner and serves up the traditionals—prime rib, roast game hen, filet—for business diners. Seasonings are distinct without being overwhelming and the garnishes are well chosen.

MATUBA

			QUALITY
Japanese	★★★½	Inexpensive	**85**
			VALUE
			B

2915 Columbia Pike, Arlington
  (703) 521-2811   Zone 11B, Virginia suburbs
4918 Cordell Avenue, Bethesda
  (301) 652-7449   Zone 10A, Maryland suburbs

Reservations: Accepted
When to go: Monday, when many
  menu items are $1; alternate Tues-
  days for specials on sushi platters
  or teriyakis
Entree range: $6.95–16.50
Payment: VISA, MC, AMEX
Service rating: ★★★

Friendliness rating: ★★★★
Parking: Street
Bar: Beer and wine only
Wine selection: House
Dress: Casual, informal
Disabled access: Fair
Customers: Local, ethnic

Lunch: Monday–Friday, 11:30 A.M.–2:30 P.M.; Saturday, noon–3 P.M.
Dinner: Monday–Thursday, 5:30–10 P.M.; Friday and Saturday,
  5–10:30 P.M.; Sunday, 5–9:30 P.M.

Atmosphere/Setting: Small and traditional but uncomplicated, with a lot of blond wood and a few woodblock reproductions.

House Specialties: Oyaku donburi, the homey chicken-and-egg (literally, "parent and child") variation on chicken and rice stew not often seen after lunch; "wedding sushi," a marriage of scallops and shrimp; soft-shell crab tempura in season.

Other Recommendations: Unagi donburi; grilled teriyaki squid; sea urchin; grilled fresh fish.

Summary & Comments: Matuba (pronounced "MAT-su-ba") in Arlington was one of the first Japanese restaurants in the area that Japanese patrons recommended, although being honest and dependable is not always enough to keep up in such a competitive market. It's the sort of place that rewards regular attention: For unfamiliar customers, sushi portions can be small in comparison to many other bars, though the quality is high; but known faces are treated generously. Many of the custom rolls are delicious; the Alaska roll mixes smoked salmon and scallops.

MELROSE

Modern American	★★★½	Moderate	QUALITY
			87
			VALUE
			C

24th and M Streets, NW
(202) 955-3899   Zone 5, Georgetown

Reservations: Recommended
When to go: Anytime
Entree range: $21–28
Payment: VISA, MC, AMEX, CB, DC, D
Service rating: ★★★
Friendliness rating: ★★½
Parking: Valet, street

Bar: Full service
Wine selection: Good
Dress: Business, informal
Disabled access: Good
Customers: Local, business

Breakfast: Every day, 6:30–10:30 A.M.
Brunch: Sunday, 11 A.M.–2:30 P.M.
Lunch: Monday–Saturday, 11 A.M.–2:30 P.M.
Dinner: Every day, 5:30–10:30 P.M.

Atmosphere/Setting: At first glance, it's almost plain, but after so many overdecorated restaurants, it becomes soothing: a simple room, light and bright, with pastels, florals, marble, and magnificent flowers; glass walls along two sides allow diners to look out toward fountains, cafe-style umbrella tables, flowering shrubs, and the herb garden.

House Specialties: Roasted twin medallions of pepper-crusted tuna and foie gras; poached salmon with bok choy and vanilla-and-cardamom-flavored vinaigrette; and a signature dish of steamed lobster and angelhair pasta with mascarpone sauce. Among the appetizers: house-cured gravlax stuffed with crab and crème fraîche; shrimp ravioli.

Other Recommendations: Grilled seafood; duck breast with dates.

Entertainment & Amenities: A quartet for dancing on Saturday nights; no corkage fee on Sunday nights.

Summary & Comments: Chef Brian McBride has a light-bright attitude toward cooking that is a perfect match for the atmosphere here; he's especially good with seafood, which dominates the menu. His sauces are complements, not covers, and although the attitude is generally classic, his combinations often provide a gentle surprise. (Occasionally he wants to cover too many bases at once, but that's an explorer's risk.) The chef's choice is usually five courses for about $55.

MESKEREM

			QUALITY
Ethiopian	★★★½	Inexpensive	**86**
			VALUE
			A

2434 18th Street, NW
  (202) 462-4100   Zone 6, Dupont Circle/Adams-Morgan

Reservations: Suggested
When to go: Anytime
Entree range: $8.50–11.95
Payment: VISA, MC, AMEX, DC
Service rating: ★★★
Friendliness rating: ★★★

Parking: Street
Bar: Full service
Wine selection: Minimal
Dress: Casual
Disabled access: Good
Customers: Locals, tourists

Open: Sunday–Thursday, noon–midnight; Friday and Saturday, noon–1 A.M.

Atmosphere/Setting: Simple but cheerful, with "skylight" rays painted blue and white and Ethiopian-style seating (for the limber) on leather cushions at balcony basket-weave tables.

House Specialties: Kitfo (tartare with chili sauce, but it can be ordered lightly cooked, or you can have a similar hot chopped beef stew called kay watt); lamb tibbs (breast and leg meat sautéed with onions and green chiles); shrimp watt; beef or lentil and green chile sambussa (fried pastries); tikil gomen: cabbage, potatoes, and carrots in a gentle sauce.

Other Recommendations: Chicken or shrimp alicha for the spice-intimidated; zilbo (lamb and collard greens); a honey-wine version of kitfo called gored-gored.

Summary & Comments: There are three things novices need to know about Ethiopian food: First, it's eaten with the hands, using a spongy pancake called injera as plate, spoon, and napkin all in one; second, "alicha" is the name of the milder stew or curry preparation; and third, "watt" is the spicier one. Washington's many Ethiopian restaurants (there may be a dozen in Adams-Morgan alone) offer similar menus, in some cases without much distinction between stews, but Meskerem is one of the best. If you want a sampler—a tray-sized injera palette—order the "mesob" for $7.25. "Meskerem," incidentally, is the first month of the 13-month Ethiopian calendar, the one that corresponds to September, which in Ethiopia is the end of the rainy season and thus is akin to springtime.

MISS SAIGON

Vietnamese	★★½	Inexpensive	QUALITY
			79

			VALUE
			B

1847 Columbia Road, NW
   (202) 667-1900   Zone 6, Dupont Circle/Adams-Morgan
M Street, NW
   (202) 333-5545   Zone 5, Georgetown

Reservations: Helpful
When to go: Anytime
Entree range: $6.95–11.95
Payment: VISA, MC, AMEX, D, DC
Service rating: ★★
Friendliness rating: ★★★

Parking: Free lot
Bar: Full service
Wine selection: House
Dress: Casual
Disabled access: Good
Customers: Local, ethnic

Lunch/Dinner: Monday–Thursday, 11:30 A.M.–10:30 P.M.; Friday and Saturday, 11:30 A.M.–11 P.M.; Sunday, noon–10:30 P.M.

Atmosphere/Setting: The Dupont Circle branch leans more toward the Franco-Viet style, with Art Deco–cafe furniture and pink and green carpeting (plus a great view of the sidewalk life), while the Georgetown branch is more like the mother shop in Arlington, with lots of greenery and wood.

House Specialties: A spectacular soup with quail, shiitake mushrooms, and noodles and topped with bits of pork fat; roast quail by itself as an appetizer; a good version of pho (though without all the options available at a pure pho house); egg noodles topped with oyster sauce–flavored seafood.

Other Recommendations: Pumpkin in coconut-milk curry; hearty "hot pots"; beef in grape leaves.

Summary & Comments: Thanks to their trendier locations, these two offspring of Arlington's Little Viet Garden have outstripped their parent in publicity; similarly, though the family resemblance is clear from the menu, there are some flashier dishes here. And to be frank, every new generation seems to be a little better—the Georgetown kitchen is the best. Vegetarians will be happy as well; like more and more savvy Asian restaurants, the Misses Saigon are using not only their noodles, but their mock goose and veggie duck to attract health- and animal-conscious diners.

MORRISON-CLARK INN

Modern American	★★★	Moderate	QUALITY
			83
			VALUE
			B

1015 L Street, NW (Massachusetts and 11th)
  (202) 898-1200   Zone 3, Downtown

Reservations: Recommended	Parking: Valet
When to go: Anytime	Bar: Full service
Entree range: $16.50–21.50	Wine selection: Good
Payment: VISA, MC, AMEX, DC, D	Dress: Business; coat and tie
Service rating: ★★★	Disabled access: No
Friendliness rating: ★★★	Customers: Local, business

Brunch: Sunday, 11:30 A.M.–2 P.M.
Lunch: Monday–Friday, 11:30 A.M.–2 P.M.
Dinner: Monday–Thursday, 6–9:30 P.M.; Friday and Saturday,
  6–10 P.M.; Sunday, 6–9 P.M.

Atmosphere/Setting: For many years, this was the home of a Civil War–era government supplier, and in the late 19th century it was purchased by a traveler who added a Chinese Chippendale porch and Shanghai mansard roof. In the '20s, it was the Soldiers, Sailors, Marines and Airmen's Club, and the furnishings somehow pay tribute to all that old seafaring romance—Victorian mixed with chinoiserie that recalls the tea trade, brightened with sunny yellow wallpaper and made gracious by marble fireplaces. The combination sort of suits the menu, too, which is mostly old-fashioned but with the occasional Eastern spice.

House Specialties: Loin of rabbit stuffed with greens and topped with a whiskey sauce; curry-flour-dusted catfish in tomato-sherry sauce; lemon-chive pasta with asparagus and poached salmon (lunch); calamari in fennel and orange sauce; shrimp however prepared.

Other Recommendations: Hearty but not heavy meat dishes, such as marinated pork chop with adobe sauce or rack of lamb rubbed with balsamic vinegar.

Summary & Comments: Chef Susan McCreight Lindeborg is interested in recasting traditional foods, particularly Southern ones, in a modern light—cornmeal-fried catfish with black-eyed peas and corn relish; herb-studded biscuits with country ham; chicken smothered in mustard gravy. (Obviously, "light" is not a pun here.)

MORTON'S OF CHICAGO

			QUALITY
Steak	★★★½	Expensive	**89**
			VALUE
			B

3251 Prospect Street, NW
  (202) 342-6258   Zone 5, Georgetown

Connecticut and L Streets, NW
  (202) 955-5997   Zone 3, Downtown

8075 Leesburg Pike (Fairfax Square Shopping Center), Tysons Corner
  (703) 883-0800   Zone 11A, Virginia suburbs

Reservations: Recommended	Bar: Full service
When to go: Early for prime rib	Wine selection: Good
Entree range: $19.95–49.95	Dress: Business, dressy
Payment: VISA, MC, AMEX, CB, DC	Disabled access: Prospect Street, fair;
Service rating: ★★★	downtown and Leesburg Pike,
Friendliness rating: ★★★	good
Parking: Valet	Customers: Business, local, tourist

Lunch: Monday–Friday, 11:30 A.M.–2 P.M. (Virginia and downtown only)

Dinner: Monday–Saturday, 5:30–11 P.M.; Sunday, 5–10 P.M.

Atmosphere/Setting: These loud, brash gentlemen's club–cum-chophouses with LeRoy Neiman sports art and carts of raw meat rolling around are almost as much a competition as a dining experience. And, with the vigor of the bartending, waiting for a table (likely even with a reservation) is also a test of endurance.

House Specialties: Porterhouse; smoked salmon; lobsters by the pound; the broiled veal chop that is becoming a steakhouse standard.

Other Recommendations: Swordfish; lamb chops.

Summary & Comments: This is the original cholesterol test, steak as straight as it comes, and as prime as it comes. Prime rib is one of the signature dishes here, but some people never make it in time, as it sells out early in the evening. Another special is the 48-ounce "double porterhouse" for couples, family groups, or *Guinness Book* aspirants. All the classics are here—New York strip, filet mignon so large it belies the name, Delmonico —and the vegetables are just as predictable: mountainous baked potatoes, spinach, tomatoes (problematic), asparagus. In classic old-boys' style, Morton's offers minicatalogs of cigars, single-malt Scotches, and more than three dozen types of martinis: After all, if you're going to hit the artery superhighway, you might as well go first-class.

Note: For disabled access at the Tysons Corner location, tell the valet to notify the dining staff that you will be using the elevator.

NEW HEIGHTS

				QUALITY
Modern American		★★★½	Moderate	**88**
				VALUE
				C

2317 Calvert Street, NW
(202) 234-4110   Zone 6, Dupont Circle/Adams-Morgan

Reservations: Recommended
When to go: Anytime
Entree range: $17–25
Payment: VISA, MC, AMEX, DC, D
Service rating: ★★½
Friendliness rating: ★★★

Parking: Valet
Bar: Full service
Wine selection: Good
Dress: Informal, business
Disabled access: Fair
Customers: Local

Brunch: Sunday, 11 A.M.–2:30 P.M.
Dinner: Sunday–Thursday, 5:30–10 P.M.; Friday and Saturday,
5:30–11 P.M.

Atmosphere/Setting: A small Woodley Park townhouse simply decorated and opened up to take advantage of the light and the glorious view down Connecticut Avenue to Dupont Circle.

House Specialties: The menu changes seasonally, but typical dishes include bouillabaisse with lemongrass; Provençal brandade of salt cod with tomatoes and truffle oil; lobster flan with wild mushrooms; pan-roasted pheasant with coffee barbecue.

Other Recommendations: Marlin "layered" traditional Japanese style with miso and pearl rice; poached salmon with roast mushrooms and artichokes.

Summary & Comments: This is a back-to–modern basics kitchen with an Asian slant and an even bigger Mediterranean wanderlust. Even nicer, several of the entrees can be ordered in appetizer portions. Some people find its eclecticism off-putting, but currently it's strongly on track: Chef Matthew Lake was named one of the ten most promising chefs of 1996 by *Food & Wine* magazine. In fact, the owner here, Umbi Singh, has a great eye for chefs and a willingness to give them room to stretch; Lake is the fifth success story here, following Alison Swope (Sante Fe East, Stella's), Melissa Balinger (Clyde's group corporate chef), Greggory Hill (Gabriel), and Dean Winning (Red Sage, the Turning Point Inn).

NORA

Modern American	★★★	Moderate	QUALITY
			80
			VALUE
			C

2132 Florida Avenue, NW
(202) 462-5143   Zone 6, Dupont Circle/Adams-Morgan

Reservations: Recommended	Parking: Street, valet
When to go: Anytime	Bar: Full service
Entree range: $18.95–25.95	Wine selection: Good
Payment: VISA, MC	Dress: Business, casual
Service rating: ★★★½	Disabled access: No
Friendliness rating: ★★★★	Customers: Locals

Dinner: Monday–Thursday, 6–10 P.M.; Friday and Saturday, 6–10:30 P.M.; Sunday, closed

Atmosphere/Setting: A pretty corner townhouse with exposed brick walls and a gallery of handicrafts, quilt pieces, and faux naif art in the dining rooms; an enclosed greenhouse balcony in the rear is the prettiest area.

House Specialties: The menu changes frequently, but look for shellfish, such as a lobster-shellfish pan roast; organ meats from additive-free animals; seared squab or tuna appetizers; home-cured gravlax or trout; veal or lamb; honey-and-spice-glazed pheasant; roasted salmon; vegetarian platters.

Summary & Comments: Nora, the neighborhood hangout of the Dupont Circle A and B lists, was haute organic before organic was chic. The back of the menu, which changes daily, lists the specific farms where the meat, produce, dairy products, and eggs—naturally low in cholesterol, according to the supplier—are raised. Nora's own all-edible flower and herb garden alongside the restaurant is indicative. The cost of acquiring such specialized ingredients is passed on, but not unreasonably. Nora was also ahead of the crowd by introducing alternative grains and pastas, and it was the first restaurant to make lentils that didn't taste like a Zen penance. Its only drawback is an odd tendency to weightiness—the meals sometimes feel heartier than they taste. Now that the Clintons and Gores have been publicized dining here, it may become more of a tourist attraction.

OBELISK

			QUALITY
Italian	★★★½	Expensive	**89**
			VALUE
			B

2029 P Street, NW

  (202) 872-1180   Zone 6, Dupont Circle/Adams-Morgan

Reservations: Recommended	Parking: Street
When to go: Anytime	Bar: Full service
Entree range: Prix fixe only, about $40	Wine selection: Good
	Dress: Business, informal
Payment: VISA, MC, DC	Disabled access: No
Service rating: ★★★	Customers: Local, business
Friendliness rating: ★★★½	

Dinner: Monday–Saturday, 6–10 P.M.; Sunday, closed.

Atmosphere/Setting: A tiny room that's elegant and good-humored; the customers, staff, and accoutrements—not only the room's floral centerpiece and silver chest but the astonishingly light breadsticks and bottles of grappa—work intimately elbow to elbow.

House Specialties: Chef Peter Pastan has figured out the cure for overlong, overrich menus—he offers a fixed-price menu, four to five courses with only two, maybe three, choices per course. Among typical antipasti: marinated anchovies and fennel; artichokes with goat cheese; caramel-soft onion and cheese tart; crostini; a thick soup; quail terrine; crispy fried cheese; polenta with Gorgonzola; potato or rice balls. The *primi* course is apt to be seafood or pasta (red pepper noodles with crab and pungent chive blossoms; gnocchi with pesto; wheat noodles with rabbit ragout) or soup; the *secondi*, veal (particularly tenderloin prepared with artichokes or chanterelles), fish (pompano with olives; black sea bass with grilled radicchio), or perhaps game bird or a mixed grill. After that comes a fine bit of cheese, with or without a dessert course following. Whatever the price—it varies with the daily menu—it's a quality bargain in this town.

Summary & Comments: Pastan's hand is so deft he doesn't need to overdress anything; sauces are more like glazes, and pungent ingredients—olives, pine nuts, garlic, and greens—are perfectly proportioned to their dish. Above all, it shows the value of letting a chef who knows exactly what he likes do as he likes. Pastan, who also owns Pizzeria Paradiso next door, is co-owner of the new Blue Plate.

OLD ANGLER'S INN

Modern American   ★★★½   Expensive

QUALITY
89

VALUE
C

10801 MacArthur Boulevard, Potomac
(301) 299-9097   Zone 10B, Maryland suburbs

Reservations: Required
When to go: Anytime
Entree range: $23–30
Payment: VISA, MC, AMEX, DC
Service rating: ★★★
Friendliness rating: ★★★
Parking: Free lot

Bar: Full service
Wine selection: Brief
Dress: Dressy, business, jacket
and tie
Disabled access: No
Customers: Locals

Brunch: Sunday, noon–2:30 P.M.
Lunch: Tuesday–Saturday, noon–2:30 P.M.
Dinner: Tuesday–Friday, 6–10:30 P.M.; Saturday, 5:30–10:30 P.M.;
Sunday, 5:30–9:30 P.M.; Monday, closed.

Atmosphere/Setting: A beautiful, old-fashioned inn above the river, with a blazing fireplace in the parlor bar downstairs and a huddle of small dining rooms up a narrow iron spiral staircase (and bathrooms out of the servants' quarters). The stone terrace and gazebo levels are open in good weather.

House Specialties: Ostrich and venison; lobster; buttery (but butterless) pumpkin soup or asparagus bisque with lump crabmeat; roast monkfish with macadamia crust; stuffed grilled quail or Cornish hen; rabbit sausage with couscous; shrimp with a fresh, coarse salsa; roast pheasant with spinach spaetzle.

Summary & Comments: This has always been a beautiful site, but years of haphazard service and pretentious, overpriced food had nearly ruined Old Angler's reputation. (The wine list is still underconsidered.) But under chef Jeffrey Tomchek, this has settled down to a consistently satisfying, unobtrusively healthful kitchen, light on butters and creams but big on flavor and contrast. Altogether, Tomchek is pushing close on his fourth star. Improv is close to Tomchek's heart: Upon request, the kitchen will provide a much more intriguing, five-course tasting dinner for $55 a head (or seven courses for $75), which you may request with all or no seafood, red meat, etc. One all-vegetarian version included a butternut squash ravioli, potato-cheese soup, and beautifully orchestrated mixed salad with truffles.

OLD EBBITT GRILL

			QUALITY
American	★★★	Moderate	**80**

	VALUE
	C

675 15th Street, NW
  (202) 347-4801   Zone 3, Downtown

Reservations: Recommended
When to go: Sunday brunch; after
  work for power-tripping
Entree range: $9.95–14.95
Payment: VISA, MC, AMEX, DC, D
Service rating: ★★★
Friendliness rating: ★★★
Parking: Pay lots (validated after
  6 P.M.)

Bar: Full service
Wine selection: Good
Dress: Business, informal
Disabled access: Very good (through
  G Street atrium)
Customers: Business, feds, locals,
  tourists

Breakfast: Monday–Friday, 7:30–11 A.M.; Saturday, 8–11:30 A.M.
Brunch: Sunday, 9:30 A.M.–4 P.M.
Lunch/Dinner: Monday–Saturday, 11 A.M.–midnight; Sunday,
  4 P.M.–midnight

Atmosphere/Setting: An updated old-boys' club, but with equal opportunity hospitality: a few horsey accoutrements (bridles, snaffles) in front, lots of greenery and etched glass dividers in the main room, and a classic oyster bar.

House Specialties: Linguine with shrimp, basil, and fresh tomatoes; pork chops with homemade applesauce; black pepper–rubbed leg of lamb with papaya relish; old-fashioned pepperpot beef; steamed mussels; smoked salmon (a company signature) and smoked bluefish when available. Annually, during the brief halibut season in Alaska, the Old Ebbitt and its Clyde's cousins have a halibut celebration that is a command performance for seafood lovers. For brunch, fat old-style French toast and corned beef hash.

Entertainment & Amenities: Occasional piano music at happy hour.

Summary & Comments: This is one restaurant whose whole experience is somehow better than the food might indicate by itself. The Old Ebbitt— actually, the new Old Ebbitt for those who remember the fusty Back Bay–style original around the corner and its stuffed owls and scuffed bar rails—takes its White House neighborhood location seriously, but not too seriously. That is, it gives out pagers to patrons waiting for tables, but the staff democratically seats the ties and T-shirts side by side.

OLD GLORY

			QUALITY
Barbecue	★★½	Moderate	**78**

	VALUE
	B

3139 M Street, NW
  (202) 337-3406   Zone 5, Georgetown

Reservations: Parties of 6 or more
  only, for lunch or weekday dinner
When to go: Afternoon
Entree range: $6.25–14.95
Payment: VISA, MC, AMEX, D, DC
Service rating: ★★½
Friendliness rating: ★★★

Parking: Pay lots, street
Bar: Full service
Wine selection: Minimal
Dress: Casual, informal
Disabled access: Good
Customers: Local, tourist

Brunch: Sunday, 11 A.M.–3 P.M.
Lunch/Dinner: Monday–Thursday, 11:30 A.M.–1:30 A.M.; Friday and
  Saturday, 11:30 A.M.–2:30 A.M.; Sunday, 11 A.M.–1:30 A.M.; late-night
  menu available every day, 11:30 P.M. until close

Atmosphere/Setting: A chic and cheeky take on roadhouse diner decor
with a sort of Six Flags theme: The state colors of Tennessee, Texas, Georgia, Kentucky, Kansas (which used to be Arkansas), and the Carolinas hang
overhead, while each table is armed with bottles of six different barbecue
sauces—mild, sweet, vinegary, multi-chili'd, mustardy, tomatoey—named
for the same six states. A mix of old and new country and honky-tonk
music plays on the PA.
House Specialties: Pork ribs or beef short ribs; "pulled" (shredded rather
than chopped) pork shoulder; smoked chicken; grilled summer sausages;
smoked ham; and various combinations or sandwich versions thereof.
Daily specials often include pit-fired steaks or fresh seafood.
Other Recommendations: Pit-grilled burgers with cheddar and smoked
bacon; marinated and grilled skewered vegetables; hot barbecued shrimp.
Entertainment & Amenities: Live music Tuesday, Thursday, and Saturday.
Summary & Comments: This trendy finger-lickers' stop is surprisingly
good, particularly when it comes to the sort of Southern side dishes that
rarely travel well. The biscuits are fine (the cornbread isn't) and the hoppin' John—black-eyed peas and rice—is better than authentic; it's neither
mushy nor greasy.

PIZZERIA PARADISO

			QUALITY
Pizza	★★★	Inexpensive	**83**
			VALUE
			A

2029 P Street, NW
   (202) 223-1245   Zone 6, Dupont Circle/Adams-Morgan

Reservations: Not accepted
When to go: Anytime except about
   8–10 P.M.
Entree range: $5.50–15.95
Payment: VISA, MC, DC
Service rating: ★★★
Friendliness rating: ★★★

Parking: Street
Bar: Beer and wine
Wine selection: Limited
Dress: Casual
Disabled access: No
Customers: Local, tourist, student

Open: Monday–Thursday, 11 A.M.–11 P.M.; Friday and Saturday,
   11 A.M.–midnight; Sunday, noon–10 P.M.

Atmosphere/Setting: As tiny as this upper room is, it's hilariously decorated, with trompe l'oeil stone walls opening at the "ruined roof" to a blue sky; columns with capitals of papier-mâché veggies; a wood-burning stove painted like a smokestack; and semi-impressionistic painted cardboard pizzas like Amish hexes around the walls (a sly comment on the mass-market competition, perhaps?).

House Specialties: Pizzas with four cheeses or "the atomica," with salami, black olives, and hot peppers; zucchini, eggplant, peppers, and fresh buffalo mozzarella; mussels (surprisingly, yes); and potato with pesto sauce and Parmesan.

Other Recommendations: Thick sandwiches made with focaccia, including roast lamb and roasted veggies, as well as multimeat Italian subs and pork with hot peppers.

Summary & Comments: It may seem extravagant to give such high marks to a pizzeria, but pizza this good—shoveled in and out of the deep oven, with a splash of extra-virgin olive oil and a handful of cheese tossed on at the last moment—makes most American takeout blush. It's almost a redefinition of pizza. This restaurant also has real attitude—not commercial camp, just an irresistible New Wave nonchalance. No larger than its next-door sibling, Obelisk, Pizzeria Paradiso shoehorns them in and rolls them out at an astonishing but validating rate.

PROVENCE

French (Provençal)	★★★½	Moderate	QUALITY
			87
			VALUE
			C

2401 Pennsylvania Avenue, NW
  (202) 296-1166   Zone 6, Dupont Circle/Adams-Morgan

Reservations: Recommended
When to go: Lunch
Entree range: $18.95–29.95
Payment: VISA, MC, AMEX, DC, CB
Service rating: ★★½
Friendliness rating: ★★★
Parking: Pay lot, valet at dinner

Bar: Full service
Wine selection: Good
Dress: Business, informal
Disabled access: Good
Customers: Local, business, tourist

Lunch: Monday–Friday, noon–2 P.M.
Dinner: Monday–Thursday, 6–10 P.M.; Friday and Saturday,
  5:30–11:30 P.M.; Sunday, 5:30–9:30 P.M.

Atmosphere/Setting: Aristo-rustic, with huge windows, flagstone flooring, dried flowers, artfully weathered hutches, iron trellises, shutters, and trompe l'oeil stonework—a sunny French South villa of a fashion magazine's dreams.

House Specialties: Grilled langoustines (appetizer), squid stuffed with lavender or wild mushrooms, hare-stuffed ravioli, grilled monkfish with anchovies, grilled squab with capers, grilled lobsters with truffle oil, pheasant with figs, rolled stuffed loin of rabbit, stewed veal tongue, whole fish with fennel seed. Daily specials are particularly good but can be extremely pricey, too.

Summary & Comments: This Provençal haven is the creation of local star chef Yannick Cam, first of the cutting-edge nouvelle French, Le Pavillion, and now co-owner of the Brazilian Coco Loco and the regional Spanish El Catalan. Unfortunately, such intellectual and culinary restlessness means that Cam doesn't keep his finger in the sauce as often as might be desired. But in most ways, this is truly an indulgent experience. Its heavy reliance on grilling, aromatic herbs, chard, figs, and citrus is evidence of the close relationship between Tuscan and Provençal cooking—and just because Mediterranean food is trendy doesn't mean it can't be good for you. If you like real hearty, garlicky seafood dishes, Cam has a bourride for you, a seafood stew with aïoli. Execution is somewhat erratic, and service can be wildly condescending, but when it's good, it's very, very good.

RAKU: AN ASIAN GRILL

			QUALITY
Pan Asian	★★★	Inexpensive	**82**
			VALUE
			A

1900 Q Street, NW
   (202) 265-7258   Zone 6, Dupont Circle/Adams-Morgan

7240 Woodmont Avenue, Bethesda
   (301) 718-8680   Zone 10A, Maryland suburbs

Reservations: Not accepted	Parking: Street, lot
When to go: Anytime	Bar: Wine, beer, and Japanese saké
Entree range: $6.50–8.75	Wine selection: Limited
Payment: VISA, MC	Dress: Business, casual
Service rating: ★★★	Disabled access: Good
Friendliness rating: ★★★	Customers: Hip local, tourist

Open: D.C.: Monday–Thursday, 11:30 A.M.–11 P.M.; Friday and
Saturday, 11:30 A.M.–midnight; Sunday, 11:30 A.M.–10 P.M.; Bethesda:
Sunday–Thursday, 11:30 A.M.–10 P.M.; Friday and Saturday,
11:30 A.M.–11 P.M.

Atmosphere/Setting: A very lively, loud crowd in a chic, cheeky, modern
Asian mix, with bamboo shades, Asian music and videos, slate floors, all-
exhibition cooking on grills, and dumpling steamers imported from Japan.
Some tables are communal (i.e., family-style), as they are in Japan; or you
can sit at the "bar" right across from the grill. Glass walls slide back for
deck-style sidewalk dining in Dupont Circle.

House Specialties: "Peking duck" dumplings, wrapped in Vietnamese rice
papers instead of moo shi pancakes; gyoza, dumplings simultaneously
steamed and griddled; a very light and cooling mound of organic soba
noodles with dipping sauce; Indonesian satays; noodle soups.

Other Recommendations: Korean chile-fired strips of beef in broth and,
for the fat-fearless, coconut curries and shrimp-paste "lollipops" on sugar
cane.

Entertainment & Amenities: Sidewalk cafe seating in Dupont Circle.

Summary & Comments: Creator Mark Miller of Coyote Cafe fame calls
these first of a projected national chain (outlets in New York and San Fran-
cisco so far) alternatives to business delis and carryouts, with "fast, fun, and
flavorful foods." Nothing will take more than five minutes to prepare, and
the entire menu is nondairy and low-fat except for deep-fried foods, which
are even made with low-saturated oil. The menu is divided into five food
groups: noodle dishes, "wrapped" dishes, skewered foods, fried foods, and
desserts. And three broths, one traditional pork and chicken, one seaweed,
and one coconut, allow vegans, vegetarians, and carnivores to dine together.

RED SAGE

			QUALITY
New Southwestern	★★★★	Expensive	**94**
			VALUE
			B

605 14th Street, NW
  (202) 638-4444   Zone 3, Downtown

Reservations: Essential for dining room; not accepted in chili bar	Parking: Pay lots (validated)
When to go: Anytime	Bar: Full service
Entree range: $19–36	Wine selection: Good
Payment: VISA, MC, AMEX, DC, D	Dress: Dressy, informal
Service rating: ★★★	Disabled access: Excellent
Friendliness rating: ★★★	Customers: Local, tourist, gourmet mag groupies

Lunch: Monday–Friday, 11:30 A.M.–2:15 P.M.; Chili bar: Monday–Friday, 11:30 A.M.–11:30 P.M.

Dinner: Monday–Thursday, 5:30–9:45 P.M.; Friday and Saturday, 5:30–10:30 P.M.; Sunday, 5–9:45 P.M.; Chili bar: Saturday, 5:30–midnight; Sunday, 4:30–11:30 P.M.

Atmosphere/Setting: A fun and funny $5-million-plus New Wave slant on Santa Fe chic, with cast-iron lizard door handles, plaster clouds with "lightning" in the chili bar, and $100,000 worth of glass etched with campfires and broncos.

House Specialties: Wild mushroom–Swiss chard ravioli; cinnamon-smoked or roasted quail with pecans and ham; wood-roasted duck; house-smoked salmon or tuna carpaccio with habanero pesto; bourbon rabbit; a vegetarian plate with poblano tamales and wood-roasted mushrooms; sausage of the day (venison, duck, rabbit, even wild boar); venison chili in the chili bar.

Other Recommendations: The Cubana Torta, griddled pork loin with ham and cheese; blue cornmeal oysters. At lunch, the upstairs cafe has a choice of fascinating salads, small chic pizzas, four flavors of rotisserie chicken, etc.

Summary & Comments: After the biggest preopening ballyhoo of the decade, and the inevitable deflation, Red Sage has found its feet, and its heat, gloriously. The roasted-chiles cuisine made famous by owner Mark Miller is a pungent panoply rather than a painful blur; each dish is seasoned with just the right flavor of pepper and to just the right degree, so that you are constantly astonished by the nuances. All meats and game are steroid-free.

RIO GRANDE CAFE

			QUALITY
Tex-Mex	★★½	Moderate	**78**
			VALUE
			C

4919 Fairmont Avenue, Bethesda
  (301) 656-2981   Zone 10A, Maryland suburbs

4301 North Fairfax Drive, Ballston
  (703) 528-3131   Zone 11B, Virginia suburbs

1827 Library Street (Reston Town Center), Reston
  (703) 904-0703   Zone 11B, Virginia suburbs

Reservations: Not accepted	Friendliness rating: ★★★½
When to go: Thursday for goat; early or late dinner	Parking: Street
	Bar: Full service
Entree range: $7.25–16.50	Wine selection: House
Payment: VISA, MC, AMEX, CB, DC, D	Dress: Casual
	Disabled access: Good
Service rating: ★★½	Customers: Local, tourist

Open: Monday–Thursday, 11 A.M.–10:30 P.M.; Friday, 11 A.M.–11:30 P.M.; Saturday, 11:30 A.M.–11:30 P.M.; Sunday, 11:30 A.M.–10:30 P.M.

Atmosphere/Setting: Cheeky tortilla warehouse with crates of Southwestern beer on the floor, exposed industrial ducts overhead, jokey "native" art (and even jokier graffiti on the bright walls, which is unfortunately reminiscent of South of the Border billboards), and an improbably torturous Rube Goldberg of a tortilla machine grinding out the pancakes.

House Specialties: Cabrito, barbecued baby goat and goat ribs, available only on Thursdays; grilled quail; chiles rellenos.

Other Recommendations: Frog legs; grilled shrimp; enchiladas.

Summary & Comments: Rio Grande may not have invented the frozen-margarita-in-a-machine technique, but they perfected it and got a pretty good recipe going, too. You almost never have to wait for a refill—which is a good thing, since you may be waiting for a table. On the other hand, it may make you feel as if you're drinking on an assembly line.

ROCKLANDS

			QUALITY
Barbecue	★★★	Inexpensive	**80**
			VALUE
			C

2418 Wisconsin Avenue, NW
(202) 333-2558   Zone 5, Georgetown
4000 North Fairfax Drive, Arlington
(703) 528-9663   Zone 11B, Virginia suburbs

Reservations: Not accepted	Parking: Limited street meters
When to go: Afternoon, late dinner	Bar: None
Entree range: $3.95–15.75	Wine selection: None
Payment: AMEX	Dress: Casual
Service rating: ★★½	Disabled access: No
Friendliness rating: ★★★	Customers: Locals

Open: Georgetown: Monday–Saturday, 11:30 A.M.–10 P.M.; Sunday, 11 A.M.–9 P.M.; Arlington: Monday and Tuesday, 11:30 A.M.–9 P.M.; Wednesday, 11:30 A.M.–10 P.M.; Thursday, 11:30 A.M.–11 P.M.; Friday, 11:30 A.M.–midnight; Saturday, 11 A.M.–11 P.M.; Sunday, 11 A.M.–9 P.M.

Atmosphere/Setting: Its small storefront size, and the fact that most of the room is taken up by pit space, kitchen, and grill, mean that this is authentically a stand-up or bolt-and-carryout spot; there's only one communal service table and six or eight stools at the window counter, and the food is served in burger-shop paper dishes. The primary decor is supplied by the two wall cabinets of trendy pepper and super-hot chili sauces, chutneys, etc. The Arlington branch is really the kitchen partner of an auto dealership–turned–billiard parlor called, appropriately, the Car Pool.

House Specialties: Chopped-pork sandwiches (actually almost everything, including the marinated sliced lamb loin, trout, and catfish, except the ribs and chicken wings, is served as a sandwich); racks in quarter, half, and full sizes; and frequently "exotic" meats or fresh fish such as salmon and swordfish.

Other Recommendations: Most of the old-style side dishes, such as the greens (mustard, turnip, etc., available in pints and quarts), potato salad, slaw, fresh green beans, and red beans and rice are very good. The corn pudding is more like Stovetop Stuffing, although there are those who swear by the Caesar salad. A yuppie-ish side dish, perhaps, and one that seems to go strangely with the crew, but hey, this is Glover Park, after all.

Summary & Comments: Amid the tidal wave of authentic (and only "authentic-style") pit barbecue, Rocklands might be considered a nouveau-retro meat counter, attracting both barbecue heads and food trendies. Owner John Snedden not only stocks a huge selection of super-hot chili sauces—and sets out several at a time for taste-testing—but he also likes to serve up meats more interesting than the usual pig. He's experimented with elk, boar, venison, and ostrich, and he often throws out a whole carcass (of whatever) as happy-hour fare.

SAM & HARRY'S

			QUALITY
Steak	★★★	Expensive	**84**
			VALUE
			C

1200 19th Street, NW
(202) 296-4333   Zone 6, Dupont Circle/Adams-Morgan

Reservations: Recommended
When to go: Anytime
Entree range: $19–31.95
Payment: VISA, MC, AMEX, CB, DC, D
Service rating: ★★★★
Friendliness rating: ★★★★

Parking: Street, lot, valet (dinner only)
Bar: Full service
Wine selection: Very good
Dress: Business, dressy
Disabled access: Good
Customers: Business, local

Lunch: Monday–Friday, 11:30 A.M.–2:30 P.M.
Dinner: Monday–Saturday, 5:30–10:30 P.M.; Sunday, closed.

Atmosphere/Setting: Dark columns and woodwork pun on (or provide protective camouflage for) the silk-stocking law and lobby firms that surround this expense-account parlor; glass and French doors make seating flexible.

House Specialties: The signature steak is a two-inch-thick New York strip, and there is also a two-pound Delmonico house favorite; also, prime rib, lobsters in the three- to four-pound range, and crab cakes. Sam & Harry's has an amazing special between Fourth of July and Labor Day: Every bottle of wine in the cellar is half-price on Friday and Saturday nights.

Other Recommendations: Veal T-bones; shrimp and scallop salad (lunch only).

Summary & Comments: Modeled on Morton's of Chicago, where one of the owners once worked, Sam & Harry's serves everything in giant portions, including triple-sized salads and baked potatoes the size of small pets. The staff is so used to splitting meals, even those potatoes, that they sometimes bring extra plates without waiting for you to ask—and you'll still need a doggie bag. Potatoes are offered in six or seven versions. Salads offer a little variety, too; one features goat cheese, apples, pecans, and endive. Play to the kitchen's strength; don't expect too much of the fish here.

SEA CATCH

			QUALITY
Seafood	★★★	Moderate	**83**

	VALUE
	B

1054 31st Street, NW
  (202) 337-8855   Zone 5, Georgetown

Reservations: Recommended	Parking: Valet
When to go: Early	Bar: Full service
Entree range: $15.75–23	Wine selection: Good
Payment: VISA, MC, AMEX, DC, D	Dress: Casual, business
Service rating: ★★★	Disabled access: Good
Friendliness rating: ★★½	Customers: Local, business

Lunch: Monday–Saturday, noon–3 P.M.
Dinner: Monday–Saturday, 5:30–10:30 P.M.; Sunday, closed.

Atmosphere/Setting: Sleekly elegant, with a white marble raw bar, polished-wood dining room with fireplace and, in good weather, a balcony overlooking the Chesapeake and Ohio Canal.

House Specialties: House-smoked salmon and big-eye tuna; lobster specials, such as medallions over fettuccine or steamed lobster, mussels, oysters, clams, and shrimp; shrimp with saffron; soft-shell crabs with pesto; scallops with black olive and tomato tapenade; the low-fat, catfish-flavored Amazon fish called pirarucu.

Other Recommendations: A personal "off the menu" favorite is the lobster sashimi, which is only available when the raw bar isn't too busy.

Summary & Comments: This is an underrated seafood establishment particularly ideal for people who suffer from fear of frying. The key here is balance: The kitchen likes to play with its presentations, but not to the point where the quality or texture of the shellfish is obscured. Those who prefer the straighter stuff may order lobster steamed, grilled, broiled, baked, or poached; a variety of fresh fish (there is no freezer in the kitchen, proof of the chef's dedication to freshness) brushed with oil and grilled; or an updated surf-and-turf of tenderloin and crab-stuffed mushrooms. However, for dedicated carnivores, the Thai-marinated roast chicken or the steaks are very dependable. There is also a pretheater menu for $18.95.

SEASONS

					QUALITY
Modern American		★★★★		Expensive	**93**
					VALUE
					B

Four Seasons Hotel, 2800 Pennsylvania Avenue
  (202) 944-2000   Zone 5, Georgetown

Reservations: Recommended	Parking: Valet (validated)
When to go: Anytime	Bar: Full service
Entree range: $19.97–34	Wine selection: Very good
Payment: VISA, MC, AMEX, DC	Dress: Business, informal
Service rating: ★★★★	Disabled access: Good
Friendliness rating: ★★★	Customers: Business, tourist, local

Breakfast: Monday–Friday, 7–11 A.M.; Saturday and Sunday, 8–noon
Lunch: Monday–Friday, noon–2:30 P.M.
Dinner: Daily, 6–10:30 P.M.

Atmosphere/Setting: A classic grand-hotel dining room as far as service and setting is concerned, but with lots of plants to up the intimacy level.

House Specialties: The menu changes almost constantly, but characteristic dishes include wild mushroom ravioli, carpaccio with sun-dried tomato tapenade, duck foie gras with apple and grape compotes, mushroom and barley-stuffed quail or richly colored grilled vegetable terrine (all appetizers); loin of rabbit with braised endive and tangerines; loin of venison with porcini risotto; crispy oriental duck with ginger–stir fried vegetables; grilled Chilean bass with tapenade.

Summary & Comments: It's almost incomprehensible that chef Doug McNeill, who can maintain a suitably MOR hotel menu while investing it with so much interest, could be so under-celebrated in his own city except by his industry peers. (He's so admired by some more critically acclaimed chefs, in fact, that it recalls the old saying, "Plagiarism is the sincerest form of flattery.") It's also hard to imagine a place that has introduced more consumer-friendly ideas, such as the long list of moderately priced good wines by the glass, the business-oriented "$19.97 express lunch," and really good vegetarian and low-cal/low-fat/low-sodium dishes. In fact, this was one of the first restaurants in Washington to put any real thought into alternative cuisine. The chef's tasting dinner for $55 is a must.

SEVEN SEAS

			QUALITY
Chinese	★★★½	Moderate	**85**

VALUE
B

1776 East Jefferson Street (1776 Plaza Shopping Center),
   Rockville (301) 770-5020   Zone 10B, Maryland suburbs

Reservations: Only for 5 or more
When to go: Early on weekends
Entree range: $9.95–25
Payment: VISA, MC, AMEX, D
Service rating: ★★★
Friendliness rating: ★★½

Parking: Free lot
Bar: Full service
Wine selection: House
Dress: Informal, casual
Disabled access: No
Customers: Ethnic, local

Open: Every day, 11 A.M.–1 A.M.

Atmosphere/Setting: A large, bustling series of rooms divided by oriental archways and a few paintings; sushi bar and bar to one side.

House Specialties: Fresh seafood and fish, particularly blue and Dungeness crabs available in your choice of spicy black bean, ginger, or mild Cantonese sauce; tiny Manila or giant razorback clams; live Pacific scallops looking and tasting more like mild oysters and topped with julienned scallions and ginger; steamed whole fish, particularly the slightly fatty black cod (it stays moist and the fatty layer drops away), simmered at the table in light ginger and soy broth.

Other Recommendations: Jumbo shrimp in ginger sauce; squid in black bean sauce; wrap-it-yourself lettuce rolls with minced seafood and water chestnut filling; lovely delicate bok choy with mushrooms. On weekends, some dim sum.

Summary & Comments: The first thing you see in this Shanghai palace is the tanks of live lobsters, crabs, and shellfish and the menu board of seafood specials: pink scallops; green-shelled mussels; Manila clams; Ice Island cod; and red, blue, and Dungeness crabs among them. Take that as a strong hint: Although this is a full-range Chinese restaurant, seafood is what they do best. Beef or pork dishes are better elsewhere. There are also Japanese items on the menu, but stick to sashimi: The cold, pasty, and poorly seasoned sushi rice doesn't pass muster.

1789

Modern American	★★★	Expensive	QUALITY
			83
			VALUE
			C

1226 36th Street, NW
  (202) 965-1789   Zone 5, Georgetown

Reservations: Recommended	Parking: Valet
When to go: Anytime	Bar: Full service
Entree range: $18–29	Wine selection: Good
Payment: VISA, MC, AMEX, DC, D	Dress: Jacket required
Service rating: ★★★	Disabled access: No
Friendliness rating: ★★★	Customers: Local, business, tourist

Dinner: Sunday–Thursday, 6–10 P.M.; Friday, 6–11 P.M.; Saturday, 5–11 P.M.

Atmosphere/Setting: A meticulously maintained Federal townhouse with blazing fireplaces, polished silver, and historic poise; a certain formality is implied rather than expressed.

House Specialties: Pan-roasted lobster with ginger and cilantro; rockfish with carrots and fennel; grilled barbecued duck breast with greens; venison medallions with black trumpet mushrooms.

Other Recommendations: Rack of lamb with polenta; lobster risotto; three-way salmon appetizers (smoked, salt-cured, and tartare); pan-seared salmon with cherries.

Summary & Comments: This menu, inspired by seasonal availability, showcases regional game and seafood with care and respect. The kitchen aims to re-create and reclaim classic dishes—grilled quail with oysters and bacon, venison medallions, rack of lamb—and update them rather than invent novel treatments. In other words, it's more of a culinary tender of the flame than an innovator, which suits its old-money clientele. However, under the direction of chef Ris Lacoste, the kitchen is moving with increasing confidence into a middle ground, still classic but fresh. Vegetarian options are especially intriguing.

SUSHI-KO

			QUALITY
Japanese	★★★★	Moderate	92
			VALUE
			B

2309 Wisconsin Avenue, NW
(202) 333-4187   Zone 5, Georgetown

Reservations: Recommended on weekends	Parking: Street, valet (dinner only)
When to go: Anytime	Bar: Full service
Entree range: $8.50–18.50	Wine selection: House
Payment: VISA, MC, AMEX	Dress: Business, casual
Service rating: ★★★	Disabled access: No
Friendliness rating: ★★★	Customers: Local, ethnic

Lunch: Tuesday–Friday, noon–2:30 P.M.
Dinner: Monday–Friday, 6–10:30 P.M.; Saturday, 5–10:30 P.M.; Sunday, 5–10 P.M.

Atmosphere/Setting: Sushi bar to the max: a simple but natty, samurai-print-and-varnished-wood, two-story establishment with the sushi bar in the rear.

House Specialties: Sushi, especially seasonal dishes such as ankimo (monkfish liver) and toro (fatty tuna); and any of head chef Kaz Okochi's original recipes, such as a "Napoleon" of chopped sea trout layered in fried wontons and smoked ankimo over mesclun with purple potato vinaigrette. These are usually chalked up on a board near the sushi bar.

Other Recommendations: Broiled eel; soft-shell crabs; octopus salad; grilled fish.

Summary & Comments: Thanks to its upper Georgetown location, an early jump on the sushi bandwagon, and smart, selective pampering, Sushi-Ko attracts a broad, generally knowledgeable and fairly affluent crowd. This has made it possible for owner Daisuke Utagawa and Okochi to offer a more flexible style of cooking, both traditional and improvisational — that is, based on market availability and traditional seasonal factors. However, while the "ordinary" sushi is reasonable, those specials can make dinner somewhat more pricey than a meal at most other sushi bars, so don't waste it on someone who's happy with grocery-store California roll. Utagawa is also intrigued with the notion of matching Japanese food to wines and with offering higher quality sakés.

TABERNA DEL ALABARDERO

			QUALITY
Spanish	★★★½	Expensive	**88**

VALUE
C

1776 I Street, NW (entrance on 18th Street)
(202) 429-2200   Zone 3, Downtown

Reservations: Recommended
When to go: Anytime for tapas;
  lunch for fixed-price meals
Entree range: $18–25
Payment: VISA, MC, AMEX, DC, D
Service rating: ★★★★
Friendliness rating: ★★★

Parking: Free next door
Bar: Full service
Wine selection: Very good
Dress: Jacket and tie suggested
Disabled access: Good
Customers: Local, embassy, ethnic

Lunch: Monday–Friday, 11:30 A.M.–2:30 P.M.
Dinner: Monday–Thursday, 6–10 P.M.; Friday and Saturday, 6–11 P.M.;
  Sunday, closed.

Atmosphere/Setting: Lace curtain and velvet old-world elegance, with ornate moldings and a magnificent private room (like a chapel) in the center.

House Specialties: Lobster paella at night, as well as traditional paella and the pasta version called fideua (there is a variety of versions at lunch); venison; rabbit casserole or boneless rabbit and lobster medallions dealt alternately on the plate; duck confit; stuffed squid in ink; sweetbreads.

Other Recommendations: Daily specials, particularly game, and at least a half-dozen seafood specials every day; quail or pheasant; halibut with mussels.

Summary & Comments: This is a very old-world-style restaurant and quite dignified; some people may find it weighty as well. One alternative is to dabble in Taberna's riches via the tapas menu, a selection of a dozen smaller-sized dishes, including a serving of the paella, for $3.50 to $6.50 apiece (and you can linger as long as you like). Other choices include artichoke bottoms baked with ham; empanadas; grilled chorizo; poached calamari in a salad of sweet peppers. There is also a list of a dozen sherries by the glass and red or white sangria. Taberna now offers ten set lunch menus, ranging from $28–38, making it a little quicker, if not less expensive. And it's also getting into the special-events trend, with wine dinners and imported guest chefs.

TACHIBANA

			QUALITY
Japanese	★★★½	Moderate	**88**
			VALUE
			B

6715 Lowell Avenue, McLean
  (703) 847-1771   Zone 11A, Virginia suburbs

Reservations: Recommended on weekends	Parking: Large lot
When to go: Anytime	Bar: Full service
Entree range: $8.95–25	Wine selection: House
Payment: VISA, MC, AMEX, DC, D	Dress: Informal, casual
Service rating: ★★★	Disabled access: Good
Friendliness rating: ★★★	Customers: Local, ethnic

Lunch: Monday–Friday, 11:30 A.M.–2 P.M.
Dinner: Monday–Thursday, 5–10 P.M.; Friday and Saturday,
  5–10:30 P.M.

Atmosphere/Setting: A sophisticated though not particularly traditional room: slightly split-level, mostly dark green and polished wood, but with two separate sushi bars. The larger front one is a sleek lacquer-like curve, and the second, in the back room, is smaller and simpler, with two slabs of what appear to be polished driftwood hanging overhead instead of the usual cloth flags.

House Specialties: Teriyaki jaw of yellowtail; squid tempura; shabu shabu (requires 24 hours' notice); soft-shell crabs in season.

Other Recommendations: One-pot meals such as nabeyaki or sukiyaki, available in vegetarian versions; traditional grilled salmon over rice with green tea poured over it.

Summary & Comments: This may not be one of the grandest sushi bars in the area, but it's one of the best. Although some of the high-quality sushi here has American names, it tends to be authentic under the seaweed skin: "Washington roll," for example, is broiled eel with scallions and shiso, the basil-like Japanese herb. Tachibana's seafood is fresh and generously sliced, and the teriyaki jaw of yellowtail enormous. The homier soups and stews, not available in more trend-minded shops, are not only fine bargains but real comfort food; after all, Japanese mothers have been making nabe-mono as long as Jewish mothers have been making chicken soup.

TAKO GRILL

			QUALITY
Japanese	★★★★	Moderate	**92**
			VALUE
			B

7756 Wisconsin Avenue, Bethesda
(301) 652-7030   Zone 10A, Maryland suburbs

Reservations: Not accepted
When to go: Before 7
Entree range: $7.50–16.50
Payment: VISA, MC, AMEX
Service rating: ★★★★
Friendliness rating: ★★★
Parking: Street, public garages, free lot
(dinner only)

Bar: Wine and beer
Wine selection: House
Dress: Casual, informal
Disabled access: Very good
Customers: Local, business

Lunch: Monday–Friday, 11:30 A.M.–2 P.M.
Dinner: Monday–Thursday, 5:30–10 P.M.; Friday and Saturday,
5:30–10:30 P.M.; Sunday, 5–9:30 P.M.

Atmosphere/Setting: A cool, hip, very '90s-Tokyo room, a study in white, black, and scarlet, but with deft artistic touches (the flower arrangements) and almost hallucinatory "script" versions of Japanese verses hung on the walls. (The chefs, particularly the younger ones, are very Tokyo-stylish, too—check out the bleached and reddened hair.)

House Specialties: Grilled jaw of yellowtail; ankimo, a monkfish liver pâté; soft-shell crabs tempura-fried and chopped into hand rolls.

Other Recommendations: Grilled whole red snapper or rainbow trout; glazed grilled eel; tiny candied whole octopus.

Summary & Comments: Of the three best Japanese restaurants in the area, each has a different slant: Makoto's classic; Sushi-Ko's cutting-edge; and Tako's cool. In addition to some of the best and freshest sushi and sashimi in the area, Tako has a hot-stone grill called a robotai, on which whole fish, large shrimp, and a variety of fresh vegetables are cooked. The line of customers waiting to get in—the recent expansion notwithstanding—is the surest evidence of Tako's quality. Weekday lunches are a business special: soup, salad, rice, and a daily entree (orange roughy, chicken teriyaki, pork cutlet), plus six pieces of rolled sushi for $5.95. And since several of the waitresses are vegetarian or vegan, Tako is especially well-equipped to satisfy customers with special diets.

TARA THAI

Thai	★★★½	Moderate	QUALITY
			85
			VALUE
			A

226 Maple Avenue West, Vienna
 (703) 255-2467   Zone 11A, Virginia suburbs
4828 Bethesda Avenue, Bethesda
 (301) 657-0488   Zone 10A, Maryland suburbs

Reservations: Helpful
When to go: Weekdays
Entree range: $7.95–12.95
Payment: VISA, MC, AMEX, DC, D
Service rating: ★★★
Friendliness rating: ★★★½

Parking: Free lot
Bar: Full service
Wine selection: House
Dress: Informal, casual
Disabled access: Fair
Customers: Ethnic, local

Lunch: Monday–Friday, 11:30 A.M.–3 P.M.; Saturday and Sunday, noon–3:30 P.M.

Dinner: Sunday–Thursday, 5–10 P.M.; Friday and Saturday, 5–11 P.M.

Atmosphere/Setting: "Tara" has nothing to do with the Old South. It means "blue," and these charming restaurants are marine blue and swimming in fantastical creatures and lacquered tables. The original Vienna branch is quite small, but so friendly that it seems cheerfully crowded rather than annoyingly so. The Bethesda branch draws a more mixed 20- and 30-something crowd to its cheeky murals, window-box bar, and chrome touches.

House Specialties: Whole fish, either fried with chili sauce or steamed in banana leaves with black mushrooms and ginger; soft-shell crabs; "wild" lamb curry; red curry beef; green eggplant curry with chicken.

Other Recommendations: Nua sawan: thin, dried but tender beef, fried and served with slaw—sort of Thai barbecue; honey-glazed duck. For a light meal or shared appetizer, try the "heavenly wings," chicken drumettes scraped back into rattle shapes, stuffed with crab and green onion, then battered and fried.

Summary & Comments: These cheerful in-circle kitchens (the staff began at the equally cerulean Busara) have quickly become area favorites; the food is extremely fresh and clean-tasting, with a variety of sauces and heat levels.

TASTE OF SAIGON

			QUALITY
Vietnamese	★★★½	Moderate	**86**
			VALUE
			A

410 Hungerford Drive, Rockville
   (301) 424-7222   Zone 10B, Maryland suburbs

8201 Greensboro Drive, McLean
   (703) 790-0700   Zone 11A, Virginia suburbs

Reservations: Accepted	Parking: Free lot
When to go: Anytime	Bar: Full service
Entree range: $8–13	Wine selection: Limited
Payment: VISA, MC, AMEX, CB, DC, D	Dress: Informal
Service rating: ★★★	Disabled access: Good
Friendliness rating: ★★★★	Customers: Local, business, ethnic

Open: Monday–Thursday, 11 A.M.–10 P.M.; Friday and Saturday, 11 A.M.–11 P.M.; Sunday, 11 A.M.–9:30 P.M.

Atmosphere/Setting: An intriguingly angular, sleek, gray-and-black-lacquer room slyly tucked into the back of a plain office building.

House Specialties: Stuffed baby squid; steamed whole rockfish served with rice crêpes and vegetables for rolling up; grilled pork meatballs, also served with crêpes and dipping sauce; caramelized soft-shell crabs (in season) with black beans; choice of seafoods—lobster, soft shells, scallops, or shrimp—in a house special black pepper sauce.

Other Recommendations: Cornish hen stuffed with pork; boneless roast quail; grilled pork with mushrooms, peanuts, and cellophane noodles; pho and other noodle soups in appetizer or entree sizes; rich venison curry; pork-stuffed Cornish hen.

Entertainment & Amenities: Patio dining in good weather.

Summary & Comments: The specials here are interesting dishes; it's as if the kitchen were as intrigued as the diners. The beef dishes are only fair, but the seafood and game bird entrees are particularly good. Some of the sauces are quite heavy, but if you stick to the steamed fish or bountiful soup choices, Vietnamese dinner can be a dieter's dream.

TONY CHENG'S MONGOLIAN RESTAURANT

			QUALITY
Chinese	★★½	Inexpensive	**75**

VALUE
A

619 H Street, NW
  (202) 842-8669   Zone 3, Downtown

Reservations: Accepted
When to go: Anytime
Entree range: $8.50–13.95
Payment: VISA, MC, AMEX
Service rating: ★★½
Friendliness rating: ★★★

Parking: Street
Bar: Full service
Wine selection: House
Dress: Informal, casual
Disabled access: Fair
Customers: Local, tourist, ethnic

Open: Sunday–Thursday, 11 A.M.–11 P.M.; Friday and Saturday,
  11 A.M.–midnight

Atmosphere/Setting: A big, bright, open room with woven chairs and a giant iron grill in the center surrounded by coolers.

House Specialties: Mongolian hot pot, a stockpot of broth with vegetables and noodles to which one adds more ingredients—clams, squid, oysters, chicken, even tripe—at $1.95 to $3.95 per ingredient plus $5 for the pot; or the all-you-can-eat Mongolian barbecue, a sort of similar pick-your-flavor arrangement, but cooked on the grill, for $13.95.

Other Recommendations: None—it's a two-item menu, in effect.

Summary & Comments: The barbecue is the more fun choice: Customers fill a serving bowl with meats, seafood, or vegetables from the cooler trays, then hand it over to the chef, who dumps the whole plateful onto the grill and stir-fries it—the Mongolian version of Benihana. The cooked dish is flavored with soy sauce, ginger, rice wine, garlic, or chili oil and eaten at the table by stuffing it into little sesame rolls. Tony Cheng's has become an all-you-can-eat indulgence for dieters, especially the hot pot. A good seafood restaurant is upstairs, incidentally, which serves not only a variety of set-price lunches or dinners for parties of four or more and a very serious broad Chinese menu, but also dim sum daily from 11 to 3.

VEGETABLE GARDEN

			QUALITY
Chinese (vegetarian)	★★★	Moderate	**80**

	VALUE
	B

11618 Rockville Pike (White Flint Station Shopping Center),
   Rockville (301) 468-9301   Zone 10B, Maryland suburbs

Reservations: Accepted	Parking: Free lot
When to go: Anytime	Bar: Full service
Entree range: $6.75–12.95	Wine selection: House
Payment: VISA, MC, AMEX	Dress: Casual
Service rating: ★★½	Disabled access: Good
Friendliness rating: ★★★	Customers: Local, ethnic

Lunch: Monday–Friday, 11:30 A.M.–2:30 P.M.
Dinner: Sunday–Thursday, 5–10 P.M.; Friday and Saturday, 5–10:30 P.M.

Atmosphere/Setting: Light suburban Asian, with pink walls, pink and green carpeting and floral upholstery, and nice poster art of the chain-gallery variety.

House Specialties: A really good "vegi-goose" dish, thin soy crêpes wrapped around minced vegetables and mushrooms; crunchy sesame "chicken" nuggets (all the meats are soy foods, with slightly differing textures); carved shiitake mushrooms with asparagus and a little chile bite; spinach-stuffed tofu-skin rolls fried with asparagus and sweet-and-sour sauce.

Other Recommendations: Crispy (fried) spicy eggplant or braised eggplant in hot sauce; and noodle choices of soba, rice noodles, and lo mein. There are also a variety of appetizers, such as steamed or pan-fried dumplings, spinach "knishes" and "latkes" (this is Rockville, after all), and spaghetti squash patties.

Summary & Comments: The Vegetable Garden is beginning to be noticed by national magazines catering not only to vegetarians and vegans but also to young, nutrition-conscious women. Nothing is really strong-tasting, even the dishes marked spicy (unless you make a point of it), but it's surprisingly soothing—a different concept of comfort food. And much, though not all, is low-cal, as a fringe benefit. The menu follows Buddhist rules, so it eliminates dairy foods entirely; if you ask, the staff will even tell you which dishes are made with only organic ingredients. You also have a choice of brown or white rice.

VIDALIA

			QUALITY
Modern American	★★★★	Expensive	**93**
			VALUE
			B

1990 M Street, NW
   (202) 659-1990   Zone 6, Dupont Circle/Adams-Morgan

Reservations: Recommended
When to go: Anytime
Entree range: $19–22
Payment: VISA, MC, AMEX, D
Service rating: ★★★★
Friendliness rating: ★★★
Parking: Street, garage, valet (dinner
   only)

Bar: Full service
Wine selection: Very good
Dress: Business, dressy, casual
Disabled access: Good
Customers: Business, local, tourist

Lunch: Monday–Friday, 11:30 A.M.–2:30 P.M.
Dinner: Monday–Thursday, 5:30–10 P.M.; Friday and Saturday,
5:30–10:30 P.M.; Sunday, 5–9:30 P.M.

Atmosphere/Setting: Although this is actually a below-stairs establishment (disabled access is through the office lobby elevators), it's remarkably bright for a basement and as new–Southern Revival as a Martha Stewart magazine: sponged buttercup walls (the chef's wife's handiwork), dried flower wreaths, stripped-wood banisters and dowels.

House Specialties: Roasted sweetbreads with morels and a tang of bacon and chard; salmon seared in a fennel-seed crust; fried squid with blackened fennel; a Provençal-style round-bone lamb steak with artichokes, olives, and roast garlic; double "porterhouse" pork chop with pears and currants at dinner and a cornbread-and-sausage-stuffed chop at lunch.

Other Recommendations: Monkfish roasted in a mushroom crust; a lunchtime steak salad with arugula, fennel, and shiitakes; breast of duck with duck confit; a seared but rare salmon appetizer with marinated scallops and Southwestern spices. For light fare, go into the Onion Bar and check out the $4 tapas.

Summary & Comments: Jeff Buben is another of those chefs who delight in native American ingredients based on sheer flavor rather than tradition. His luxuriant sauces aren't low-cal but he serves them with a light touch. Particularly if you dally over the big first-course salads and the scones, Vidalia can be a bargain.

VINCENZO AL SOLE

			QUALITY
Italian	★★★	Expensive	82
			VALUE
			C

1606 20th Street, NW
   (202) 667-0047   Zone 6, Dupont Circle/Adams-Morgan

Reservations: Recommended
When to go: Anytime
Entree range: $15.75–21.75
Payment: VISA, MC, AMEX, DC,
   CB
Service rating: ★★★
Friendliness rating: ★★½

Parking: Street, valet (dinner only)
Bar: Full service
Wine selection: Good but limited
Dress: Casual, business
Disabled access: Good
Customers: Local, business, tourist

Lunch: Monday–Friday, noon–2 P.M.
Dinner: Monday–Saturday, 6–10 P.M.; Sunday, closed.

Atmosphere/Setting: An elegant old Dupont Circle mansion whose small, intimate rooms are given unusual warmth by huge floral arrangements and the glassed-in patio-cum-conservatory. The casual place settings make it seem like your rich uncle's country estate.

House Specialties: Although seafood is no longer the only choice, it's still the best: antipasto di mare with marinated shrimp, steamed clams, and fried squid; sea bass with olives; shrimp fried with fennel; squid with Swiss chard. The next best choice is pasta. Among meats, sweet-and-sour rabbit with polenta; braised veal.

Other Recommendations: Daily specials; grilled mackerel.

Summary & Comments: Once D.C.'s best Italian seafood specialist, Vincenzo had slipped from its longtime prominence with the influx of showier Italian restaurants; and a couple of ill-conceived image retoolings—not only of the menu but a bewildering merry-go-round of names and levels of formality—had confused and even alienated some of its clientele. So it is gradually doing what it probably should have done the first time—gotten back to its basics. It still conveys an odd sense of ambivalence, however: The kitchen alternates between a sort of brash confidence and a longing for security, which results in first-rate food one night, merely satisfying fare another. Disabled access is through the rear.

WOO LAE OAK

			QUALITY
Korean	★★★	Moderate	**82**

	VALUE
	A

1500 South Joyce Street, Arlington
  (703) 521-3706   Zone 11B, Virginia suburbs

Reservations: Accepted, suggested on weekends	**Parking:** Free lot
When to go: Anytime	**Bar:** Full service
Entree range: $8.50–15	**Wine selection:** Fair
Payment: VISA, MC, AMEX, DC	**Dress:** Casual, informal
Service rating: ★★★★	**Disabled access:** No
Friendliness rating: ★★★	**Customers:** Ethnic, local

Open: Every day, 11:30 A.M.–10:30 P.M.

Atmosphere/Setting: California Asian, this freestanding section of an apartment complex is a big curving slice of a room on stilts, with modernized versions of traditional wood-slat-and-rice-paper decor. All tables have barbecue grills built in.

House Specialties: Shin sun ro, a fancy hot pot (Korean shabu shabu) that requires 24 hours' notice; saeng sun jun, battered and grilled fish; bulgoki, the familiar sweet-soy beef barbecue; spicy fish stew in a pot; yook hwe bibimbap, marinated raw sirloin strips with spinach, bean sprouts, zucchini, etc., in sesame oil; boneless short rib cubes.

Other Recommendations: Beef liver, heart, tongue, and tripe for the more intrepid barbecuers; broiled salmon; sliced raw fish, cut in generous, steak-fry-sized pieces, not the thin Japanese layers. Modum yori, a combination grill platter, including a whole fish, shrimp, chicken, and beef, is a huge family meal, but requires a day's advance notice.

Summary & Comments: This is not food to eat alone. The fun is barbecuing (or in the case of the many hot-pot dishes, dipping) with friends. Besides, many of the dishes are made for two, and the sashimi appetizer is so big—about 24 pieces, and cut Korean-style, meaning large—that it's either a meal or a first course for several. Many dishes cost less at lunch. The one real disappointment about this restaurant for non-Asian diners is that staffers frequently doubt that you know what you're ordering, or don't take it seriously; for example, even with the 24 hours' notice, it can be hit-or-miss whether you get your shin sun ro.

Hotel	Room Star Rating	Zone	Street Address
American Inn of Bethesda	★★	10	8130 Wisconsin Avenue Bethesda, MD 20814
ANA Hotel	★★★★½	5	2401 M Street, NW Washington, DC 20037
Arlington Virginia Hilton	★★★½	11	950 N. Stafford Street Arlington, VA 22203
Best Western Arlington Inn	★★½	11	2480 S. Glebe Road Arlington, VA 22206
Best Western Key Bridge	★★½	11	1850 N. Fort Myer Drive Arlington, VA 22209
Best Western New Hampshire Suites	★★★	6	1121 New Hampshire Avenue, NW Washington, DC 20037
Best Western Old Colony Inn	★★	11	615 First Street Alexandria, VA 22314
Best Western Skyline Inn	★★½	9	10 "I" Street, SW Washington, DC 20024
Best Western Tyson's Westpark	★★½	11	8401 Westpark Drive McLean, VA 22102
Bethesda Court Hotel	★★½	10	7740 Wisconsin Avenue Bethesda, MD 20814
Canterbury Hotel	★★★★	6	1733 N Street, NW Washington, DC 20036
Capitol Hilton	★★★★½	3	16th and K Streets, NW Washington, DC 20036
Carlton Hotel	★★★★½	3	923 16th Street & K Street, NW Washington, DC 20006
Carlyle Suites Hotel	★★½	6	1731 New Hampshire Avenue, NW Washington, DC 20009
Channel Inn Hotel	★★★	1	650 Water Street, SW Washington, DC 20024
Clarion Hampshire Hotel	★★★½	6	1310 New Hampshire Avenue, NW Washington, DC 20036
Comfort Inn Alexandria	★★½	11	5716 S. Van Dorn Street Alexandria, VA 22310
Comfort Inn Arlington	★★½	11	1211 N. Glebe Road Arlington, VA 22201
Comfort Inn Vienna	★★½	11	1587 Spring Hill Road Vienna, VA 22182
Courtyard Alexandria	★★★½	11	2700 Eisenhower Avenue Alexandria, VA 22314

Local Phone	Fax	800 Reservations	Rack Rate	No. of Rooms	On-site Dining	Pool
(301) 656-9300	(301) 656-2907	(800) 323-7081	$$$+	76	Yes	Yes
(202) 429-2400	(202) 457-5010	(800) 262-4683	$$$ $$$–	415	Yes	Yes
(703) 528-6000	(703) 528-4386	(800) 445-8667	$$$$+	209	Yes	Yes
(703) 949-4400	(703) 685-0051	(800) 528-1234	$$$–	326	Yes	Yes
(703) 522-0400	(703) 524-5275	(800) 528-1234	$$$$+	178	Yes	Yes
(202) 457-0565	(202) 331-9421	(800) 762-3777	$$$$–	75	No	No
(703) 739-2222	(703) 549-2568	(800) 528-1234	$$$–	151	Yes	Yes
(202) 488-7500	(202) 488-0790	(800) 458-7500	$$$$–	203	No	Yes
(703) 734-2800	(703) 821-8872	(800) 533-3301	$$$$–	312	Yes	Yes
(301) 656-2100	(301) 986-0375	(800) 874-0050	$$$–	76	No	No
(202) 393-3000	(202) 785-9581	(800) 424-2950	$$$$–	99	Yes	No
(202) 393-1000	(202) 639-5784	(800) HILTONS	$$$$ $$$$+	546	Yes	No
(202) 638-2626	(202) 638-4231	(800) 562-5661	$$$$ $$$+	192	Yes	No
(202) 234-3200	(202) 387-0085	(800) 964-5377	$$$$$–	170	Yes	No
(202) 554-2400	(202) 863-1164	(800) 368-5668	$$$$+	100	Yes	Yes
(202) 296-7600	(202) 293-2476	(800) 368-5691	$$$$+	82	Yes	No
(703) 922-9200	(703) 922-0132	(800) 999-7680	$$+	187	No	Yes
(703) 247-3399	(703) 524-8739	(800) 221-2222	$$$$	126	Yes	No
(703) 448-8020	(703) 448-0343	(800) 221-2222	$$$+	250	No	Yes
(703) 329-2323	(703) 329-6853	(800) 321-2211	$$$$–	176	Yes	No

Hotel	Room Star Rating	Zone	Street Address
Courtyard Crystal City	★★★★	11	2899 Jefferson Davis Highway Arlington, VA 22202
Courtyard New Carrollton	★★★¹/₂	10	8330 Corporate Drive Landover, MD 20785
Courtyard Rosslyn	★★★¹/₂	11	1533 Clarendon Boulevard Rosslyn, VA 22209
Courtyard Washington	★★★¹/₂	6	1900 Connecticut Avenue, NW Washington, DC 20009
Days Hotel Crystal City	★★¹/₂	11	2000 Jefferson Davis Highway Arlington, VA 22202
Days Inn Camp Springs	★★¹/₂	10	5001 Mercedes Boulevard Camp Springs, MD 20746
Days Inn Connecticut Avenue	★★¹/₂	7	4400 Connecticut Avenue, NW Washington, DC 20008
Days Inn Downtown	★★¹/₂	3	1201 K Street, NW Washington, DC 20005
Doubletree Guest Suites Alexandria	★★★★	11	100 S. Reynolds Street Alexandria, VA 22304
Doubletree Guest Suites New Hampshire Avenue	★★★¹/₂	4	801 New Hampshire Avenue, NW Washington, DC 20037
Doubletree Guest Suites Pennsylvania Avenue	★★★★	5	2500 Pennsylvania Avenue, NW Washington, DC 20037
Doubletree Hotel National Airport	★★★★	11	300 Army Navy Drive Arlington, VA 22202
Doubletree Hotel Park Terrace	★★★¹/₂	7	1515 Rhode Island Avenue, NW Washington, DC 20005
Doubletree Hotel Tysons Corner	★★★¹/₂	11	7801 Leesburg Pike Falls Church, VA 22043
DuPont Plaza Hotel	★★★	6	1500 New Hampshire Avenue, NW Washington, DC 20036
Econolodge National Airport	★★¹/₂	11	2485 S. Glebe Road Arlington, VA 22206
Econolodge West Arlington	★★¹/₂	11	6800 Lee Highway Arlington, VA 22213
Embassy Inn	★★¹/₂	6	1627 16th Street, NW Washington, DC 20009
Embassy Row Hilton	★★★★	6	2015 Massachusetts Avenue, NW Washington, DC 20036
Embassy Square Summerfield Suites	★★★¹/₂	6	2000 N Street, NW Washington, DC 20036

Local Phone	Fax	800 Reservations	Rack Rate	No. of Rooms	On-site Dining	Pool
(703) 549-3434	(703) 549-7440	(800) 847-4775	$$$$–	272	Yes	Yes
(301) 577-3373	(301) 577-1780	(800) 321-2211	$$$–	150	Yes	Yes
(703) 528-2222	(703) 528-5920	(800) 321-2211	$$$–	162	Yes	Yes
(202) 332-9300	(202) 328-7039	(800) 842-4211	$$$$$–	147	Yes	Yes
(703) 920-8600	(703) 920-2840	(800) 329-7466	$$$+	247	Yes	Yes
(301) 423-2323	(301) 702-9420	(800) DAYS-INN	$$$–	122	Yes	Yes
(202) 244-5600	(202) 244-6794	(800) 325-2525	$$$+	155	Yes	No
(202) 842-1020	(202) 289-0336	(800) 325-2525	$$$+	220	Yes	Yes
(703) 370-9600	(703) 370-0467	(800) 222-TREE	$$$$	225	Yes	Yes
(202) 785-2000	(202) 785-9485	(800) 222-8733	$$$$–	101	Yes	Yes
(202) 333-8060	(202) 338-3818	(800) 222-TREE	$$$$–	123	No	No
(703) 416-4100	(703) 416-4126	(800) 222-TREE	$$$$$–	632	Yes	Yes
(202) 232-7000	(202) 332-7152	(800) 222-TREE	$$$+	219	Yes	No
(703) 893-1340	(703) 749-8528	(800) 222-TREE	$$$$$–	404	Yes	Yes
(202) 483-6000	(202) 265-1680	(800) 841-0003	$$$$+	314	Yes	No
(703) 979-4100	(703) 979-6120	(800) 424-7777	$$+	163	Yes	Yes
(703) 538-5300	(703) 538-2110	(800) 78-LODGE	$$$–	47	No	No
(202) 234-7800	(202) 234-3309	(800) 423-9111	$$$–	38	No	No
(202) 265-1600	(202) 328-7526	(800) 445-8667	$$$$+	196	Yes	Yes
(202) 659-9000	(202) 429-9546	(800) 424-2999	$$$$$+	250	No	Yes

Hotel	Room Star Rating	Zone	Street Address
Embassy Suites Alexandria	★★★★	11	1900 Diagonal Road Alexandria, VA 22314
Embassy Suites Chevy Chase	★★★★	10	4300 Military Road, NW Washington, DC 20015
Embassy Suites Crystal City	★★★★	11	1300 Jefferson Davis Highway Arlington, VA 22202
Embassy Suites Downtown	★★★★	6	1250 22nd Street, NW Washington, DC 20037
Embassy Suites Tysons Corner	★★★★	11	8517 Leesburg Pike Vienna, VA 22182
Four Seasons Hotel	★★★★¹/₂	5	2800 Pennsylvania Avenue, NW Washington, DC 20007
George Washington University Inn	★★★★	4	824 New Hampshire Avenue, NW Washington, DC 20037
Georgetown Dutch Inn	★★★¹/₂	5	1075 Thomas Jefferson Street, NW Washington, DC 20007
Georgetown Inn	★★★★	5	1310 Wisconsin Avenue, NW Washington, DC 20007
The Governor's House Hotel	★★★¹/₂	6	1615 Rhode Island Avenue, NW Washington, DC 20036
Grand Hyatt Washington	★★★★	3	1000 H Street, NW Washington, DC 20001
Hampton Inn Alexandria	★★★	11	4800 Leesburg Pike Alexandria, VA 22302
Hay-Adams Hotel	★★★★¹/₂	3	800 16th Street, NW Washington, DC 20006
Henley Park Hotel	★★★★	3	926 Massachusetts Avenue, NW Washington, DC 20011
Holiday Inn Arlington	★★★¹/₂	11	4610 N. Fairfax Drive Arlington, VA 22203
Holiday Inn Bethesda	★★★	10	8120 Wisconsin Avenue Bethesda, MD 20814
Holiday Inn Camp Springs	★★¹/₂	10	4783 Allentown Road Camp Springs, MD 20746
Holiday Inn Capitol	★★★	2	550 C Street, SW Washington, DC 20024
Holiday Inn Central	★★★	7	1501 Rhode Island Avenue, NW Washington, DC 20005
Holiday Inn Chevy Chase	★★★¹/₂	10	5520 Wisconsin Avenue Chevy Chase, MD 20815

Local Phone	Fax	800 Reservations	Rack Rate	No. of Rooms	On-site Dining	Pool
(703) 684-5900	(703) 684-1403	(800) EMBASSY	$$$$$$–	268	No	Yes
(202) 362-9300	(202) 686-3405	(800) EMBASSY	$$$$$$+	198	No	Yes
(703) 979-9799	(703) 920-5947	(800) EMBASSY	$$$$$+	267	Yes	Yes
(202) 857-3388	(202) 293-3173	(800) EMBASSY	$$$$$$$–	318	Yes	Yes
(703) 883-0707	(703) 883-0694	(800) EMBASSY	$$$$$+	232	Yes	Yes
(202) 342-0444	(202) 944-2076	(800) 332-3442	$$$$$$ $$$$$$–	196	Yes	Yes
(202) 337-6620	(202) 298-7499	(800) 426-4455	$$$$$–	95	Yes	No
(202) 337-0900	(202) 333-6526	(800) 388-2410	$$$$+	47	Yes	No
(202) 333-8900	(202) 333-8308	(800) 424-2979	$$$$$+	95	Yes	No
(202) 296-2100	(202) 331-0227	(800) 821-4367	$$$+	152	Yes	Yes
(202) 582-1234	(202) 637-4781	(800) 233-1234	$$$$ $$$$	891	Yes	Yes
(703) 671-4800	(703) 671-2442	(800) HAMPTON	$$$+	130	No	Yes
(202) 638-6600	(202) 638-2716	(800) 424-5054	$$$$$ $$$$+	143	Yes	No
(202) 638-5200	(202) 638-6740	(800) 222-8474	$$$$+	96	Yes	No
(703) 243-9800	(703) 527-2677	(800) HOLIDAY	$$$–	221	Yes	Yes
(301) 652-2000	(301) 652-4525	(800) HOLIDAY	$$$+	270	Yes	Yes
(301) 420-2800	(301) 735-5235	(800) HOLIDAY	$$+	149	No	No
(202) 479-4000	(202) 479-4353	(800) HOLIDAY	$$$$+	529	Yes	Yes
(202) 483-2000	(202) 797-1078	(800) 248-0016	$$$+	213	Yes	Yes
(301) 656-1500	(301) 656-5045	(800) HOLIDAY	$$$$–	216	Yes	Yes

Hotel	Room Star Rating	Zone	Street Address
Holiday Inn and Suites	★★★	11	2460 Eisenhower Avenue Alexandria, VA 22314
Holiday Inn Franklin Square	★★★	3	1155 14th Street, NW Washington, DC 20005
Holiday Inn Georgetown	★★★	7	2101 Wisconsin Avenue, NW Washington, DC 20007
Holiday Inn Hotel and Suites	★★★½	11	625 First Street Alexandria, VA 22314
Holiday Inn National Airport	★★★	11	1489 Jefferson Davis Highway Arlington, VA 22202
Holiday Inn Old Town	★★★	11	480 King Street Alexandria, VA 22314
Holiday Inn on the Hill	★★★	3	415 New Jersey Avenue, NW Washington, DC 20001
Holiday Inn Silver Spring	★★★	10	8777 Georgia Avenue Silver Spring, MD 20910
Holiday Inn Westpark	★★½	11	1900 N. Fort Myer Drive Arlington, VA 22209
Hotel Lombardy	★★★½	4	2019 "I" Street, NW Washington, DC 20006
Hotel Sofitel	★★★★	6	1914 Connecticut Avenue, NW Washington, DC 20009
Hotel Washington	★★★½	3	515 15th Street, NW Washington, DC 20004
Howard Johnson Hotel and Suites	★★★	7	1430 Rhode Island Avenue, NW Washington, DC 20005
Howard Johnson National Airport	★★½	11	2650 Jefferson Davis Highway Arlington, VA 22202
Hyatt Arlington	★★★½	11	1325 Wilson Boulevard Arlington, VA 22209
Hyatt Regency Bethesda	★★★★	10	7400 Wisconsin Avenue Bethesda, MD 20814
Hyatt Regency Capitol Hill	★★★½	3	400 New Jersey Avenue, NW Washington, DC 20001
Hyatt Regency Crystal City	★★★★	11	2799 Jefferson Davis Highway Arlington, VA 22202
J.W. Marriott Hotel	★★★★	3	1331 Pennsylvania Avenue, NW Washington, DC 20004
Jefferson Hotel	★★★★½	3	1200 16th Street, NW Washington, DC 20036

Local Phone	Fax	800 Reservations	Rack Rate	No. of Rooms	On-site Dining	Pool
(703) 960-3400	(703) 329-0953	(800) HOLIDAY	$$$$–	202	Yes	Yes
(202) 737-1200	(202) 783-5733	(800) HOLIDAY	$$$$	208	Yes	Yes
(202) 338-4600	(202) 338-4458	(800) HOLIDAY	$$$$$–	296	Yes	Yes
(703) 548-6300	(703) 548-8032	(800) HOLIDAY	$$$$$–	175	Yes	Yes
(703) 416-1600	(703) 416-1615	(800) HOLIDAY	$$$$–	306	Yes	Yes
(703) 549-6080	(703) 684-6508	(800) 368-5047	$$$$$+	225	Yes	Yes
(202) 638-1616	(202) 638-0707	(800) HOLIDAY	$$$–	341	Yes	Yes
(301) 589-0800	(301) 587-4791	(800) HOLIDAY	$$$$–	222	Yes	Yes
(703) 527-4814	(703) 522-8864	(800) 368-3408	$$$$–	300	Yes	Yes
(202) 828-2600	(202) 872-0503	(800) 424-5486	$$$+	126	Yes	No
(202) 797-2000	(202) 462-0944	(800) 424-2464	$$$ $$$–	145	Yes	No
(202) 638-5900	(202) 638-4275	(800) 424-9540	$$$$+	350	Yes	No
(202) 462-7777	(202) 332-3519	(800) 368-5690	$$$–	329	Yes	Yes
(703) 684-7200	(703) 684-3217	(800) IGOHOJO	$$$$$–	279	Yes	Yes
(703) 525-1234	(703) 875-3393	(800) 233-1234	$$$ $$$–	302	Yes	No
(301) 657-1234	(301) 657-6453	(800) 233-1234	$$$$ $$+	381	Yes	Yes
(202) 737-1234	(202) 737-5773	(800) 233-1234	$$$ $$$	834	Yes	Yes
(703) 418-1234	(703) 418-1289	(800) 233-1234	$$$ $$$+	685	Yes	Yes
(202) 393-2000	(202) 626-6991	(800) 228-9290	$$$ $$$$+	772	Yes	Yes
(202) 347-2200	(202) 331-7982	(800) 368-5966	$$$$ $$$$+	100	Yes	No

Hotel	Room Star Rating	Zone	Street Address
Kalorama Guest House	★★★	6	1854 Mintwood Place Washington, DC 20009
Latham Hotel Georgetown	★★★★	5	3000 M Street, NW Washington, DC 20007
Lincoln Suites	★★★★	3	1823 L Street, NW Washington, DC 20036
Loew's L'Enfant Plaza	★★★★½	1	480 L'Enfant Plaza, SW Washington, DC 20024
Madison	★★★½	3	1177 15th Street, NW Washington, DC 20005
Marriott Crystal City	★★★★	11	1999 Jefferson Davis Highway Arlington, VA 22202
Marriott Crystal Gateway	★★★★	11	1700 Jefferson Davis Highway Arlington, VA 22202
Marriott Hotel Bethesda	★★★	10	5151 Pooks Hill Road Bethesda, MD 20814
Marriott Hotel Key Bridge	★★★½	11	1401 Lee Highway Arlington, VA 22209
Marriott Metro Center	★★★★	3	775 12th Street, NW Washington, DC 20005
Marriott Tysons Corner	★★★★	11	8028 Leesburg Pike Vienna, VA 22182
Morrison House	★★★★	11	116 S. Alfred Road Alexandria, VA 22314
Morrison-Clark Inn	★★★★½	7	1015 L Street, NW Washington, DC 20001
Normandy Inn	★★½	6	2118 Wyoming Avenue, NW Washington, DC 20008
Omni Shoreham Hotel	★★½/ ★★★★	7	2500 Calvert Street, NW Washington, DC 20008
One Washington Circle Hotel	★★★★	4	One Washington Circle, NW Washington, DC 20037
Park Hyatt	★★★★½	5	1201 24th Street, NW Washington, DC 20037
Phoenix Park Hotel	★★★	2	520 N. Capitol Street, NW Washington, DC 20001
Quality Hotel Downtown	★★½	6	1315 16th Street, NW Washington, DC 20036
Quality Hotel Silver Spring	★★½	10	8727 Colesville Road Silver Spring, MD 20910

Local Phone	Fax	800 Reservations	Rack Rate	No. of Rooms	On-site Dining	Pool
(202) 667-6369	(202) 319-1262	None	$$$	31	No	No
(202) 726-5000	(202) 337-4250	(800) 368-5922	$$$$+	143	Yes	Yes
(202) 223-4320	(202) 223-8546	(800) 424-2970	$$$$–	99	Yes	No
(202) 484-1000	(202) 646-4456	(800) 635-5065	$$$$+	370	Yes	Yes
(202) 862-1600	(202) 785-1255	(800) 424-8577	$$$$+	353	Yes	No
(703) 413-5500	(703) 413-0192	(800) 228-9290	$$$ $$$+	340	Yes	Yes
(703) 920-3230	(703) 271-5212	(800) 228-9290	$$$ $$$+	700	Yes	Yes
(301) 897-9400	(301) 897-0192	(800) 228-9290	$$$$$+	407	Yes	Yes
(703) 524-6400	(703) 524-8964	(800) 228-9290	$$$$$+	585	Yes	Yes
(202) 737-2200	(202) 347-5886	(800) 228-9290	$$$$ $$+	456	Yes	Yes
(703) 734-3200	(703) 734-5763	(800) 228-9290	$$$$$+	390	Yes	Yes
(703) 838-8000	(703) 684-6283	(800) 367-0800	$$$$$	45	Yes	No
(202) 898-1200	(202) 289-8576	(800) 332-7898	$$$$–	54	Yes	No
(202) 483-1350	(202) 387-8241	(800) 424-3729	$$$$–	75	No	No
(202) 234-0700	(202) 265-7972	(800) THE-OMNI	$$$$ $$$–	770	Yes	Yes
(202) 872-1680	(202) 887-4989	(800) 424-9671	$$$$	151	Yes	Yes
(202) 789-1234	(202) 457-8823	(800) 233-1234	$$$$$ $$$$$–	224	Yes	Yes
(202) 638-6900	(202) 393-3236	(800) 824-5419	$$$$ $$+	150	Yes	No
(202) 232-8000	(202) 667-9827	(800) 228-5151	$$$–	137	Yes	No
(301) 589-5200	(301) 588-6681	(800) 228-5151	$$$+	233	Yes	Yes

Hotel	Room Star Rating	Zone	Street Address
Quality Inn College Park	★★½	10	7200 Baltimore Avenue College Park, MD 20742
Quality Inn Iwo Jima	★★½	11	1501 Arlington Boulevard Arlington, VA 22209
Radisson Barceló Hotel	★★★½	6	2121 P Street, NW Washington, DC 20037
Radisson Plaza at Mark Center	★★★½	11	5000 Seminary Road Alexandria, VA 22311
Ramada Hotel Old Town	★★★	11	901 N. Fairfax Street Alexandria, VA 22314
Ramada Plaza Hotel Bethesda	★★★	10	8400 Wisconsin Avenue Bethesda, MD 20814
Ramada Seminary Plaza/ Pentagon	★★½	11	4641 Kenmore Avenue Alexandria, VA 22314
Red Roof Inn Downtown	★★½	3	500 H Street, NW Washington, DC 20001
Renaissance Mayflower Hotel	★★★★½	3	1127 Connecticut Avenue, NW Washington, DC 20036
Residence Inn Bethesda	★★★★	10	7335 Wisconsin Avenue Bethesda, MD 20814
Residence Inn Pentagon City	★★★★	11	550 Army / Navy Drive Arlington, VA 22202
Ritz-Carlton Pentagon City	★★★★½	11	1250 S. Hayes Street Arlington, VA 22202
Ritz-Carlton Washington, DC	★★★★	6	2100 Massachusetts Avenue, NW Washington, DC 20008
River Inn	★★★★	4	924 25th Street, NW Washington, DC 20037
Savoy Suites Hotel	★★★½	7	2505 Wisconsin Avenue, NW Washington, DC 20007
Sheraton City Centre	★★★★	6	1143 New Hampshire Avenue, NW Washington, DC 20037
Sheraton Crystal City	★★★½	11	1800 Jefferson Davis Highway Arlington, VA 22202
Sheraton National Hotel	★★★½	11	900 S. Orme Street Arlington, VA 22204
Sheraton Premiere Tysons Corner	★★★★½	11	8661 Leesburg Pike Vienna, VA 22182
Sheraton Suites Alexandria	★★★★½	11	801 N. St. Asaph Street Alexandria, VA 22314

Local Phone	Fax	800 Reservations	Rack Rate	No. of Rooms	On-site Dining	Pool
(301) 864-5820	(301) 927-8634	(800) 228-5151	$$$–	154	No	Yes
(703) 524-5000	(703) 522-5484	(800) 228-5151	$$$+	141	Yes	Yes
(202) 293-3100	(202) 857-0134	(800) 333-3333	$$$$–	294	Yes	Yes
(703) 845-1010	(703) 845-7662	(800) 333-3333	$$$$+	500	Yes	Yes
(703) 683-6000	(703) 683-7597	(800) 272-6362	$$$+	258	Yes	Yes
(301) 654-1000	(301) 654-0751	(888) 770-0900	$$$$+	160	Yes	Yes
(703) 751-4510	(703) 751-9170	(800) 228-2828	$$$–	193	Yes	Yes
(202) 289-5959	(202) 682-9152	(800) 843-7663	$$$$–	197	Yes	No
(202) 347-3000	(202) 776-9188	(800) HOTELS-1	$$$$ $$$$+	659	Yes	No
(301) 718-0200	(301) 718-0679	(800) 331-3131	$$$$ $$–	187	No	Yes
(703) 413-6630	(703) 418-1751	(800) 331-3131	$$$$$+	299	No	Yes
(703) 415-5000	(703) 415-5061	(800) 241-3333	$$$ $$$+	345	Yes	Yes
(202) 293-2100	(202) 293-0641	(800) 241-3333	$$$$ $$$+	206	Yes	No
(202) 337-7600	(202) 337-6520	(800) 424-2741	$$$$+	127	Yes	No
(202) 337-9700	(202) 337-3644	(800) 944-5377	$$$$$+	150	Yes	No
(202) 775-0800	(202) 331-9491	(800) 526-7495	$$$$+	351	Yes	No
(703) 486-1111	(703) 920-5827	(800) 325-3535	$$$$ $$$–	220	Yes	Yes
(703) 521-1900	(703) 521-0332	(800) 468-9090	$$$$$–	417	Yes	Yes
(703) 448-1234	(703) 893-8193	(800) 572-ROOM	$$$$ $$+	437	Yes	Yes
(703) 836-4700	(703) 548-4514	(800) 325-3535	$$$$$	249	Yes	Yes

Hotel	Room Star Rating	Zone	Street Address
Sheraton Washington Hotel	★★★★	7	2660 Woodley Road, NW Washington, DC 20008
St. James	★★★★	4	950 24th Street, NW Washington, DC 20037
State Plaza Hotel	★★★½	4	2117 E Street, NW & 2116 F Street Washington, DC 20037
Tabard Inn	★★★½	6	1739 N Street, NW Washington, DC 20036
Travelodge City Center	★★½	7	1201 13th Street, NW Washington, DC 20005
Washington Court Hotel	★★★★	3	525 New Jersey Avenue, NW Washington, DC 20001
Washington Hilton	★★★½	6	1919 Connecticut Avenue, NW Washington, DC 20009
Washington Marriott Hotel	★★★★	6	1221 22nd Street at M Street, NW Washington, DC 20037
Washington National Airport Hilton	★★★½	11	2399 Jefferson Davis Highway Arlington, VA 22202
Washington Plaza Hotel	★★★	3	10 Thomas Circle, NW Washington, DC 20005
Washington Premier Hotel	★★½	4	2601 Virginia Avenue, NW Washington, DC 20037
Washington Renaissance Hotel	★★★★	3	999 9th Street, NW Washington, DC 20001
Watergate Hotel	★★★★½	4	2650 Virginia Avenue, NW Washington, DC 20037
Westin City Center Hotel	★★★★½	3	1400 M Street, NW Washington, DC 20005-2750
Westin Hotel of Washington	★★★★★	5	2350 M Street, NW Washington, DC 20037
Willard Inter-Continental	★★★★½	3	1401 Pennsylvania Avenue, NW Washington, DC 20004
Windsor Park Hotel	★★½	6	2116 Kalorama Road, NW Washington, DC 20008
Wyndham Bristol Hotel	★★★★	5	2430 Pennsylvania Avenue, NW Washington, DC 20037

Local Phone	Fax	800 Reservations	Rack Rate	No. of Rooms	On-site Dining	Pool
(202) 328-2000	(202) 234-0015	(800) 325-3535	$$$+	1,505	Yes	Yes
(202) 457-0500	(202) 659-4492	(800) 852-8512	$$$$$–	196	No	Yes
(202) 861-8200	(202) 659-8601	(800) 424-2859	$$$$–	225	Yes	No
(202) 785-1277	(202) 785-6173	None	$$$$+	40	Yes	No
(202) 682-5300	(202) 371-9624	(800) 578-7878	$$$+	100	No	No
(202) 628-2100	(202) 879-7918	(800) 321-3010	$$$$ $$+	266	Yes	No
(202) 483-3000	(202) 232-0438	(800) HILTONS	$$$ $$$+	1,123	Yes	Yes
(202) 872-1500	(202) 872-1424	(800) 228-9290	$$$$$+	418	No	Yes
(703) 418-6800	(703) 418-3763	(800) HILTONS	$$$$+	386	Yes	Yes
(202) 842-1300	(202) 371-9602	(800) 424-1140	$$$$$–	340	Yes	Yes
(202) 965-2700	(202) 337-5417	(800) IGOHOJO	$$$+	192	Yes	Yes
(202) 898-9000	(202) 289-0947	(800) 228-9898	$$$$ $$$–	800	Yes	Yes
(202) 965-2300	(202) 337-7915	(800) 424-2736	$$$ $$$+	235	Yes	Yes
(202) 429-1700	(202) 785-0786	(800) WESTIN-1	$$$ $$$–	399	Yes	No
(202) 429-0100	(202) 429-9759	(800) 228-3000	$$$ $$$–	263	Yes	Yes
(202) 628-9100	(202) 637-7326	(800) 327-0200	$$$ $$$–	368	Yes	No
(202) 483-7700	(202) 332-4547	(800) 247-3064	$$$+	43	No	No
(202) 955-6400	(202) 955-5765	(800) WYNDHAM	$$$$$	239	Yes	No

INDEX

1998 *Unofficial Guide* Reader Survey

If you would like to express your opinion about Washington, D.C. or this guidebook, complete the following survey and mail it to:

> *Unofficial Guide* Reader Survey
> P.O. Box 43059
> Birmingham, AL 35243

Inclusive dates of your visit _____

Members of your party:	Person 1	Person 2	Person 3	Person 4	Person 5
Gender (M or F)	_____	_____	_____	_____	_____
Age	_____	_____	_____	_____	_____

How many times have you been to Washington, D.C.? _____

On your most recent trip, where did you stay? _____

Concerning accommodations, on a scale with 100 best and 0 worst, how would you rate:

The quality of your room? _____   The value for the money? _____

The quietness of your room? _____   Check-in/checkout efficiency? _____

Shuttle service to the parks? _____   Swimming pool facilities? _____

Did you rent a car? _____   From whom? _____

Concerning your rental car, on a scale with 100 best and 0 worst, how would you rate:

Pickup processing efficiency? _____   Return processing efficiency? _____

Condition of the car? _____   Cleanliness of the car? _____

Airport shuttle efficiency? _____

Concerning your dining experiences:

How many restaurant meals (including fast food) did you average per day? _____

How much (approximately) did your party spend on meals per day? _____

Favorite restaurants in Washington, D.C.? _____
_____

Did you buy this guide: Before leaving? _____ While on your trip? _____

How did you hear about this guide?

Loaned or recommended by a friend _____   Radio or TV _____

Newspaper or magazine _____   Bookstore salesperson _____

Just picked it out on my own _____   Library _____

Internet _____

What other guidebooks did you use on this trip? _____

_____

On the 100 best and 0 worst scale, how would you rate them? _____

_____

Using the same scale, how would you rate the *Unofficial Guide?* _____

Are *Unofficial Guides* readily available in bookstores in your area? _____

Have you used other *Unofficial Guides?* _____ Which one(s)? _____

Comments about your Washington, D.C. trip or about the *Unofficial Guide:*

_____

_____

_____

_____

_____

_____

_____

_____

_____

_____